⊚ Harden's

London
Restaurants
2017

Survey driven reviews of over 1,000 re...

Put us in your client's pocket!

Branded gift books and editions for iPhone
call to discuss the options on 020 7839 4763.

© **Harden's Limited 2016**

ISBN 978-0-9929408-5-0

British Library Cataloguing-in-Publication data:
a catalogue record for this book is available from
the British Library.

Printed in Italy by Legoprint

Client relations manager: Clare Burnage
Assistant editors: Karen Moss, Bruce Millar
Database manager: Antonia Russell

London Restaurant Awards Photography: Darren Bell

Harden's Limited
The Brew, Victoria House, 64 Paul Street, London, EC2A 4NA

Would restaurateurs (and PRs) please address
communications to 'Editorial' at the above address,
or ideally by email to: editorial@hardens.com

SURVEY HIGHEST RATINGS

AMBIENCE

1 The Ritz Restaurant
2 Sketch (Lecture Rm)
3 Galvin at Windows
4 Le Gavroche
5 The Ledbury

1 Clos Maggiore
2 Hutong
3 Rules
4 Scott's
5 Chutney Mary

1 La Poule au Pot
2 Petersham Hotel
3 Dean Street Townhouse
4 Bob Bob Ricard
5 Summerhouse

1 The Lighterman
2 Andrew Edmunds
3 Brasserie Zédel
4 José
5 Joe Allen

1 The Begging Bowl
2 Blanchette
3 Churchill Arms
4 Department of Coffee
5 Princi

OVERALL

1 The Ledbury
2 The Ritz Restaurant
3 Le Gavroche
4 Sketch (Lecture Rm)
5 The Araki

1 The Five Fields
2 Gauthier Soho
3 Chez Bruce
4 The Guinea Grill
5 Scott's

1 Sushi Tetsu
2 Oslo Court
3 Chotto Matte
4 Quo Vadis
5 Café Spice Namaste

1 The Lighterman
2 José
3 Jin Kichi
4 The Palomar
5 Andrew Edmunds

1 The Begging Bowl
2 Blanchette
3 A Wong
4 Department of Coffee
5 Paradise Hampstead

SURVEY BEST BY CUISINE

These are the restaurants which received the best average food ratings (excluding establishments with a small or notably local following).

Where the most common types of cuisine are concerned, we present the results in two price-brackets. For less common cuisines, we list the top three, regardless of price.

For further information about restaurants which are particularly notable for their food, see the cuisine lists starting on page 244. These indicate, using an asterisk*, restaurants which offer exceptional or very good food.

British, Modern

£55 and over
1 The Ledbury
2 The Five Fields
3 Chez Bruce
4 The Clove Club
5 Trinity

Under £55
1 The Dairy
2 Lamberts
3 The Anglesea Arms
4 Rabbit
5 Oldroyd

French

£55 and over
1 Gauthier Soho
2 Le Gavroche
3 La Petite Maison
4 Pied à Terre
5 Sketch (Lecture Rm)

Under £55
1 Brawn
2 Blanchette
3 Casse-Croute
4 Cigalon
5 Comptoir Gascon

Italian/Mediterranean

£55 and over
1 Bocca Di Lupo
2 The River Café
3 Assaggi
4 Murano
5 Locanda Locatelli

Under £55
1 Dehesa
2 L'Amorosa
3 Opera Tavern
4 Princi
5 500

Indian & Pakistani

£55 and over
1 Trishna
2 Tamarind
3 Café Spice Namaste
4 Gymkhana
5 Amaya

Under £55
1 Ganapati
2 Potli
3 Lahore Kebab House
4 Dishoom
5 Hoppers

Chinese

£55 and over
1 Hunan
2 HKK
3 Yauatcha W1
4 Min Jiang
5 Royal China Club

Under £55
1 Silk Road
2 A Wong
3 Royal China W2
4 Shikumen
5 Yming

Japanese

£55 and over
1 The Araki
2 Sushi Tetsu
3 Zuma
4 Dinings
5 Umu

Under £55
1 Jin Kichi
2 Kurobata W2
3 Tsunami SW4
4 Shackfuyu
5 Sticks n Sushi SW19

British, Traditional
1 St John
2 Wiltons
3 Scott's

Vegetarian
1 The Gate EC1
2 Vanilla Black
3 Mildred's

Burgers, etc
1 Tommi's
2 Patty & Bun W1
3 Honest Burger SW9

Pizza
1 Santa Maria
2 Pizza Pilgrims W1
3 Franco Manca SW9

Fish & Chips
1 Olympus
2 Golden Hind
3 The Sea Shell

Thai
1 The Begging Bowl
2 Sukho Fine Thai Cuisine
3 Smoking Goat

Steaks & Grills
1 The Guinea Grill
2 Hawksmoor W1
3 Goodman W1

Fish & Seafood
1 One-O-One
2 Outlaw's
3 Wiltons

Fusion
1 Chotto Matte)
2 Bubbledogs (Kitchen Table
3 Sushisamba

Spanish
1 Barrafina
2 José
3 Donostia

Turkish
1 Oklava
2 Kazan
3 Haz

Lebanese
1 Mezzet
2 Meza
3 Arabica

THE RESTAURANT SCENE

This year we list a record 200 newcomers – the largest ever in the 26-year history of the guide, comfortably overtaking last year's record of 179.

Closings – muted in recent years – also grew significantly to 76. Although this is well below the record of 113 seen in 2004, it is the third-highest level we have recorded.

Combining the two factors, the level of net openings this year (openings minus closings) set a new peak (just!): at 124, the figure exceeds last year's record total of 123 by 1!

Although the proportion of openings to closings, at 2.6:1, remains historically high – in fact, the fifth highest on record – this ratio is a good deal lower than last year's spike of 3.2:1. If you put these figures on a graph, then despite this year's record figures (as detailed above) it is not hard to paint a picture of a peak being passed.

Brexit being the hot topic it is, it would be tempting to see the record figures noted above as proof of the resilience of the London restaurant market to Brexit. It is no such thing of course. The time it takes to cook up a new restaurant is at least nine months (securing the site, recruiting staff, etc).

It will take till next year to have any idea whether Brexit is going to hit the confidence of restaurant investors. And even if there is a decline, there will be many factors in play. For example, Brexit aside, many in the trade are already worried about a potential over-supply of new openings, and perhaps rightly so given the rising number of closures.

"Without Europeans, we're f##ked"

These memorable words were spoken by Bruce Poole, at the inaugural Harden's London Restaurant Awards, held at the Hippodrome Casino on 12 September 2016.

In receiving his lifetime achievement award, the proprietor of Chez Bruce used his time on the stage to stress the vital contribution made by migrants from Europe in both boosting the quality of London dining, but also in providing the unskilled foot soldiers on which the trade depends.

Another attendee at the awards who employs 60, noted that in the last 15 years of running restaurants, perhaps 5% of his job applications for the post of kitchen porter had come from UK citizens. Where will they come from in future?

The restaurant trade is no stranger to friction with the home office. Never mind European migrants: any restaurateur involved with cuisine from further afield will attest to the difficulty in getting chefs into the country.

Of course, some will argue that catering to such sybaritic whims are elite concerns. But tourism accounts for about

10% of UK GDP and the importance of having an improving reputation for gastronomy – and cosmopolitan gastronomy at that – shouldn't be understated in building London to being the world's leading in-bound tourist destination. Let's hope the efforts to cope with the referendum result and underlying immigration concerns don't screw up this 'crown-jewel' feature.

East End Meat Feast

When it comes to migration within London, then – after Central London – the East End continues to be the destination of choice for restaurant openings. That noted, West London did stage something of a fight-back this year, with 3/4 the number of openings to the East. North London remains the laggard with the lowest level of activity.

According to our categorisations, Modern British and Italian cuisines remain the most popular for newcomers. But if you lump various categories such as "American", "Burgers" and "Steak & Grills" into a single meatylicious one, then this eco-unfriendly cuisine is as popular as Italian for new openings, and more so in the hipster-heavy eastern postcodes.

The popularity of Japanese cuisine also continues to be a major trend. Nipponese openings again exceeded those of the next most popular cuisines: French, Indian and Spanish.

Despite the huge Chinese community in London and China's immense culinary traditions, its cuisine continues to be poorly represented, especially in fashionable new openings. This remains a massive opportunity for anyone who can dream up winning Chinese-inspired formats.

The hottest of the hot

Every year, we choose what to us seem to be the most significant openings of the year. This year, our selection is as follows:

Anglo	Frenchie
Black Axe Mangal	Hoppers
The Barbary	Padella
Clipstone	Som Saa
Elystan Street	Vineet Bhatia

Prices

The average price of dinner for one at establishments listed in this guide is £51.37 (compared to £50.51 last year). Prices have risen by 1.7% in the past 12 months: again, a lower rate than in the preceding 12 months. This continues a 3-year trend of a slowing rate that nevertheless exceeds the very low rate of inflation generally (effectively zero). This year's real level of above-inflation restaurant price rises is very similar to last year's.

OPENINGS AND CLOSURES

Openings (200)

Ahi Poké
Albion Clerkenwell (EC1)
Anglo
Anzu
Aquavit
Assaggi
Le Bab
Bá nh Bá nh
Bao Fitzrovia (W1)
The Barbary
Barbecoa, Nova (SW1)
Berber & Q Shawarma Bar
Bernardi's
Billy & The Chicks
Bird Camden (NW1)
Black Axe Mangal
Black Roe
Blanchette East (E1)
Blandford Comptoir
Bob Bob Exchange
Bombetta
Boondocks
Bronte
Bukowski Grill (W1, SW9)
Buoni Amici
Cacio & Pepe
Café Monico
Canto Corvino
Caravan Bankside (SE1)
Casita Andina
Céleste, The Lanesborough
Chicama
The Chipping Forecast
Chriskitch (N1)
Chuck Burger
Chucs (W11)
Clipstone
CôBa
Cocotte
Coin Laundry
The Collins Room
Corner Kitchen
Counter Culture
Curio + Ta Ta
Dalloway Terrace, Bloomsbury
    Hotel
Darbaar
Dickie Fitz
Dip & Flip (SW17)
Dominique Ansel Bakery
    London
Duende
Dynamo
Elystan Street
Eneko at One Aldwych, One

Aldwych Hotel
Enoteca Turi
Escocesa
Estiatorio Milos
Farang
Farley Macallan
Farmacy
La Ferme
Figlio Del Vesuvio
Flora Indica
Foley's
Foxlow (W4)
Frenchie
The Frog
Fumo
Galley
Galvin HOP
Gotto Trattoria
Gourmet Goat
Gunpowder
Hanger
The Harcourt
Hatchetts
Hill & Szrok Public House (N1)
Homeslice (EC1)
The Hour Glass
Humble Grape
Ichiryu
The Ivy Brasserie, One Tower
    Bridge
The Ivy Café (NW8, SW19)
Jamavar
Jikoni
Joe Public
Kanada-Ya (SW1)
Kiln
Kiru
Kojawan, Hilton Metropole
Kricket (W1)
Legs
The Lighterman
Little Taperia
Lotus
Lucky Chip
MacellaioRC (SW7, EC1)
Maison Eric Kayser
Mamie's
Mangal 1.1 (EC2)
Margot
Martha Ortiz
MEATliquor (SE22)
MeatUp
Mere
Mister Lasagna
MNKY HSE

Openings (continued)

Morito *(E2)*
Mr Bao
Mustard
Nanban
Native
The Ninth
Nirvana Kitchen
No 197 Chiswick Fire Station
Noble Rot
Oklava
Oliver Maki
On The Bab *(EC4)*
100 Wardour Street
Orée
Ormer Mayfair, Flemings
   Mayfair Hotel
Osteria, Barbican Centre
Osteria 60
Ostuni *(N6)*
Padella
Parabola
Park Chinois
El Pastór
Patty and Bun *(E2)*
Pear Tree Cafe
Perilla
Petit Pois Bistro
Peyotito
Pharmacy 2, Newport Street
   Gallery
Picture Marylebone *(W1)*
Pidgin
Pique Nique
Pitt Cue Co
Poco *(E2)*
Poppies *(W1)*
Rail House Café
Randy's Wing Bar
Restaurant Ours
Rök *(N1)*
Romulo Café
Rubedo
Sagardi
Saint Luke's Kitchen, Library
Sakagura
Salut
Samarkand
Santa Maria *(SW6)*
Sardine
Savini at Criterion
Shepherd Market Wine House
Shuang Shuang
Six Portland Road
Smoke and Salt (Residency)

Smokestak *(E1)*
Som Saa
Sosharu, Turnmill Building
Spring Workshop
Squirrel
The Stable
Strut & Cluck
Sushi Masa
Sushisamba *(WC2)*
Sutton And Sons *(N16)*
Sutton And Sons *(E8)*
Tabun Kitchen
Takahashi
Talli Joe
Tate Modern Restaurant,
   Switch House
temper
Theo's
Theo's Simple Italian
Tokimeite
Tommi's Burger Joint *(W1)*
Uli
Upstairs at John the Unicorn
Urban Coterie, M By
   Montcalm
Veneta
Viet Food
View 94
Vineet Bhatia
VQ *(W11)*
Walter and Monty
Wazen
The Woodford
Xi'an Impression
Yard Sale Pizza *(N4)*
Yumi Izakaya
Zayane
Zelman Meats *(W1, SW1)*
Zia Lucia
Zima

Closures (76)

Abbeville Kitchen SW4
Amico Bio WC1
Apollo Banana Leaf SW17
Arbutus W1
Bangkok SW7
Blackfoot EC1
Bonnie Gull
  Seafood Bar EC1
Bouillabaisse W1
Brasserie Chavot W1
Bumpkin W11
Bunnychow W1
Canta Napoli W4, TW11
Carom at Meza
Ceru SE1
Chez Patrick W8
Copita del Mercado E1
Cuckoo N1
Delancey & Co W1
Dub Jam WC2
Fabrizio EC1
Garnier SW5
Gin Joint EC2
Green's SW1
Harbour City W1
Hibiscus W1
Izgara N3
Inside SE10
Joint W1
Kateh SW1
Kopapa WC2
Linnea TW9
Little Bay EC1
Lockhart W1
Lolo Rojo SW11
Megan's NW8
Mill Lane Bistro NW6
Mishkins WC2
Morden & Lea W1
Moti Mahal WC2
Newman Street Tavern W1
Nozomi SW3

Old Tom & English W1
One Sixty Smokehouse
  NW6
Only Running Footman W1
Pescatori W1
Piquet W1
Poissonnerie de
  l'Avenue SW3
Princess Garden W1
Rasoi SW3
Rex & Mariano W1
Rextail W1
Rocket W1 & WC2
Rooftop Café,
  The Exchange SE1
Roots at N1
Sackville's W1
Sea Cow SE22
Sesame WC2
Shanghai Blues WC1
Shoe Shop NW5
Source SW11
Stock Pot W1, SW1
Strand Dining Rooms WC2
Suk Saran SW19
Sushi-Say NW2
Tentazioni SE1
Terra Virgine SW10
The Terrace W8
Tinello SW1
Truscott Arms W9
Truscott Cellar NW3
Verden E5
White Rabbit N16
Zucca SE1

DIRECTORY

A Cena TW1 £50 3 3 3
418 Richmond Rd 020 8288 0108 1–4A
"Original cooking and an interesting wine list" combined with "efficient and friendly service" have long made this St Margaret's local a fave rave. "Good pre-rugby as well" if you're Twickers-bound. / TW1 2EB; www.acena.co.uk; @acenarestaurant; 10 pm; closed Mon L & Sun D; booking max 6 may apply; set weekday L £29 (FP).

A Wong SW1 £35 5 5 4
70 Wilton Rd 020 7828 8931 2–4B
"Breathtakingly skilful" dim sum – "a very exciting and intriguing mix of the traditional and innovative" – win huge esteem for Andrew Wong's "jammed-to-the-rafters" Pimlico canteen. "It's great to eat Chinese with such friendly staff" too. Top menu tip – "duck egg custard buns TO DIE FOR!" / SW1V 1DE; www.awong.co.uk; @awongSW1; 10.15 pm; closed Mon L & Sun; credit card deposit required to book.

The Abingdon W8 £62 3 3 3
54 Abingdon Rd 020 7937 3339 6–2A
"Totally reliable" and "always a treat", this stalwart, posh gastropub in an agreeable Kensington backstreet gets "very busy, so allow time for your order". Top Tip – nab a booth for the best seats. / W8 6AP; www.theabingdon.co.uk; @TheAbingdonW8; 10.30 pm, Fri & Sat 11 pm, Sun 10 pm; set weekday L £33 (FP), set Sun L £35 (FP).

About Thyme SW1 £52 3 3 3
82 Wilton Rd 020 7821 7504 2–4B
"The Spanish-orientated cuisine (including the wine list) remains reliable and interesting" at this Pimlico stalwart. "Amiable service and ambience" ensure that it's popular with locals as well as visitors. / SW1V 1DL; www.aboutthyme.co.uk; 10 pm; closed Sun.

L'Absinthe NW1 £49 2 3 2
40 Chalcot Rd 020 7483 4848 9–3B
Run by ebullient Burgundian Jean-Christophe Slowik, this popular corner bistro in Primrose Hill serves "traditional French cuisine", "Franglais-style". Not all reporters are impressed, but for a majority it's "delightful". / NW1 8LS; www.labsinthe.co.uk; @absinthe07jc; 10 pm, Sun 9 pm; closed Mon D.

Abu Zaad W12 £23 3 3 2
29 Uxbridge Rd 020 8749 5107 8–1C
"Delicious Middle Eastern cuisine" at very affordable prices makes it worth remembering this "authentic" Syrian café, near the top of Shepherd's Bush Market. / W12 8LH; www.abuzaad.co.uk; 11 pm; no Amex.

Adams Café W12 £33 3 5 3
77 Askew Rd 020 8743 0572 8–1B
"Tagines to die for in very generous portions" are the surprise in store at this Shepherd's Bush caff when it "turns into a North African restaurant by night". "It's the most friendly, hospitable, inexpensive place". / W12 9AH; www.adamscafe.co.uk; @adamscafe; 10 pm; closed Sun.

Addie's Thai Café SW5 £34 4 4 3
121 Earl's Court Rd 020 7259 2620 6–2A
"It's very cheap and we're very cheerful afterwards!" say fans of this "pretty authentic" Earl's Court café. Top Menu Tip – "especially recommended are the sizzling dishes". / SW5 9RL; www.addiesthai.co.uk; 11 pm, Sun 10.30 pm; no Amex.

The Admiral Codrington SW3 £57 1 2 3
17 Mossop St 020 7581 0005 6–2C
This popular, backstreet Chelsea boozer is still "a good old pub" to its fans,
but an increasing number of regulars are calling time on its food. "I made
the mistake of having a burger, once a Cod speciality. It isn't now", moaned
one. "How can a place go downhill so quickly?" asked another. / SW3 2LY;
www.theadmiralcodrington.co.uk; @TheAdCod; 10 pm, Thu-Sat 11 pm, Sun 9 pm;
no trainers.

Afghan Kitchen N1 £28 3 2 2
35 Islington Grn 020 7359 8019 9–3D
"Very good value" Afghan café, by Islington Green where you squash into
one of its two miniature floors, decorated Ikea-style, to enjoy a small menu
of simple stews. / N1 8DU; 11 pm; closed Mon & Sun; cash only.

Aglio e Olio SW10 £43 4 3 2
194 Fulham Rd 020 7351 0070 6–3B
This "everyday Italian" near Chelsea & Westminster Hospital is "a firm
favourite" with "very reasonable prices for the area". "The food
is exceptionally consistent – as it should be since the menu doesn't seem
to have changed in 14 years!" / SW10 9PN; 11.30 pm.

Ahi Poké W1 NEW £11
3 Percy Street no tel 3–1D
New, little (25-cover) café/takeaway in the streets near Tottenham Court
Road catering to London's latest food craving: Hawaiian-style raw fish
(poké). It opened in mid 2016. / W1T 1DE; www.ahipoke.co.uk;
@ahipokelondon; 8 pm.

Al Duca SW1 £49 3 4 3
4-5 Duke of York St 020 7839 3090 3–3D
This low-key Italian is a well-established fixture – particularly on the
St James's business lunch scene – with a "mainstream, satisfying" menu
of modern classics that "never disappoints", and which is "good value" for
this part of town. / SW1Y 6LA; www.alduca-restaurant.co.uk; 11 pm; closed Sun;
set pre theatre £33 (FP).

Al Forno £34 2 4 4
349 Upper Richmond Rd, SW15 020 8878 7522 11–2A
2a King's Rd, SW19 020 8540 5710 11–2B
"Rustic and delicious Italian cooking" including "terrific pizzas" plus
a "wonderful atmosphere" make these "fun" locals across
southwest London a good bet for a "great night out". / 10 pm-11 pm.

Alain Ducasse at The Dorchester W1 £129 2 4 3
53 Park Ln 020 7629 8866 3–3A
"3 stars .... not in my eyes!" – Michelin continue to mis-rate the world-
famous Gallic chef's Mayfair temple. True, fans do wax lyrical over its
"easy luxury" and cuisine with "perfect balance", and the "un-snooty"
service in particular is "exceptional". But there are too many doubters who
find it feels "corporate" with "inspiration-free" cooking, and "you need
to bring ALL your money!" / W1K 1QA; www.alainducasse-dorchester.com;
9.30 pm; closed Mon, Sat L & Sun; jacket required; set weekday L £84 (FP).

Albertine W12
£38 244

1 Wood Ln 020 8743 9593 8–1C
*A perfect escape from the nearby Westfield shopping centre –
this "traditional wine bar" is the antithesis of the shiny retail complex
opposite, and provides a "good, descriptive list", "knowledgeable service
and great cheeses", plus some light, "home-cooked" dishes. / W12 7DP;
www.albertinewinebar.co.uk; @AlbertineWIne; 11 pm, Thu-Sat midnight; closed
Sat L & Sun; no Amex.*

The Albion N1
£48 213

10 Thornhill Rd 020 7607 7450 9–3D
*"Very handsome" Islington neighbourhood gastro-boozer with "lots of
outdoor space" that's long been a "Sunday lunch favourite". "Dire service"
too often ruins the experience however: "the staff are positively hostile,
especially if you are stupid enough to complain". / N1 1HW;
www.the-albion.co.uk; @thealbionpub; 10 pm, Sun 9 pm.*

Albion
£51 222

NEO Bankside, Holland St, SE1 020 3764 5550 10–3B
2-4 Boundary St, E2 020 7729 1051 13–1B
63 Clerkenwell Road, EC1 020 3862 0750 10–1A NEW
*"A borderline entry" – Sir Terence Conran's group of all-day pit-stops
in Shoreditch, Clerkenwell and Bankside are "relaxed and agreeable"
venues, but it's "hard to be fantastically enthusiastic – they're not
overpriced but a bit bland". / 11 pm.*

Ali Baba NW1
£25 324

32 Ivor Pl 020 7723 5805 2–1A
*"If you want the food and ambience of an Egyptian cafe, you'll find it here",
at this living-room-style operation behind a Marylebone takeaway ("the TV
is likely to be on only If there is an important football game in Egypt").
"Interesting" home-cooked fare, and you can BYO. / NW1 6DA; midnight;
cash only.*

Almeida N1
£63 322

30 Almeida St 020 7354 4777 9–3D
*This long-running D&D London venue opposite the eponymous theatre
nowadays serves modern British cuisine (rather than its old Gallic-style
fare). It's a dependable rather than an exciting choice, most notable for its
"excellent pre-theatre menu". / N1 1AD; www.almeida-restaurant.co.uk;
10.30 pm; closed Mon L & Sun D; set weekday L & pre-theatre £25 (FP).*

Alounak
£33 324

10 Russell Gdns, W14 020 7603 1130 8–1D
44 Westbourne Grove, W2 020 7229 0416 7–1B
*"Wonderful Persian food at very reasonable prices" keeps these bustling
and atmospheric cafés in Bayswater and Olympia busy throughout the
week. "Bring your own bottle works well", too. / 11.30 pm; no Amex.*

Alquimia SW15
£51 332

30 Brewhouse Ln 020 8785 0508 11–2B
*"Shades of Pamplona rather than Putney" attract diners to this tapas bar
in a newish Thames-side development by the bridge. There are some gripes
that the "more limited" menu's "not as exciting as it was" ("too many old
favourites"), but even so "the standard's still pretty good". / SW15 2JX;
www.alquimiarestaurant.co.uk; @Alquimia_RestUK; 11.30 pm, Sun 10.30 pm.*

Alyn Williams, Westbury Hotel W1 £93 4|5|3
37 Conduit St 020 7183 6426 3–2C
"Consistently punching above its weight" – Alyn Williams's "inventive" cuisine and "the most charming service" are often "in excess of expectations" at this windowless hotel dining room, off Bond Street, whose "widely spaced tables are ideal for a discreet business meal". / W1S 2YF; www.alynwilliams.com; @Alyn_Williams; 10.30 pm; closed Mon & Sun; jacket required; set weekday L £53 (FP), set always available £65 (FP).

Amaya SW1 £78 5|3|3
Halkin Arc, 19 Motcomb St 020 7823 1166 6–1D
"As far from your local cuzza as Buckingham Palace is from a bedsit!" This stylish Belgravian – with "theatrical" open kitchen – provides tapas-style cuisine that, "even for London, is amazingly sophisticated", and "with a superb variety of flavours". Top Menu Tip – "amazing grilled meats". / SW1X 8JT; www.amaya.biz; @theamaya_; 11.30 pm, Sun 10.30 pm.

Ametsa with Arzak Instruction, Halkin Hotel SW1 £90 4|3|2
5 Halkin St 020 7333 1234 2–3A
"The strange taste combinations always work better than you expect" – "incredible" – and come with "very good wine pairings" ("interesting Spanish wines never seen or heard of before") at this Belgravia outpost of star Basque chef, Juan Mari Arzak. A disgruntled minority of reporters deliver the opposite verdict however, and the setting is "rather dull". / SW1X 7DJ; www.comohotels.com/thehalkin/dining/ametsa; @AmetsaArzak; 10 pm; closed Mon L & Sun.

L'Amorosa W6 £43 4|4|3
278 King St 020 8563 0300 8–2B
"How lucky we are that Andy Needham decided to open an accessible, neighbourhood Italian on the Hammersmith/Chiswick borders!" "Service shines", and the realisation of the "short but tempting" menu is "extremely competent" – in particular the "brilliant pasta – consistently al dente and combined with strong, gutsy flavours". And all at "sensible prices" too. / W6 0SP; www.lamorosa.co.uk; @LamorosaLondon; 9.30 pm, Fri & Sat 10 pm; closed Mon & Sun D.

Anarkali W6 £36 3|4|3
303-305 King St 020 8748 1760 8–2B
"Freshly cooked food by chef Rafiq is always a pleasure – fairly standard Indian, but done so well", say fans of this age-old, comfortably traditional Hammersmith curry house. "Great service" too ("attentive when they needed to be, otherwise left us alone"). / W6 9NH; www.anarkalifinedining.com; midnight; closed Mon L & Sun L; no Amex.

The Anchor & Hope SE1 £52 4|3|3
36 The Cut 020 7928 9898 10–4A
"The gastropub against which all others are judged!" – the survey's No. 1 boozer, a short walk from Waterloo, continues to wow with its "confident, robust, mostly meaty cooking", often enjoyed "at shared table so you meet interesting people". On the downside, it can be a "scrum", with no bookings (aside from Sunday lunch) leading to "endless waits". Top Menu Tip – "the shared lamb for five is divine!" / SE1 8LP; www.anchorandhopepub.co.uk; @AnchorHopeCut; 10.30 pm; closed Mon L; no Amex; no bookings; set weekday L £29 (FP).

Andina E2 £48 4 3 4
1 Redchurch St   020 7920 6499   13–1B
This "café-style" Shoreditch hotspot serves "wonderful, intriguing Peruvian tapas for sharing". It can be "extremely busy and noisy", but when all is considered the staff "manage to do an excellent job". / E2 7DJ; www.andinalondon.com; @AndinaLondon; 10.30 pm; booking max 6 may apply.

The Andover Arms W6 £46 3 5 5
57 Aldensey Rd   020 8748 2155   8–1B
"I may have had better food elsewhere, but haven't enjoyed a meal more" – this "well-managed and run", "traditional pub" in Brackenbury Village is "extremely friendly, cosy and welcoming" and "you couldn't get a better neighbourhood pub". Don't go expecting gastro fireworks though, despite its "bizarrely positive TripAdvisor ratings". / W6 0DL; www.theandoverarms.com; @theandoverarms; 10 pm, Sun 9 pm; no Amex.

ANDREW EDMUNDS W1 £52 3 4 5
46 Lexington St   020 7437 5708   4–2C
"To 'seal the deal' with a date", this "old world", "rickety" Soho "haunt" – "all flickering candlelight and rustic Bohemian style" – has few equals. The "ever-changing", "simple", "seasonal" fare is "honest" and "always reliable", but "the wine makes a meal exceptional" – "an amazing choice" from arguably "the best-value list in London". / W1F 0LW; www.andrewedmunds.com; 10.45 pm, Sun 10.30 pm; no Amex; booking max 6 may apply.

Angelus W2 £68 3 4 3
4 Bathurst St   020 7402 0083   7–2D
"A good find in an otherwise uninspiring area" – Thierry Tomassin's "classy and serious" venture – "a grown-up, converted pub with white tablecloths" – is an unexpected find near Lancaster Gate tube. The Gallic cooking can be "divine" (although "prices are high"), but the prime attraction is the "wine buff's" wine list one might expect of Le Gavroche's ex-sommelier. / W2 2SD; www.angelusrestaurant.co.uk; @AngelusLondon; 11 pm, Sun 10 pm; set weekday L £44 (FP).

Angler, South Place Hotel EC2 £84 3 3 3
3 South Pl   020 3215 1260   13–2A
Despite the odd quibble that it feels "corporate", this D&D London rooftop venture near Moorgate leaves most reporters "very surprised by how good it is" – "a lovely setting, with lots of windows and sunshine" and "beautifully cooked and presented" fish. / EC2M 2AF; www.anglerrestaurant.com; @southplacehotel; 10 pm; closed Sat L & Sun.

The Anglesea Arms W6 £51 3 4 4
35 Wingate Rd   020 8749 1291   8–1B
"Panic set in when it closed for a while", but this "top-class neighbourhood gastropub" near Ravenscourt Park is "in great form" again according to most (if not quite all) reports, combining "hospitable" service with a "charming" setting and "interesting" cooking. / W6 0UR; www.angleseaarmspub.co.uk; @_AngleseaArmsW6; 10 pm, Sun 9 pm; closed weekday L; no bookings.

Anglo EC1 NEW
£69   4 3 2
30 St Cross Street   020 7430 1503   10–1A

"If Noma were to move to London... this is it!" Most early reports on Mark Jarvis and Jack Cashmore's Hatton Garden newcomer – on the modest site vacated by Fabrizio (RIP) – describe *"a superb dining experience"*, particularly the *"INCREDIBLE tasting menu of beautifully presented dishes"* (anchored in British ingredients and cuisine). Its ratings are capped by a minority of refuseniks though who just decry *"ridiculously small portions... at a price"*. / EC1N 8UH; www.anglorestaurant.com; 10.30 pm; closed Mon, Sat L & Sun; booking max 4 may apply.

L'Anima EC2
£74   3 3 3
1 Snowden St   020 7422 7000   13–2B

"Crisp, all-white" City venue near Liverpool Street – *"echoey"* when full but *"a bit of a mausoleum"* at quiet times – that's *"perfect for a business lunch"*, especially *"if someone else is paying"*. The Italian cooking can be *"superlative"*, but since Francesco Mazzei left in 2015 *"its precision has declined"*. / EC2A 2DQ; www.lanima.co.uk; @lanimalondon; 11 pm, Sat 11.30 pm; closed Sat L & Sun; set weekday L & dinner £59 (FP).

L'Anima Café EC2
£53   3 2 3
10 Appold St   020 7422 7080   13–2B

"Hearing is easier, and it's more relaxed" than at its namesake restaurant around the corner, but this *"busy and bustling"* café/deli near Liverpool Street is *"pretty slick in terms of overall quality"*, serving simple southern Italian dishes, snacks and coffee in an *"industrial"*-style setting. / EC2A 2AP; www.lanimacafe.co.uk; @LAnimacafe; 10 pm; closed Sat & Sun.

Anima e Cuore NW1
£44   4 2 1
129 Kentish Town Rd   020 7267 2410   9–2B

This tiny shopfront in Kentish Town *"couldn't be more basic"*, but the *"authentic Italian food"* and home-made gelato served from a blackboard menu are *"absolutely fantastic"*. Better still, *"you bring your own wine, which keeps the total bill down considerably"*. / NW1 8PB; @animaecuoreuk; 9 pm, Sun 2.30 pm.

Annie's
£46   2 3 4
162 Thames Rd, W4   020 8994 9080   1–3A
36-38 White Hart Ln, SW13   020 8878 2020   11–1A

A *"cosy atmosphere in a pretty room"*, plus *"warm, welcoming, flexible staff"*, and *"great-value"* prices create a winning combination for this pair of neighbourhood faves in Barnes and Strand-on-the-Green. The food's only *"standard"*, but there's *"plenty on offer"* from brunch to supper, and its quality is *"reliably consistent"*. / www.anniesrestaurant.co.uk; 10 pm, Sat 10.30 pm, Sun 9.30 pm.

The Anthologist EC2
£47   2 2 3
58 Gresham St   0845 468 0101   10–2C

"Bustling", large bar/restaurant near the Guildhall, whose *"different"* look for the Square Mile *"makes for a good atmosphere"*. The food's somewhere between *"just right for a business meeting"* and *"pretty average"*, and service-wise it can be *"a slight case of it just being plonked down"*. / EC2V 7BB; www.theanthologistbar.co.uk; @theanthologist; 11 pm, Thu & Fri 1 am; closed Sat & Sun; SRA-2 star.

L' Antica Pizzeria NW3 £37 4 3 3
66 Heath St 020 7431 8516 9–1A
"Permanently heaving with Italians", this "cramped and buzzy little pizzeria on Hampstead High Street" serves "fantastic wood-fired pizza", and you catch "wafts of the most delicious smells whenever the oven opens". / NW3 1DN; www.anticapizzeria.co.uk; @AnticaHamp; 10.30 pm; Mon-Thu D only, Fri-Sun open L & D

Antico SE1 £47 3 4 3
214 Bermondsey St 020 7407 4682 10–4D
"Makes up for the sad demise of Zucca (RIP)"! A "great neighbourhood Italian spot" in Bermondsey, with "consistent food" and "particularly good risottos". It's "family-friendly" too, if "rather noisy" when lunch is in full flow. / SE1 3TQ; www.antico-london.co.uk; @AnticoLondon; 10.30 pm, Sun 9.30 pm; closed Mon.

Antidote W1 £62 2 2 2
12a Newburgh St 020 7287 8488 4–1B
"Lovely, cosy but airy wine bar that's a welcome retreat from the bustle of Carnaby Street's environs". "It's great for a glass of wine and some charcuterie/cheese" (the wine list is excellent), but since Mikael Jonsson stopped consulting here, recommendations for the more ambitious fare in the slightly "dreary" upstairs dining room have become mixed: to fans "exceptional", to sceptics "a bit overpriced and not all dishes work". / W1F 7RR; www.antidotewinebar.com; @AntidoteWineBar; 10.30 pm; closed Sun.

Anzu SW1 NEW
St James's Market, 1 Norris Street no tel 3–3D
From the owners of Tonkotsu – the ramen bar group – a new format: a Japanese brasserie, inspired by contemporary Tokyo dining, which is expected to open in St James's Market in autumn 2016 (alongside a raft of other eateries, including Aquavit London and Duck & Waffle). / SW1Y 4SB.

Applebee's Café SE1 £56 4 4 2
5 Stoney St 020 7407 5777 10–4C
"The best fish pie ever…", "The best scallops ever…", "The best fish 'n' chips ever…" – this "vibrant" café and fish shop provides "memorable" dishes. It's "excellent value" too, even if "it's edged upmarket since Borough Market became so highly fashionable". / SE1 9AA; www.applebeesfish.com; @applebeesfish; Mon-Wed 10 pm, Thu-Sat 11 pm; closed Sun; no Amex.

Apulia EC1 £39 3 3 3
50 Long Ln 020 7600 8107 10–2B
This "straightforward, good-value Puglian" local is a popular option near the Barbican – useful for a working lunch or pre-show supper, with a "great menu of delicious" southern Italian dishes. / EC1A 9EJ; www.apuliarestaurant.co.uk; 10 pm, Sun 3.30 pm; closed Sun.

aqua nueva W1 £66 1 2 2
240 Regent St (entrance 30 Argyll St) 020 7478 0540 4–1A
This "impressive" nightclubby rooftop (with terrace) Spanish venue near Oxford Circus has "changed for the worse", losing ratings across the board. "The bars have become the focal points, food that was good now seems nothing special", and "the music is cranked up too high". (Little feedback this year on the adjoining Japanese, aqua kyoto). / W1B 3BR; www.aqua-london.com; @aqualondon; 10.30 pm, Thu-Sat 11 pm, Sun 8.30 pm.

Aqua Shard SE1 £95 1 1 3
Level 31, 31 St Thomas St 020 3011 1256 10–4C
"Only go for the view!" (admittedly "spectacular") to this swish
(but "soulless") chamber on the Shard's 31st floor, where "average food
is indifferently served" at extortionate expense. "If you go, go on a deal".
/ SE1 9RY; www.aquashard.co.uk; @aquashard; 10.45 pm.

Aquavit SW1 NEW
1 St James's Market, 1 Carlton St awaiting tel 3–3D
Manhattan's famous Nordic fine dining restaurant (est. 1987), with an
emphasis on tasting and prix-fixe menus, is opening a London
outpost in Haymarket's new St James's Market development in autumn
2016. Exec chef is Emma Bengtsson, whose claim to fame is being the
second US female chef to win two Michelin stars. / SW1Y 4QQ;
www.aquavitrestaurants.com; @aquavitlondon.

Arabica Bar & Kitchen SE1 £49 3 3 3
3 Rochester Walk 020 3011 5151 10–4C
"Excellent Middle Eastern fare" – "delicious, authentic and good value" –
can be found at this bustling Lebanese outfit in the "great location"
of foodie Borough Market. / SE1 9AF; www.arabicabarandkitchen.com;
@ArabicaLondon; 10.30 pm, Thu 11 pm, Fri & Sat 11.30 pm; closed Sun D.

The Araki W1 £380 5 5 4
Unit 4 12 New Burlington St 020 7287 2481 4–3A
"Peerless" (and that goes for the bill too…). Given the bankruptcy-inducing
set price of a meal – half as expensive again as a meal at The Fat Duck –
it would be easy to feel let down by this Mayfair 9-seater, where "world-
leading expert in his field Chef Mitushiro Araki" (who earnt three Michelin
stars in Tokyo, and gave them up to move to London) "prepares and serves
the sushi, right in front of you". However, not one of the reports
we received on this "stunning, intimate, authentic, and completely unique
experience" were anything other than totally rapturous, and it scored the
survey's highest food mark this year: "bliss… if at a cost". / W1S 3BH;
www.the-araki.com; 8.30 pm; D only, closed Mon; booking essential.

Ariana II NW6 £30 3 2 2
241 Kilburn High Rd 020 3490 6709 1–2B
This "family-run" Kilburn BYO is popular for a "cheap and cheerful" bite,
and "handy for the Tricycle Theatre" – "simple Afghan food (grilled meat
or veg with rice and salad) at amazing prices". / NW6 7JN;
www.ariana2restaurant.co.uk; @Ariana2kilburn; midnight.

Ark Fish E18 £44 4 4 2
142 Hermon Hill 020 8989 5345 1–1D
This South Woodford chippy serves "good fresh fish in casual
surroundings", and provides "excellent value". "I go there when I need
cheering up – the staff are all mates and seem to be having a good time!"
/ E18 1QH; www.arkfishrestaurant.co.uk; 9.45 pm, Fri & Sat 10.15 pm,
Sun 8.45 pm; closed Mon; no Amex; no bookings.

Artigiano NW3 £48 2 3 3
12a Belsize Ter 020 7794 4288 9–2A
You'll find "excellent service and a very good ambience, with high ceilings
and large windows", at this friendly Italian local in Belsize Park. "For the
price, the food is good but not great". / NW3 4AX;
www.etruscarestaurants.com; @artigianoesp; 10 pm; closed Mon L

L'Artista NW11 £37 2 4 4
917 Finchley Rd 020 8731 7501 1–1B
"The best pizzas for miles around" draw a family crowd to this festive Italian in the railway arches near Golders Green tube station. There's "always a friendly welcome for children of all ages, and they're very accommodating in adapting the menu". / NW11 7PE; www.lartistapizzeria.com; 11.30 pm.

L'Artiste Musclé W1 £49 2 2 5
1 Shepherd Mkt 020 7493 6150 3–4B
This "perfect French bistro" in Shepherd Market is arguably "a bit of a parody of itself", but reporters young and old "love the place": "I've been going back for 45 years and am never disappointed!" The wine is "well-priced" and "you can drink all afternoon!" / W1J 7PA; @lartistemuscle; 10 pm, Fri-Sun 10.30 pm.

Artusi SE15 £46 3 3 3
161 Bellenden Rd 020 3302 8200 1–4D
"The menus are short, the food excellent" at this two-year-old Italian, seemingly "home-from-home for Peckham hipsters: last time I dined there, twice as many men had beards as were clean-shaven!" / SE15 4DH; www.artusi.co.uk; @artusipeckham; Mon-Sat 10 pm, Sun 8 pm; closed Mon L.

Asakusa NW1 £36 5 3 2
265 Eversholt St 020 7388 8533 9–3C
"Really authentic" Japanese, set in beamed, mock-Tudor premises near Mornington Crescent, impressively highly rated by its fans for outstanding sushi and other fare. / NW1 1BA; 11.30 pm, Sat 11 pm; D only.

**Asia de Cuba,
St Martin's Lane Hotel WC2** £88 1 2 2
45 St Martin's Ln 020 7300 5588 5–4C
"The food is a pale reflection of what it used to be" in the ever-more "canteen-like" dining space of this glossy West End boutique-hotel, where the "overpriced" Cuban-Oriental fare has been "lost in translation" – a "fusion which doesn't fuse"; "good cocktails though". / WC2N 4HX; www.morganshotelgroup.com; @asiadecuba; 11 pm, Fri & Sat midnight, Sun 10.30 pm; set pre-theatre & Sun L £52 (FP).

Assaggi W2 NEW £73 4 4 3
39 Chepstow Pl 020 7792 5501 7–1B
"We were thrilled when it re-opened last November!" This "perfect, rustic Italian" in a simple upstairs dining room above a converted Bayswater pub has recently been resurrected, and most reporters are "so glad it's back" as it's just "as good as ever!" – "Pietro is gone, but it's still the same old Assaggi": "warm and welcoming" staff and "authentic south Italian food" ("wonderful, simple but fresh ingredients, deliciously prepared"), "albeit at authentic London prices". / W2 4TS; www.assaggi.co.uk; 11 pm; closed Sun; no Amex.

Assunta Madre W1 £106 2 2 2
8-10 Blenheim St 020 3230 3032 3–2B
While diners generally give this Mayfair branch of a Roman seafood specialist the benefit of the doubt on the food front, its "ridiculous" prices remain a major brake on all-round enthusiasm levels. / W1S 1LJ; www.assuntamadre.com; @assuntamadre; midnight.

Atari-Ya £30
20 James St, W1 020 7491 1178 3–1A
7 Station Pde, W3 020 8896 1552 1–2A
1 Station Pde, W5 020 8896 3175 1–3A
595 High Rd, N12 020 8446 6669 9–1B
31 Vivian Ave, NW4 020 8202 2789 1–1B
75 Fairfax Road, NW6 020 7328 5338 9–2A
The sushi is "exceptional" ("every piece is delicious!") and comes "at a
reasonable cost" at these "authentic" outfits, operated by a Japanese food
importer, and scattered around the parts of London frequented
by Nipponese expats ("they're always heaving with folks from Japan").
On the downside, "service is woolly", and "they're not the most glamorous"
places ("St James's is basically a takeaway with a waiting room, with service
on a plastic tray!"). / www.atariya.co.uk; W1 8 pm, NW4 & NW6 9.30 pm,
W9 9 pm; NW4, NW6 closed Mon.

L'Atelier de Joel Robuchon WC2 £112
13-15 West St 020 7010 8600 5–2B
"Gorgeously decorated" Covent Garden outpost of the star Parisian chef's
global empire, which offers a "sumptuous" experience, from cocktails
in the plush, rooftop bar and terrace to the exquisite series of "little taste
bombs" served in either of the two luxuriously appointed dining rooms.
(On the darker ground floor you perch on high stools, and there's a counter
where you can watch the kitchen – the second floor is more conventional).
Its culinary performance is "average compared to the past", however –
even some who say their meal "was not bad by any measure" feel
"the taste of the dishes didn't match their looks", or feel its mega prices
are "not worth it". / WC2H 9NE; www.joelrobuchon.co.uk; @latelierlondon;
11.30 pm, Sun 10 pm; no trainers.

The Atlas SW6 £48
16 Seagrave Rd 020 7385 9129 6–3A
A "hidden gem tucked away at the back of West Brompton tube" –
"a fantastic pub (and yes, it's still a pub)", with "outstanding" Med-
influenced cuisine, "lots of great ales" and staff who are "soooo friendly";
terrace garden in summer. / SW6 1RX; www.theatlaspub.co.uk; @theatlasfulham;
10 pm.

Augustine Kitchen SW11 £46
63 Battersea Bridge Rd 020 7978 7085 6–4C
A "great little gem of a French bistro in Battersea" specialising in "high-
quality" Savoyard dishes, such as fera fish from Lake Geneva: "the smoked
variety is to be recommended"; "fair prices" too. / SW11 3AU;
www.augustine-kitchen.co.uk; @augustinekitchen; 10.30 pm; closed Mon & Sun D.

Aurora W1 £52
49 Lexington St 020 7494 0514 4–2C
This low-profile stalwart makes a particularly "cosy" choice for a sociable
meal in central Soho and provides "very enjoyable" modern European
dishes ("though the menu could vary more often"); cute rear courtyard too.
/ W1F 9AP; www.aurorasoho.co.uk; 10 pm, Wed-Sat 10.30 pm, Sun 9 pm.

L'Autre Pied W1 £80
5-7 Blandford St 020 7486 9696 2–1A
"The more casual baby sister of Pied à Terre" is "everything a top
restaurant should be, but with no fuss" – providing "outstanding cuisine"
at "a very reasonable price", plus "professional yet informal service". But
not everyone's wowed by the "slightly cramped" and low-key interior.
/ W1U 3DB; www.lautrepied.co.uk; @LAutrePied; 10 pm; closed Sun D.

L'Aventure NW8 £67   3 3 5
3 Blenheim Ter 020 7624 6232 9–3A
"Magnifique!" – Catherine Parisot's "special" St John's Wood treasure is "so French, fun and romantic" and continues to deliver "dependable, high-quality" cuisine bourgeoise. Service from La Patronne and her team can be "attitude-y" or slow, but on most accounts: "who cares?" / NW8 0EH; 11 pm; closed Sat L & Sun.

The Avenue SW1 £63   1 2 2
7-9 St James's St 020 7321 2111 3–4D
D&D London's spacious Manhattan-esque brasserie in St James's is tipped by fans as a "stunning and comfortable" business venue, and also for pre-theatre dining. It is perennially accused of being "soulless and overpriced" however, and one or two meals here this year were "a fiasco". / SW1A 1EE; www.avenue-restaurant.co.uk; @avenuestjames; 10.30 pm; closed Sun D; set always available £36 (FP).

Awesome Thai SW13 £28   3 4 3
68 Church Rd 020 8563 7027 11–1A
"Super-fresh, very tasty cooking at good prices" has made this "authentic Thai" opposite Barnes's popular Olympic Studios cinema a long-time favourite among local families. "The set lunch is excellent value", too. / SW13 0DQ; www.awesomethai.co.uk; 10.30 pm, Sun 10 pm; Mon-Thu D only, Fri-Sun open L & D.

Le Bab W1 NEW £42   5 4 3
2nd Floor, Kingly Ct 020 7439 9222 4–2B
"Just what street food crossovers should be like"; this "gourmet take on the kebab" – now permanently housed at the top of the food court off Carnaby Street – is "awesome". The "owners are engaging and passionate" and the food's "a wonderful seasonal and flavourful twist on an old favourite". / W1B 5PW; www.eatlebab.com; @EatLeBab; 11 pm, Sun 7 pm.

Babaji Pide W1 £39   2 2 3
73 Shaftesbury Ave 020 3327 3888 5–3A
Hakkasan founder Alan Yau's year-old concept on Shaftesbury Avenue already "seems to have lost its first flush of fine food and enthusiasm". Fans do still say its "filled Turkish pizza (pide) are really quite special", but even they can find it "less memorably original" than it first was, and service can be "terrible" ("you just get forgotten!") / W1D 6EX; www.babaji.com.tr; 11 pm, Fri & Sat 11.30 pm, Sun 10 pm.

Babur SE23 £53   5 5 4
119 Brockley Rise 020 8291 2400 1–4D
It's "worth the trek" across south London to this "sensory experience" in Forest Hill. The modern Indian cuisine – amongst London's best – has huge "subtlety of flavour" and the "unfailingly friendly and positive staff" are "exceptional". / SE23 1JP; www.babur.info; @BaburRestaurant; 11.30 pm.

Babylon, Kensington Roof Gardens W8 £72   2 2 3
99 Kensington High St 020 7368 3993 6–1A
"Wonderful views over west London" are a pull at this "specially situated" and "moodily decorated" Kensington penthouse, where you can cap off a meal with a stroll around the incredible roof gardens. Reactions to the modern British cuisine are mixed – to fans "ambitious and well executed", to foes "pretentious style over substance". / W8 5SA; www.virginlimitededition.com/en/the-roof-gardens/b; 10.30 pm; closed Sun D; set weekday L £46 (FP), set Sun L £51 (FP); SRA-3 star.

Bacco TW9 £49 3 3 3
39-41 Kew Rd 020 8332 0348 1–4A
This "unpretentious" Italian local is "convenient for both the Orange Tree and Richmond theatres" – as well as being close to the station. "Unfortunately, it's not always consistent", but "homemade pasta is a strong suit", and "when on form it's fabulous". / TW9 2NQ; www.bacco-restaurant.co.uk; @BaccoRichmond; 11 pm; closed Sun.

Bageriet WC2 £14 3 4 3
24 Rose St 020 7240 0000 5–3C
"Swinging a cat would be hard" at this "tiny" Swedish café in Covent Garden with "excellent coffee", "incredible cakes and pastries"… and just eight chairs: "I just wish I could get a seat more often!" There's always take-away, and "the loaves they sell are pretty good, too". / WC2E 9EA; www.bageriet.co.uk; @BagerietLondon; 7 pm; closed Sun.

The Balcon, Sofitel St James SW1 £65 2 2 2
8 Pall Mall 020 7968 2900 2–3C
As a "good bet for a business lunch" or other West End rendezvous, this ex-bank off Trafalgar Square offers "wonderful architecture" and "a posh French bistro-style menu", which most – if not all – reporters say is "better than your typical, upmarket, chain-hotel brasserie". / SW1Y 5NG; www.thebalconlondon.com; @TheBalcon; 10.45 pm, Sun 9.45 pm.

Balthazar WC2 £69 1 1 3
4-6 Russell St 020 3301 1155 5–3D
"Riding the wave of its superior NYC cousin", Keith McNally's "buzzy" Grand Café in Covent Garden "could never live up to the hype that was built up around it, and it consistently falls flat". Sure, the "ornate" interior looks "spectacular", but the brasserie fare – no better than "fine" – is "horrendously expensive", and the room can become "chaotic and noisy", not helped by "service that manages to be simultaneously over-pushy and neglectful". Top Tip – "a classic for brunch". / WC2B 5HZ; www.balthazarlondon.com; @balthazarlondon; midnight, Sun 11 pm.

Baltic SE1 £54 3 4 4
74 Blackfriars Rd 020 7928 1111 10–4A
"Don't be distracted by the large list of homemade flavoured vodkas" and you can enjoy some "surprisingly interesting and varied Polish and Eastern European food" ("a cut above the usual stodge") at this "deceptively spacious" venue ("cocktail bar at the front, more formal dining area beyond"), whose "high ceilings and sparse modern look" result from the conversion of a Georgian factory near The Cut. / SE1 8HA; www.balticrestaurant.co.uk; @balticlondon; 11.15 pm, Sun 10.30 pm; closed Mon L.

Bandol SW10 £67 3 3 2
6 Hollywood Rd 020 7351 1322 6–3B
"High quality" Niçoise and Provençal sharing plates with wine from the region are the draw at this Chelsea yearling (from the people behind nearby Margaux). "Always great for delicious, light food – I could go back every week!" / SW10 9HY; www.barbandol.co.uk; @Margaux_Bandol; 11 pm, Sun 10 pm.

Bánh Bánh SE15 NEW £33

46 Peckham Rye no tel 1–4D

"Beautifully prepared Vietnamese food" from "a well-executed short menu" has won instant raves for this "absolutely charming" Peckham Rye newcomer – "only recently evolved from pop-up to permanent" and run "exceptionally well" by five siblings from the Nguyen family (plus mum). "Delicious cocktails too". / SE15; www.banhbanh.com; @BanhBanhHQ; 10 pm, Fri & Sat 10.30 pm, Sun 9 pm; closed Mon, Tue-Fri D only, Sat & Sun open L & D.

Banners N8 £43

21 Park Rd 020 8348 2930 1–1C

This hallowed all-day Crouch End stalwart majors on "big portions and big flavours", with a strong Caribbean bias on its menu of world food. It's particularly "great for breakfast/brunch" (perhaps less distinguished at other times), and has "a wonderful community feel". / N8 8TE; www.bannersrestaurant.com; 11 pm, Fri 11.30 pm, Sat midnight, Sun 10.30 pm; no Amex.

Bao £28

31 Windmill St, W1 01442 510 520 5–1A NEW

53 Lexington St, W1 awaiting tel 4–2C

"Pillowy-soft" and "very more-ish" Taiwanese steamed buns – "sublime pockets of taste" filled with "fabulously spiced meats" – justify the ever-present queues for this Soho phenomenon. "They like you in and out quickly", and "the tiny premises and jam-packed tables don't encourage lingering". (A second Fitzrovia branch opened in mid-2016 in the premises that were Boopshis.) / see web for detail.

Baozi Inn WC2 £24

26 Newport Ct 020 7287 6877 5–3B

This "cheap, kitsch and wacky" Chinatown caff "hung with Chairman Mao memorabilia" serves "great steamed buns, dandan noodles and dumplings" and "is ideal both for a snack or to fill up". Disclaimers: "you may have to wait", "it will never win points for service or comfortable chairs", it's "cash only, and don't expect to linger". / WC2H 7JS; www.baoziinnlondon.com; 10 pm, Fri & Sat 10.30 pm; cash only; no bookings.

Bar Boulud, Mandarin Oriental SW1 £71

66 Knightsbridge 020 7201 3899 6–1D

"The gourmet burgers are worth all the hype" at this relatively "casual" Belgravia outpost of the NYC super-chef, and although it's "full of suits and monied types", other dishes on the "Lyon-via-Manhattan" menu are "reasonable value for the ultra-luxe location" (in the basement of a super-swanky Knightsbridge hotel). / SW1X 7LA; www.barboulud.com; @barbouludlondon; 10.45 pm, Sun 9.45 pm; set weekday L & dinner £37 (FP).

Bar Esteban N8 £39

29 Park Rd 020 8340 3090 1–1C

"Fabulous, lip-smacking tapas and great service" bring the Crouch End crowd to this "busy, fun" local – "we're so lucky to live nearby!" / N8 8TE; www.baresteban.com; @barestebanN8; Mon-Thu 9.30 pm, Fri & Sat 10.30 pm, Sun 9 pm.

Bar Italia W1 £32

22 Frith St 020 7437 4520 5–2A

"When in London, I just HAVE to go for my espresso fix!" – this legendary Italian pitstop in the heart of Soho is "not the absolute best for coffee, nor the best for service, but still the winner on ambience, style and history", and rammed at all hours. / W1D 4RF; www.baritaliasoho.co.uk; @TheBaristas; open 24 hours, Sun 4 am; no Amex; no bookings.

Bar Termini W1 £35 3 4 5
7 Old Compton St   awaiting tel   5–2B
"What it lacks in size it makes up in for in substance…" Tony Conigliaro's "tiny" Soho joint is "a reminder of how bars work in Italy – great cappuccino in the morning and then exquisitely prepared aperitifs, digestivi and cocktails". "The bar food's authentic and the Negronis short and sharp as they should be!" / W1D 5JE; www.bar-termini.com; @Bar_Termini; Mon-Thu 11.30 pm, Fri & Sat 1 am, Sun 10.30 pm.

The Barbary WC2 NEW £44
16 Neal's Yard   awaiting tel   5–2C
From the team behind smash-hit, The Palomar, comes a new summer 2016 venture celebrating the tastes of the Barbary Coast, from North Africa to Jerusalem. The tiny, 24-cover venue in Neal's Yard doesn't take bookings, unfortunately: we suggest you start queuing now. / WC2H 9DP; www.thebarbary.co.uk; no bookings.

Barbecoa £66 2 2 2
Nova, Victoria St, SW1   no tel   2–4C NEW
194-196 Piccadilly, W1   awaiting tel   4–4C
20 New Change Pas, EC4   020 3005 8555   10–2B
For "a good, if expensive" business lunch, numerous expense accounters recommend Jamie Oliver's "rather American-feeling shed of a space, in a shopping centre, overlooking St Paul's" (with branches in Victoria and Piccadilly), whose speciality is US-style BBQ. Even some fans feel "it's really not worth the price you pay" however, and to sceptics it's just totally "uninspiring and average". / @Barbecoa_london; see web for detail.

La Barca SE1 £75 2 2 2
80-81 Lower Marsh   020 7928 2226   10–4A
An "unassuming-looking" age-old trattoria near Waterloo station capable of some "quality, traditional Italian" cooking; even fans advise care when ordering however – "order a pasta and a glass of decent vino and you can escape with a modest bill", otherwise it can be "ridiculously expensive". / SE1 7AB; www.labarca-ristorante.com; @labarca1976; 11.30 pm; closed Sat L & Sun.

Il Baretto W1 £74 2 2 2
43 Blandford St   020 7486 7340   2–1A
Despite pukka backing and high prices, this "noisy" basement Italian in Marylebone continues to inspire a mixed rep. As a business venue it has its fans, but scores are mixed given a pizza and pasta offering that can seem "hideously expensive for what it really is". / W1U 7HF; www.ilbaretto.co.uk; @IlBarettoLondon; 10.15 pm, Sun 9.45 pm; set weekday L £50 (FP).

Barnyard W1 £44 2 3 3
18 Charlotte St   020 7580 3842   2–1C
Ollie Dabbous's "deliberately barn-like" Fitzrovia "novelty" hasn't particularly made waves of late, but escaped the harsh critiques of last year, with fans "more than impressed" by its eclectic comfort-food small plates (although they're too small for some tastes… especially at the price). / W1T 2LZ; www.barnyard-london.com; Mon-Wed 10 pm, Thu-Sat 10.30 pm, Sun 8.30 pm.

Barrafina £42 5 5 5
54 Frith St, W1 020 7813 8016 5–2A
10 Adelaide St, WC2 020 7440 1456 5–4C
43 Drury Ln, WC2 020 7440 1456 5–2D

"It's a theatrical experience to watch your food being prepared with such artistic delicacy and loving care" at the Hart Bros' "rightly celebrated" bars, whose "utterly brilliant" tapas is "better even than in Barcelona". Despite "a queue visible from the space station" (at W1 especially), the food is "totally worth the wait every time" and the "terrific and very kind" staff add to the "wonderfully dynamic" atmosphere. "Exceptionally, the spin-offs are as good as the original" (each is "subtly different"), but in autumn 2016, change is afoot, as the original Frith Street branch moves site into the redeveloped ground floor of nearby Quo Vadis (see also). Top Menu Tip – "everything is bloomin' marvellous and fresh, but anything out of the sea most especially so". / www.barrafina.co.uk; 11 pm, Sun 10 pm; no booking.

Barrica W1 £55 3 3 3
62 Goodge St 020 7436 9448 2–1B

"Utterly reliable Goodge Street tapas and wine bar, serving much more interesting and substantial offerings than the norm". With "scrumptious plates and a strong wine list", it's "as close to authentic as you'll get". / W1T 4NE; www.barrica.co.uk; @barricatapas; 10.30 pm; closed Sun.

Barshu W1 £56 4 2 2
28 Frith St 020 7287 6688 5–3A

"If you like really good spicy food, look no further" – this Sichuan café in Soho shows a "rare fidelity" to the fiery cuisine, and provides "a good alternative to the standard Chinese in nearby Chinatown". "Favourites include numbing and hot dried beef, and dry wok pig intestines". / W1D 5LF; www.barshurestaurant.co.uk; 10.30 pm, Fri & Sat 11 pm.

Bbar SW1 £54 3 4 3
43 Buckingham Palace Rd 020 7958 7000 2–4B

"A handy pitstop within the Victoria area" – overlooking the Royal Mews – this bar/restaurant "provides a good selection of South African wines and tasty bar snacks", with "great moist burgers" the highlight of the "South African-inspired menu". / SW1W 0PP; www.bbarlondon.com; @bbarlondon; 10 pm; closed Sun D; no shorts.

Bea's Cake Boutique WC1 £39 3 2 3
44 Theobalds Rd 020 7242 8330 2–1D

"The best cupcakes in London", swoon fans of the Bloomsbury original – a cosy café near Gray's Inn. Naturally it's "absolutely fantastic for afternoon tea". / WC1X 8NW; www.beasofbloomsbury.com; @beas_bloomsbury; 7 pm; L only.

Beast W1 £115 2 2 2
3 Chapel Pl 020 7495 1816 3–1B

"Huge" portions of high-quality surf 'n' turf – served in "the most dramatic setting" of candlelit communal tables – is the bold proposition of this Goodman-owned two-year-old off Oxford Street. But even if "the food is excellent, prices are way OTT", and very "hard to justify". And it's not a place for an "intimate date" – more of an "expensive team night out" if you've got a boss with deep pockets. / W1G 0BG; www.beastrestaurant.co.uk; @beastrestaurant; 10.30 pm; closed Mon L, Tue L, Wed L & Sun.

Beer & Buns EC2 £36 **3** **3** **4**
3 Appold St   020 7539 9209   13–2B
*"A wide selection of Japanese beers with the musical backdrop of heavy
rock" sets the scene at this (permanent) 'pop up izakaya', above K10 –
"so much fun", with buns and spicy wings that are "so tasty". / EC2A 2AF;
www.beerandbuns.co.uk; @Beer_And_Buns; Mon-Fri 11 pm; closed Mon L, Tue L,
Wed L, Sat & Sun.*

The Begging Bowl SE15 £37 **5** **4** **3**
168 Bellenden Rd   020 7635 2627   1–4D
*"Way above the level of anything else Thai for miles around Peckham" –
this no-booking hotspot may be "more cramped than a hamster's cage
thanks to its popularity" (and "is not cheap") but provides "friendly,
accommodating service" and superbly "tasty, spicy food". / SE15 4BW;
www.thebeggingbowl.co.uk; @thebeggingbowl; Mon-Sat 9.45 pm, Sun 9.15 pm;
no bookings.*

Bel Canto, Corus Hotel Hyde Park W2 £58 **2** **3** **4**
1 Lancaster Gate   020 7262 1678   7–2C
*Expect to have your dinner punctuated by professionally sung operatic arias
if you dine at this Bayswater basement dining room, solidly-rated (albeit
on limited feedback) in all aspects of its operation. / W2 3LG;
www.belcantolondon.co.uk; 10.30 pm; D only, closed Mon & Sun.*

Bellamy's W1 £61 **3** **4** **3**
18-18a Bruton Pl   020 7491 2727   3–2B
*"The tucked-away location adds to the charm" of Gavin Rankin's
"very clubbable", "art-lined" brasserie, in a "picturesque mews" –
"a delightful choice for a civilised lunch, whether for business or pleasure",
serving "a limited choice" of "very good, bistro-style dishes", which are
"reasonably priced… for Mayfair". (One of a handful of London
restaurants ever visited by The Queen.) / W1J 6LY;
www.bellamysrestaurant.co.uk; 10.30 pm; closed Sat L & Sun.*

Bellanger N1 £58 **2** **2** **3**
9 Islington Grn   020 7226 2555   9–3D
*"Finally a 'grown-up' restaurant on Upper Street" – fans of Corbin & King's
replacement for Browns (RIP) on Islington Green adore this "elegant", large
yearling, with its "enveloping wood and brass interior". "The hype is a little
overdone" though – the "kind-of-Alsatian menu" (lots of tartes flambées
and choucroute) can seem "a tad underwhelming" (and "if you don't like
this style of food, you have to pick your way through the menu") and all-in-
all standards seem "reliable but unremarkable". / N1 2XH;
www.bellanger.co.uk; @BellangerN1; 11 pm, Sun 10.30 pm.*

Belvedere W8 £69 **2** **2** **4**
Holland Pk, off Abbotsbury Rd   020 7602 1238   8–1D
*"Nothing beats this venue" – a grand 17th-century former ballroom inside
Holland Park – "for a summer lunch, it just has all the ingredients". But
even fans concede that it's "not cheap" and that "the food won't blow your
mind", and sceptics say "it should be wonderful, but needs a relaunch".
/ W8 6LU; www.belvedererestaurant.co.uk; 10.30 pm; closed Sun D.*

Benares W1   £95   1 1 2
12a Berkeley Square House,   020 7629 8886   3–3B
Fans still laud the "subtle, gorgeous flavours" of Atul Kochar's cuisine which have made this "classy" if slightly "oddly furnished (shades of the '70s)" gourmet Indian, in rambling first-floor premises by Berkeley Square, one of London's best-known dining destinations. However, its ratings have cratered in recent times due to too many experiences of "Keystone Kops" service and food that just seems "expensive and very average". / W1J 6BS; www.benaresrestaurant.co.uk; @benaresofficial; 10.45 pm, Sun 9.45 pm; closed Sun L.

Bentley's W1   £82   3 4 4
11-15 Swallow St   020 7734 4756   4–4B
"Steeped in history", this 100-year-old institution near Piccadilly Circus is "most atmospheric in the downstairs oyster bar" (there's also a more stately first-floor restaurant). Richard Corrigan presides over "a fab choice of the finest fish, with oysters to die for". / W1B 4DG; www.bentleys.org; @bentleys_london; 10.30 pm, Sun 9.30pm; no shorts; booking max 8 may apply; set weekday L & pre-theatre £57 (FP).

Berber & Q E8   £42   4 3 5
Arch 338 Acton Mews   020 7923 0829   14–2A
"It looks like style-over-substance, but it's the real deal!" – this "simply brilliant" North African-inspired grill in an oh-so-hip Haggerston railway arch continues to surf the zeitgeist with its lovely cocktails and "amazing, smoky, unctuous meat and stunning vegetable sides" (and, sadly, also its no bookings policy). / E8 4EA; www.berberandq.com; @berberandq; 10.30 pm, Sun 9.30 pm; D only, closed Mon.

Berber & Q Shawarma Bar EC1 NEW   £30
Exmouth Market   020 7837 1726   10–1A
From Hackney's Berber & Q founders, Josh & Paul Katz and Mattia Bianchi, this Exmouth Market shawarma bar specialising in slow cooked, spit-roasted lamb and Middle Eastern-style rotisserie chicken opened post-survey in June 2016. / EC1R 4QL; www.berberandq.com; @berberandq; Tue-Sat 10.30 pm, Sun 9.30 pm; closed Mon; no bookings.

Bernardi's W1 NEW   £60   3 4 3
62 Seymour Street   020 3826 7940   2–2A
"There's a lot to like about this smart but fairly traditional Italian newcomer" in the calm corner of Marylebone off Seymour Place: "a great neighbourhood spot" where "everything is done properly" in a "modern Italian classic style without pretentions or a big bill". It's "huge" however, and when busy "would be transformed enormously by installing carpets to deaden noise", and "when empty has no atmosphere". / W1H 5BN; www.bernardis.co.uk; @BernardisLondon; 10.30 pm, Fri & Sat 11 pm, Sun 9 pm.

The Berners Tavern,
London Edition W1   £73   2 2 4
10 Berners St   020 7908 7979   3–1D
"A wow of a space" ("formerly a vast, voluminous banking hall") provides "a stunning backdrop" to a meal at what fans say is "London's chicest dining room", north of Oxford Street. It can seem like a case of "style over substance" though – the food (overseen by Jason Atherton) is "good but not amazing", and at the punishing price can seem "a huge let down". / W1T 3NP; www.bernerstavern.com; 11.45 pm, Sun 10.15 pm.

Best Mangal £36 **4** **3** **2**
619 Fulham Rd, SW6   020 7610 0009   6–4A
104 North End Rd, W14   020 7610 1050   8–2D
66 North End Rd, W14   020 7602 0212   8–2D
"Not your average kebab joints" – this Turkish trio in west London are popular "cheap 'n' cheerful" pitstops due to their "very good charcoal-grilled meats and super-fresh salads", in "very generous" portions. / www.bestmangal.com; midnight, Sat 1 am; no Amex.

Bibendum SW3 £76
81 Fulham Rd   020 7581 5817   6–2C
"One of London's great dining spaces" – this "spacious room in an iconic site" (the old Michelin Building on Brompton Cross) is best enjoyed at lunchtime when "the daylight filtering through the skylight is lovely". Its "refinement and elegance" and "very fine" wine list make it a still-popular business treat, but – in contrast to the physical refurbishment this year – "a shake-up of the kitchen is overdue": the food is too often "rather ordinary", especially at the "OTT prices". STOP PRESS – the longed for shake-up is coming soon – chef Claude Bosi is rumoured to be moving here in February 2017! / SW3 6RD; www.bibendum.co.uk; @bibendumltd; 11 pm, Sun 10.30 pm; booking max 12 may apply.

Bibendum Oyster Bar SW3 £53 **4** **2** **4**
81 Fulham Rd   020 7589 1480   6–2C
This "wonderful tiled room" off the foyer of Michelin House is a well-known Chelsea rendezvous for "good seafood and a glass of wine". "The shellfish platter is still superb, as is their petit pot de chocolat". STOP PRESS – the Claude Bosi managed makeover of the main restaurant is likely to involve this ground floor space: details are as yet unknown. / SW3 6RD; www.bibendum.co.uk; @bibendumrestaurant; 10 pm; no bookings.

Bibimbap £29 **2** **2** **2**
10 Charlotte St, W1   020 7287 3434   2–1C
11 Greek St, W1   020 7287 3434   5–2A
39 Leadenhall Mkt, EC3   020 7283 9165   10–2D
"Grab a cheap, fast bite in a spendy part of town", at these "bustling no-frills Korean canteens" in Soho and Fitzrovia (plus 'To Go' in the City). There's the odd cautionary report though: "I've been coming for years and am really disappointed with my last 2 visits – dry rice in the signature dish, and heavy handed on the soy!" / see web for detail.

Bibo SW15 £51 **3** **3** **3**
146 Upper Richmond Rd   020 8780 0592   11–2B
"Interesting Italian food" (for example, "spicy n'duja croquettes, rabbit ragu and Amalfi lemon doughnuts") make this Putney sibling to Sonny's in Barnes "a high-end and accomplished" modern Italian: "not just the usual pasta but proper cooking". / SW15 2SW; www.biborestaurant.com; @biborestaurant; 10.45 pm.

Big Easy   £54   2 2 3
12 Maiden Ln, WC2   020 3728 4888   5–3D
332-334 King's Rd, SW3   020 7352 4071   6–3C
Crossrail Pl, E14   020 3841 8844   12–1C
Fans report "an adequate meat-fest" and "great lobsters and shrimp" too
at these "fun" US-style BBQ shacks, although "given the proliferation
of other smokehouses nowadays" even supporters acknowledge "there's
better BBQ elsewhere". Both Covent Garden and the Chelsea original
outscore their huge new Canary Wharf sibling, which divides opinion;
enthusiasts say "it's a great night out, with a stunning bar and top live
music" – sceptics just feel it provides "horrible everything".
/ www.bigeasy.co.uk; @bigeasytweet; Mon-Thu 11 pm, Fri-Sat 11.30, Sun 10.30 pm.

Bill or Beak NW1   £14   4 4 –
Inside King's Boulevard   07791 787567   n/a–n/a
"Worth a detour and a rain-soaked lunch" – these habitués
of (amongst other venues) Street Feast, Model Market, and Kerb stand out
for reporters: "the Vietnamese pork and duck burger with truffle and
Parmesan fries is worth a trip alone!" / NW1; www.billorbeak.co.uk;
@BillorBeak.

Billy & The Chicks W1 NEW   £29   3 3 2
27-28 St Anne's Ct   020 7287 8111   5–2A
More "nicely seasoned fancy chicken" in Soho (opposite Zelman Meats) –
this time deep-fried by Billy Stock (latterly of St John and Salt Yard Group),
and as is now de rigueur using only free-range British birds (in this case
Cotswold Whites). / W1F 0BN; www.billyandthechicks.com; @Billyandthechix;
11 pm; closed Sun.

The Bingham TW10   £66   3 4 4
61-63 Petersham Rd   020 8940 0902   1–4A
"Always a joy", this "delightful restaurant in the elegant surroundings" of a
Richmond boutique hotel "has a balcony overlooking the garden and the
River Thames" – "a treat for lunch or evening romance". There's also
"afternoon tea to match anything in central London!" / TW10 6UT;
www.thebingham.co.uk; 10 pm; closed Sun D; no trainers.

Bird   £38   3 2 2
81 Holloway Rd, N7   020 3195 8788   9–2D
21-22 Chalk Farm Rd, NW1   020 3195 4245   9–2B NEW
Westfield Stratford, Montfichet Road, E20   no tel   14–1D NEW
42-44 Kingsland Rd, E2   020 7613 5168   13–1B
"You get exactly what you'd expect – tasty chicken, nothing more!" – at this
"fun fried-chicken place" in Shoreditch (now with branches in Islington,
Camden and Westfield). "The beer on hand isn't bad, either…" / see web
for detail.

Bird in Hand W14   £46   3 3 4
Brook Green   020 7371 2721   8–1C
"The pizzas are wonderful" ("if hardly cheap") and "the setting even
better" at this "fun and lively" backstreet haunt in Olympia (sibling to The
Oak in W11 and SW12). / W14 0LR; www.thebirdinhandlondon.com;
@TBIHLondon; 10 pm, Sun 9.15 pm.

Bird of Smithfield EC1   £64   2 2 2
26 Smithfield St   020 7559 5100   10–2B
"It's popular with business lunchers", but this five-storey Georgian
townhouse in Smithfield (with summer roof terrace) attracts somewhat
mixed reviews ("OK"… "fine but unremarkable"). "Nice bar though".
/ EC1A 9LB; www.birdofsmithfield.com; @BirdoSmithfield; 10 pm; closed Sun.

Bistro Aix N8   £54   **4 3 3**
54 Topsfield Pde, Tottenham Ln   020 8340 6346   9–1C
"When you walk through the door you feel as though you're in France" at this small Crouch End bistro where *"the cuisine is always good and the service exceptional"*. Fans agree it's *"one of the best locals"* – *"I've been going for years and always get the same good quality food"*. / N8 8PT; www.bistroaix.co.uk; @bistroaixlondon; 10 pm, Fri & Sat 11 pm; Mon-Thu D only, Fri-Sun open L & D; no Amex.

Bistro Union SW4   £46   **3 3 3**
40 Abbeville Rd   020 7042 6400   11–2D
Adam Byatt's bistro spinoff from Trinity in Clapham is a "relaxed place for good British food" – *"terrific value, great for the kids, excellent food and friendly staff"*. Top Tip – *"Their Sunday Supper offering is a huge winner"*, BYO and kids eat free. / SW4 9NG; www.bistrounion.co.uk; @BistroUnion; 10 pm, Sun 8 pm.

Bistrotheque E2   £58   **3 3 4**
23-27 Wadeson St   020 8983 7900   14–2B
Critics may say it's "trading on its five minutes of fame as the original hipster hangout ten years ago", but most reports say this East End warehouse-conversion is *"hard to find, but worth the effort"* – *"a light and airy space, with a solid range of offerings (particularly drinks…)"* / E2 9DR; www.bistrotheque.com; @bistrotheque; 10.30 pm, Fri & Sat 11 pm; closed weekday L; set pre theatre £39 (FP).

Black Axe Mangal N1   NEW   £50   **5 3 2**
156 Canonbury Road   no tel   9–2D
"Heavy metal kebabs!" – *"The soundtrack is not for everyone"* but *"if you can handle the loud metal and strong spices"*, you can enjoy some *"mindblowingly good"* and unexpectedly audacious cooking at KISS-fan and owner Lee Tiernan's (ex-head chef of St John Bread & Wine) tiny, off-the-wall Highbury Corner newcomer. *"Amazing"* flatbread starters are followed up with extremely *"different"* kebab mains, many featuring offal. / N1; www.blackaxemangal.com; @blackaxemangal; Tue-Sat 10.30 pm, Sun 3 pm; closed Mon, Tue L, Wed L, Thu L, Fri L & Sun D; no bookings.

Black Roe W1   NEW   £66   **3 3 3**
4 Mill Street   020 3794 8448   3–2C
"Kicking off a new London craze for poké (a Hawaiian raw fish dish)" – Kurt Zdesar's (of Chotto Matte fame) *"on-trend"* newcomer in the heart of Mayfair also provides more substantial fare from a Kiawe (mesquite tree) wood grill. It's *"very expensive"*, but *"the food is zingy and fresh"* and it has a good *"clubby vibe"*. / W1S 2AX; www.blackroe.com; @blackroe; 10.45 pm; closed Sun.

Blacklock W1   £35   **5 4 4**
25 Great Windmill St   020 3441 6996.   4–2D
"The best chops in London", draw devotees to this *"simple but winning"* two-year-old in a bare-brick Soho basement that sells very little else. *"Meat overload (in a good way)"* – *"smokey grilled chops, chips and wine: what's not to like?"* The no-reservations policy is *"a hassle, but they send you a text to come back from the pub when they're ready"*. / W1D 7LH; www.theblacklock.com; @blacklocksoho; 11.30 pm; closed Sun; may need 6+ to book.

F S A

Blanchette £39 `4` `4` `5`
9 D'Arblay St, W1   020 7439 8100   4–1C
204 Brick Lane, E1   020 7729 7939   13–1C **NEW**
"A touch of France in the centre of London" – this "buzzing" two-year-old
"feels like it's been in Soho for years" and is "an excellent place for the
price". "Traditional-ish Gallic dishes with a tapas twist" – "rustically
presented and packed with flavour" – include "a good selection of regional
French cheeses and charcuterie". 'Blanchette East' opened in mid-
August 2016 on east London's curry mile, with a similar menu, but also
new Southern French and North African dishes. / see web for detail.

Blandford Comptoir W1 **NEW** £53 `4` `4` `4`
1 Blandford Street   020 7935 4626   2–1A
"A superb wine list, well laid out, and fairly priced" (with 250 bins and
50 champagnes) is the cornerstone of this small Marylebone newcomer –
from Texture and 28°-50° co-founder Xavier Rousset – but its varied
menus of small and large plates gets a strong thumbs up too. / W1U 3DA;
www.blandford-comptoir.co.uk; @BlandfordCompt; 10 pm.

Bleecker Street Burger E1 £16 `5` `2` `2`
Unit B Pavilion Building, Spitalfields Mkt   077125 40501   13–2B
"Undeniably the best burger in London, if not the UK and/or world!" –
so claim devotees of former New York corporate lawyer Zan Kaufman's
"basic" pop-up-gone-permanent in Spitalfields (and still also trading
at various market locations). Their "simple, juicy beef patty in a bun
doesn't try to be fancy or different, but ticks all the burger boxes". / E1 6AA;
www.bleeckerburger.co.uk; @bleeckerburger; 9 pm.

Bleeding Heart Restaurant EC1 £64 `3` `3` `5`
Bleeding Heart Yd, Greville St   020 7242 8238   10–2A
"Time just flows away irrelevantly" at this "olde-worlde" warren, "hidden
away in a yard" on the fringe of the City. Its "dark", Dickensian interior has
"bucket loads of charm" and provides both "a propitious atmosphere for
client deals" over "a lengthy lunch", and also a perfect spot "for a quiet
tryst". The "fabulous wine list" ("with an Antipodean twist") outshines what
is nevertheless "solid" French cuisine, delivered by "proper French waiters".
/ EC1N 8SJ; www.bleedingheart.co.uk; @bleedingheartyd; 10.30 pm; closed
Sat & Sun.

Blixen E1 £52 `3` `4` `4`
65a Brushfield St   020 7101 0093   13–2B
This all-day Spitalfields brasserie (no relation to the Out of Africa writer)
offers a "very enjoyable" menu from brunch to dinner, with "entertaining
and helpful service". "The basement private dining area feels like a retro
drinking den". / E1 6AA; www.blixen.co.uk; @BlixenLondon; 11 pm, Sun 8 pm.

Bluebird SW3 £64
350 King's Rd   020 7559 1000   6–3C
"Never again!" is still too often the verdict on this prominent D&D London
landmark of nearly 20 years' standing on the King's Road whose airy
interior should be "good for all occasions", but too often falls short when
it comes to the "snooty" service or "limited and mediocre" food.
In September 2016 it relaunched after a £2m refit – perhaps they will
have finally sorted this one out. / SW3 5UU; www.bluebird-restaurant.co.uk;
@bluebirdchelsea; 10.30 pm, Sun 9.30 pm.

Blueprint Café, Design Museum SE1 £51   2 2 5
28 Shad Thames, Butler's Wharf   020 7378 7031   10–4D
"The setting has lost none of its wow-factor" at this "river-view" dining room – a stunning vantage-point (binoculars are provided!) Since Jeremy Lee left a couple of years ago, some reports suggest the cooking has "lost its pizazz", but ratings aren't so bad, and in truth the food's never been the main point here. / SE1 2YD; www.blueprintcafe.co.uk; @BlueprintCafe; 10.30 pm; no bookings.

Bob Bob Exchange EC3 NEW
122 Leadenhall Street   no tel   10–2D
This sibling to Soho's Bob Bob Ricard is to open in April 2017, occupying the entire third floor of 'The Cheesegrater'. More 'press for champagne' buttons are promised, alongside grills, bites, wine auctions and a sushi bar. One thing we know already: it won't be understated. / EC3V 4PE.

Bob Bob Ricard W1 £66   3 4 5
1 Upper James St   020 3145 1000   4–2C
"An emergency champagne button.... what more can you ask for!?" – Leonid Shutov's splendidly "OTT" Soho venue, with its conspiratorial and "romantic" booths, provides a "gorgeous setting for a fun night out" or "enjoyable brunch". Critics fear its "comfort" food is "expensive and ordinary", but most reporters feel it's "very enjoyable". / W1F 9DF; www.bobbobricard.com; @BobBobRicard; Sun-Fri 11.15 pm, Sat midnight; closed Sat L; jacket required.

The Bobbin SW4 £46   3 4 4
1-3 Lillieshall Rd   020 7738 8953   11–1D
This sidestreet gastropub "caters charmingly to everyone from the Clapham cool crowd to mums and dads with buggies". A "lovely little garden" and airy conservatory are ideal for "long and chilled Sunday lunches", but there's "plenty of vibe on Friday nights". / SW4 0LN; www.thebobbinclapham.com; @bobbinsw4; 10 pm, Sun 9 pm.

Bobo Social W1 £45   4 4 3
95 Charlotte St   020 7636 9310   2–1C
"Highest quality" rare-breed burgers – "I am American, so you must take it as an article of faith that the Bobo burger is the best burger ever" – win high praise for this small town-house conversion in Fitzrovia. Critics say the decor is "too try-hard" but fans find it "refreshing". / W1T 4PZ; www.bobosocial.com; @BoboSocial; 10.30 pm; closed Sun.

Bocca Di Lupo W1 £59   5 4 4
12 Archer St   020 7734 2223   4–3D
"Discover what REAL Italian food is all about" at Jacob Kennedy and Victor Hugo's "buzzing and exciting" venue, a short walk from Piccadilly Circus: its "inventive" tapas-style plates – an ever-changing selection "from the remotest corners of Italy" – are "unbelievably good" and backed up by a "gorgeous" wine list "full of regional gems". Sitting it at the bar, "watching the skill and intensity of the chefs" is a favourite perch. / W1D 7BB; www.boccadilupo.com; @boccadilupo; 11 pm, Sun 9.30 pm; booking max 10 may apply.

Bocconino W1 £72   3 3 3
19 Berkeley St   020 7499 4510   3–3C
"A real sensibly priced gem in Mayfair" – who'd have thought a Russian-owned yearling in this eurotrashiest heart of town would be this "very pleasant venue with good pizza and pasta"? "You could pay a lot more for poorer quality food just around the corner". / W1J 8ED; www.bocconcinorestaurant.co.uk; @BocconcinoUK; 11.30 pm, Sun 10.30 pm.

Al Boccon di'vino TW9 £68 4 4 5
14 Red Lion St 020 8940 9060 1–4A
"Lucky Richmond" to have this "memorably amazing culinary experience"
– "fabulous Italian food", but "no menu, no choices, no prices", just "a wild
ride with a surprise for every course". "Only visit when you're hungry" –
"you get a lot of food"; and "be prepared to share your happiness with the
strangers at adjoining (very closely adjoining) tables". / TW9 1RW;
www.nonsolovinoltd.co.uk; 8 pm; closed Mon, Tue L & Wed L; no Amex.

Bodean's £44 2 2 2
10 Poland St, W1 020 7287 7575 4–1C
25 Catherine St, WC2 020 7257 2790 5–3D **NEW**
4 Broadway Chambers, SW6 020 7610 0440 6–4A
348 Muswell Hill Broadway, N10 no tel 1–1C **NEW**
225 Balham High St, SW17 020 8682 4650 11–2C **NEW**
169 Clapham High St, SW4 020 7622 4248 11–2D
201 City Rd, EC1 020 7608 7230 13–1A
16 Byward St, EC3 020 7488 3883 10–3D
"A carnivore's paradise", these Kansas City-style BBQ joints have become
a fixture after more than a decade in London, and they're still "great fun"
if "a tiny bit formulaic" – even those who say the food's "only OK" say "it'll
win you over if you're a meat-lover". / www.bodeansbbq.com; 11 pm,
Sun 10.30 pm; booking: min 8.

La Bodega Negra W1 £51 3 3 4
16 Moor St 020 7758 4100 5–2B
"Fun", "low-lit" basement Mexican in Soho – it gets mixed reviews for its
food, but is "so funky that you almost forget about it". / W1D 5NH;
www.labodeganegra.com; 1 am, Sun midnight.

Boisdale SW1 £63 2 2 3
13-15 Eccleston St 020 7730 6922 2–4B
Ranald Macdonald's "civilised and fun" Belgravia bastion – if you like all
things hearty and male – is known for its meaty Scottish fare ("splendid
grouse" and other game in season), marvellous wines and whiskies,
"excellent cigar terrace", and live jazz. Even those who feel prices are
excessive, or have encountered "poor service", say they use "superb quality
meat" and admit that results are "pretty good". / SW1W 9LX;
www.boisdale.co.uk; @boisdaleCW; midnight; closed Sat L & Sun.

Boisdale of Bishopsgate EC2 £66 2 2 2
202 Bishopsgate, Swedeland Ct 020 7283 1763 10–2D
"Down a narrow alley" near Liverpool Street, this City-outpost of the
Victoria original has a ground floor bar, and below it "a very red,
almost gothic-themed banquette-style dining room". Most often tipped as a
business venue: even those who felt "the bill was rather high",
say "the food was generally good, and steak excellent". / EC2M 4NR;
www.boisdale.co.uk; @Boisdale; 11 pm, Sat midnight; closed Sat & Sun.

Boisdale of Canary Wharf E14 £67 2 2 3
Cabot Pl 020 7715 5818 12–1C
The Canary Wharf spin-off from the Belgravia original is a popular
expense-accounter choice thanks to its views, meaty Scottish fare
("not complex but good"), spacious interior and Thames-side cigar terrace.
It does have its critics though, who say it's "hyped", or "OK but nothing
special". / E14 4QT; www.boisdale.co.uk; @boisdaleCW; 11 pm; closed Sun D.

Bombay Brasserie SW7 £60 3 3 3
Courtfield Road   020 7370 4040   6–2B

This "still stylish" South Kensington stalwart – known for its "bright and airy" conservatory – remains a "benchmark" for its fans, with its "subtle use of spices" and "comfortable" colonial decor. Its recent refurb doesn't wow everyone though, and some long-term fans feel "it's a shadow of its former self". / SW7 4QH; www.bombayb.co.uk; @bbsw7; 11 pm, Sun 10.30 pm; closed weekday L.

Bombay Palace W2 £49
50 Connaught St   020 7723 8855   7–1D

"Will it ever re-open?", sigh fans of this beloved – if monumentally dull-looking – Bayswater Indian. After a summer 2015 fire, its website has continued to promise that it will… and a date we understand has now been set as this guide goes to press (in autumn 2016). / W2 2AA; www.bombay-palace.co.uk; @bombaypalaceW2; 11 pm.

Bombetta E11 NEW
Station Approach   020 3871 0890   1–1D

A group of local foodies (including food writer Suzannah Butcher) have teamed up with owners of online Italian food suppliers The Chef's Deli, to open this new grill a short walk from Snaresbrook tube station, named for the Pugliese cheesy-meat street food bites that form part of its menu. It opened post-survey, but initial feedback suggests it's worth a try… especially if you're in Wanstead! / E11 1QE; www.bombettalondon.com; @bombettaLondon.

Bone Daddies £34 4 4 4
Nova, Victoria St, SW1   no tel   2–4C NEW
14a, Old Compton St, W1   020 7734 7492   5–2B
30-31 Peter St, W1   020 7287 8581   4–2D
Whole Foods, Kensington High St, W8   020 7287 8581   6–1A
The Bower, Baldwin St, EC1   020 7439 9299   13–1A

"Power-packed flavours" ("you'll never be able to touch Wagamama noodles again!") inspire drooling reviews for these "very hip Japanese-Western hybrids" in Soho, in High Street Ken's Whole Foods, and now also in Shoreditch and Victoria. "Service is by staff who are laid-back, but still know their stuff". / www.bonedaddies.com; see web for detail.

Bonhams Restaurant,
Bonhams Auction House W1 £69 4 5 3
101 New Bond St   020 7468 5868   3–2B

"Such a delight in a surprising location" – this "top-class" two-year-old sits off the back of the famous Mayfair auction house (with its own entrance). It's "a quiet and spacious" room in which to enjoy both Tom Kemble's accomplished cuisine and a "fantastic all-round wine list". / W1S 1SR; www.bonhams.com/locations/res; 8.30 pm; closed Sat & Sun.

Bonnie Gull W1 £59 4 4 3
21a Foley St   020 7436 0921   2–1B

"There's a real seaside feel to this small and cramped Fitzrovia dining room", whose "lovely and relaxed service", "casual, low-key appearance and nautical clichés belie the very tasty and sophisticated seafood that's served". / W1W 6DS; www.bonniegull.com; @BonnieGull; 9.45 pm, Sun 8.45 pm.

The Booking Office,
St Pancras Renaissance Hotel NW1   £67   ②②④
Euston Rd   020 7841 3566   9–3C
A "fantastic location" in the beautifully converted former St Pancras station
ticket office, with a "quiet and comfy lounge" attached makes this a "great
place to start the day with brunch" or for business meetings. The food? –
"nothing exotic" but "reasonable". / NW1 2AR;
www.bookingofficerestaurant.com; 11 pm.

Boondocks EC1 NEW
205 City Rd   07912 345678   13–1A
A follow-up to Bea Vo's Stax (which opened in Carnaby Street's Kingly Court
last year) – this sizeable, two-floor newcomer north of the Old Street
roundabout offers more American diner fare, and opened in late summer
2016. / EC1V 1JT; midnight.

Boqueria SW2   £34   ③④④
192 Acre Ln   020 7733 4408   11–2D
"Bustling and busy" tapas bar between Clapham and Brixton, now with
a Battersea offshoot. Both offer a "jolly" and "fun-packed" destination for
"interesting tapas, drawing inspiration from the traditional (patatas bravas
and tortilla) and beyond (tuna with almond and soy sauce)". / SW2 5UL;
www.boqueriatapas.com; @BoqueriaTapas; 11 pm, Fri & Sat midnight, Sun 10 pm;
closed weekday L.

Il Bordello E1   £51   ③④⑤
81 Wapping High St   020 7481 9950   12–1A
"Cosy, friendly, lively, jolly" – this "quintessential neighbourhood Italian
restaurant in Wapping is always overcrowded (a good sign)" and has
particularly "enthusiastic" service. "It churns out huge portions
of wholesome grub" (in particular "brilliant pizza") – "even when you are
at your hungriest, you will find it hard to finish your plate!" / E1W 2YN;
www.ilbordello.com; 11 pm, Sun 10.30 pm; closed Sat L.

Boro Bistro SE1   £42   ③③③
Montague Cl, 6-10 Borough High St   020 7378 0788   10–3C
Limited reports on this small Gallic bistro (with outside terrace),
by picturesque Southwark Cathedral – all are positive however on its food
offering, which includes charcuterie boards and cheese platters. / SE1 9QQ;
www.borobistro.co.uk; @borobistro; 10.30 pm.

The Botanist   £64   ②①②
7 Sloane Sq, SW1   020 7730 0077   6–2D
Broadgate Circle, EC2   020 3058 9888   13–2B
Attractive bar/restaurant on Sloane Square inspiring very mixed feelings:
fans say it delivers "a buzzy atmosphere and surprisingly good food" but
for its harshest critics "it's a package made in hell": "slow, crowded,
with indifferent service" and "awful, expensive cooking". (Limited feedback
on its Broadgate sibling). / thebotanist.uk.com; @botanistchester; see web for
detail.

Boudin Blanc W1   £59   ②③④
5 Trebeck St   020 7499 3292   3–4B
The "magical" Shepherd Market location "guarantees it will be full
most of the time" and – "if you can get an outside table in the sunshine" –
this "very very French" bistro is "hard to beat". Its cooking is quite well-
rated, but "the menu could do with a refresh", and "there's little sign
of flair". / W1J 7LT; www.boudinblanc.co.uk; 11 pm.

Boulestin SW1 £70 [2][2][2]
5 St James's St   020 7930 2030   3–4D
*Mixed views on Joel Kissin's St James's two-year-old, which revives the name
of a famous French basement in Covent Garden and serves classic Gallic
dishes. Fans proclaim it a "surprisingly chirpy and casual venue for SW1"
with a "lovely courtyard" (and "excellent breakfasts" too), but one or two
reports are dire, citing "dismal" results. / SW1A 1EF; www.boulestin.com;
@BoulestinLondon; 10.30 pm; closed Sun; no trainers; set weekday L, dinner &
pre-theatre £45 (FP).*

The Boundary E2 £64 [1][1][3]
2-4 Boundary St   020 7729 1051   13–1B
*"There's an amazing roof terrace, but the basement space is wonderful
too" at Sir Terence Conran's Shoreditch operation. Supporters claim the
food is likewise "excellent, with interesting combinations", but a worrying
number just find it "boring and badly presented". / E2 7DD;
www.theboundary.co.uk; @boundaryldn; 10.30 pm; D only, ex Sun L only.*

The Brackenbury W6 £53 [3][4][3]
129-131 Brackenbury Rd   020 8741 4928   8–1C
*"It's good having the Brack' back", say locals who love Ossie Gray's
relaunched "perfect local" in the backstreets of Hammersmith, with its
"interesting French/Italian dishes" and attractive summer terrace. It was
refurbished this year, to make one of the two rooms a more informal,
tapas-style bar. / W6 0BQ; www.brackenburyrestaurant.co.uk; @BrackenburyRest;
10 pm; closed Mon & Sun.*

Bradley's NW3 £60 [3][2][2]
25 Winchester Rd   020 7722 3457   9–2A
*"A mildly posh place, really convenient for Hampstead Theatre" –
this backstreet stalwart in Swiss Cottage "lacks buzz" but its cooking
is "worthwhile" and very "reliable". / NW3 3NR; www.bradleysnw3.co.uk;
10 pm; closed Sun D.*

Brady's SW18 £34 [3][3][3]
Dolphin Hs, Smugglers Way   020 8877 9599   11–2B
*"A great, local 'upmarket' fish 'n' chip restaurant" – "standards have stayed
high at the Brady family's newish, much larger location near the river"
in Battersea, which is "less manic" than its old longstanding home (which
it vacated a couple of years ago). / SW18 1DG; www.bradysfish.co.uk;
@Bradyfish; 10 pm; closed Mon, Tue L, Wed L, Thu L & Sun; no Amex; no bookings.*

La Brasserie SW3 £56 [2][2][4]
272 Brompton Rd   020 7581 3089   6–2C
*An "excellent French brasserie in the heart of Chelsea" – "reliable, unflashy
and cosy", although even fans admit it's "not cutting-edge" and "the food
quality could be improved". And it's "not the cheapest" either,
but "stop complaining – you'd pay more for less in Paris!" / SW3 2AW;
www.labrasserielondon.com; @labrasserie272; Mon-Sat 11.30 pm, Sun 11 pm.*

Brasserie Blanc £52 [1][2][2]
*"How does Raymond Blanc put his name to cooking of this quality?" This
bland modern brasserie chain does have its fans as a business standby,
but "it's gone downhill" in recent times – the food can be "very ordinary",
service "perfunctory" and "there's no sense of emotional ownership".
/ www.brasserieblanc.com; most branches close between 10 pm & 11 pm; SE1 closed
Sun D, most City branches closed Sat & Sun; SRA-2 star.*

Brasserie Gustave SW3 £62 **3** **4** **3**
4 Sydney St 020 7352 1712 6–2C
"Interesting variations on French classics" and "a really warm welcome from the owners and wait staff" help this Chelsea brasserie two-year-old draw "a lively and eclectic crowd". Named for Gustave Eiffel – he of the famous Parisian tower – it happily plays up to the national stereotype. / SW3 6PP; www.brasserie-gustave.com; @brassergustave; 10.30 pm; closed weekday L; set weekday L & pre-theatre £38 (FP).

Brasserie Toulouse-Lautrec SE11 £45 **3** **3** **3**
140 Newington Butts 020 7582 6800 1–3C
"Solid" Gallic bistro cooking founds the appeal of this oasis in a gloomy quarter of Kennington; it also has "a superb little jazz bar upstairs", and "if you're lucky enough to sit on the tiny roof terrace, then it's like a tiny slice of Paris". / SE11 4RN; www.btlrestaurant.co.uk; @btlrestaurant; 10.30 pm, Sat & Sun 11 pm.

BRASSERIE ZÉDEL W1 £40 **1** **3** **5**
20 Sherwood St 020 7734 4888 4–3C
For "glamour-on-the-cheap", nowhere matches Corbin & King's "so dazzling", gilded Art Deco basement – "an approximation to a huge Paris brasserie" just seconds from Piccadilly Circus, where "keen prices for this location" amount to "unbeatable value". It is a trade-off though – service can be "rushed" and the brasserie fodder is "so mediocre". / W1F 7ED; www.brasseriezedel.com; @brasseriezedel; 11.45 pm.

Bravas E1 £44 **3** **3** **2**
St Katharine Docks 020 7481 1464 10–3D
A "favourite" choice in St Katharine Docks for all who report – a Hispanic two-year-old, with dependable tapas and the picturesque backdrop of boats in the marina. / E1W 1AT; www.bravastapas.co.uk; @Bravas_Tapas; 10 pm.

Brawn E2 £51 **5** **4** **4**
49 Columbia Rd 020 7729 5692 13–1C
Ed Wilson's "intelligently thought-out" dishes "always give the same hearty, down-to-earth impression" ("simple, with no pretension, but clearly demonstrating a superb level of skill and creativity, and great ingredients") at his East End venture (nowadays under his sole ownership). "It's a light and bright room" epitomising "the best of East London design hype – an ex-workshop, with exposed brick, and zinc things", and "those who dine in the back room have the benefit of being able to see the open kitchen". The "unusual and intriguing" wine list "is not a brief read, but it rewards those who select 'off piste' options". / E2 7RG; www.brawn.co; @brawn49; 11 pm; closed Mon L & Sun D; no Amex.

Bread Street Kitchen EC4 £68 **2** **2** **3**
10 Bread St 020 3030 4050 10–2B
A "stylish" space and "lovely" breakfasts are two winning features of Gordon Ramsay's "enormous", "bustling" venue in a City shopping mall, most popular with expense-accounters. Scores have improved across the board in the last year, but there are still a fair few reporters who find it "noisy, expensive and totally uninspiring". / EC4M 9AJ; www.breadstreetkitchen.com; @breadstreet; 11 pm, Sun 8 pm.

Breakfast Club £27 3 3 2
33 D'Arblay St, W1   020 7434 2571   4–1C
2-4 Rufus St, N1   020 7729 5252   13–1B
31 Camden Pas, N1   020 7226 5454   9–3D
12-16 Artillery Ln, E1   020 7078 9633   13–2B
"Quirky, retro-fit" '80s-nostalgia diners which seem to be "popping up all over the capital". They do have their critics ("can't even pull off being a funky greasy spoon") but for most reporters the main problems are crazy waits and being "squeezed-in". "So long as you get there early – before the queues form round the block – you'll find easy and informal service and enough tasty scoff to last you a whole day" – "everyone happy!"

Briciole W1 £40 3 3 3
20 Homer St   020 7723 0040   7–1D
A "favourite discovery", this "small slice of Italy" in Marylebone (little brother of Latium), is a "deli with a relaxing restaurant" serving "hearty dishes from delicious ingredients". / W1H 4NA; www.briciole.co.uk; @briciolelondon; 10.15 pm.

Brick Lane Beigel Bake E1 £6 4 1 1
159 Brick Ln   020 7729 0616   13–1C
"Hectic at weekends but great fun" – this legendary 24-hour Brick Lane takeaway is redolent of a vanished East End... as are its prices. / E1 6SB; open 24 hours; cash only; no bookings.

The Bright Courtyard W1 £60 5 3 2
43-45 Baker St   020 7486 6998   2–1A
The food at this modern Marylebone outfit "is absolutely epic" – "up there with the best Chinese in London, and much more reasonably priced than Hakkasan, etc". Dim sum are "very good and not very expensive", but the room is "a bit antiseptic" and the service "hit and miss". / W1U 8EW; www.lifefashiongroup.com; @BrightCourtyard; 10.45 pm, Thu-Sat 11.15 pm.

Brilliant UB2 £38 3 4 3
72-76 Western Rd   020 8574 1928   1–3A
"Authentic dishes from the Punjab" draw fans from far and wide to the distant 'burbs of Southall, and this big and "buzzy" institution of over 40 years' standing. This family catering outfit was founded in Nairobi, adding a "heavy East African bias" to the cooking. / UB2 5DZ; www.brilliantrestaurant.com; @brilliantrst; 11 pm, Fri & Sat 11.30 pm; closed Mon, Sat L & Sun L.

Brinkley's SW10 £57 1 2 3
47 Hollywood Rd   020 7351 1683   6–3B
A very "Chelsea crowd" is a defining feature of this "lively" bar/restaurant (near the C&W Hospital), as is John Brinkley's "excellent wine list", which is notably reasonably priced. No great prizes for the "brasserie-type fare" however – "it can be terrible". / SW10 9HX; www.brinkleys.com; @BrinkleysR; 11 pm, Sun 10.30 pm; closed weekday L.

Bronte WC2 NEW
Grand Buildings, 1-3 Strand   awaiting tel   2–3C
On the site of the Strand Dining Rooms (RIP), this large newcomer has recently debuted off Trafalgar Square. It opened too late for survey feedback: early reviews suggest that despite a fairly wacky-sounding Pacific-fusion menu, the food is eclipsed by the dazzling Tom Dixon interior design. / WC2N 5EJ; www.bronte.co.uk; @bronte_london; no bookings.

The Brown Dog SW13 £51 3 2 3

28 Cross St 020 8392 2200 11–1A

"On a pretty terraced backstreet in Barnes", this countrified pub is packed
out on Sundays for "the best roasts in the vicinity, and one of the
best sticky toffee puddings anywhere". "As the name suggests, it helps
to like hounds as customers bring 'em in". / SW13 0AP;
www.thebrowndog.co.uk; @browndogbarnes; 10 pm, Sun 9 pm.

**Brown's Hotel,
The English Tea Room W1** £70 3 4 4

Albemarle St 020 7493 6020 3–3C

"Let yourself be transported away from the madding crowd to this peaceful
haven of afternoon tea!", say fans of this very "traditional" hotel lounge,
"with the tinkling piano in the background". "It may not be the
most innovative, but the quality and quantity is second to none, and they
really look after you". / W1S 4BP; www.roccofortehotels.com; 6.30 pm; no trainers.

Brown's Hotel, HIX Mayfair W1 £72 2 3 3

Albemarle St 020 7518 4004 3–3C

For "a grand hotel dining room experience", this "civilised" Mayfair
landmark fits the bill, and its "well-spaced tables" and "professional"
service add to its appeal "for a discreet business conversation". Its "classic
British cuisine" is dependable for fans, but to critics it's "disappointing".
/ W1S 4BP; www.thealbemarlerestaurant.com; 11 pm, Sun 10.30 pm; set weekday
L & dinner £55 (FP).

Brunswick House Café SW8 £48 2 3 5

30 Wandsworth Rd 020 7720 2926 11–1D

"A huge, OTT architectural salvage and antiques shop" in a massive
Georgian house in Vauxhall makes "a quirky and unusual setting" for this
modern bistro. Service can be "a bit slow" and even fans find the food
"variable", but hit lucky and a meal here is "fantastic". / SW8 2LG;
www.brunswickhouse.co; 10 pm; closed Sun D.

Bubbledogs, Kitchen Table W1 £104 5 4 3

70 Charlotte St 020 7637 7770 2–1C

11/10 for originality to James Knappett and his "amazing" chef's table,
tucked away at the back of his and his wife's adjoining hot dog place.
"What an experience" – "a floor-show, gastronomical extravaganza and
a bit of a mystery tour all combined. You'll find out what the main
ingredient in each course is, but not know what you'll eat until it is
presented to you by the chef". "Seeing it prepared is revelatory" and the
flavours "jump out on your tongue!" / W1T 4QG; www.kitchentablelondon.co.uk;
@bubbledogsKT; 6 pm & 7.30 pm seatings only; D only, closed Mon & Sun; credit
card deposit required to book.

Buddha-Bar London SW1 £70 2 2 3

145 Knightsbridge 020 3667 5222 6–1D

With its "hip club" vibe, this Knightsbridge outpost of a Paris-based
franchise is "let down a little by the pan-Asian food, but the atmosphere
makes up for it"; "amazing cocktails (including one that arrived still
smoking!)" too, along with "Asian afternoon tea that's a delicious
alternative to the traditional variety". / SW1X 7PA; www.buddhabarlondon.com;
@BuddhaBarLondon; 10 pm.

Buen Ayre E8   £53   4 2 2
50 Broadway Mkt   020 7275 9900   14–2B
"Steaks as good as some of the opulent chains, but served with authentic Argentinian flair and taste", can be found at this Hackney 'parilla'. The décor is simple and there's a "good wine list", but "the focus is the food". / E8 4QJ; www.buenayre.co.uk; 10.30 pm; no Amex.

The Builders Arms SW3   £48   2 2 4
13 Britten St   020 7349 9040   6–2C
Generous ratings this year for this attractively modernised pub in a cute Chelsea backstreet – fantastic atmosphere and acceptable scoff. / SW3 3TY; www.geronimo-inns.co.uk/london-the-builders; @BuildersChelsea; 10 pm, Thu-Sat 11 pm, Sun 9 pm; no bookings.

Bukowski Grill   £38   4 3 2
10-11 D'Arblay St, W1   020 3857 4756   4–1C NEW
Brixton Market, SW9   020 7733 4646   11–2D NEW
Boxpark, Unit 61, 4-6 Bethnal Green Rd, E1   020 7033 6601   13–2B
"Good burgers, ribs, shakes and no vitamin C in sight" pretty well sums up the appeal of this highly rated US-style mini-chain, with grills in Brixton, Shoreditch and Soho. / see web for detail.

The Bull N6   £46   2 3 4
13 North Hill   020 8341 0510   9–1B
This "revived microbrewery" pub in Highgate is particularly known for being "great for a family Sunday lunch" – even the only reporter who found the food "disappointing" said "the atmosphere, service and beer filled the gap". / N6 4AB; thebullhighgate.co.uk; @Bull_Highgate; 10 pm.

Bull & Last NW5   £61   3 2 3
168 Highgate Rd   020 7267 3641   9–1B
"For a hearty meal after a walk on the heath", this "beaut' of a local" in Kentish Town, with its "spacious, shabby-chic interior" is a classic. However, even some who say "it sets the standard for revived north London boozers" feel "it's getting expensive now"… "a safe bet, but it doesn't reach the heights it once did". / NW5 1QS; www.thebullandlast.co.uk; @thebullandlast; 10 pm, Sun 9 pm.

Bumpkin   £53   2 2 2
119 Sydney St, SW3   020 3730 9344   6–3C
102 Old Brompton Rd, SW7   020 7341 0802   6–2B
Westfield Stratford City, The Street, E20   020 8221 9900   14–1D
"Some days are really good, other days distinctly ordinary" at this rustically styled chain, where the odd report is of total disaster, but the best praise a "buzzy" atmosphere, plus "good and typically British" dishes. / www.bumpkinuk.com; 11 pm; closed Mon.

Buona Sera   £42   3 3 3
289a King's Rd, SW3   020 7352 8827   6–3C
22 Northcote Rd, SW11   020 7228 9925   11–2C
"Perfect for a quick plate of pasta" or pizza – this "still reliable (and cheap)" Clapham café is "as lively as ever" after all these years. Less feedback on its "cosy" Chelsea spin-off with fun double-decker seating, but what we have says it is likewise "dependable and very noisy!" / midnight; SW3 11.30 pm, Sun 10 pm; SW3 closed Mon L.

Buoni Amici W12 [NEW] £42 333
170 Goldhawk Road   020 8743 7335   8–1C
Trying hard in an under-developed corner of Shepherd's Bush: this Italian newcomer – a simple but attractive shop conversion – offers "a large menu (though not everything seems to be 'on' all the time)" and "pleasant service that's keen you should have a good time". / W12 8HJ; www.buoniamici.co.uk; @BuoniAmici; closed Mon; set weekday L £14 (FP).

Burger & Lobster £45 333
Harvey Nichols, SW1   020 7235 5000   6–1D [NEW]
26 Binney St, W1   020 3637 5972   3–2A [NEW]
29 Clarges St, W1   020 7409 1699   3–4B
36 Dean St, W1   020 7432 4800   5–2A
6 Little Portland St, W1   020 7907 7760   3–1C
High Holborn, WC1   020 7432 4805   1–1D
40 St John St, EC1   020 7490 9230   10–1B
Bow Bells Hs, 1 Bread St, EC4   020 7248 1789   10–2B
"If you have the lobster, it's a top deal", according to the massive fanclub of this "so simple, so well-executed" concept. "It's less of a bargain for the burger", but they're "surprisingly good" too. / www.burgerandlobster.com; @Londonlobster; 10.30 pm; Clarges St closed Sun D, Bread St & St John St closed Sun.

Busaba Eathai £39 223
What Alan Yau did next after Wagamama: these handsome, communal Thai canteens remain an "easy" and "reliable" cheap 'n' cheerful choice. On the food front, "compromises over the years have resulted in less authenticity", but they are "approachably priced". / www.busaba.co.uk; 11 pm, Fri & Sat 11.30 pm, Sun 10 pm; W1 no booking; WC1 booking: min 10.

**Butler's Restaurant,
The Chesterfield Mayfair W1** £82 343
35 Charles St   020 7958 7729   3–3B
Perhaps it is "sedate" and old-fashioned in its styling, but this Mayfair dining room inspires a dedicated fanclub with its "informative" service and Ben Kelliher's quality, traditional British cuisine. / W1J 5EB; www.chesterfieldmayfair.com; @chesterfield_MF; 10 pm; jacket required.

Butlers Wharf Chop House SE1 £60 222
36e Shad Thames   020 7403 3403   10–4D
"Pleasant enough by the side of the Thames" – a harsh but fair verdict on this D&D group property near the better-known Pont de la Tour. The focus is on "fairly straightforward" grills, which are most "acceptable as long as you aren't paying". / SE1 2YE; www.chophouse-restaurant.co.uk; @bwchophousetowerbridge; 11 pm, Sun 10 pm.

La Buvette TW9 £42 333
6 Church Walk   020 8940 6264   1–4A
This "small neighbourhood bistro" attractively "out of the way" off the alleys surrounding St Mary Magdalene has become a fixture in the old heart of Richmond, serving a "limited but nicely prepared menu" of "heavily French-accented" regional cuisine (with occasional forays into Spain, Italy or Switzerland). Top Tip – "good value set menu". / TW9 1SN; www.labuvette.co.uk; @labuvettebistro; 10 pm.

Byron £38 2 3 3

"Still love it when a burger is needed!"; the leading 'posh patties' chain is *"not what it was"* when it first started, but the styling of its individually-designed branches are *"a cut above other burger bars"* and – while *"it offers nothing mindblowing, it's the best failsafe"* for its huge armies of fans.* / www.byronhamburgers.com; most branches 11 pm.

C London W1 £102 1 1 3

25 Davies St 020 7399 0500 3–2B
"The crowd is from another planet" at this eurotrashy Mayfair haunt, which can seem *"fun"* if you've money to burn. The *"simple"* cooking isn't so much bad as *"massively overpriced"* – *"service on the other hand is truly dreadful"* – *"do they have to train the staff to be so inattentive?"* / W1K 3DE; www.crestaurant.co.uk; 11.45 pm.

C&R Cafe £35 4 2 2

3-4 Rupert Ct, W1 020 7434 1128 5–3A
52 Westbourne Grove, W2 020 7221 7979 7–1B
"I get frustrated if people want to eat anywhere else!" – its small fanclub adores this little, *"cheap 'n' cheerful"* Malaysian café in Chinatown (its glossier Bayswater offshoot never inspires much feedback). Top Menu Tip – *"fabulous Laksa"*. / www.cnrrestaurant.com; 10.30 pm; W2 closed Tue.

Caboose, The Old Truman Brewery E1 £31 2 3 4

Ely's Yd, Brick Ln 07437 209 275 13–2C
"Great fun" street food BYO, with burgers (and a few other dishes) served from a custom-built railway cabin outside Brick Lane's Old Truman Brewery. Get together a dozen or so friends, and you can have it to yourself for a 3-courser. / E1 6QR; www.wearecaboose.com; @WeAreCaboose; 11 pm.

Cacio & Pepe SW1 NEW £54 4 4 4

46 Churton Street 020 7630 7588 2–4B
"In an underserved backwater of Pimlico", *"a fine new addition to the ever-improving local restaurant scene"*, on the former site Mekong (RIP). Owned and run by former Fiorentina footballer Mauro Della Martira (father of 2013 Italian MasterChef winner Enrica Della Martira), it provides *"excellent food with a Roman accent"* and a *"bustly and friendly atmosphere"* (although the basement is *"a little dark and less atmospheric"*). / SW1V 2LP; www.cacioepepe.co.uk; 11 pm.

Café Below EC2 £40 2 2 3

St Mary-le-Bow, Cheapside 020 7329 0789 10–2B
"Simple, cheap, good-quality" cooking is on the menu at this *"delightful"* venue – but the trump card is its *"setting in the atmospheric crypt of Bow Bells church"*. *"When busy, conversation can be hard"*. / EC2 6AU; www.cafebelow.co.uk; 9 pm; closed Mon D, Tue D, Sat & Sun.

Café del Parc N19 £43 5 5 4

167 Junction Road 020 7281 5684 9–1C
"This tiny Tuffnell Park spot is an absolute winner", serving *"interesting North African/Spanish tapas-style food"*. *"No menu to speak of"*, *"but you're in safe hands with a really confident and inspired chef"* who sends out *"a splendid succession of delicious and very varied surprises"*. / N19 5PZ; www.delparc.com; 10.30 pm; closed Mon, Tue, Wed L, Thu L, Fri L, Sat L & Sun L; no Amex.

Café du Marché EC1   £56   3 3 4
22 Charterhouse Sq   020 7608 1609   10–1B
"A cosy, candlelit piece of France" – this "delightfully atmospheric building",
"tucked away" off Charterhouse Square, is "particularly lovely when there's
live music at night", and even if its "traditional, French-bistro-style cooking"
can seem "a bit old-fashioned", it's "honest" and "appetising". Still tipped
for business lunching, but its prime forte nowadays is being "great for
a date". / EC1M 6DX; www.cafedumarche.co.uk; @cafedumarche; 3.30 pm; L only,
closed Sat & Sun.

Café East SE16   £23   4 2 2
100 Redriff Rd   020 7252 1212   12–2B
"Wonderful, fresh and healthy Vietnamese food" makes this Bermondsey
canteen a regular stop for devotees of pho and other Viet classics. "It's the
real thing and at a very reasonable price" – "certain dishes are just in a
league of their own". / SE16 7LH; www.cafeeastpho.co.uk; @cafeeastpho;
10.30 pm, Sun 10 pm; closed Tue; no Amex.

Café in the Crypt,
St Martin's in the Fields WC2   £33   2 2 4
Duncannon St   020 7766 1158   2–2C
The self-service crypt of St Martin-in-the-Fields, right on Trafalgar Square,
makes a "delightful place to stop for a quick lunch in this busy part
of London". It's "always buzzy, and so much better than a lot of the chains
nearby" – and even if its soup, sarnies and light dishes are "not very
special" they come in "good-sized portions", "and at very reasonable
prices". / WC2N 4JJ; stmartin-in-the-fields.org/cafe-in-the-crypt; @smitf_london;
8 pm, Thu-Sat 9 pm, Sun 6 pm; no Amex; no bookings.

Café Monico W1 NEW   £61   2 3 4
39-45 Shaftesbury Avenue   020 3727 6161   5–3A
Soho House's latest West End foray in the thick of Theatreland aims
to look like its been there for decades, with its carefully distressed, vintage
looks, and brasserie menu overseen from afar by Rowley Leigh. "Its feel
is not dissimilar to Les Deux Salons, but the food is much better and
cheaper". / W1D 6LA; www.cafemonico.com; @cafemonico; midnight, Fri & Sat
1 am.

Cafe Murano   £54   3 3 3
33 St James's St, SW1   020 3371 5559   3–3C
34-36 Tavistock St, WC2   020 3371 5559   5–3D
"Straightforward cooking, with a twist beyond the staple dishes" and
"professional" service – all "without the mothership's high prices" –
win high popularity for Angela Hartnett's spin-offs in St James's and Covent
Garden. Some reports are sceptical though: "sure the food's fine,
but mainstream, and do we need another star chef's standard West End
option where the biggest excitement is their name?"
/ www.cafemurano.co.uk; see web for detail.

Café Pistou EC1   £46   3 2 2
8-10 Exmouth Mkt   020 7278 5333   10–1A
"Very enjoyable Provençal food" makes this all-day bistro a handy option
even in happening Exmouth Market. The service is "very friendly",
"even when the place is crowded". / EC1R 4QA; www.cafepistou.co.uk;
@CafePistou; 10.30 pm.

Café Spice Namaste E1 £57
16 Prescot St   020 7488 9242   12–1A

Cyrus Todiwala's "genuine, exotic and intriguing" Parsi cuisine "relies on spices rather than heat (though you can get that too)" and delivers some "perfect flavours". "The man himself is very jolly as he works the room" at his Whitechapel HQ, where there's "always a cheerful welcome, and great service". / E1 8AZ; www.cafespice.co.uk; @cafespicenamast; 10.30 pm; closed Sat L & Sun.

Caffè Caldesi W1 £61
118 Marylebone Ln   020 7487 0754   2–1A

"Wonderful, authentic Italian food" with an emphasis on robust Tuscan flavours makes this "no-nonsense" Marylebone fixture "a treat". "It's always full of Italians, which speaks volumes for the quality on offer". / W1U 2QF; www.caldesi.com; 10.30 pm, Sun 9.30 pm.

La Cage Imaginaire NW3 £49
16 Flask Walk   020 7794 6674   9–1A

"Such a pretty", "tiny bistro on a Hampstead backstreet"; try it in a forgiving frame of mind however – the "traditional Gallic cuisine" is "not the most exciting" (and can be "terribly bland" nowadays), and service is "friendly", but can have "shades of Fawlty Towers". / NW3 1HE; www.la-cage-imaginaire.co.uk; 11 pm.

Cah-Chi £37
394 Garratt Ln, SW18   020 8946 8811   11–2B
34 Durham Rd, SW20   020 8947 1081   11–2B

In the Korean enclaves of Raynes Park and Earlsfield, these "buzzy venues" are "very popular with ex-pats". Their "fresh" cooking delivers "super flavours" at "reasonable prices"; BYO. / www.cahchi.com; SW20 11 pm; SW18 11 pm, Sat & Sun 11.30 pm; SW20 closed Mon; cash only.

The Camberwell Arms SE5 £56
65 Camberwell Church St   020 7358 4364   1–3C

"A good reason to go to Camberwell!" – this Anchor & Hope sibling goes "from strength to strength", with fans even "daring to suggest" it outshines its stablemate. Not only do you get "excellent, well-sourced, seasonal British food", but "as a bonus, you can even get a table!" / SE5 8TR; www.thecamberwellarms.co.uk; @camberwellarms; closed Mon L & Sun D.

Cambio de Tercio SW5 £70
161-163 Old Brompton Rd   020 7244 8970   6–2B

"Superb, modern Spanish cooking complemented by an astonishing wine list, full of mouthwatering options" – plus notably "charming" service – maintain Abel Lusa's "fun and inviting" Earl's Court venture as "one of London's best". On the downside though, it can seem "too crowded" and "expensive". / SW5 0LJ; www.cambiodetercio.co.uk; @CambiodTercio; 11.15 pm, Sun 11 pm.

Camino £47
3 Varnishers Yd, Regent Quarter, N1   020 7841 7330   9–3C
The Blue Fin Building, 5 Canvey St, SE1   020 3617 3169   10–4A
15 Mincing Ln, EC3   020 7841 7335   10–3D
33 Blackfriars Ln, EC4   020 7125 0930   10–2A

"A good standby!" – these "fun" tapas stops (they can be "loud") offer "well-prepared dishes" ("sometimes way above average"), and a "decent modestly priced list of wines", beers and sherries. / www.camino.uk.com; EC3 & EC4 closed Sat & Sun.

Canada Water Cafe SE16 £39 **3 4 3**
40 Surrey Quays Road   020 3668 7518   12–2B
Very handy for Canada Water tube – an "efficient and friendly"
(and "family-friendly") café, most popular for its "great sourdough pizzas"
(though other fare is available). / SE16; www.canadawatercafe.com; 10.30 pm
Mon-Sat, Sun 9 pm.

Cannizaro House, Hotel du Vin SW19 £58 **2 3 3**
West Side, Wimbledon Common   0871 943 0345   11–2A
This "romantic" and "plush" venue on the edge of Wimbledon Common,
nowadays part of the Hotel du Vin group, offers dining in its bistro
or Orangerie. Opinion is split on the experience, ranging from
"very enjoyable" to "terrible". / SW19 4UE;
www.hotelduvin.com/locations/wimbledon; @HotelduVinBrand; 10 pm.

Cantina Laredo WC2 £53 **3 2 3**
10 Upper St Martin's Ln   020 7420 0630   5–3C
"Upmarket" Mexican operation in Covent Garden, with "very fresh-tasting"
dishes (guacamole a speciality); reporters do gripe however that it's
"pricey". / WC2H 9FB; www.cantinalaredo.co.uk; @CantinaLaredoUK; 11.30 pm,
Fri & Sat midnight, Sun 10.30 pm.

Canto Corvino E1 NEW £62 **4 4 4**
21 Artillery Lane   020 7655 0390   13–2B
This "bright and sparse modern Italian", with its "very posh" decor
is "a superb addition to the restaurant scene" around Spitalfields Market.
The cooking – "an excellent range of small plates" – is "very fine",
and service is "top class". Top Tip – "highly recommended for larger groups
looking for a special dining experience". / E1 7HA; www.cantocorvino.co.uk;
@cantocorvinoe1.

Canton Arms SW8 £48 **4 3 4**
177 South Lambeth Rd   020 7582 8710   11–1D
"Be prepared to wait for a table and then possibly to share it", if you visit
this "jammed" Stockwell gastropub (sibling to the epic Anchor & Hope) –
"it still feels like a proper pub", and serves "huge portions of rustic hearty
cuts of meat" and other "distinctive British dishes". / SW8 1XP;
www.cantonarms.com; @cantonarms; 10.30 pm; closed Mon L & Sun D; no Amex;
no bookings.

Canvas SW1 £71 **2 3 2**
1 Wilbraham Pl   020 7823 4463   6–2D
Limited feedback nowadays on this ambitious basement off Sloane Street
(once Le Cercle, RIP). Fans still say it's "romantic", but rate its
contemporary cuisine highly, but some reports are of "bizarre dishes that
do not work". / SW1X 9AE; www.canvaschelsea.com; @CanvasbyMR; 9.30 pm,
Fri & Sat 10 pm; D only, closed Mon.

Capote Y Toros SW5 £49 **3 4 4**
157 Old Brompton Rd   020 7373 0567   6–2B
"The croquetas are the best this side of the Pyrenees", claim fans
of Cambio de Tercio's perhaps "over-noisy" but "superbly atmospheric"
neighbouring bar, serving "delightful" tapas, with "a joy" of a
"comprehensive (if, to be fair, not cheap) wine list and gin menu".
/ SW5 0LJ; www.cambiodetercio.co.uk; @CambiodTercio; 11.30 pm; D only, closed
Mon & Sun.

Le Caprice SW1 £75 3 4 4
Arlington Hs, Arlington St 020 7629 2239 3–4C
"The magic never fades" at this *"island of casual sophistication and understatement"* near the Ritz – *"still wonderfully fashionable after all these years"*, and charmingly presided over by *"the amazing Mr Jesus Adorno"*. That said, while the cooking has always been *"nursery"* style, it has become more *"unexciting"* during the tenure of current owner, Richard Caring. / SW1A 1RJ; www.le-caprice.co.uk; @CapriceHoldings; 11.30 pm Mon-Sat, Sun 10.30 pm.

Caraffini SW1 £54 3 5 4
61-63 Lower Sloane St 020 7259 0235 6–2D
"Marvellous, long-surviving, honest Italian", near Sloane Square, *"which can be recommended without fear of disappointment"*. The *"home-cooked"* food *"never shines but never misses"*, while *"it's the service that lifts the experience to the next level"* and lends the place its *"happy"* atmosphere – *"even first-timers are greeted as regulars"*, and *"waiters are equally charming with your 12-year-old as with your gran"*. / SW1W 8DH; www.caraffini.co.uk; Mon-Fri 11.30 pm, Sat 11 pm; closed Sun.

Caravaggio EC3 £62 2 3 3
107-112 Leadenhall St 020 7626 6206 10–2D
This *"City lunchtime favourite"* (a spacious Italian, near Leadenhall Market) scored hits and misses this year – some disappointments were recorded, but other reports applaud its *"well-cooked fare and very efficient service"*. / EC3A 4DP; www.etruscarestaurants.com; 10 pm; closed Sat & Sun.

Caravan £52 3 2 3
1 Granary Sq, N1 020 7101 7661 9–3C
Metal Box Factory, Great Guildford Street, SE1 no tel 10–4B **NEW**
11-13 Exmouth Mkt, EC1 020 7833 8115 10–1A
"Crazy eclectica rubs shoulders with family favourites" on the sometimes *"bizarre"* menu of these *"bustling"* *"cheek-by-jowl"* fusion haunts, whose *"phenomenal coffee by itself would score a 6/5!"* and helps establish them both as major brunch hangouts. Nowadays the *"ever-busy"* Exmouth Market branch is eclipsed by its huge, *"super-cool"* Granary Square sibling in King's Cross, where *"media types from The Guardian and students from adjacent St Martin's"* bolster the *"hip and trendy"* vibe. STOP PRESS – a third branch is to open on Bankside. / www.caravanonexmouth.co.uk; EC1 10.30 pm, Sun 4 pm; closed Sun.

Carob Tree NW5 £35 3 5 3
15 Highgate Rd 020 7267 9880 9–1B
"The terrific fish is the thing to go for" (although the meat is *"well cooked"* too) at this very busy local Greek in Dartmouth Park, where *"the owners treat you as a long-lost friend even if you have never been in their place before"*. / NW5 1QX; 10.30 pm, Sun 9 pm; closed Mon; no Amex.

Carousel W1 £54 4 5 4
71 Blandford St 020 7487 5564 3–1A
"A different guest chef every week" makes this *"engaging and informal"* (*"shared trestle tables"*) Marylebone merry-go-round a *"fabulous way to try new cuisines"* from around the world; on a good night here, the food is *"a revelation!"* / W1U 8AB; www.carousel-london.com; 11.30 pm.

Casa Brindisa SW7 £46 2 2 2
7-9 Exhibition Rd 020 7590 0008 6–2C
*"Convenient for the museums", this outpost of the Brindisa group near
South Kensington station offers a menu of Spanish small plates, wines and
sherries familiar from the Borough Market original, but as a tapas bar
it feels a bit "formulaic", and its marks lag behind accordingly. / SW7 2HE;
www.brindisatapaskitchens.com/casa-brindisa; @TapasKitchens; 11 pm, Sun 10 pm.*

Casa Cruz W11 £48 2 4 4
123 Clarendon Rd 020 3321 5400 7–2A
*This lavish pub conversion with a copper bar and "shiny gold mirrors"
on the edge of Notting Hill was opened last year by Argentinian
restaurateur Juan Santa Cruz. While reporters generally favour its
performance including the Argentinian-inspired European food, even fans
can find it "overpriced". / W11 4JG; www.casacruz.london; @CasaCruzrest,
12.30 am, Sun 5 pm; closed Mon.*

Casa Malevo W2 £57 3 4 2
23 Connaught St 020 7402 1988 7–1D
*"Very good steaks" headline the Latino menu at this cosy, tucked-away
Argentinian, in Bayswater; also praised for its "very good service". / W2 2AY;
www.casamalevo.com; @casamalevo; 10.30 pm, Sun 10 pm.*

Casita Andina W1 NEW
Great Windmill Street 020 3327 9464 4–3D
*Martin Morales (the restaurateur behind Ceviche and Andina) launched
a fourth London Peruvian post-survey in Soho in summer 2016. Apparently
it's inspired by Peru's 'picanterias': family-run, traditional restaurants,
serving Andean dishes and small bites. / W1F 9UE;
www.twitter.com/casitaandina; @CasitaAndina.*

Casse-Croute SE1 £45 4 3 4
109 Bermondsey St 020 7407 2140 10–4D
*"Are you sure this isn't really in a French suburb?" – this "real Gallic bistro
in Bermondsey" serves "classic bistro fare with a twist" from a "simple and
well-executed menu" on "a daily changing blackboard". "You'll have
to breathe in to sit down in this tiny place when it's busy, but it's worth it!"
/ SE1 3XB; www.cassecroute.co.uk; @CasseCroute109; 10 pm, Sun 4 pm; closed
Sun D.*

Cau £49 1 2 2
10-12 Royal Pde, SE3 020 8318 4200 1–4D
33 High St, SW19 020 8318 4200 11–2B
1 Commodity Quay, E1 020 7702 0341 10–3D
*Ratings have dipped at this national Argentinian-themed steakhouse chain,
of which the Wimbledon Village branch is by far the best known. Some
"yummy steaks" are reported, but there are a concerning number of let-
downs ("it looked great, but wasn't properly prepared").
/ @CAUrestaurants; see web for detail.*

The Cavendish W1 £60 3 3 3
35 New Cavendish St 020 7487 3030 2–1A
*With its comfortable leather banquettes, upmarket brasserie menu, cigars
and cocktails, this Marylebone pub-conversion is consistently well rated as a
"pricey-but-good" experience. / W1G 9TR; 35newcavendish.co.uk;
@35newcavendish; 10.30 pm, Sun 5.45 pm.*

Caxton Grill SW1 £75
2 Caxton St   020 7227 7773   2–4C
Adam Handling's brief stint in the "glorious" dining room of this tucked-away Westminster Hotel has at least put it back on London's culinary map – after his May 2016 departure, whether it stays remains to be seen… / SW1H 0QW; www.caxtongrill.co.uk; 10.30 pm.

Cây Tre £36
42-43 Dean St, W1   020 7317 9118   5–2A
301 Old St, EC1   020 7729 8662   13–1B
"Fresh, zingy Vietnamese food" makes these "affordable" Soho and Shoreditch venues a "trusty option", especially for an "excellent-value set lunch" or "quick pre-theatre meal". / www.vietnamesekitchen.co.uk; 11 pm, Fri & Sat 11.30 pm, Sun 10.30 pm; booking: min 8.

Cecconi's W1 £78 2️⃣2️⃣3️⃣
5a Burlington Gdns   020 7434 1500   4–4A
"Always buzzing with pretty and interesting people" – Richard Caring's "classy" Venetian brasserie near Old Bond Street is a "classic" Mayfair rendezvous, especially for schmoozing by Hedge Fund types. Expansion to Miami, LA etc has done nothing for standards though, and a "slide downhill" this year has tipped the always precarious balance here towards seeming complacent and overpriced. Breakfast though is "superior to other meals" and amongst the best in town: "truffled scrambled eggs – yum!" / W1S 3EP; www.cecconis.co.uk; @SohoHouse; 11.30 pm, Sun 10.30 pm.

Céleste, The Lanesborough SW1 NEW £100 2️⃣3️⃣2️⃣
Hyde Park Corner   020 7259 5599   2–3A
"Refurbished along very classic lines" (part of a £60m refit of the whole property) – the "grand but soulless" atrium dining space of this luxurious Hyde Park Corner hotel perennially "promises great things" but never quite gets its act together. This latest incumbent (overseen by the management of Paris's Le Bristol) seems cut from the same cloth: "there are some glimmers of Frechon's signature dishes but it doesn't quite make the grade". / SW1X 7TA; www.lanesborough.com/eng/restaurant-bars/celeste; @TheLanesborough; 10.30 pm.

Cellar Gascon EC1 £33 3️⃣3️⃣3️⃣
59 West Smithfield Rd   020 7600 7561   10–2B
The little sibling of Smithfield stalwart Club Gascon, next door, still wins fans with its "stand-out regional French wines" and elegant (slightly "tired"?) style. One or two reporters feel that "some dishes don't quite hit the mark", but it's overall still well rated. / EC1A 9DS; www.cellargascon.com; midnight; closed Sat & Sun; no Amex.

Ceviche £46 3️⃣3️⃣3️⃣
17 Frith St, W1   020 7292 2040   5–2A
Alexandra Trust, Baldwin St, EC1   020 3327 9463   13–1A
"Bring your tastebuds alive!", say fans of the "great food and even better Pisco sours" at these "cool" and "lively-if-noisy" hangouts ("like a holiday in Peru!"), in Soho and near Old Street. But while "interesting, not all dishes are entirely successful". / www.cevicheuk.com; @cevicheuk; see web for detail.

Chakra W8 £56 4️⃣2️⃣3️⃣
33c Holland Street   020 7229 2115   7–2B
"Absolutely stunning food in a perfect (Notting Hill) location" (complete with chandeliers) is "not what you would normally get in an Indian restaurant", although it's sometimes let down by "disappointing" service. / W8 4LX; www.chakralondon.com; @ChakraLondon; 11 pm, Sun 10.30 pm.

Chamberlain's EC3   £63   2 3 2
23-25 Leadenhall Mkt   020 7648 8690   10–2D
The "lovely fish" at this seafood specialist in Leadenhall Market comes at very City prices – "I almost choked on the bill!" But it has its fans, who praise the "great location, happy staff and interesting food" (if from an "essentially static" menu). / EC3V 1LR; www.chamberlains.org; @Chamberlainsldn; Mon-Sat 9.30 pm; closed Sun.

Champor-Champor SE1   £52   4 4 5
62 Weston St   020 7403 4600   10–4C
This "ever wonderful" outfit (the name means 'mix and match'), tucked away behind London Bridge station, is adored by its small fanclub for its funky decor as much as the distinctive Thai-Malay cooking. / SE1 3QJ; www.champor-champor.com; @ChamporChampor; 10 pm; D only.

The Chancery EC4   £66   4 4 3
9 Cursitor St   020 7831 4000   10–2A
Graham Long's "very interesting, high quality" and "always reliable" cuisine is the hallmark of this "friendly but formal enough" fixture near Chancery Lane – tipped as often as a gastronomic destination as it is for its natural business appeal. / EC4A 1LL; www.thechancery.co.uk; @chancerylondon; 10.30 pm; closed Sat L & Sun.

Chapters SE3   £51   2 2 2
43-45 Montpelier Vale   020 8333 2666   1–4D
"A great choice of brekkies"… "lovely steaks from the Josper grill" – this longstanding modern brasserie by Blackheath Common remains a popular and useful local amenity. / SE3 0TJ; www.chaptersrestaurants.com; @Chapters_ADD; 11 pm, Sun 9 pm.

Charlotte's   £52   3 5 3
6 Turnham Green Ter, W4   020 8742 3590   8–2A
"For excellent casual dining" this "cosy" (tightly packed) Chiswick haunt hits the spot, boosted by a cute bar by the entrance; value-wise, "you get what you've paid for and more". No feedback on its laid-back W5 sibling, but see also Charlotte's Place W5. / www.charlottes.co.uk; see web for detail.

Charlotte's Place W5   £55   3 3 3
16 St Matthew's Rd   020 8567 7541   1–3A
Fans of this "favourite local" say it's "the best in Ealing by far" – a "lovely place" where "high-quality produce and cooking" are complemented by "attentive, friendly service". See also its spin-offs Charlotte's in W4 and W5. / W5 3JT; www.charlottes.co.uk; @CharlottesW5; 10.30 pm, Fri & Sat 11 pm, Sun 9 pm.

Cheneston's Restaurant,
The Milestone Hotel W8   £88   2 3 4
1 Kensington Ct   020 7917 1000   6–1A
"Charming", traditional dining room, offering a tranquil refuge from Kensington. It is particularly recommended for its "feast" of a breakfast and splendid afternoon teas ("scones are perfect – crisp on the outside and fluffy on the inside!") / W8 5DL; www.milestonehotel.com; @milestonehotel; 10pm; no jeans.

F S A

Chettinad W1 £38 4 2 3
16 Percy St   020 3556 1229   2–1C
*"Not a standard Indian restaurant by any means", this Fitzrovia venue
named after a village in Tamil Nadu features a "delicious" menu
"almost entirely based on southern Indian dishes" (including dosa
pancakes). It's "always busy", with "quite a few Indian diners". / W1T 1DT;
www.chettinadrestaurant.com; @chettinadlondon; 11 pm, Sun 10 pm; no Amex.*

Cheyne Walk Brasserie SW3 £68 3 3 3
50 Cheyne Walk   020 7376 8787   6–3C
*"Where the beautiful people go" near the Thames in Chelsea, this chic
Gallic brasserie serves "delicious BBQ" – most notably "meat grilled on the
wood fire in the open restaurant". "Surprisingly family-friendly, too, at
least at lunchtime" – although it's certainly "not for anyone who counts
their pennies". / SW3 5LR; www.cheynewalkbrasserie.com; @CheyneWalkBrass;
10.30 pm, Sun 9.30 pm; closed Mon L.*

Chez Abir W14 £38 3 2 3
34 Blythe Rd   020 7603 3241   8–1D
*"Tabbouleh as good as I've ever tasted" typifies the "wonderfully tasty and
fresh" Lebanese cuisine at this backstreet café – "not to be missed"
if you're near Olympia. It made its reputation as Chez Marcelle (she retired
a couple of years ago), and is still "well up to snuff". / W14 0HA;
www.chezabir.co.uk; 11 pm; closed Mon.*

CHEZ BRUCE SW17 £74 5 5 4
2 Bellevue Rd   020 8672 0114   11–2C
*"You can see why people rave!"; Bruce Poole's "casual yet elegant"
neighbourhood classic by Wandsworth Common is – for the umpteenth
year – the survey's No. 1 favourite by dint of doing "everything
effortlessly… and just right", all at a price that makes it "6/5 for value".
The modern British cuisine is "unfailingly outstanding, but never over-
elaborate: it just tastes intensely of what it is". Service is "first class, helpful
and welcoming", the interior is "stylish, but not over-styled", and there's
an "enormous, eclectic and excellent wine list". / SW17 7EG;
www.chezbruce.co.uk; @ChezBruce; 10 pm, Fri & Sat 10.30 pm, Sun 9 pm;
set weekday L £33 (FP), set Sun L £39 (FP), set dinner £53 (FP).*

Chicama SW10 NEW
383 King's Road   020 3874 2000   6–3C
*From the team behind Marylebone's Pachamama, a new Peruvian seafood
restaurant opened in Chelsea in mid-summer 2016. Chef Erren Nathaniel
(who has worked at Viajante, as well as Maido in Peru) heads up the
kitchen. As well as a 72-cover dining room there's a 16-seater chef's table
in the kitchen and 30-cover terrace. / SW10 0LP; www.chicamalondon.com;
@chicamalondon.*

Chick 'n' Sours E8 £32 3 2 3
390 Kingsland Rd   020 3620 8728   14–2A
*"Crispy and spicy Korean-style fried chicken" and "well-considered
cocktails" are the deal at this Dalston joint with "all the hipster credentials
– dark interior, bearded staff and mono menu". Portions are "surprisingly
big". / E8 2AA; www.chicknsours.co.uk; @chicknsours; 10 pm, Fri & Sat 10.30 pm,
Sun 9.30 pm; may need 6+ to book.*

Chicken Shop £35 ②②❸
199-206 High Holborn, WCI   020 7661 3040   2–1D
274-276 Holloway Rd, N7   020 3841 7787   9–2D **NEW**
79 Highgate Rd, NW5   020 3310 2020   9–1B
128 Allitsen Rd, NW8   020 3757 4849   9–3A **NEW**
7a Chestnut Grove, SW12   020 8102 9300   11–2C
141 Tooting High St, SW17   020 8767 5200   11–2B
27a Mile End Rd, E1   020 3310 2010   13–2D
"Does what it says on the tin!" – these "cool-feeling" pitstops offer "tasty chicken that won't break the bank", and win praise for a formula that's "simple, delicious, fun and very reasonable". (For the odd cynic however, "Nick Jones knows exactly where the 'just-good-enough-for-the-masses' level is".) / Mon-Sun 10.30 pm ; WC1V closed Sun.

Chilli Cool WCI £33 ❹②❶
15 Leigh St   020 7383 3135   2–1D
The "best dandan noodles this side of Chengdu" and other lip-tinglingly spicy dishes make this Bloomsbury cafe a Xanadu for lovers of fiery Sichuan scoff. / WC1H 9EW; 10.15 pm; no Amex.

The Chiltern Firehouse W1 £86 ❶②❸
1 Chiltern St   020 7073 7676   2–1A
"I CAN see what the fuss is about", insist fans of this "beautiful people hangout" in Marylebone, who go ape for its "relaxed cool", its "lovely" interior, "gorgeous outside area", and "inventive" menu. For far too many spoilsport critics though, it's "totally overhyped", "astronomically expensive" and "not that enjoyable" given the "nondescript and noisy" setting, and "prosaic" cuisine. / W1U 7PA; www.chilternfirehouse.com; 10.30 pm.

China Tang, Dorchester Hotel W1 £74 ❸②❸
53 Park Ln   020 7629 9988   3–3A
Sir David Tang's homage to '30s Shanghai (particularly the marvellous cocktail bar) is "a weird-but-interesting basement space that feels a bit dated now", but is nevertheless "elegant beyond 99% of Chinese restaurants". "The Peking duck especially is delicious", but the food standards have long divided opinion here and prices give nothing away. / W1K 1QA; www.chinatanglondon.co.uk; @ChinaTangLondon; 11.45 pm.

Chinese Cricket Club EC4 £63 ❸❸❶
19 New Bridge St   020 7438 8051   10–3A
"Plate after plate of delightful, well-balanced Chinese food" emerge from the kitchen of this hotel dining room near Blackfriars Bridge. But while "the quality is up there with high-end Hong Kong", it's "a bit pricey" and "a shame it feels like an airport departure lounge". / EC4V 6DB; www.chinesecricketclub.com; @chinesecclub; 10 pm; closed Sat & Sun L.

The Chipping Forecast W11 NEW £36
29 All Saints Road   020 7460 2745   7–1B
After trading for eight months as a stall at Soho's Berwick Street market, this fish 'n' chip shop (serving sustainably caught Cornish fish), launched its first standalone restaurant in deepest Notting Hill – early feedback says it's outstanding. / W11 1HE; www.chippingforecast.com; @CForecast; 10.30 pm, Fri & Sat 11.30 pm, Sun 10 pm; closed Mon; no bookings.

Chisou £52 4 4 2
4 Princes St, W1   020 7629 3931   3–1C
31 Beauchamp Pl, SW3   020 3155 0005   6–1D
*"One of the best proper Japanese restaurants in London" – both the calm
and "easily overlooked" Mayfair original and its "secret hideaway"
Knightsbridge offshoot offer "excellent" sushi and sashimi backed up by
a "very good range of izakaya-style dishes" and an interesting sake
selection. / www.chisourestaurant.com; Mon-Sat 10.30 pm, Sun 9.30 pm.*

Chiswell Street Dining Rooms EC1 £62 2 2 2
56 Chiswell St   020 7614 0177   13–2A
*This reasonably "stylish" operation near the Barbican can be "very good for
a business lunch", although it's "a bit expensive" and there's repeated
sentiment that "the experience is decent but should be better". / EC1Y 4SA;
www.chiswellstreetdining.com; @chiswelldining; 11 pm; closed Sat & Sun.*

Chor Bizarre W1 £63 3 2 4
16 Albemarle St   020 7629 9802   3–3C
*"A lovely ambience created by Indian antiques" helps win fans for this bric-
a-brac-infested Mayfair fixture. "OK, the food's not at the heights of the
very best Indians going, but good quality across the board". / W1S 4HW;
www.chorbizarre.com; @ChorBizarreUK; 11.30 pm, Sun 10.30 pm.*

Chotto Matte W1 £60 4 3 5
11-13 Frith St   020 7042 7171   5–2A
*"Buzzy, very hip and classy", "club-like" Soho two-year-old, which
is regularly "heaving" thanks to its "fabulous cocktails" and "superb" food
that's a "fantastic combination of Peruvian and Japanese cuisines".
/ W1D 4RB; www.chotto-matte.com; @ChottoMatteSoho; Mon-Sat 1 am,
Sun 11 pm.*

Chriskitch £27 4 4 3
7 Tetherdown, N10   020 8411 0051   1–1C
5 Hoxton Market, N1   020 7033 6666   13–1B NEW
*"It's opposite my house and it never disappoints!" – Chris Kitch's Muswell
hill yearling in a converted front room continues to inspire love for its
"fabulous salads, cakes and really good coffee"; fans "just wish it was
bigger!" Owner Christian Honor's more ambitious new venture with open
kitchen in hipster-central Hoxton opened too late for the survey –
the cooking gets the thumbs up in the press. / see web for detail.*

Christopher's WC2 £77 3 2 3
18 Wellington St   020 7240 4222   5–3D
*The "exceptional, spacious and stylish" interior is the special draw of this
"wonderful" Covent Garden townhouse, where "very good but very
expensive steaks" are the best feature of its American menu. Other
attractions? – a good downstairs bar; and "a fabulous brunch, with a great
array of choices". / WC2E 7DD; www.christophersgrill.com; @christopherswc2;
11.30 pm, Sun 10.30 pm; booking max 14 may apply.*

Chuck Burger E1 NEW £25
4 Commercial Street   020 7377 5742   13–2C
*Little sister to Spitalfield's BBQ spot Hot Box, this burger bar opened
in summer 2016 in a renovated 'classic East End London caff'
in Whitechapel after a stint at Street Feast's Hawker House. / E1 7PT;
www.chuckburgerbar.com; 10 pm.*

Chucs £66 353
30b Dover St, W1   020 3763 2013   3–3C
226 Westbourne Grove, W11   020 7243 9136   7 1B **NEW**
Spin-offs from the up-and-coming luxury menswear brand (inspired by Ian Fleming's look in the '50s and '60s) – this new duo of comfortable, clubbable cafés brings a hint of St Tropez (its third branch) to Mayfair and – now also – Notting Hill. Both serve "solid, classic Italian food": the former is a "tiny", "very intimate" space next to the boutique, the latter (on the ground floor below the shop, with outside terrace) is more "buzzing" and "ladies-who-lunch" in style. Notably "impeccable service" at both locations. / see web for detail.

Churchill Arms W8 £37 335
119 Kensington Church St   020 7792 1246   7–2B
"Such a cute, little quirky place at the back of a pub" off Notting Hill, and "unbelievable value"; this "fun, butterfly-filled conservatory" ("the floral display is worth the trip alone") "never fails to deliver some of the tastiest Asian scoff this side of Thailand" and is so damn "cheap". Meanwhile "the pub itself is always cheerful with an authentic pub atmosphere" that's "popular with locals and tourists alike". / W8 7LN; www.churchillarmskensington.co.uk; @ChurchillArmsW8; 10 pm, Sun 9.30 pm.

Chutney Mary SW1 £82 434
73 St James's St   020 7629 6688   3–4D
"I needn't have been apprehensive about the move from the King's Road!" – this re-located Indian stalwart (in its new "grown-up" St James's premises for over a year now) continues to delight its large fanclub with its "exceptional, deeply flavoured and superbly textured" cuisine. / SW1A 1PH; www.chutneymary.com; @thechutneymary; 10.30 pm; closed Sat L & Sun.

Chutneys NW1 £31 322
124 Drummond St   020 7388 0604   9–4C
"Seriously good value" Keralan veggie food makes this BYO one of the stars of Euston's 'Little India'. "Quality remains consistent, with good spicing", while the lunchtime and Sunday evening buffet is one of London's top deals. / NW1 2PA; www.chutneyseuston.co.uk; 11 pm; no Amex; may need 5+ to book.

Ciao Bella WC1 £42 235
86-90 Lamb's Conduit St   020 7242 4119   2–1D
"Chaotic and charming" (like Boris Johnson, for whom apparently it's a favourite) – this "full-to-bursting", "old school Italian (like stepping back into the '70s)" in Bloomsbury is the epitome of a "cheap 'n' cheerful" trattoria. It's the "verve and enthusiasm" of the staff and "slightly manic atmosphere" that stand out though, rather than the "family-sized portions of simple classics". / WC1N 3LZ; www.ciaobellarestaurant.co.uk; @CiaobellaLondon; 11.30 pm, Sun 10.30 pm.

Cibo W14 £55 453
3 Russell Gdns   020 7371 6271   8–1D
"If you don't have time to go to Italy..." this "very enjoyable and most-relaxed" stalwart local on a sidestreet near Olympia station will do the trick: "it really does feel the part", the "food is superb and such good value for money", and there's a "great wine list". / W14 8EZ; www.ciborestaurant.net; 10.30 pm; closed Sat L & Sun D.

Cigala WC1 £50   2 2 2
54 Lamb's Conduit St   020 7405 1717   2–1D
"Admirable" tapas has won a foodie reputation for this this long-serving Spanish joint, in a quaint corner of Bloomsbury. Quibbles persist, though: the food can disappoint, service can be "careless", and "I do wish they'd do something about the ambience" (although it can be "lovely outside watching the world go by"). / WC1N 3LW; www.cigala.co.uk; 10.45 pm, Sun 9.45 pm.

Cigalon WC2 £53   3 4 3
115 Chancery Ln   020 7242 8373   2–2D
Created originally as an auction house – the "lovely airy space" creates a "classy" but "refreshingly unstuffy atmosphere" at this favourite legal-land rendezvous (whose best seats are in the "wonderful booths"). Service is "swift", and the Provençal cooking is "exceptionally good (and never too heavy)". / WC2A 1PP; www.cigalon.co.uk; @cigalon_london; 10 pm; closed Sat & Sun.

THE CINNAMON CLUB SW1 £74   3 3 3
Old Westminster Library, Great Smith St   020 7222 2555   2–4C
For "inspirational Indian cuisine in a very classy setting", this "impressive", "airy" edifice that originally housed Westminster Public Library, would be many reporters' top choice in London. It can seem "a little stuffy", and even fans agree "you pay the price", but disappointments are rare. / SW1P 3BU; www.cinnamonclub.com; @cinnamonclub; 10.30 pm; no trainers; booking max 14 may apply; set weekday L £49 (FP), set Sun L £61 (FP).

Cinnamon Kitchen EC2 £59   3 2 3
9 Devonshire Sq   020 7626 5000   10–2D
"Inventive and subtle" dishes with "just the right amount of spice" win praise for this "high-endish Indian" – the City cousin of the famous Cinnamon Club – within a large covered atrium near Liverpool Street. Its ratings have been higher though, and critics say: "it's perfectly adequate, but it was far better than adequate once-upon-a-time". / EC2M 4YL; www.cinnamon-kitchen.com; @cinnamonkitchen; 10.45 pm; closed Sat L & Sun.

Cinnamon Soho W1 £45   4 2 2
5 Kingly St   020 7437 1664   4–2B
"Not like the other Cinnamons – this is a truly casual one" (the styling is "adequate"), just off Regent Street. It "breaks the stereotypes of Indian food" with dishes such as "rogan josh shepherd's pie and vindaloo ox cheek – highly recommended". / W1B 5PE; www.cinnamon-kitchen.com/soho-home; @cinnamonsoho; 11 pm, Sun 4.30 pm; closed Sun D.

City Barge W4 £50   3 3 4
27 Strand-on-the-Green   020 8994 2148   1–3A
A "wonderful location, right on the river" is the trump card of this refurbished boozer in Strand-on-the-Green. "Tasty food and helpful, engaging staff" complete its hand. / W4 3PH; www.citybargechiswick.com; @citybargew4; Mon-Thu 11 pm, Fri & Sat midnight, Sun 10.30 pm.

City Càphê EC2 £18   3 2 1
17 Ironmonger St   no tel   10–2C
"Expect a queue noon–2pm" at this "authentic Vietnamese with good báhn mi and pho" near Bank – it can be "crazy busy". The "genuine" scoff mostly inspires raves, but some fear that "high demand has led to lower quality". / EC2V 8EY; www.citycaphe.com; 3 pm; L only, closed Sat & Sun.

City Social EC2 £84 3 3 5
Tower 42 25 Old Broad St 020 7877 7703 10–2C
"Perfect with a client" – especially on a clear day when there's an "exceptional vista" – Jason Atherton's 24th floor perch, in the City's Tower 42, provides "first-rate" cuisine in "swish" surroundings. To some extent though, "you're paying for the view not the food". / EC2N 1HQ; www.citysociallondon.com, 9 pm; closed Sat & Sun.

Clarke's W8 £64 4 4 4
124 Kensington Church St 020 7221 9225 7–2B
"Still delivering exceptional food after all these years: amazing!" Sally Clarke's "very grown up" temple to seasonal cuisine off Notting Hill ("everything is carefully chosen by Sally herself") delivers "simple and wonderful" cooking – "very fresh" and prepared with "a gentle rarity of touch and seasoning". Old-timers may complain that "the enlarged eating area has removed the special intimacy of old" but "the packed house says she's called it right" and it's "a safe bet for business" and "romantic" too. / W8 4BH; www.sallyclarke.com; @SallyClarkeLtd; 10 pm; closed Sun; booking max 14 may apply.

Claude's Kitchen, Amuse Bouche SW6 £51 4 3 3
51 Parsons Green Ln 020 7371 8517 11–1B
Claude Compton's "enjoyably idiosyncratic" dining room upstairs from Amuse Bouche champagne bar (and opposite Parsons Green tube station) has a "short menu of very good food". "An unexpected treat to eat so well – and so inventively – in Fulham". / SW6 4JA; www.claudeskitchen.co.uk, @AmuseBoucheLDN; 11 pm, Sun 9.30 pm; closed weekday L.

Clipstone W1 NEW
5 Clipstone Street 020 7637 0871 2–1B
From the team behind Fitzrovia's outstanding Portland comes a new, hard-edged and minimalist venture just a few streets away. It launched in September 2016 – too late for survey feedback – but to say that press reviews have been ecstatic would be an understatement. / W1W 6BB; www.clipstonerestaurant.co.uk; @clipstonerestaurant; 11 pm; closed Sun.

Clives Midtown Diner WC1 £23 3 4 2
49 Museum Street 020 7405 3182 2–1C
"New kid on the block: hope it sticks around!" – owned by an American, this "stoic attempt at a quality diner" near the British Museum, has won instant praise for its "jolly good burgers" in particular (including a veggie option) and dishes such as "excellent chicken wings... and all the usual trimmings". / WC1A; www.clivesmidtown.co.uk; @clivesmidtown; 6 pm, Fri & Sat 9.30 pm.

CLOS MAGGIORE WC2 £74 3 4 5
33 King St 020 7379 9696 5–3C
"A man on the next table got on one knee and proposed... she said yes!" This "joyful oasis" remains London's No. 1 romantic destination thanks to its "magical" interior – in particular its "extraordinarily pretty" rear conservatory. A "well-oiled, very professional operation", "the food quality is high for Covent Garden too, but gastronomically speaking it's the enormous wine list that really sings" ("allow an hour to digest it fully!") / WC2E 8JD; www.closmaggiore.com; @closmaggiorewc2; 11 pm, Sun 10 pm.

The Clove Club EC1 £95 5 4 4
Shoreditch Town Hall, 380 Old St 020 7729 6496 13–1B
"Beyond amazing!!!!" Isaac McHale's "playful" and "exquisitely crafted"
cuisine provides one of London's best trendy gastronomic experiences.
Despite the hipster street cred of this "slightly sparse and echoey" chamber
inside Shoreditch's fine old town hall, staff are "attentive and not
overbearing", but the "pay-in-advance policy" can seem "irritating".
/ EC1V 9LT; www.thecloveclub.com; @thecloveclub; 9.30 pm; closed Mon L & Sun.

Club Gascon EC1 £87 4 3 2
57 West Smithfield 020 7600 6144 10–2B
"The exciting things they do with foies gras can miss, but when they hit:
WOW!" – "Beautiful dishes with amazing combinations of flavour and
colours", all "rooted in SW France", together with "a comprehensive range
of lesser-known but delicious Gallic wines" maintain the culinary standing
of this "serious" and "business-friendly" French venue, near Smithfield
Market, even if the interior can seem "a bit '90s". / EC1A 9DS;
www.clubgascon.com; @club_gascon; 10 pm, Fri & Sat 10.30 pm; closed
Sat L & Sun.

CôBa N7 NEW £38 4 3 3
244 York Way 0749 596 3336 9–2C
"An excellent addition to a slightly dead area in terms of food" – Damon
Bui's has shifted attention from supper clubs to this new sparse pub-
conversion in Barnsbury, which wins all-round praise, not least for its "tasty
Vietnamese BBQ". / N7 9AG; www.cobarestaurant.co.uk; @cobafood; 10 pm;
closed Sun.

Cocotte W2 NEW £48 4 3 3
95 Westbourne Grove 020 3220 0076 7–1B
"Of course it helps if you like chicken, but this simple rôtisserie concept
works a treat" – "tasty roast birds, all from the same farm in France,
are served with a variety of sauces and some original and delicious salads"
at this new outlet on the Notting Hill/Bayswater border. "Not for Michelin-
stye gourmets, but hard to beat for a tasty, healthy and good-value family
supper out". / W2 4UW; www.mycocotte.uk; @cocotte_rotisserie; 10 pm, Fri & Sat
11 pm.

Coin Laundry EC1 NEW £48
70 Exmouth Mkt 020 7833 9000 10–1A
Despite its prime Exmouth Market location, survey feedback totally ignores
this new bar/restaurant whose website boasts 'comfort food, 70's revival
cocktails and a big slice of nostalgia' – despite favourable press critiques
from Giles Coren and Grace Dent, it has all the hallmarks of somewhere
that makes super copy but not such super food. / EC1R 4QP;
www.coinlaundry.co.uk; @coinlaundryem; 11 pm, Thu-Sat 2 am; SRA-2 star.

Colbert SW1 £59 1 1 2
51 Sloane Sq 020 7730 2804 6–2D
The dud of the Corbin & King stable – a prime, Sloane Square corner-
location ensures this handsome Parisian-brasserie-style haunt is "always
buzzing", but "they need to get a grip": the classic fare is "so uneven"
(some dishes are "a total failure") and service is too often "bored and
lackadaisical". / SW1W 8AX; www.colbertchelsea.com; @ColbertChelsea;
Sun 10.30 pm, Mon-Thu 11 pm, Fri & Sat 11.30 pm.

La Collina NW1 £54 3 3 3
17 Princess Rd 020 7483 0192 9–3B
"Excellent home-made pasta" gets top billing at this *"obliging"* local Italian on the fringes of Primrose Hill. *"Top marks for ambience in the garden (but rather less indoors)"*, so it comes into its own in the summer.
/ NW1 8JR; www.lacollinarestaurant.co.uk; @LacollinaR; 10.15 pm, Mon & Tue 9.15 pm; closed Mon L.

The Collins Room SW1 NEW £86 2 4 5
Wilton Place 020 3137 1302 6–1D
"A girlie afternoon not to be missed!" is to be had at this re-named Knightsbridge chamber (formerly The Caramel Room). Its *"Pret-a-Portea has to be the best-looking afternoon tea in London and somehow manages not to sacrifice deliciousness at the temple of style"*. *"Go with your mum, granny, daughter or girlfriend!"* / SW1X 7RL; www.the-berkeley.co.uk; 10.45 pm, Sun 10.15 pm.

Le Colombier SW3 £66 3 4 3
145 Dovehouse St 020 7351 1155 6–2C
"Everyone's perfect idea of a Gallic brasserie!" – Didier Garnier's *"dependable old favourite"* is *"tucked away on a corner of a Chelsea backstreet"*, and *"feels like you were in France, except for so many elderly Rosbifs"*. The *"classic French cuisine"* is *"always more-ish"*, and *"service is impeccably well-mannered in the best French way"*. / SW3 6LB; www.le-colombier-restaurant.co.uk; 10.30 pm, Sun 10 pm.

Colony Grill Room, Beaumont Hotel W1 £65 3 4 4
Brown Hart Gdns 020 7499 1001 3–2A
"Utterly professional service and fabulous surroundings" help win votes for Corbin & King's *"serious"*, *"panelled"* Mayfair dining room, particularly as an ideal venue *"for an understated or confidential business meeting"*. Its *"throwback menu"* of *"classic American dishes"* fits the bill too – *"proper chaps' food"*. / W1K 6TF; www.colonygrillroom.com; @ColonyGrillRoom; midnight, Sun 11 pm.

Como Lario SW1 £54 2 2 2
18-22 Holbein Pl 020 7730 2954 6–2D
Some regulars still *"feel part of the family"* at this age-old trattoria near Sloane Square, but there are growing signs that it's *"no longer quite the place it was"*: *"I've been going for years but after last night may not go again"*. / SW1W 8NL; www.comolario.co.uk; 11.30 pm, Sun 10 pm.

Comptoir Gascon EC1 £45 3 3 3
63 Charterhouse St 020 7608 0851 10–1A
"Interesting regional French dishes (if in slightly modest portions for the price)" inspire lots of affection for this *"cute little French bistro"* in Smithfield (near its parent, Club Gascon). *"It's great for business lunches"*, but the *"lovely casual Gallic ambience"* is also *"perfect for date night"* too. Top Menu Tip – *"the foie gras duck burger is worth the coronary!"* / EC1M 6HJ; www.comptoirgascon.com; @ComptoirGascon; 10 pm, Thu & Fri 10.30 pm; closed Mon & Sun.

Comptoir Libanais £34 2 2 3
"Delicious mezze" top the bill at this *"cheap, fast and tasty"* Lebanese chain with *"bright and quirky interiors"*. There is a school of thought though, which feels the food is *"OK, but that's all"*. / www.lecomptoir.co.uk; W12 9 pm, Thu & Fri 10 pm, Sun 6 pm; W1 9.30 pm; W12 closed Sun D; no bookings.

Il Convivio SW1 £62 3 3 4
143 Ebury St   020 7730 4099   2–4A
A "hidden gem" in Belgravia, this "quiet" stalwart "never disappoints" its fans – the interior is "absolutely lovely" and it serves "honest, Italian-inspired food". / SW1W 9QN; www.etruscarestaurants.com/il-convivio; 10.45 pm; closed Sun.

Coopers Restaurant & Bar WC2 £49 2 3 3
49 Lincoln's Inn Fields   020 7831 6211   2–2D
"Very useful for the area" – this "low-key" operation in the thinly provided environs of Lincoln's Inn Fields feeds both legal types and academics from the nearby LSE. Arguably its "classic" dishes "could be more inspiring", but its performance is "sound". / WC2A 3PF; www.coopersrestaurant.co.uk; @coopers_bistro; 10.30 pm; closed Sat & Sun; no bookings.

Le Coq N1 £42 3 3 3
292-294 St Paul's Rd   020 7359 5055   9–2D
"The signature rôtisserie chicken is delicious" at this straightforward Islington two-year-old. Service is "efficient and friendly", while the "occasional guest-chef takeover nights are good fun, too". / N1 2LH; www.le-coq.co.uk; @LeCOQrestaurant; 10.15 pm.

Coq d'Argent EC2 £86 2 2 2
1 Poultry   020 7395 5000   10–2C
"Ideal for City entertaining" – D&D London's central landmark, right by Bank, boasts a wonderful rooftop location (and you can drink outside in the bar). It perennially seems "expensive for what it is" however, mixing "average food, with some good views, and silly prices". / EC2R 8EJ; www.coqdargent.co.uk; @coqdargent1; 9.45 pm; closed Sun D.

Cork & Bottle WC2 £55 2 3 4
44-46 Cranbourn St   020 7734 7807   5–3B
"One of the only good places to eat near Leicester Square", this age-old "cellar, bistro-style wine bar" is a venerable haven in tourist-land, "but would be great anywhere!" The "reliably good food", including more than a dozen cheeses, is simple and straightforward – top draw is the "exceptional wine list". / WC2H 7AN; www.thecorkandbottle.co.uk; @corkbottle1971; 11.30 pm, Sun 10.30 pm; no bookings at diner.

Corner Kitchen E7 NEW £40 3 2 3
58 Woodgrange Road   020 8555 8068   14–1D
"A recent addition to the Forest Gate eating scene – a deli, café and shop" tipped for its "great pizza". / E7; cornerkitchen.london; @CornerKitchenE7; Mon-Thu 10 pm, Sat 10.30 pm, Sun 9 pm.

Cornish Tiger SW11 £52 3 3 3
1 Battersea Rise   020 7223 7719   11–1C
"An Asian slant on Cornish produce" has made this "lively" two-year-old "an interesting addition to the Battersea dining options". A minority is unconvinced by the fusion though ("the random addition of chilli and sometimes coriander"). / SW11 1GH; www.cornishtiger.com; @cornishtiger; 11 pm, Sun 6 pm; closed Mon.

Corrigan's Mayfair W1 £92 344
28 Upper Grosvenor St 020 7499 9943 3–3A
Richard Corrigan's "clubby" Mayfair HQ is "an opulent place with fine cuisine", but also a "manly" and business-friendly destination ("the decor shouts hunting, shooting, fishing!") "The menu reads as a homage to gutsy, comfort stalwarts, and though the food looks more delicate than you might imagine, there's nothing dainty about the flavours". "Great private dining options". / W1K 7EH; www.corrigansmayfair.com; @CorriganMayfair; 10 pm; closed Sat L & Sun D; booking max 10 may apply.

Côte £48 222
"As a useful port of call", these "safe" all-day French brasseries remain immensely popular, especially for their "bargain set lunch", and pre-theatre deals. However, even many fans would concede that the "straightforward" fare is "solid but unspectacular". / www.cote-restaurants.co.uk; 11 pm.

Counter Culture SW4 NEW £32 444
16 The Pavement 020 8191 7960 11–2D
"New from the Dairy (next door). Tapas food... no bookings". As the name suggests the focus is on kitchen counter-style dining with just 15 seats (six right on the pass) and its "excellent" pintxos are "full of flavour"; you can even BYO. / SW4 0HY; www.countercultureclapham.co.uk; @culturesnax; 11 pm; D only, closed Mon & Sun; no bookings.

Counter Vauxhall Arches SW8 £48 233
Arch 50, South Lambeth Pl 020 3693 9600 11–1D
A "hipster" railway arch near Vauxhall tube (at 60m long, it claims to be London's longest restaurant) houses this funky yearling. It serves a versatile array of brasserie dishes, plus cocktails, with top billing going to the "American style brunch". / SW8 1SP; www.counterrestaurants.com; @eatatcounter; 12.30 am, Fri & Sat 1.30 am.

The Cow W2 £55 324
89 Westbourne Park Rd 020 7221 0021 7–1B
"A bit rough around the edges but a proper boozer" – Tom Conran's "busy" Irish pub in Bayswater makes "a refreshing change from most glammed-up pubs", and provides "simple seafood cooked well, great Guinness and a buzzing atmosphere": "I always have a whole crab and spend hours eating it!" / W2 5QH; www.thecowlondon.co.uk; @TheCowLondon; 10 pm, Sun 10 pm; no Amex.

Coya W1 £76 324
118 Piccadilly 020 7042 7118 3–4B
"Fabulous atmosphere" is the highlight of this happening haunt in Mayfair ("the main room can get noisy"). Praise too for its "amazing and beautifully presented" Peruvian dishes, even if a vocal minority feel they are "far too expensive". / W1J 7NW; www.coyarestaurant.com; @coyalondon_; Sun-Wed 10.30 pm, Thu-Sat 11 pm.

Craft London SE10 £65 433
Peninsula Sq 020 8465 5910 1–3D
"Exceptional food in the culinary desert of the O2", brought to the Greenwich Peninsular by hip-crowd chef Stevie Parle in a "beautiful three-storey venue" topped by a bar. The restaurant is "a great locally sourced concept", while the "buzzing" ground-floor café scores for "rustic pizzas" and "great coffee and cardamom buns". / SE10 0SQ; www.craft-london.co.uk; @CraftLDN; café 6 pm, restaurant 10.30 pm, Sun 4 pm.

Crate Brewery & Pizzeria E9   £28   3 2 3

7, The White Building, Queens Yard   020 8533 3331   14–1C

Grungily-groovily located on the canalside looking over to the Olympic Park, this hipster craft brewery and pizzeria, in Hackney Wick's White Building, is one of the area's best-established hangouts thanks to its handy standard of pizza. / E9 5EN; www.cratebrewery.com; @cratebrewery; 10 pm, Fri & Sat 11 pm.

Crazy Bear W1   £66   2 2 4

26-28 Whitfield St   020 7631 0088   2–1C

"Quirky", swish venue hidden away off Tottenham Court Road, whose glam basement bar is the crown jewel feature. The ground floor restaurant lacks the verve it once displayed, but some still admire its "fun" style and "great Thai food". / W1T 2RG; www.crazybeargroup.co.uk; @CrazyBearGroup; 10.30 pm; closed Mon L & Sun; no shorts.

Crocker's Folly NW8   £56   2 2 3

23-24 Aberdeen Pl   020 7289 9898   9–4A

The "gorgeous interior" and "spectacular Victorian features" justify a visit to this "ornately decorated" former hotel in St John's Wood (Frank Crocker built it anticipating a railway terminus opposite, but went bust when they decided to end the line in Marylebone instead). Shame that the food – British, despite the Lebanese Maroush group ownership – is "too pricey". / NW8 8JR; www.crockersfolly.com; @Crockers_Folly; 10.30 pm.

The Crooked Well SE5   £49   3 3 4

16 Grove Ln   020 7252 7798   1–3C

"Confidence and skill in the kitchen" helps inspire numerous favourable reports for this spacious, very "pleasant" gastroboozer in Camberwell. / SE5 8SY; www.thecrookedwell.com; @crookedwell; 10.30 pm; closed Mon L; no Amex.

The Cross Keys SW3   £54   3 3 4

1 Lawrence St   020 7351 0686   6–3C

This "stylish dining pub" – Chelsea's oldest boozer, now revamped as a stablemate of the Sands End in Fulham – wins consistent praise for its "high-quality, reliable cooking". / SW3 5NB; www.thecrosskeyschelsea.co.uk; @CrossKeys_PH; midnight.

The Culpeper E1   £43   2 2 3

40 Commercial St   020 7247 5371   13–2C

After a wizard start, this year-old Spitalfields "hipster hangout" – "a carefully curated, shabby-chic dining room over a frenetic bar" – put in a more mixed showing this year. Fans still praise its "simple", "innovative" dishes and "efficient service", but sceptics are scathing about the staff's "cavalier attitude" and food that's "really nothing to write home about given the hype". / E1 6LP; www.theculpeper.com; @TheCulpeper; Mon-Thu midnight, Fri & Sat 2 am, Sun 11 pm.

Cumberland Arms W14   £44   4 4 3

29 North End Rd   020 7371 6806   8–2D

An "epic pub in the barren streetscape of Olympia" – "so reliable", with "accurate cooking of a Med-inspired menu", "(best Italian sausages and mash)", and "a great rotating selection of beers and fine wines". / W14 8SZ; www.thecumberlandarmspub.co.uk; @thecumberland; 10 pm, Sun 9.30 pm.

CURIO + TA TA E8 NEW
258 Kingsland Road   020 7254 4945   14–2A
A summer 2016 opening — cx-Viajante chefs behind street food phenomenon TA TA Eatery have teamed up with Curio Cabal coffee shop to bring their 'Chinese family style' rice fix (with a Portuguese twist to Haggerston). / E8 4DG; www.curioandtata.co.uk; @curioandTaTa; Thu 11 pm, Fri & Sat midnight; D only, closed Mon-Wed & Sun.

Cut, 45 Park Lane W1   £118   1 2 2
45 Park Ln   020 7493 4545   3–4A
"Good steaks at eye-watering prices" sums up the limited appeal of US celeb-chef Wolfgang Puck's "oddly proportioned" venture, off the foyer of a boutique hotel. "It could only survive on Park Lane" — "it's one for misguided travelling businessmen": "do any Londoners actually go there?" / W1K 1PN; www.45parklane.com; @the_cut_bar; 10.30 pm.

Da Mario SW7   £48   2 3 4
15 Gloucester Rd   020 7584 9078   6–1B
"Deservedly popular", this Italian stalwart near the Royal Albert Hall "may be cheesy, with its Princess Di connections", but "it's so nice to get away from chains": "they do make a really good pizza", the "pasta dishes are consistently good", and the "wine prices are sensible". / SW7 4PP; www.damario.co.uk; 11.30 pm.

Da Mario WC2   £43   3 3 3
63 Endell St   020 7240 3632   5–1C
"Old-fashioned", "crowded and very noisy" neighbourhood Italian — a "star in the largely ho-hum Covent Garden gastronomic firmament". "There's always a warm welcome from the hosts", along with "plenty of daily specials" at prices that are "easy on the wallet". / WC2H 9AJ; www.da-mario.co.uk; 11.15 pm; closed Sun.

Dabbous W1   £87   3 3 2
39 Whitfield St   020 7323 1544   2–1C
Ollie Dabbous's "loft-style" Fitzrovia haunt again divides reporters sharply. To advocates, it combines "precision cooking, with brilliant tastes and textures" and has an "excellent and unfussy" approach — to detractors, "portions are minuscule", dishes are "sometimes a little too wacky", and the interior's too "stark". / W1T 2SF; www.dabbous.co.uk; @dabbous; 9.30 pm (bar open until 11.30 pm); closed Sun.

The Dairy SW4   £40   5 4 4
15 The Pavement   020 7622 4165   11–2D
"Like a mini-Noma on Clapham Common" — this "creative" three-year-old draws fans from across town for its "exceptional" and "clever" small plates. Service is "brisk and helpful", and most (if not quite all) reporters love its "relaxed" style. / SW4 0HY; www.the-dairy.co.uk; @thedairyclapham; 9.45 pm; closed Mon, Tue L & Sun D.

Dalloway Terrace, Bloomsbury Hotel WC1 NEW   £56
16-22 Great Russell St   020 7347 1221   2–1C
It's easy to feel disoriented if you stumble across this new restaurant, with lovely leafy terrace (and fully retractable roof) — how can it be so close to grungy old Centre Point! We don't yet have sufficient feedback for a rating, but one early report is all-round positive. / WC1B 3NN; www.dallowayterrace.com; @DallowayTerrace; 10.30 pm.

Daphne's SW3 £73 2 2 3
112 Draycott Ave 020 7589 4257 6–2C
Thanks to its "lovely and romantic" interior, this "appealing" Chelsea old-timer has been a "special" favourite since time immemorial (it was once famously Princess Di's top spot). Its Italian cuisine has slipped notably in recent times though: "preparation could be vastly improved". / SW3 3AE; www.daphnes-restaurant.co.uk; @DaphnesLondon; 11 pm, Sun 10 pm.

Daquise SW7 £49 2 2 2
20 Thurloe St 020 7589 6117 6–2C
This Polish veteran by South Ken tube station clocks up its 70th anniversary next year, and its overall appeal somehow exceeds the sum of its parts: "it's like meeting a friend from the distant past and discovering there's still something special". / SW7 2LT; www.daquise.co.uk; @GesslerDaquise; 11 pm; no Amex.

Darbaar EC2 NEW £60 4 4 3
1 Snowden Street 020 7422 4100 13–2B
On the site near Liverpool Street that was formerly a svelte Japanese venture (Chrysan, RIP), this Indian newcomer is the work of Abdul Yaseen, ex-head chef of nearby Cinnamon Kitchen. It wins high ratings for its "generous dishes, delicately spiced"; and "varied tasting menus giving you the opportunity of trying different options" (including "lovely 'nanza'" – naan meets pizza). / EC2A 2DQ; www.darbaarrestaurants.com; @DarbaarbyAbdul; 10.45 pm; closed Sun.

The Dartmouth Castle W6 £47 3 4 4
26 Glenthorne Rd 020 8748 3614 8–2C
"There's nothing bang-whizz about this place" – a very "solid" little gastropub bordering Hammersmith's one-way system. But "it gets the basics perfectly right" and "everything's served with a smile". / W6 0LS; www.thedartmouthcastle.co.uk; @DartmouthCastle; 10 pm, Sun 9.30 pm; closed Sat L

Darwin Brasserie, Sky Garden EC3 £68 2 2 4
20 Fenchurch St 033 3772 0020 10–3D
"You can't beat the views over London on a beautiful day" from this large all-day operation on the top of the Walkie Talkie and although "the food's not outstanding" it's "surprisingly good" given the location. Top Tip – its "value-for-money brunch" ("but additional drinks on top of the set price are expensive"). / EC3M 3BY; skygarden.london/darwin; @SG_Darwin; 10.30 pm, Sun 8.30 pm.

Daylesford Organic £54 2 2 3
44b Pimlico Rd, SW1 020 7881 8060 6–2D
Selfridges & Co, 400 Oxford St, W1 0800 123 400 3–1A
6-8 Blandford St, W1 020 3696 6500 2–1A
208-212 Westbourne Grove, W11 020 7313 8050 7–1B
"You feel like the food's doing you good (although it probably isn't!)", at Lady Bamford's "bright" (but "crowded" and slightly "chaotic") organic-branded cafés, hailed by fans for their "fresh and healthy" dishes, including "lovely breakfasts served in quirky metal pans". / www.daylesfordorganic.com; SW1 & W11 7 pm, Sun 4 pm – W1 9 pm, Sun 6.15 pm; W11 no booking L

Dean Street Townhouse W1 £61 **2 3 5**

69-71 Dean St 020 7434 1775 5–2A

Soho House Group's versatile brasserie in the heart of Soho itself, remains hugely popular. "It's the buzzy feel of the place that makes it a great hangout", although "the food's fine" and "service is attentive and friendly for such a busy place". / W1D 3SE; www.deanstreettownhouse.com; @deanstreettownhouse; 11.30 pm, Fri & Sat midnight, Sun 10.30 pm.

Defune W1 £72 **4 3 1**

34 George St 020 7935 8311 3–1A

"I was staggered to find it's had the same owner for 40 years!" – this "quiet" Marylebone "classic" is "just like being in Japan" (not such a boon on the ambience front...) and still delivers "outstanding" teppanyaki and "marvellously inventive" sushi. Breathe deeply when the bill arrives though – it's "pricey". / W1U 7DP; www.defune.com; 10.45 pm, Sun 10.30 pm.

Dehesa W1 £51 **4 2 3**

25 Ganton St 020 7494 4170 4–2B

"Lovely, little dining room and outdoor terrace" off Carnaby Street which serves "brilliant" Spanish and Italian tapas and "great wine" in a "laid-back, intimate atmosphere". / W1F 9BP; www.dehesa.co.uk; @SaltYardGroup; 10.45 pm.

THE DELAUNAY WC2 £58 **2 3 4**

55 Aldwych 020 7499 8558 2–2D

Like its sibling, The Wolseley, Corbin & King's "bustling and luxurious" venue on Aldwych "gives a very good impression of a middle-European café in the grand style", and makes a supremely business-friendly choice. But aside from "wonderful old-school breakfasts" and "lovely afternoon teas", the somewhat "unimaginative" cooking is "only OK for the price", and has seemed even more "ordinary" of late. Next door, 'The Counter' is "The Delaunay's little brother, serving light meals, coffee and cakes". / WC2B 4BB; www.thedelaunay.com; @TheDelaunayRest; midnight, Sun 11 pm.

Delfino W1 £49 **4 3 2**

121a Mount St 020 7499 1256 3–3B

"Top pizza and great value" win fans for this straightforward venue, by the Connaught – "small", hectic and "slightly squished" at peak times, but "long may it continue". / W1K 3NW; www.finos.co.uk; 10.45 pm; closed Sun.

Delhi Grill N1 £35 **3 2 2**

21 Chapel Mkt 020 7278 8100 9–3D

"Fast, furious, tasty, cheap!" This "buzzy" Chapel Market canteen, with its "Indian street food and Bollywood posters" is the best bet for "simple curries in Islington". "Set lunch for just over a fiver: irresistible!" / N1 9EZ; www.delhigrill.com; @delhigrill; 10.30 pm; cash only.

La Delizia Limbara SW3 £40 **3 2 2**

63-65 Chelsea Manor St 020 7376 4111 6–3C

"Tucked away off the King's Road", this is a "locals' hangout worth searching out" for "cracking pizzas and pasta banged out with little fuss"; "always a squeeze but always worth it". / SW3 5RZ; www.ladelizia.org.uk; @ladelizia; 11 pm, Sun 10.30 pm; no Amex.

Department of Coffee & Social Affairs EC1 £15   3 5 4
14-16 Leather Ln 020 7419 6906 10–2A
"They're serious about their caffeine" – "some of the best and smoothest coffee in London" – at these "vibey" haunts (also offering "a small collection of delicious, simple cakes"). The site listed is the original Leather Lane branch (a converted old ironmongers) – "a cool hangout for young media start-up types which contrasts with the old-school market traders outside". / EC1N 7SU; www.departmentofcoffee.co.uk; @DeptOfCoffee; 6 pm, Sat & Sun 4 pm; L only.

The Depot SW14   £44   2 2 5
Tideway Yd, Mortlake High St 020 8878 9462 11–1A
"A wonderfully unspoilt location overlooking the Thames" guarantees a "magical" experience at this fixture near Barnes Bridge. "We always have a lovely time here", say regulars – even if the quality of the food "varies a bit too much". STOP PRESS – in October 2016 it was announced that the business was being purchased by Rick & Jill Stein (of Padstow fame) – no immediate changes are planned but these are likely in 2017. / SW14 8SN; www.depotbrasserie.co.uk; @TheDepotBarnes; 10 pm, Sun 9.30 pm.

Les Deux Salons WC2   £62   1 2 1
40-42 William IV St 020 7420 2050 5–4C
Yikes! – "Things have not improved under Sir Terence Conran's new ownership", at this large venue, just off Trafalgar Square, which nowadays combines an upstairs restaurant with ground floor 'café, bistro, épicerie and cave à vin'. OK, some reports do applaud its "very passable" Gallic fare, but the consensus is "don't bother" – it's "all a bit limited and lacking in ambience" with food that's "just factory catering". / WC2N 4DD; www.lesdeuxsalons.co.uk; @lesdeuxsalons; 10.45 pm, Sun 5.45 pm; closed Sun D.

Dickie Fitz W1 NEW   £62   2 2 2
48 Newman St 020 3667 1445 3–1D
Mixed reports on this Antipodean-influenced brasserie newcomer with striking yellow-leather banquettes, on the former site of The Newman Street Tavern (RIP). Its Aussie breakfasts and Pacific-inspired all-day menu do win some praise, but one or two disasters were also reported, and service can be "apathetic". / W1T 1QQ; www.dickiefitz.co.uk; @DickieFitzrovia; 10.30 pm, Sun 6 pm; closed Sun D.

Dinings W1   £57   4 3 1
22 Harcourt St 020 7723 0666 9–4A
"Every single bite is memorable" at this Marylebone venue where Tomonari Chiba provides some of "the best quality and most innovative Japanese food in London!" The decor – either sit at the ground floor counter or in the bunker-like basement – is decidedly "iffy" however, and critics fear it is becoming "embarrassingly expensive". / W1H 4HH; www.dinings.co.uk; @diningslondon; 10.30 pm; closed Sun.

Dinner, Mandarin Oriental SW1   £106   3 3 4
66 Knightsbridge 020 7201 3833 6–1D
Heston Blumenthal's "theatrical" menu "loosely based on historic British recipes" has won fame for this large, swish dining room, with "magnificent views over Hyde Park". Arguably the shtick "relies more on history-telling than cooking" however, and "now that the original hype is over" reporters divide between the majority for whom the cuisine is still plain "incredible" and a sizeable minority for whom "the original 'ooooohs' and 'aaaahs' have been superseded by 'so whats'". / SW1X 7LA; www.dinnerbyheston.com; 10.30 pm.

Dip & Flip £25 3 2 2
87 Battersea Rise, SW11 no tel 11–2C
115 Tooting High St, SW17 no tel 11–2C NEW
62 The Broadway, SW19 no tel 11–2B
64-68 Atlantic Road, SW9 no tel 11–2D NEW
*This burger concept – with gravy, and a kitchen roll instead of forks –
is hailed by locals as a "tremendous addition to the food scene"
in southwest London, where it's grown fast (Battersea, Wimbledon, Tooting
and Brixton). But not everyone is a convert: "where do the good reviews
come from? Too many people are squashed into a tiny place, and the
food's unexciting". / see web for detail.*

Dirty Burger £14 3 2 2
78 Highgate Rd, NW5 020 3310 2010 9–2B
Arch 54, 6 South Lambeth Rd, SW8 020 7074 1444 2–4D
13 Bethnal Green Rd, E1 020 7749 4525 13–1C
27a, Mile End Rd, E1 020 3727 6165 13–2D
*"For a quick in/out visit when you're looking for something dirty", or "for a
late night munch to soak up the alcohol", the "always impressive burgers"
at these "always busy and buzzy" shacks are "how fast food should be".
/ www.eatdirtyburger.com; Mon-Thu 11 pm-midnight, Fri & Sat 1 am-2 am,
Sun 8 pm-11 pm.*

Dishoom £40 4 3 4
Kingly St, W1 020 7420 9322 4 2B
12 Upper St Martins Ln, WC2 020 7420 9320 5–3B
Stable St, Granary Sq, N1 020 7420 9321 9–3C
7 Boundary St, E2 020 7420 9324 13–1B
*"Buzzy, bordering on frenetic" – these "wonderful replicas of Mumbai's
Parsi cafés" have exceptional energy levels for a fast-expanding chain,
and offer "deeply satisfying, colonially-inspired, street-food style dishes"
(including "terrifically interesting breakfasts"), plus "excellent cocktails".
The catch? – the limited-bookings policy leads to "massive" queues "out of
all proportion to reality". Top Menu Tip – "the black dhal is a must".
/ www.dishoom.com; @Dishoom; 11 pm, Sun 10 pm.*

Diwana Bhel-Poori House NW1 £27 3 2 1
121-123 Drummond St 020 7387 5556 9–4C
*"An institution" of Euston's 'Little India': this "never changing" veggie
canteen wouldn't win any prizes for interior design (unless the category was
for authentically '60s decor). It has survived for decades on its "delicious
dosas", and is known for its "excellent value buffet lunch". / NW1 2HL;
www.diwanabph.com; @DiwanaBhelPoori; 11.45 pm, Sun 11 pm; no Amex;
may need 10+ to book.*

**The Dock Kitchen,
Portobello Dock W10** £60 3 2 3
342-344 Ladbroke Grove, Portobello Dock 020 8962 1610 1–2B
*Stevie Parle serves an "eclectic", ever-changing, global menu at his
Victorian dockside warehouse conversion at the north end of Ladbroke
Grove, to general – but not universal – acclaim. "It's wonderful in summer
and autumn, sitting outside on the deck". / W10 5BU;
www.dockkitchen.co.uk/contact.php; @TheDockKitchen; 9.30 pm; closed Sun D.*

Dominique Ansel Bakery London SW1 NEW
17-21 Elizabeth Street   020 7324 7705   2–4B
Famous US baker, Dominique Ansel brings some of his most famous pastries – the Cronut and the DKA (Dominique's Kouign Amann) – across the Pond as he opens his first London site in autumn 2016 (although this Belgravia site is somewhat in contrast to its relatively hip SoHo NYC roots). / SW1W 9RP; www.dominiqueansellondon.com; @DominiqueAnsel.

The Don EC4   £66   3 3 2
20 St Swithin's Ln   020 7626 2606   10–3C
"Tucked away in a cobbled mews, but just a stone's throw from the Bank of England", this "handily located" fixture is one of the Square Mile's top business choices. Ratings don't hit the highs they once did, but it's a "reliable" and "efficient" operation, with a smart and spacious (if perhaps slightly "sterile") interior. See also Sign of the Don. / EC4N 8AD; www.thedonrestaurant.com; @thedonlondon; 10 pm; closed Sat & Sun; no shorts.

Donna Margherita SW11   £45   3 3 2
183 Lavender Hill   020 7228 2660   11–2C
"Authentic Naples pizza (stone-baked too giving it a lovely crust)" wins a thumbs up for this Battersea Italian – "noisy, but that makes it fun". One minor gripe: the wine list can seem a mite "predictable". / SW11 5TE; www.donna-margherita.com; @DMargheritaUK; 10.30 pm, Fri & Sat 11 pm; Mon-Thu D only, Fri-Sun open L & D.

Donostia W1   £49   5 3 4
10 Seymour Pl   020 3620 1845   2–2A
"Sensational" Basque tapas (Donostia = San Sebastián) – "true to the region and featuring seasonal specials" – win ongoing acclaim for this "casual" bar, arranged around an open kitchen, whose "enthusiastic" owners also run nearby Lurra. "Sitting outside on a summer's evening feels like another world from the hectic hellhole that is Marble Arch". / W1H 7ND; www.donostia.co.uk; @DonostiaW1; 11 pm; closed Mon L.

Doppio NW1   £6   3 3 3
177 Kentish Town Rd   020 7267 5993   9–2B
"Brilliant, expert coffee" is to be had in a "really laid back warehouse setting (it literally is a warehouse!)" at these "trendy" concepts in Camden Town and Shoreditch; alongside brews there's "a huge range of coffee, and coffee-making equipment for sale". / NW1 8PD; www.doppiocoffee.co.uk; @doppiocoffeeltd; 6 pm.

Dorchester Grill,
Dorchester Hotel W1   £104   3 3 3
53 Park Lane   020 7629 8888   3–3A
The bonkers former tartan-riot decor has given way to tasteful luxury at this grand chamber, nowadays overseen from afar by Alain Ducasse, with a blameless modern French menu. There's little to criticise – especially on business – but for those spending their own hard-earned lucre, little to distinguish it from so many other expensive Mayfair dining experiences. / W1K 1QA; www.thedorchester.com; @TheDorchester; 10.15 pm, Sat 10.45 pm, Sun 10.15 pm; no trainers.

Dotori N4   £28   4 3 2
3a Stroud Green Rd   020 7263 3562   9–1D
Packed outfit near Finsbury Park station: "go for authentic Korean and some Japanese dishes, but book in advance – it's small and sells out quickly". / N4 2DQ; www.dotorirestaurant.wix.com/dotorirestaurant; 10.30 pm; closed Mon; no Amex.

The Dove W6
£46   2 2 **4**

19 Upper Mall   020 8748 5405   8–2B

"It's one of the best pubs in London", "with a lovely terrace right on the Thames", but this small 18th-century tavern in a cute Hammersmith alley is "not really gastro" – "the food's OK, but you come for the beer and the atmosphere". / W6 9TA; www.fullers.co.uk; @thedovew6; 11 pm; closed Sun D; no bookings.

Dragon Castle SE17
£36   **3** 3 2

100 Walworth Rd   020 7277 3388   1–3C

"Excellent for an area which frankly doesn't have much, and good overall!" – a big, cavernous Cantonese near Elephant & Castle whose dim sum are "freshly prepared and very good value". What sets it apart are the "more interesting regional dishes" introduced by "a new chef who has revitalised the menu". / SE17 1JL; www.dragon-castle.com; @Dragoncastle100; Mon-Sat 11 pm, Sun 10 pm.

Dragon Palace SW5
£30   **4** 3 2

207 Earls Court Rd   020 7370 1461   6–2A

"More than just a neighbourhood local" – this inconspicuous modern Chinese café north of Earl's Court tube draws fans from across neighbouring postcodes for its "excellent all-day dim sum". / SW5; www.thedragonpalace.com; 11 pm.

Drakes Tabanco W1
£49   **4 4 4**

3 Windmill St   020 7637 9388   2–1C

"Sherry served straight from the cask" and "top-notch" tapas are the main attractions at this "easy-to-miss" Fitzrovia spot off Charlotte Street, inspired by (and named after) the sherry taverns of Andalucia. / W1T 2HY; www.drakestabanco.com; @drakestabanco; 10 pm.

The Drapers Arms N1
£50   **3** 2 2

44 Barnsbury St   020 7619 0348   9–3D

"Excellent pub food" ("love the pies!") lives up to the high reputation of this Islington gastro-boozer, although the "interesting, regularly changing menu" is "sometimes let down by surly service". Top tip for the summer: "there's a fabulous sun-trap garden at the back". / N1 1ER; www.thedrapersarms.com; @DrapersArms; 10.30 pm; no Amex.

The Duck & Rice W1
£59   **4** 3 **4**

90 Berwick St   020 3327 7888   4–2C

"Very impressive… and I don't even like Chinese food!" Wagamama-creator, Alan Yau maybe onto another winning format with his year-old Soho gastropub makeover, which combines "stylish decor, good-quality Chinese classics, plus dim sum and amazing bao buns". / W1F 0QB; www.theduckandrice.com; @theduckandrice; Mon -11.30 pm, midnight, Sun 10.30 pm.

Duck & Waffle EC2
£70   2 2 **5**

110 Bishopsgate, Heron Tower   020 3640 7310   10–2D

"You are admittedly paying for the astonishing views", at this arguably "completely over-priced", 24/7 neighbour to SushiSamba, on the 40th-floor of the Heron Tower. No one disputes the "wow factor" though, and many reports are surprisingly complimentary regarding its "chunky, meaty fashionable food and sharing plates", including "the eponymous signature dish". Top Tip – "really delicious breakfast". (Coming soon: a second branch is set to open in late 2016 in the new St James's Market development). / EC2N 4AY; www.duckandwaffle.com; @DuckandWaffle; open 24 hours.

Ducksoup W1 £55 3 3 4

41 Dean St 020 7287 4599 5–2A

A "tasty, if not overchallenging hybrid of Italian and North African" dishes along with "unusual wines" win fans for this "nicely buzzing" Soho spot. / W1D 4PY; www.ducksoupsoho.co.uk; @ducksoup; 10.30 pm; closed Sun D.

Duende WC2 NEW £45 4 2 2

16 Maiden Ln 020 7836 5635 5–4D

"Love, love, love" the "amazing and inventive tapas", say fans of Victor Garvey's inspiring, early-2016, solo venture in Covent Garden. "Amateur service" and a "cramped" space are drawbacks though, and not everyone is wowed: "I was hoping for the same quality as his original hangout, Tapas Bravas" but "the food looked better than it tasted (even though it looked fantastic…)" / WC2E 7NJ; www.duendelondon.com; @duendelondon; 11.30 pm; D only, closed Sun.

Duke of Sussex W4 £46 3 3 4

75 South Pde 020 8742 8801 8–1A

This substantial Victorian tavern beside Acton Common Green serves an "excellent Spanish menu" of "dependable" tapas and larger plates in its grand, rear dining room. / W4 5LF; www.metropolitanpubcompany.com; @thedukew4; 10.30 pm, Sun 9.30 pm.

Duke's Brew & Que N1 £55 4 2 3

33 Downham Rd 020 3006 0795 14–2A

"Bring your appetite – you won't regret it", when you visit this "hip, crowded (with great music blasting)" Texan BBQ in Dalston. "Fred Flintstone-esque ribs (the size of your forearm), juicy, fat burgers, and spicy fries will make you salivate just thinking about them"; "fantastic beers" too. / N1 5AA; www.dukesbrewandque.com; @dukesJoint; 10 pm, Sun 9.30 pm; closed weekday L.

Dynamo SW15 NEW £35 3 3 3

200-204 Putney Bridge Rd 020 3761 2952 11–2B

"Things seem to have taken off" at this new "cycle-themed café in Putney": it serves "excellent sourdough pizza", and "breakfasts and brunches are really delicious, with proper barista coffee". / SW15; www.the-dynamo.co.uk; @WeAreTheDynamo; 10 pm, Thu-Sat 11 pm.

The Dysart Petersham TW10 £69 4 4 3

135 Petersham Rd 020 8940 8005 1–4A

"A great surprise" – Kenneth Culhane cooks "wonderful food" at this Arts & Crafts pub between Richmond Park and the Thames. If there's a gripe it is that it "could feel more lively" (especially at lunch). / TW10 7AA; www.thedysartarms.co.uk; @dysartpetersham; 9.30 pm; closed Sun D.

E&O W11 £56 3 3 3

14 Blenheim Cr 020 7229 5454 7–1A

"Still full and fun!" – Will Ricker's "vibrant" Notting Hill hangout may be "a bit predictable" nowadays in terms of its "well seasoned and spiced" pan-Asian tapas, but no-one very much minds, and its yummy cocktails still slip down very nicely. / W11 1NN; www.rickerrestaurants.com; 11 pm, Sun 10.30 pm; booking max 6 may apply.

The Eagle EC1   £33   **4** **3** **5**
159 Farringdon Rd   020 7837 1353   10–1A
"The grandfather of gastropubs" near Exmouth Market "is still showing the
way after all these years". "The gastro dining experience elsewhere has
become dull, but the Eagle remains true to its roots" – "loud crowd,
open kitchen, stubbly chefs, short Anglo-Med menu on blackboard,
good beer: brilliant!" / EC1R 3AL; www.theeaglefarringdon.co.uk;
@eaglefarringdon; 10.30 pm; closed Sun D; no Amex; no bookings.

Ealing Park Tavern W5   £52   **3** **3** **4**
222 South Ealing Rd   020 8758 1879   1–3A
This expansive South Ealing venue – nowadays part of the ETM group –
is sometimes thought "quite pricey" for a gastropub, but "they can
definitely cook" and the food's "usually very good". / W5 4RL;
www.ealingparktavern.com; @Ealingpark; 10 pm, Sun 9 pm.

Earl Spencer SW18   £45   **3** **2** **4**
260-262 Merton Rd   020 8870 9244   11–2B
"Lovely unpretentious food from a daily changing menu" in a "very friendly
proper local pub" – a substantial Edwardian roadhouse in Wandsworth.
"They've recently added 50 gins to their drinks menu" (which has "a good
selection of local ales") – "what's not to love?" / SW18 5JL;
www.theearlspencer.co.uk; @TheEarlSpencer; 11 pm; Mon-Thu D only, Fri-Sun open
L & D; no booking Sun.

Eat 17   £39   **4** **4** **3**
28-30 Orford Rd, E17   020 8521 5279   1–1D
64-66 Brooksbys Walk, E9   020 8986 6242   14–1C
"Overlooked in 'The Stow'", but worth discovering – a British brasserie-style
operation in the heart of Walthamstow Village that's part of a local food
empire incorporating the award-winning SPAR in Hackney. / www.eat17.co.uk;
@eat_17; see web for detail.

Eat Tokyo   £24   **4** **2** **2**
50 Red Lion St, WC1   020 7242 3490   2–1D
15 Whitcomb St, WC2   020 7930 6117   5–4B
169 King St, W6   020 8741 7916   8–2B
18 Hillgate St, W8   020 7792 9313   7–2B
14 North End Rd, NW11   020 8209 0079   1–1B
"Hype-free, authentic Japanese cuisine", inspires "popularity amongst ex-
pats" and "queues out of the door" at these "unpretentious" ("noisy" and
"crowded") cafés. The menu is "voluminous", but "they understand
Japanese food: tastes are fresh and genuine and come at low prices".
/ Mon-Sat 11.30 pm, Sun 11 pm.

Ebury Restaurant & Wine Bar SW1   £58   **2** **2** **3**
139 Ebury St   020 7730 5447   2–4A
This comfy, old-school wine bar near Victoria station is "a great place
to meet business colleagues" in an area that doesn't offer much choice –
a "fab, everyday option", if one without huge culinary pretentions.
/ SW1W 9QU; www.eburyrestaurant.co.uk; @EburyRestaurant; 10.15 pm.

Eco SW4   £36   **3** **3** **4**
162 Clapham High St   020 7978 1108   11–2D
This long-serving Clapham haunt (owned by one of the Franco Manca co-
founders) is an "excellent local", even more so "since being revamped",
with a new wood-burning oven and modishly stripped-to-brickwork walls:
"friendly, excellent, quick, and good value for money". / SW4 7UG;
www.ecorestaurants.com; @ecopizzaLDN; 11 pm, Fri & Sat 11.30 pm.

Edera W11 £62
148 Holland Park Ave 020 7221 6090 7–2A
A "high standard" of Italian cooking is to be found at this "low-key"
Sardinian right on Holland Park Avenue – "not cheap" but "top rate". Top
Menu Tip – "their truffle dishes are extremely good". / W11 4UE;
www.edera.co.uk; 11 pm, Sun 10 pm.

Edwins SE1 £49
202-206 Borough High St 020 7403 9913 10–4B
This bistro two-year-old above a mock-Tudor pub next door to Borough
tube station is a "favourite local" and consistently rated as an "all-round
good option". / SE1 1JX; www.edwinsborough.co.uk; @edwinsborough; 11.30 pm,
Sat midnight, Sun 4 pm; closed Sun D.

8 Hoxton Square N1 £54
8-9 Hoxton Sq 020 7729 4232 13–1B
A Hoxton "fave" serving "great value wines" including "unusual bottles"
available to drink by the glass, carafe or half-bottle. The "short menu
changes daily and the excellent cooking does justice to the quality of the
ingredients used". / N1 6NU; www.8hoxtonsquare.com; @8HoxtonSquare;
10.30 pm; closed Sun D.

Eight Over Eight SW3 £56
392 King's Rd 020 7349 9934 6–3B
Will Ricker's "always buzzy Chelsea stalwart" has a nightclubby feel and
serves "delicious small dishes reflecting a wide array of Asian cuisines",
plus very gluggable cocktails. / SW3 5UZ;
www.rickerrestaurants.com/eight-over-eight; 11 pm, Sun 10.30 pm.

Electric Diner W11 £51
191 Portobello Rd 020 7908 9696 7–1A
Rub shoulders with the Notting Hill set at this "lively, buzzy" hangout,
which in particular is "great at the weekend". "But don't go just for the
food – it's pretty average". / W11 2ED; www.electricdiner.com; @ElectricDiner;
11 pm, Fri & Sat midnight, Sun 10 pm.

Elliot's Café SE1 £55
12 Stoney St 020 7403 7436 10–4C
"Interesting tapas-style dishes" and an all-natural list of wines fit well with
the vibey Borough Market location of Brett Redman's bare-brick cafe
(sibling to The Richmond). / SE1 9AD; www.elliotscafe.com; @elliotscafe; 10 pm;
closed Sun.

Ellory, Netil House E8 £56
1 Westgate St 020 3095 9455 14–2B
Divergent feedback on this yearling, set within the achingly hip environs
of a set of creative studios in London Fields. Fans nominate Matthew
Young's ingredient-led cuisine as their best meal of the year, others say
"it's trying too hard, and needs to focus on flavour". / E8 3RL;
www.ellorylondon.com; @ellorylondon; 11 pm, Sun 5 pm; closed Mon, Tue L, Wed L,
Thu L & Sun D; booking max 6 may apply.

Elystan Street SW3 NEW
43 Elystan Street 020 7628 5005 6–2C
Chef Phil Howard, famous for his 25 years at the helm of The Square,
Mayfair, has paired up with Rebecca Mascarenhas once again to launch
a new, modern British restaurant, on the former Chelsea site of Tom Aikens
Restaurant, opening in October 2016. A 'flexitarian' approach with more
emphasis on vegetables is promised by comparison with the more protein-
led cuisine at The Square. STOP PRESS – early press critiques are very
upbeat. / SW3 3NT; www.elystanstreet.com; @elystanstreet.

Ember Yard W1   £51   4 4 4

60 Berwick St   020 7439 8057   3–1D

*Stylish Soho sibling to Salt Yard that "seems to have moved up a notch"
in recent times. Service is "really friendly and efficient" and "there's lots
of interesting dishes on the menu", when it comes to the "smoky, delicate,
BBQ-style small plates" from the char grill. / W1F 8SU; www.emberyard.co.uk;
@emberyard; 11 pm, Thu-Sat midnight, Sun 10 pm; booking max 13 may apply.*

Emile's SW15   £47   3 4 2

96-98 Felsham Rd   020 8789 3323   11–2B

*"Off the beaten track in a residential street", this "hospitable" bistro
is "a firm favourite" among Putney locals, not least because "the owner
treats everyone as personal friends". There's always an "interesting special
on the blackboard", but avoid the "quieter second room, which can
be lonely". / SW15 1DQ; www.emilesrestaurant.co.uk; 11 pm; D only, closed Sun;
no Amex.*

The Empress E9   £46   4 4 4

130 Lauriston Rd   020 8533 5123   14–2B

*"Jewel of a gastropub" beside Victoria Park, which was one of the
first to gentrify in east London and which is "just what a local should be –
friendly, good value and fit for all occasions". "The food's always good",
from "an interesting, changing menu", and "complemented by a fun, buzzy
atmosphere". / E9 7LH; www.empresse9.co.uk; @elliottlidstone; 10.15 pm,
Sun 9.30 pm; closed Mon L; no Amex.*

**Eneko at One Aldwych,
One Aldwych Hotel WC2** NEW   £76

1 Aldwych   020 7300 0300   2–2D

*A partnership between One Aldwych Hotel and the owner of the Bilbao
legend, Azurmendi – the basement site which was formerly Axis (RIP) re-
opened in late summer 2016 as a Basque restaurant and wine bar: it's
cast in a much more informal style than that which won Eneko Atxa his
three Michelin stars back home. / WC2B 4BZ; www.eneko.london;
@OneAldwych; Mon-Sat 11 pm, Sun 10 pm.*

Engawa W1   £146   4 4 4

2 Ham Yd   020 7287 5724   4–3D

*"If you don't like sushi or Kobe, don't come" to this "intimate", little shrine
to Japan's highly prized Kobe beef, in the cute environs of Soho's Ham Yard
– a "truly authentic experience of exceptional quality", featuring "stunning
food that begs to be talked about and talked over." / W1D 7DT;
www.engawa.uk; @engawaLondon; 10.45 pm, Fri & Sat 11.15 pm, Sun 10.15 pm.*

Enoteca Rabezzana EC1   £49   2 2 2

62-63 Long Ln   020 7600 0266   10–2B

*A "mind-expanding wine list" focussed on Italy at "reasonable mark-ups"
and all available by the glass is the big draw at this City wine bar, whose
owners hail from the Monferrato vineyard region in Piedmont. The "sensibly
short" food selection is "fine". / EC1A 9EJ; www.rabezzana.co.uk;
@RabezzanaLondon; midnight, Sat 1 am; closed Sun.*

Enoteca Turi SW1 NEW £66
87 Pimlico Road   020 7730 3663   6–2D
When Giuseppi and Pamela Turi lost their premises of decades' standing near Putney Bridge, who would have predicted they would undertake and pull off this "very successful move"? Still "SW15's major loss is Pimlico's gain", and their newcomer remains true to the "lovely, family-run, regional Italian" it has always been, even if the "relaxed but refined" setting is now "far superior" here. Service remains "genial" yet "dedicated", the "northern Italian menu provides regional dishes you won't find elsewhere", but the big deal remains Signor Turi's "exceptional" list of Italian wines with his own annotations – "highly educational, with superb, lesser-known vintages" and "a civilised approach to mark-ups". / SW1W 8PH; www.enotecaturi.com; @EnotecaTuri; 10.30 pm, Fri & Sat 11 pm; closed Sun; booking max 8 may apply.

The Enterprise SW3 £58
35 Walton St   020 7584 3148   6–2C
On a "film-set" Chelsea street, this "upmarket pub" with "book-lined windows and heavy drapes" offers a "super atmosphere and warm welcome". A "great menu of British fare" with a "slightly hip twist" completes the deal. / SW3 2HU; www.theenterprise.co.uk; 10.30 pm, Sun 10 pm; no booking, except weekday L; set weekday L £35 (FP).

L'Escargot W1 £62
48 Greek St   020 7439 7474   5–2A
"A long-time (and forever) favourite" (est 1927), this "romantic" Gallic classic in Soho (current owner, Brian Clivaz) retains its reputation for dependable French cuisine, "attentive" service and a "buzzy" ambience and is particularly "convenient for the theatre". / W1D 4EF; www.lescargot.co.uk; @LEscargotSoho; 11.30 pm; closed Sun D.

Escocesa N16 NEW £45
67 Stoke Newington Church Street   020 7812 9189   1–1C
"A great addition to the Stoke Newington repertoire" – this "packed-to-the-rafters" tapas-newcomer ("from the founder of Crouch End's Bar Estoban") mainlines on "serving Scottish seafood with Spanish flair" ("very pure flavours and a more interesting take on familiar dishes"). It's not so comfy though, and "you can't hear yourself think". / N16 0AR; www.escocesa.co.uk; @escocesaN16; Mon-Thu 10 pm, Fri & Sat 10.30 pm, Sun 9.30 pm.

Essenza W11 £63
210 Kensington Park Rd   020 7792 1066   7–1A
"Reliable and very friendly Italian", which – along with its nearby siblings Mediterraneo and Osteria Basilico – is 'part of the furniture' in the heart of Notting Hill; truffles are something of a speciality. / W11 1NR; www.essenza.co.uk; 11.30 pm.

Estiatorio Milos SW1 NEW £122
1 Regent St   020 7839 2080   2–3C
"Amazingly fresh fish" chosen from an icy display helps seduce devotees of this "lovely" looking new Greek fish specialist in the West End – a glamorous outpost of Costas Spiliadis's luxurious international group. Even fans note that "you could pay a small king's ransom here" however, and to cynics "it's an attempt to out-Moscow Moscow" – "stacks of dead fish on an iceberg is not decor and £15 for a teeny starter is not real life!" / SW1Y 4NR; www.milos.ca/restaurants/london; Lunch 12-3pm 11pm.

Ethos W1 £39 3 2 3
48 Eastcastle St 020 3581 1538 3–1C
"Very tasty" self-service veggie near Oxford Circus, where you pay
by weight (and less for take-away). Vegan and paleo options, as well
as alcohol. / W1W 8DX; www.ethosfoods.com; @ethosfoods; 10 pm, Sun 4 pm;
closed Sun D; may need 6+ to book.

L'Etranger SW7 £72 3 3 2
36 Gloucester Rd 020 7584 1118 6–1B
"Elegant and poised dishes combining French technique with Asian
flavours" plus an extremely impressive wine list earn a loyal following for
this offbeat fixture, tucked away near the Royal Albert Hall. "Subdued
decor and lighting lend romance" to this "serene room, with a slight air
of the '80s about it". / SW7 4QT; www.etranger.co.uk; @letrangerSW7; 11 pm;
closed Sun; credit card deposit required to book.

Everest Inn SE3 £37 4 3 3
41 Montpelier Vale 020 8852 7872 1–4D
"High-quality Gurkha dishes" and "Nepalese specialities" ("they do really
tender tandoori meats") make this Blackheath favourite "a cut above your
average curry house", even if "service can be a bit chaotic". / SE3 0TJ;
www.everestinnblackheath.co.uk; 11.30 pm, Fri & Sat midnight; set weekday L
£23 (FP).

Eyre Brothers EC2 £64 5 3 3
70 Leonard St 020 7613 5346 13–1B
"Superb food from Spain and Portugal (both as sit-down meals and light
tapas at the bar)" provides ample motivation to seek out this "warm and
stylish" haunt near Silicon Roundabout. There's also "the finest selection
of Iberian wine", including sparklers, rosés and sherry. / EC2A 4QX;
www.eyrebrothers.co.uk; @eyrebrothers2; 10.30 pm, Sun 4 pm; closed Sun D.

Faanoos £27 3 3 2
472 Chiswick High Rd, W4 020 8994 4217 8–2A
11 Bond St, W5 020 8810 0505 1–3A
481 Richmond Road, SW14 020 8878 5738 1–4A
A mini-chain serving "fab Persian-style chicken or lamb kebabs", fresh
salads and flatbreads, which has built a strong following in Chiswick, Ealing
and East Sheen. "The meat's good quality, the dishes tasty and the prices
very reasonable". / SW14 11 pm; W4 11 pm; Fri & Sat midnight.

Fairuz W1 £48 3 3 3
3 Blandford St 020 7486 8108 2–1A
This Marylebone Lebanese stalwart wins consistent praise and solid ratings
across the board for its "good Middle Eastern fare" and "attentive staff".
/ W1H 3DA; www.fairuz.uk.com; 11 pm, Sun 10.30 pm.

Falafel King W10 £9 3 2 2
274 Portobello Rd 020 8964 2279 7–1A
"Still the best falafel in London" claim fans of this simple Notting Hill
pitstop – given the pace of service though, it's not always fast food.
/ W10 5TE; 7 pm.

La Famiglia SW10 £52 2 2 4
7 Langton St 020 7351 0761 6–3B
"You can always rely on this longstanding Chelsea favourite", say fans
of this family-run and family-friendly "classic". Even they often admit that
it's "pricey", or that the food nowadays is "not particularly good", but they
treasure its "fun", "buzzy" style, and "lovely" back garden in summer.
/ SW10 0JL; www.lafamiglia.co.uk; @lafamiglia_sw10; 11 pm.

Farang SE1 NEW
Flat Iron Sq   07903 834 808   10–4B
*Head chef of Soho's tiny Thai Smoking Goat, Seb Holmes, is to open a new
Vietnamese restaurant just south of Borough Market in autumn 2016,
after testing out his menus at supper clubs in Highbury's San Daniele.
/ SE1; www.faranglondon.co.uk; @farangLDN.*

Farley Macallan E9 NEW   £34
177-179 Morning Lane   020 8510 9169   14–1B
*Hot on the heels of wine-bar-cum-café, Legs, another new vino-focused
venture landed in summer 2016 in Hackney's Morning Lane. There's
a range of biodynamic wines by the glass and bottle alongside food from
the E5 Smokehouse. Hackney's Five Points Brewery provides the beers.
/ E9 6LH; www.farleymacallan.com; @MeetFarley; midnight, Fri & Sat 1 am,
Sun 10 pm; closed Mon, Tue, Wed L, Thu L & Fri L.*

Farmacy W2 NEW   £54
74-76 Westbourne Grove   020 7221 0705   7–1B
*Plant-based newcomer (inspired by founder Camilla Al Fayed's travels
to California) in Bayswater offering health-conscious vegan cuisine –
including its signature 'Farmacy Burger' and plant-based ice cream sundaes
– and with pharmacist-inspired decor. One early-days reporter said: "Great
to see a really healthy restaurant in the 'hood. We went on their first day
and found interesting food showing that veggies can be satisfying!"
/ W2 5SH; www.farmacylondon.com; @farmacyuk; 11 pm, Sun 7 pm.*

Fenchurch Restaurant, Sky Garden EC3   £82   3|3|3
20 Fenchurch St   033 3772 0020   10–3D
*"The wonderful setting adds drama and panache" to this "contemporary
and loungey" venue, 150m above the City below; but for somewhere with
such "brilliant views" (although "oddly better on the way up") the food
(from caterers, Rhubarb) is "much better than expected". / EC3M 3BY;
skygarden.london/fenchurch-restaurant; @SG_Fenchurch.*

**FERA AT CLARIDGE'S,
CLARIDGE'S HOTEL W1**   £116   4|4|4
49 Brook St   020 7107 8888   3–2B
*"Utterly sublime on every level" – Simon Rogan's three-year-old tenure
in this "luxurious" (and "surprisingly large") Art Deco dining room has hit
an even stride, providing "mindblowing food that's experimental and fun",
"warm service" and a "glorious" atmosphere (although "the earthenware
plates do clash a bit with the decor"). "It's not a budget option" ("prices
are unjustifiable" for a few reporters) but, Top Tip – "set lunch is fantastic
value". This year Rogan also added the new Aulis '6-seat development
table' in a private room off the kitchen: "a magical, innovative dining
experience – what makes it incredible is listening to Dan talk about the
ingredients, how the team came across it, and the thinking and creative
process behind each course." / W1K 4HR; www.feraatclaridges.co.uk;
@FeraAtClaridges; 10 pm.*

La Ferme EC1 NEW   £41   3|2|2
102-104 Farrington   020 7837 5293   10–1A
*Near Exmouth Market, this new deli and restaurant's rustique styling is laid
on heavily with a pitchfork (one of the items adorning the walls). The Gallic
cooking is more ambitious than its small premises might imply – the odd
disastrous meal is reported, but it can be very good. / EC1R 3EA;
www.lafermelondon.com; @lafermelondon; 10.30 pm; closed Sun.*

Fernandez & Wells £48 **3 3 3**
16a St Anne's Ct, W1 020 7494 4242 4–1D
43 Lexington St, W1 020 7734 1546 4–2D
73 Beak St, W1 020 7287 8124 4–2C
Somerset Hs, Strand, WC2 020 7420 9408 2–2D
"Securing a chair is like fighting for a life-jacket on the Titanic (and worth it!)", say fans of these funky cafés with "always good" coffee, plus high-quality sarnies and pastries. / www.fernandezandwells.com; Lexington St & St Anne's court 10 pm, Beak St 6 pm, Somerset House 11 pm; St Anne's Court closed Sun.

Fez Mangal W11 £26 **5 4 3**
104 Ladbroke Grove 020 7229 3010 7–1A
"Delicious charcoal-grilled fish and meat as well as tasty mezze" ("comparing well with Istanbul") means there are often queues at this small Notting Hill Turk. "No licence – and no corkage charged" means it's also "incredible value". / W11 1PY; www.fezmangal.com; @FezMangal; 11.30 pm; no Amex.

Ffiona's W8 £60 **3 4 4**
51 Kensington Church St 020 7937 4152 6–1A
Diners are made to feel welcome and special by the eponymous patronne of this "romantic" Kensington stalwart, which focuses on well-cooked traditional British dishes, and is popular for weekend brunches. / W8 4BA; www.ffionas.com; @ffionasnotes; 11 pm, Sun 10 pm; closed Mon; no Amex.

Fields SW4 £32 **3 3 3**
2 Rookery Rd no tel 11–2C
"The owners of hip Balham coffee shop Milk know what they're doing", and this takeover of a park café on Clapham Common delivers some "really interesting brunch options". "It can be windy, though, so take care to find the right table". / SW4 9DD; www.fieldscafe.com; @fieldscafe; 5 pm, Fri 4 pm; L only; no bookings.

Fifteen N1 £69 **2 2 3**
15 Westland Pl 020 3375 1515 13–1A
The project which helped Jamie Oliver establish his meeja career: this Hoxton Italian continues to divide reporters (although above all else they ignore it – for all the hype it remains well off London's 'foodie map'). Fans do applaud its "delicious dishes, buzzing atmosphere and great gin list", but as ever a significant proportion dismiss it as average-to-poor across the board. / N1 7LP; www.fifteen.net; @JamiesFifteen; 10.30 pm, Sun 9.30 pm; booking max 12 may apply.

Figlio Del Vesuvio SW17 NEW £29 **4 4 2**
658 Garratt Lane 020 3609 1118 11–2B
"Never judge a book by its cover!" This "tiny, cramped" and "wholly authentic" new Neapolitan may be "lacking in location (on a roundabout in the no-mans-land between Earlsfield and Tooting Broadway) and interior aesthetics" but serves "sensational wood-fired pizzas, cooked to perfection at incredibly competitive prices". Cash only. / SW17; figlidelvesuvio.com; @figli_vesuvio; 11 pm; closed Tue.

Fischer's W1 £62

50 Marylebone High St   020 7466 5501   2–1A

Corbin & King's "meticulous interpretation of a classic Austrian/German restaurant" in Marylebone "captures the essence of Mitteleuropa perfectly" – "the food is a slightly stodgy, warm embrace", and the "beautiful, deeply coloured, panelled interior" creates a very "gemütlich" ambience. Top Menu Tip – "delicious schnitzel". / W1U 5HN; www.fischers.co.uk; @FischersLondon; 11 pm, Sun 10 pm.

Fish Cafe NW3 £38

71 Hampstead High St   020 7433 1430   9–2A

A newish venture of the Villa Bianca Group – this Hampstead two-year-old is, say fans, "a quality fish restaurant hiding behind a fish 'n' chips frontage"; the odd sceptic though accuses it of an "unimpressive" performance. / NW3; www.villabiancagroup.co.uk; 11 pm.

Fish Central EC1 £32

149-155 Central St   020 7253 4970   13–1A

"A favourite with cabbies for good reason" – this "socially diverse" and "friendly" Clerkenwell chippie is a "fantastic bargain". "High-quality specials are all fresh that day and cost less than at Borough Market, without the need to cook it yourself!" / EC1V 8AP; www.fishcentral.co.uk; 10.30 pm, Fri 11 pm; closed Sun.

Fish Club SW11 £40

189 St John's Hill   020 7978 7115   11–2C

This modern take on the classic fish 'n' chip shop in Battersea wins praise for "always fresh fish" as well as some unexpected extras: "love the sweet potato chips", and "even the Caesar salad is delicious". / SW11 1TH; www.thefishclub.com; 10 pm, Sun 10pm; closed Mon L.

Fish in a Tie SW11 £35

105 Falcon Rd   020 7924 1913   11–1C

"Decent food and wine at great prices" makes it worth remembering this "friendly" bistro – a handy "cheap 'n' cheerful" option north of Clapham Junction. / SW11 2PF; www.fishinatie.com; midnight, Sun 11 pm.

Fish Market EC2 £55

16b New St   020 3503 0790   10–2D

"The catch of the day is always a good choice" at this atmospheric converted warehouse near Bishopsgate. It's a "nice enough member of the D&D stable, though unremarkable" beyond the "well-cooked fish". / EC2M 4TR; www.fishmarket-restaurant.co.uk; @FishMarketNS; 10.30 pm, Sun 4 pm; closed Sun D.

fish! SE1 £56

Cathedral St   020 7407 3803   10–4C

Glazed shed by Borough Market capable of being "an excellent fish restaurant, with plenty to choose from in a lively atmosphere". It can feel "noisy, crowded, hot and touristy" however, and given "food that's quite basic, plus occasionally indifferent service", prices can seem "OTT". / SE1 9AL; www.fishkitchen.com; @fishborough; 11 pm, Sun 10.30 pm.

Fishworks £60

7-9 Swallow St, W1   020 7734 5813   4–4C
89 Marylebone High St, W1   020 7935 9796   2–1A

"Simply cooked, very fresh fish" is the "straightforward formula done well" at these plain West End bistros. Aside from the fact that you walk through a fishmongers to dine, they "have no pretence to be anything other than upmarket fish 'n' chip restaurants". / www.fishworks.co.uk; 10.30 pm.

The Five Fields SW3 £89 5 5 4
8-9 Blacklands Ter   020 7838 1082   6–2D
"The epitome of fine dining, minus the stuffiness" – Taylor Bonnyman's "unflashy and grown-up" three-year-old, "tucked way in Chelsea" offers "an all-round fantastic experience". The setting is "elegant", service "genuine and unpretentious"; while the cuisine is "truly exceptional – exciting, yet accessible and (most importantly) delicious" ("expect an astonishing array of amuse bouches"). Until October 2016, this was perhaps "Michelin's most shocking omission", but finally the tyre men divvied up the requisite star. / SW3 2SP; www.fivefieldsrestaurant.com; @The5Fields; 10 pm; closed Mon L, Tue L, Wed L, Thu L, Fri L, Sat & Sun; no trainers.

Five Guys £13 3 2 2
1-3 Long Acre, WC2   020 7240 2657   5–3C
71 Upper St, N1   020 7226 7577   9–3D
"McDonald's makes more effort on the decor!", but these "amped-up fast food" joints do "great customisable burgers" ("be prepared to get messy"), "massive portions of fries", and "interesting, more-ish shakes". / @FiveGuysUK; see web for detail.

500 N19 £48 3 4 2
782 Holloway Rd   020 7272 3406   9–1C
"A haven of good food in an area not famed for gastronomy" – this "sincere, friendly and convivial" Holloway Italian provides "excellent" Sicilian food, and it's "great value" too. / N19 3JH; www.500restaurant.co.uk; @500restaurant; 10.30 pm, Sun 9.30 pm; Mon-Thu D only, Fri-Sun open L & D.

Flat Iron £22 4 3 3
17 Beak St, W1   no tel   4–2B
17 Henrietta St, WC2   no tel   5–4C
9 Denmark St, WC2   no tel   5–1A
77 Curtain Road, EC2   no tel   13–1B NEW
"If you want simple steak, well-delivered at a bargain price, you can't go wrong" with these "consistent and effective" West End haunts (where "the unfashionable flat iron cut is elevated to first rank, and identified farms and rearing practices give credibility to the final product"). "Despite fairly basic surroundings, they feel somehow pleasant" even if "the queues are less great" ("they take your mobile number and text you when your table's ready"). / see web for detail.

Flat Three W11 £82 4 4 2
120-122 Holland Park Ave   020 7792 8987   7–2A
Limited feedback on this minimalistic Holland Park basement (originally a supper club) whose fusion cuisine blends Japanese and Scandi' influences – fans rate the food as absolutely outstanding, but some visitors feel it's a case of style over substance. / W11 4UA; www.flatthree.london; @infoflat3; Tue-Sat 9.30 pm; closed Mon & Sun.

Flesh & Buns WC2 £50 3 3 3
41 Earlham St   020 7632 9500   5–2C
"Packed to the gills with a loud and well-lubricated crowd", this "buzzing and cool" Soho basement (sibling to Bone Daddies) provides "fab" steamed buns that are "so good and fresh", plus "excellent hot stone rice dishes". / WC2H 9LX; www.bonedaddies.com/flesh-and-buns; @FleshandBuns; Mon & Tue 10.30 pm, Wed-Sat 9.30 pm, Sun 9.30 pm; booking max 8 may apply.

Flora Indica SW5 NEW
242 Old Brompton Rd   020 7370 4450   6–2A
Remember Mr Wing? Well, you're getting on a bit then! But this British/Indian fusion venture opened in summer 2016 on the two-floor Earl's Court site long known for its party potential. It's the work of former Benares chef Sameer Taneja and – with echoes of its distant predecessor – puts a big emphasis on cocktails. / SW5 0DE; www.flora-indica.com; @Flora_Indica.

Flotsam & Jetsam SW17
£17   **3** **4** **4**
4 Bellevue Parade   020 8672 7639   11–2C
"Australian coffee shop on the edge of Wandsworth Common" that's "a hit in a location that has always failed" – "eternally busy", with "helpful staff" serving up "very good breakfasts" (but "don't go if you take the King Herod view of young children!)" / SW17 7EQ; www.flotsamandjetsamcafe.co.uk; @_flotsam_jetsam; 5 pm; L only; no bookings.

FM Mangal SE5
£31   **3** **3** **2**
54 Camberwell Church St   020 7701 6677   1–4D
"A real gem in Camberwell", this Turk offers "fantastic value" for its "addictive grilled flatbread, smoky onions and toothsome grilled lamb in varying styles of preparation and spicing". "Deservedly, it's always busy". / SE5 8QZ; midnight; no Amex; no bookings.

Foley's W1 NEW
23 Foley Street   020 3137 1302   2–1B
Following a six-week pop-up (Foley's Tasting Kitchen) in Shepherd's Bush, this roaming operation has found a full-time home in Fitzrovia. The 70-cover restaurant is open all day and vaunts an open kitchen with counter dining and an alfresco coffee bar. Former Palomar chef Mitz Vora serves up an internationally-influenced menu inspired by the spice trail. / W1W 6DU; www.foleysrestaurant.co.uk; @foleyslondon.

Fortnum & Mason, The Diamond Jubilee Tea Salon W1
£66   **3** **3** **3**
181 Piccadilly   020 7734 8040   3–3D
"The best selection of teas in town" and "exceptional, endlessly refreshed platters" of sandwiches and cakes help establish this "stylish and beautiful" chamber on the third floor of the famous St James's grocery store as "a wonderful spot for a special celebration afternoon tea". / W1A 1ER; www.fortnumandmason.com; @fortnumandmason; 7 pm, Sun 6 pm.

Fortnum & Mason, 1707 W1
£54   **2** **2** **3**
181 Piccadilly   020 7734 8040   3–3D
Named after the year Fortnum's was founded, this basement perch below the famous food halls is perfect for "trying wines from slightly off the beaten track" that you've dug up in the adjacent F&M wine department (for a £15 corkage charge). There's a "limited menu" for food, but it's "a useful stop-off for a light meal with good vino". / W1A 1ER; www.fortnumandmason.co.uk; @fortnumandmason; 7.45 pm, Sun 5 pm; closed Sun D.

45 Jermyn St SW1 £69 3 4 4
45 Jermyn St., St. James's London 020 7205 4545 3–3D
"Like stepping back to a much more glamorous time – the champagne, the caviar, the leather booths, even the little golden coat tickets all make an evening here very special" – F&M's successful relaunch of its all-day restaurant (formerly The Fountain, RIP) has injected more pizazz into the venue, which serves *"decent if very safe food with a really good (and good-value) wine list"*. Top Tip – it's still *"a fantastic spot for breakfast"* (but doesn't do afternoon tea any more). / SW1A 6DN; www.45jermynst.com; @Fortnums; 11 pm, Sun 6 pm; closed Sun D.

40 Maltby Street SE1 £54 4 3 3
40 Maltby St 020 7237 9247 10–4D
"Carefully selected natural wines from small vineyards" are twinned with Steve Williams's *"changing blackboard menu full of delights"* that are *"served from a tiny kitchen behind the bar"* at this *"truly exceptional"* wine warehouse, in the well-known foodie enclave near London Bridge station. / SE1 3PA; www.40maltbystreet.com; @40maltbystreet; 9.30 pm; closed Mon, Tue, Wed L, Thu L & Sun; no Amex; no bookings.

The Four Seasons £50 4 1 1
12 Gerrard St, W1 020 7494 0870 5–3A
23 Wardour St, W1 020 7287 9995 5–3A
84 Queensway, W2 020 7229 4320 7–2C
"The famous roast duck may not be the world's best but it's extremely good" (as is the *"addictive crispy pork belly"*) at these Chinese *"classics"*, in Bayswater and Chinatown. *"You don't go for the surroundings, and certainly not for the service!"* / www.fs-restaurants.co.uk; Queensway 11 pm, Sun 10h45 pm; Gerrard St 1 am; Wardour St 1am, Fri-Sat 3.30 am.

The Fox & Hounds SW11 £50 4 4 4
66 Latchmere Rd 020 7924 5483 11–1C
This *"buzzy"* Battersea sibling to Earl's Court's Atlas *"assumes no airs and graces, but punches out its ever-changing Mediterranean-led menu at top standard, with, awesome real ales in great condition"*. / SW11 2JU; www.thefoxandhoundspub.co.uk; @thefoxbattersea; 10 pm; Mon-Thu D only, Fri-Sun open L & D.

The Fox & Anchor EC1 £55 3 3 4
115 Charterhouse St 020 7250 1300 10–1B
This *"wonderful"*, *"hidden-away"* Victorian pub, complete with *"cosy snugs"*, was built for meat market workers at nearby Smithfield Market – hence the 7am opening, when it's *"perfect for traditional cooked breakfast and a pint"*. There's an *"excellent range of beers on hand pump complemented by good hearty English food cooked very well with fresh ingredients"*. / EC1M 6AA; www.foxandanchor.com; @foxanchor; Mon-Sat 9.30 pm, Sun 6 pm.

Foxlow £51 2 2 2
11 Barley Mow Pas, W4 020 7680 2702 8–2A NEW
71-73 Stoke Newington Ch' St, N16 020 7014 8070 1–1C
15-19 Bedford Hill, SW12 020 7680 2700 11–2C NEW
St John St, EC1 020 7014 8070 10–2A
For a *"reliable and solid"* meat-fest, fans commend these Hawksmoor-lite spin-offs, also tipped for a *"great brunch"* and for *"going the extra mile for kids"*. Even supporters can say they are *"not exciting"* though, and critics say: *"I really, really, really want to love it, but I find the food and menu disappointing"*. / www.foxlow.co.uk; @FoxlowTweets; –; SRA-3 star.

Franco Manca £22 **4 3 3**

*"Who knew a chain could do such great pizza?!" – their "slightly chewy",
but thin, fresh and "so-darn-tasty" wood-fired, sourdough crusts
(plus "a few simple toppings packed with flavour") help maintain
surprisingly high ratings for this VC-backed brand. Branches are "chaotic
and noisy" but "for such authentic quality they still offer amazing value".
/ www.francomanca.co.uk; SW9 10.30, Mon 5 pm; W4 11 pm; E20 9 pm, Thu-Sat
10 pm, Sun 6 pm; no bookings.*

Franco's SW1 £74 **3 3 3**

61 Jermyn St 020 7499 2211 3–3C
*This "very old school St James's destination comes with starched linen
tablecloths, courteous waiters, high quality – if unadventurous – Italian
food… and astronomical prices"; ("just walking in seemingly adds £1m
to your personal net worth, but while plutocratic it carries none of the
blingy nonsense that passes for style in flashier quarters"). A natural for
local pinstripes: "sometimes I just sit and make it my office from
breakfast onwards!" / SW1Y 6LX; www.francoslondon.com; @francoslondon;
10.30 pm; closed Sun.*

Franklins SE22 £55 **4 3 3**

157 Lordship Ln 020 8299 9598 1–4D
*Well-established Dulwich neighbourhood fixture (with farm shop on the
other side of the road), very consistently praised for its above-average
modern British cooking (with a fair amount of game). "Sadly brunch is only
on a Saturday". / SE22 8HX; www.franklinsrestaurant.com; @frankinsse22;
10.30 pm, Sun 10 pm; no Amex; set brunch £29 (FP).*

Frantoio SW10 £56 **2 3 4**

397 King's Rd 020 7352 4146 6–3B
*A "huge greeting when you arrive" from flamboyant host Bucci creates
an "atmosphere more like a club", at this "bubbly and dependable"
World's End trat. The cooking is generally good, "if slightly resting on its
gastronomic laurels". / SW10 0LR; www.frantoio.co.uk; 11 pm.*

Frederick's N1 £64 **2 3 4**

106 Camden Passage 020 7359 2888 9–3D
*"Islington lacks upmarket restaurants", and this "well-spaced" and
"attractive" old veteran – complete with "good-looking conservatory and
lovely outside tables on a warm day" – has a loyal (generally silver-haired)
fanclub. It's not a foodie fave rave though, with "cooking that's more akin
to banqueting than to haute cuisine". / N1 8EG; www.fredericks.co.uk;
@fredericks_n1; 11 pm; closed Sun; set dinner £34 (FP).*

Frenchie WC2 **NEW** £72 **4 2 2**

18 Henrietta St 020 7836 4422 5–3C
*"Believe the hype!" – Grégory Marchand's "transplant direct from Paris"
(where he owns a venture of the same name) is proving "a great new
addition to Covent Garden", on the prominent, corner site (with basement)
that was for yonks Porters (nowadays transplanted to Berkhamsted). Its
appeal is his "skilled and beautiful" modern French cuisine however –
service can be "slack" and the "informal", "buzzing" interior can seem too
"noisy" and "cramped". / WC2E 8QH; www.frenchiecoventgarden.com;
@frenchiecoventgarden; 10.30 pm.*

The Frog E1 NEW
Old Truman Brewery, Hanbury St   020 3813 9832   13–2C
MasterChef finalist Adam Handling left his restaurant at St Ermin Hotel
to open his own venture in Shoreditch in summer 2016 (apparently the
first of many planned under 'The Frog' brand). His cuisine in Westminster
sometimes seemed a tad "tortured" and "pretentious" – just right for the
local hipsters? / E1 6QR; www.thefrogrestaurant.com; @TheFrogE1; closed
Mon & Sun D.

La Fromagerie Café W1 £45 322
2-6 Moxon St   020 7935 0341   3–1A
"Cheese, soups, teas… the quality is good" at this superior Marylebone
café attached to the acclaimed cheese store. "Fantastic breakfast" too –
"even if you have toast, it's the best bread, best butter,
best marmalade…!" / W1U 4EW; www.lafromagerie.co.uk; @lafromagerieuk;
7.30 pm, Sat 7 pm, Sun 6 pm; L only; no bookings.

The Frontline Club W2 £56
13 Norfolk Pl   020 7479 8960   7–1D
"In an area of fast food joints", this comfortable dining room – part of
a journalists' club for war reporters – is known for its "really consistent
food, with fine wine at affordable prices". It further upped the ante
in summer 2016, re-launching after a major revamp adding a mezzanine,
and with higher culinary ambition (so for the time being we've left it un-
rated). / W2 1QJ; www.frontlineclub.com; @frontlineclub; 11 pm; closed
Sat L & Sun.

Fumo WC2 NEW
37 St Martin's Lane   5–4C
An 'all-day Italian and chic cocktail bar' concept from the San Carlo group
(Cicchetti, Signor Sassi), Fumo is already open in Birmingham and
Manchester, and made its London debut, in Covent Garden, in September
2016. / WC2N 4JS; www.sancarlofumo.co.uk/fumo-london/.

Gaby's WC2 £33 322
30 Charing Cross Rd   020 7836 4233   5–3B
"I'm so glad it's survived!" This "iconic" and "indispensable" – if "slightly
crumbling" – caff by Leicester Square tube (Jeremy Corbyn's favourite!)
beat off the developers a couple of years ago, so saving its "absolutely
fantastic falafel", "exemplary salt beef" and "delicious healthy salads".
"The chairs and tables are vinyl and Formica covered, and service rarely
involves a smile, but at least the plentiful posters signed by stars of stage
and screen take your mind off the Spartan surroundings". / WC2H 0DE;
midnight, Sun 10 pm; no Amex.

Gallery Mess, Saatchi Gallery SW3 £52 223
Duke of Yorks HQ, Kings Rd   020 7730 8135   6–2D
The food at Charles Saatchi's Chelsea art gallery generates little
enthusiasm, but the "mess" in the former Duke of York's HQ makes
a useful venue for a business lunch, and "on a sunny day the outdoor
tables are quiet and classy". / SW3 4RY; www.saatchigallery.com/gallerymess;
@gallerymess; 11 pm, Sun 7 pm; closed Sun D.

Galley N1 NEW £58 434
105-106 Upper St   020 3670 0740   9–3D
"A lot of thought and care has gone into Galley – a new, firm Islington
favourite". The headline attractions are the "superb seafood choices, with a
mix of small and large plates" but the "very smart" interior design also
gets the thumbs up. / N1 1QN; www.galleylondon.co.uk; @Galleylondon; 11 pm.

Gallipoli £35 **3 4 4**

102 Upper St, N1	020 7359 0630	9–3D
107 Upper St, N1	020 7226 5333	9–3D
120 Upper St, N1	020 7226 8099	9–3D

These "intimate, bazaar-style" Turkish cafés with "over-the-top" Ottoman-themed décor are just a few doors apart on Islington's main drag. From "excellent mezze to breakfast" the scoff's "serviceable and good value" (and "far better than you might expect"). / www.cafegallipoli.com; 11 pm, Fri & Sat midnight.

Galvin at the Athenaeum W1 £68

Athenaeum Hotel, 116 Piccadilly   020 7640 3557   3–4B

In July 2016 (post-survey) the Galvin brothers annexed this gracious but perennially overlooked dining room in an Art Deco hotel, facing Green Park. This is their first venture to put the emphasis more on British rather than French cuisine (and will continue to offer afternoon tea – previously one of the greater attractions here). / W1J 7BJ; www.athenaeumhotel.com; @Galvin_brothers; 11 pm.

Galvin at Windows,
Park Lane London Hilton Hotel W1 £101 **2 3 5**

22 Park Ln   020 7208 4021   3–4A

"To wow a client", or to create an ambience "conducive to seduction", the "stunning" panorama from this 28th-floor park-side Mayfair chamber is – say fans – "unbeatable". "It's the view that makes it" though, "not the Identikit hotel decor", while the "decent" cuisine is in something of a supporting role. Top Tip – enjoy a better vista for the price of a cocktail at the adjacent bar! / W1K 1BE; www.galvinatwindows.com; @GalvinatWindows; 10 pm, Thu-Sat 10.30 pm, Sun 3 pm; closed Sat L & Sun D; no trainers; set weekday L £53 (FP), set Sun L £72 (FP).

Galvin Bistrot de Luxe W1 £69 **3 3 3**

66 Baker St   020 7935 4007   2–1A

"Still delivering no-nonsense, quality after more than 10 years" – the Galvin brothers' original venture, south of Baker Street tube, has built its renown on serving "consistent bistro cuisine" in a "buzzy", business-friendly setting. "It's starting to slip" though, with ratings now middling across the board. / W1U 7DJ; www.galvinbistrotdeluxe.com; @bistrotdeluxe; Mon-Wed 10.30 pm, Thu-Sat 10.45 pm, Sun 9.30 pm; set weekday L £22 (FP), set dinner & pre-theatre £24 (FP).

Galvin HOP E1 NEW £56 **4 4 3**

35 Spital Sq   020 7299 0404   13–2B

On the former site of Café à Vin – to which has been added Pilsner tanks and an open kitchen – the Galvin brothers' new posh, City-fringe gastropub is the flagship of their new company (Galvin Pub de Luxe); on early reports it's the very competent, upscale boozer you'd expect. / E1 6DY; www.galvinrestaurants.com/section/62/11/galvinhop; @Galvin_brothers; 10.30 pm, Sun 9.30 pm; booking max 5 may apply.

GALVIN LA CHAPELLE E1 £82 3 3 4

35 Spital Sq   020 7299 0400   13–2B

"The breathtaking architecture of the building" – "a beautiful, cathedral-like space" created from the "clever conversion of a Victorian school chapel" – creates a "magnificent" setting for the Galvin brothers' well-known venture, near Spitalfields. At its best, this is one of London's most "memorable" all-rounders (particularly for business) combining "smooth" service and "subtle cuisine" into a "sumptuous" overall offering. Performance was less consistent this year however, with reports of "over-stretched if well-intentioned" service, and "uneven" culinary results. / E1 6DY; www.galvinlachapelle.com; @galvin_brothers; 10.30 pm, Sun 9.30 pm; no trainers; set weekday L, dinner, pre-theatre & Sun L £35 (FP).

Ganapati SE15 £43 5 4 3

38 Holly Grove   020 7277 2928   1–4C

"The true flavours of South India, with no compromises and no frills" have won a formidable foodie reputation for "what is little more than a corner shop" in Peckham; "delightful people" too. / SE15 5DF; www.ganapatirestaurant.com; 10.30 pm, Sun 10 pm, closed Mon; no Amex.

Le Garrick WC2 £52 2 3 4

10-12 Garrick St   020 7240 7649   5–3C

"Expect candles and inviting booths" in this "quirky and romantic" bistro in the heart of Covent Garden. "It's not high-end cuisine" (on occasion a bit "second rate") but it's generally "good value" and "very handy as a pre-theatre option". / WC2E 9BH; www.legarrick.co.uk; @le_garrick; 10.30 pm; closed Sun; set pre-theatre £28 (FP), set Sun L £32 (FP).

The Garrison SE1 £51 3 2 4

99-101 Bermondsey St   020 7089 9355   10–4D

"Slightly cramped but buzzy" green-tiled former pub, once at the forefront of Bermondsey's gastro-revival with its transformation into a food-led dining venue over a decade ago. It still has a "lively atmosphere", the "fish 'n' chips are brilliant" (and there's even a cinema for private viewings in the basement). / SE1 3XB; www.thegarrison.co.uk; @TheGarrisonSE1; 10 pm, Sun 9.30 pm.

Gastronhome SW11 £67 5 4 3

59 Lavender Hill, London   020 3417 5639   11–2C

"A surprising and welcome find in Lavender Hill" – Damien Fremont and Christopher Nespoux's "homely" yet "truly exceptional" French three-year-old provides an "enthusiastic" welcome, and "adds a real level of quality" to the local eating destinations. "If you can, go for the tasting menu for some really sublime dishes, and there are some brilliant accompanying wines". / SW11; www.gastronhome.co.uk; 10:15 pm; closed Mon; no jeans.

The Gate £48 4 3 3

51 Queen Caroline St, W6   020 8748 6932   8–2C
370 St John St, EC1   020 7278 5483   9–3D

"Still producing exceptional veggie dishes after 25 years" – "the best in town" – this popular duo are "a good advertisement for meat-free food, proving it can be interesting and full of flavour". The original – an intriguing "converted artists' loft" that's "hidden away" behind Hammersmith Odeon – is "splendid in an area devoid of decent restaurants", while its younger sibling is "really convenient for Sadler's Wells". / www.thegaterestaurants.com; @gaterestaurant; EC1 10.30 pm, W6 10.30, Sat 11 pm; SRA-3 star.

Gatti's £63

1 Finsbury Ave, EC2   020 7247 1051   13–2B
1 Ropemaker St, EC2   020 7628 8375   13–2A

"You can't fault the model" of this business-friendly City duo in Br~~oa~~te
and nearby Moorgate – "Italians just like they used to be". / closed
Sat & Sun.

Gaucho £74   2 2 1

"It used to be so good, what happened?" London's first upscale
contemporary steak-house chain still wins praise for its "pretty fine
Argentinian meat", and "wonderful" Latino wines, but its glitzy (sometimes
"very loud and very dark") branches have increasingly "lost their charm".
"Stratospheric" prices are the main issue, and "with so many good steak
options at all levels these days, it's hard to see where Gaucho fits in".
/ www.gauchorestaurants.co.uk; 11 pm; EC3 & EC1 closed Sat & Sun, WC2 & EC2
closed Sat L & Sun.

GAUTHIER SOHO W1 £72   5 5 4

21 Romilly St   020 7494 3111   5–3A

"A haven in a busy part of Soho" – this "delightful" Georgian townhouse
is "made all the more special by having to ring the doorbell" to enter,
and once inside, its "peaceful" series of rooms "exude romance". However
"it's the food that's the key element" – Alexis Gauthier's "top-league French
cuisine" features "brilliant flavour combinations", and is matched by a
"varied and exciting" wine list, while staff provide "wonderful hospitality
from start to finish". Top Tip – "the lunchtime deal is amazing value".
/ W1D 5AF; www.gauthiersoho.co.uk; @GauthierSoho; Tue-Thu 9.30 pm, Fri & Sat
10.30 pm; closed Mon & Sun; booking max 7 may apply; set weekday L £46 (FP).

LE GAVROCHE W1 £132   5 5 4

43 Upper Brook St   020 7408 0881   3–2A

London's oldest temple of Gallic gastronomy narrowly missed the No. 1 slot
in this year's survey, but for its legions of fans remains "the absolute
pinnacle of fine dining". Established by Albert Roux nearly 50 years ago
(and run by his son, Michel Roux Jr for the last 25), its hallmark style
combines "richly indulgent" cuisine (overseen by head chef Rachel
Humphrey) and an "astonishing, predominantly French wine list", served
in a "classy" if "dated", "'70s-France" basement setting, while it follows
a pleasing, "slightly anachronistic" formula ("jackets required for men,
ladies' menus don't have prices"). "Ever-attentive, charming and
unostentatious" staff add further to the experience, as does the
"accessibility and personal attention" of the main man, who is much
in evidence. The price? – best not to ask, but the set lunch is "stonking
value". Top Menu Tip – soufflé Suissesse. / W1K 7QR; www.le-gavroche.co.uk;
@legavroche_; 10 pm; closed Mon, Sat L & Sun; jacket required; set weekday L
£63 (FP).

Gay Hussar W1 £50   2 3 4

2 Greek St   020 7437 0973   5–2A

The "ambience, history and wonderful caricatures lining the walls" are the
stuff of Labour party legend at this Soho Hungarian institution. "Never
mind the middling Mittel European food", it's "still reminiscent of the old
days". / W1D 4NB; www.gayhussar.co.uk; @GayhussarsSoho; 10.45 pm; closed Sun.

Gaylord W1 £60 3 4 3
79-81 Mortimer St 020 7580 3615 2–1B
"Step back into the '70s (if not at '70s prices)" at this "ultimate traditional
Indian" – a "favourite for authentic North Indian dishes" since it opened
50 years ago in Fitzrovia. The interior can feel "a little staid" but "wakes
up in the evening", and "service is hard to surpass". / W1W 7SJ;
www.gaylordlondon.com; @gaylord_london; 10.45 pm, Sun 10.30 pm; set pre theatre
£38 (FP).

Gazette £39 2 2 3
79 Sherwood Ct, Chatfield Rd, SW11 020 7223 0999 11–1C
100 Balham High St, SW12 020 8772 1232 11–2C
147 Upper Richmond Rd, SW15 020 8789 6996 11–2B
"Great fun" and "traditional" (if "pretty variable") bistro cooking have won
praise for this small family-friendly group with venues in Balham, Clapham
and Putney. "Service is not always up to scratch, but it's local and it's
French". / www.gazettebrasserie.co.uk; 11 pm.

Geales £53 1 2 2
1 Cale St, SW3 020 7965 0555 6–2C
2 Farmer St, W8 020 7727 7528 7–2B
Diehard fans still applaud this veteran (est 1939) fish 'n' chip restaurant
off Notting Hill Gate (and with a much more recent Chelsea spin-off),
but they disappoint far too many reporters nowadays: "they used to be
great... sadly no more". / www.geales.com; @geales1; 10.30 pm, Sun 9.30 pm;
Mon L.

Gelupo W1 £9 5 2 2
7 Archer St 020 7287 5555 4–3D
"Offbeat but brilliant gelateria" with branches in Soho and Cambridge
Circus – "the best ice cream I have had in the UK – and I've tried a lot!"
Service, though, can be a bit "Fawlty Towers". / W1D 7AU; www.gelupo.com;
11 pm, Fri & Sat midnight; no Amex; no bookings.

Gem N1 £34 3 4 3
265 Upper St 020 7359 0405 9–2D
"Bread being prepared in the window draws you in" to this "cracking" and
"aptly named" Turkish-Kurdish local near Angel. "You'll be welcomed like
a regular and overfed (portions are generous)" and it's "reliable", "family-
friendly" and "great value for money". / N1 2UQ; www.gemrestaurant.org.uk;
@Gem_restaurant; 11 pm, Sun 10 pm; no Amex.

German Gymnasium N1 £69 2 2 3
King's Boulevard 020 7287 8000 9–3C
The "jaw-dropping building" – "a high-ceilinged, former Victorian
gymnasium" next to King's Cross station – provides an "amazing setting"
for this D&D London yearling. Its reception has been mixed however – staff
are "charming" but can be "slow"; and the German cuisine ("wurst and
other classics") can seem "interesting", but is too often judged "beige",
"heavy" and "not very tempting". / N1C 4BU; www.germangymnasium.com;
@TheGermanGym; 11 pm, Sun 9 pm.

Giacomo's NW2 £38 3 3 2
428 Finchley Rd 020 7794 3603 1–1B
"Unpretentious rustic food" and "friendly and efficient staff" attract
a "loyal local clientele" to this trad family-run Italian in Child's Hill, where
"a ridiculously large pepper grinder is ceremoniously toted around
in almost caricature style". / NW2 2HY; www.giacomos.co.uk; 10.30 pm;
closed Mon.

Gifto's Lahore Karahi UB1 £26 3 2 2

162-164 The Broadway 020 8813 8669 1–3A

Large Pakistani canteen whose "well-priced authentic cuisine" has carved it a place as a Southall landmark; "grills are their speciality". / UB1 1NN; www.gifto.com; 11.30 pm, Sat & Sun midnight; booking weekdays only.

The Gilbert Scott, St Pancras Renaissance NW1 £74 2 3 4

Euston Rd 020 7278 3888 9–3C

"Who can resist the splendour?" of this "huge" and "iconic" dining room, not far from the Eurostar platforms? Even fans can note that Marcus Wareing's offering here is "highly priced", but ratings bounced back across the board this year for his resolutely British cuisine. / NW1 2AR; www.thegilbertscott.co.uk; @Thegilbertscott; 11 pm, Sun 9 pm; set weekday L & pre-theatre £51 (FP).

Gilgamesh NW1 £70 2 2 3

The Stables, Camden Mkt, Chalk Farm Rd 020 7428 4922 9–3B

Cecil B DeMille wouldn't have produced a more eye-catching interior than this huge and "opulent" bar/restaurant by Camden Lock, with its lavish, imported, wood-carved decoration. The pan-Asian food is "well-presented and tasty" but critics say "massively expensive". / NW1 8AH; www.gilgameshbar.com; @GilgameshBar; Sun-Thu 10 pm, Fri & Sat 11 pm.

Ginger & White £14 2 4 3

2 England's Ln, NW3 020 7722 9944 9–2A

4a-5a, Perrins Ct, NW3 020 7431 9098 9–2A

This "achingly trendy coffee shop" – "down a lane off Hampstead High Street" (there's another in Belsize Park) delivers a good caffeine fix, but won most praise this year for its "great, friendly staff"; "nice blankets to keep you warm outside on a cold day". / www.gingerandwhite.com; 5.30 pm, W1 6 pm; W1 closed Sun.

Giraffe £40 2 2 1

"I take it all back!" – "the grub seems to have gotten better of late" at these world-food diners; recently acquired by the Birmingham-based Boparan group, and scoring higher ratings across the board. "It's perfect for families", "especially those with tots... which is why no-one in their right mind would ever visit at the weekend!" / www.giraffe.net; 10.45 pm, Sun 10.30 pm; no booking, Sat & Sun 9 am-5 pm.

The Glasshouse TW9 £72 3 4 2

14 Station Pde 020 8940 6777 1–3A

Though never quite a match for its stablemate, Chez Bruce, this "sunny" ("slightly bland") dining room by Kew Gardens tube has always boasted similarly "sparkling and seasonal" modern cuisine, and "diligent and friendly" service. On most accounts it remains as "superb" as ever, but its ratings took an unexpected knock this year, due to a few reports of meals "not up to expectations" and, in particular, "tiny portions". / TW9 3PZ; www.glasshouserestaurant.co.uk; @The_Glasshouse; 10.30 pm, Sun 10 pm; booking max 8 may apply.

Gökyüzü N4 £33 4 4 4

26-27 Grand Pde, Green Lanes 020 8211 8406 1–1C

The "quality of barbecued meat is consistently high at this popular Green Lanes Turk" on Harringay's Grand Parade, with "beautiful succulent sharing platters" ("portions are enormous!"). On top of that it's fun, friendly and "good value". / N4 1LG; www.gokyuzurestaurant.co.uk; @Gokyuzulondon; midnight, Fri & Sat 1 am.

Gold Mine W2 £34 **4** **2** **2**

102 Queensway   020 7792 8331   7–2C

"When you need a Cantonese duck fix", this Bayswater café is just the job, and many fans would say it's *"better than the neighbouring Four Seasons"* (which is much better known). / W2 3RR; 11 pm.

Golden Dragon W1 £33 **3** **2** **2**

28-29 Gerrard St   020 7734 1073   5–3A

A Chinatown *"staple"* that perennially *"scores for dim sum"*. It's *"always buzzy despite the Soviet-era interior design, probably because the food quality's high"*. / W1 6JW; goldendragonlondon.com; 11.30 pm, Fri-Sun midnight; no bookings.

Golden Hind W1 £26 **4** **4** **2**

73 Marylebone Ln   020 7486 3644   2–1A

"Genuine", *"old-style fish 'n' chip restaurant in the heart of Marylebone"* that's central London's top chippy. *"It's nothing fancy, but the food is excellent"* – *"steamed dishes or fried in batter to satisfy the most hardened northerner"* – and all *"served with enthusiasm"* under the watchful eye of owner, Mr Christou. *"BYO makes it very affordable"*. / W1U 2PN; 10 pm; closed Sat L & Sun.

Good Earth £58 **3** **2** **2**

233 Brompton Rd, SW3   020 7584 3658   6–2C
143-145 The Broadway, NW7   020 8959 7011   1–1B
11 Bellevue Rd, SW17   020 8682 9230   11–2C

"High-quality", family-owned Chinese venues (in Balham, Knightsbridge and Mill Hill), long known as an *"expensive but good"* treat. The branch near Harrods especially is seen as *"not as good as it once was"* though: in particular *"the dated decor could use a makeover"*. / www.goodearthgroup.co.uk; Mon-Sat 10.30 pm, Sun 10 pm.

Goodman £88 **3** **3** **3**

24-26 Maddox St, W1   020 7499 3776   3–2C
3 South Quay, E14   020 7531 0300   12–1C
11 Old Jewry, EC2   020 7600 8220   10–2C

"For a red meat blow out" – especially *"if you want a steak for a serious business lunch"* – these *"NYC-style"*, *"testosterone-charged"* steakhouses fully fit the bill (and outscored rivals Hawksmoor in this year's survey). *"The choice of cuts – be they US, Scottish, or more 'exotic' make them a stand-out"*, with *"a good supporting cast of sides"*, and *"well-matched wines"*. Naturally *"you pay for the privilege"*. / www.goodmanrestaurants.com; 10.30 pm; E14 & EC2 closed Sat & Sun.

Gordon Ramsay SW3 £148 **2** **4** **3**

68-69 Royal Hospital Rd   020 7352 4441   6–3D

Clare Smyth's departure – with Matt Abe taking up the reins – has stymied the recovery of GR's Chelsea flagship. Fans do still laud this *"grown-up and charming"* chamber as *"amazing on every level"*, and the service in particular remains *"exceptional"*. Ratings fell back significantly this year however, with numerous attacks on modern French cuisine that's *"rather blah, fine dining-by-numbers"* and *"way, way, way too expensive"*. The chasm between reality and Michelin's three stars has never looked greater here. / SW3 4HP; www.gordonramsay.com; @GordonRamsay; 10.15 pm; closed Sat & Sun; no jeans; booking max 8 may apply; set dinner £124 (FP), set weekday L £73 (FP).

Gordon's Wine Bar WC2 £38 1️⃣2️⃣5️⃣
47 Villiers St 020 7930 1408 5–4D
This "unique" wine bar (dating from 1890) by Embankment Gardens
is "somewhere everyone should visit" once. Not for the food, which
is barely "OK", or the "grumpy bar staff", but for the marvellously gloomy
cave-like interior and huge terrace (with BBQ) in summer. / WC2N 6NE;
www.gordonswinebar.com; @GordonsWineBar; 11 pm, Sun 10 pm; no bookings.

The Goring Hotel SW1 £80 3️⃣5️⃣4️⃣
15 Beeston Pl 020 7396 9000 2–4B
"Away from the hoi polloi, and convenient for Buck Pal'", this "splendid and
unspoilt survivor" is not only "an oasis from the hustle and bustle
of Victoria" but also a bastion of unchanging values: in particular its
"impeccable" service "pandering to every whim". The Michelin star
bestowed on the "delightful dining room" is something of a distraction –
"the food is not outstandingly good, but old-fashioned and English" –
perfect for business, a "traditional British breakfast par excellence",
or "a masterclass in how to do afternoon tea". / SW1W 0JW;
www.thegoring.com; @TheGoring; 10 pm; closed Sat L; no jeans; booking max 8 may
apply; set brunch £43 (FP), set pre-theatre £53 (FP), set weekday L £67 (FP).

Gotto Trattoria E20 NEW £41
Here East, 27 East Bay Lane 020 3424 5035 14–1D
The owners of Soho's reliably fun Mele e Pere, Peter Hughes and Andrea
Mantovani, have brought culinary life to the Olympic Park as part of the
new 'Here East' development. Opened in summer 2016, press reports are
of a casual Italian trattoria, with nice al fresco tables by the canal.
/ E20 2ST; www.gotto.co.uk; @GottoTrattoria; 10.30 pm, Sun 9.30 pm.

Gourmet Burger Kitchen £30 2️⃣2️⃣2️⃣
"Overtaken by funkier rivals", but this burger franchise still wins solid
support from most reporters for its "good value, really good selection
of options, and excellent sides". / www.gbkinfo.com; most branches close
10.30 pm; no booking.

Gourmet Goat SE1 NEW £11 4️⃣4️⃣2️⃣
Borough Market 020 8050 1973 10–4C
"Great food, with a great story and people behind it!" – after two years
of trading outside at Borough Market, this rising street food star has
opened a new fixed indoor unit on one of the market's main byways,
Rochester Walk, serving Greek/Cypriot-influenced goat dishes. / SE1 9AH;
www.gourmetgoat.co.uk; @gourmet_goat; 5 pm, Fri 6 pm; closed Mon, Tue, Wed D,
Thu D, Fri D, Sat D & Sun; no bookings.

The Gowlett Arms SE15 £32 4️⃣3️⃣4️⃣
62 Gowlett Rd 020 7635 7048 1–4D
"Blimey, it's in Peckham", but this "chilled" boozer does "the best-ever
pizza" – with "tasty thin crusts", "perfectly wood-fired", and "topped with
locally smoked meats" (or try the "veggie Gowlettini"). / SE15 4HY;
www.thegowlett.com; @theGowlettArms; 10.30 pm, Sun 9 pm; cash only.

Goya SW1 £45 3️⃣3️⃣3️⃣
34 Lupus St 020 7976 5309 2–4C
"Reliable tapas" as well as "proper mains" make for a "buzzy and
reasonably priced" family-run Spaniard in a part of Pimlico that has
"very little choice". / SW1V 3EB; www.goyarestaurant.co.uk; midnight,
Sun 11.30 pm.

Grain Store N1 £58

1-3 Stable St, Granary Sq   020 7324 4466   9–3C

"In the emerging new King's Cross developments", Bruno Loubet's "vast space, with attractive, big open kitchen" has "a great buzz" (it's nice outside too). His "unusual flavour combinations" with "dishes that are vegetable-led" made a return to "fabulous" form this year. / N1C 4AB; www.grainstore.com; @GrainStoreKX; Mon-Wed 11.30 pm, Thu-Sat midnight; closed Sun D; SRA-3 star.

The Grand Imperial, Guoman Grosvenor Hotel SW1 £67

101 Buckingham Palace Rd   020 7821 8898   2–4B

This Cantonese in a strangely grand and "spacious" hotel dining room next to Victoria station "may not be the most fashionable spot, but the food is extremely good – better than many in Chinatown". "Everything to do with duck is especially good", while "the dim sum are good value". / SW1W 0SJ; www.grandimperiallondon.com; 10.30 pm, Thu-Sat 11 pm; set weekday L £33 (FP).

Granger & Co £54

175 Westbourne Grove, W11   020 7229 9111   7–1B
Stanley Building, St Pancras Sq, N1   020 3058 2567   9–3C
The Buckley Building, 50 Sekforde St, EC1   020 7251 9032   10–1A

"Crazy queues are a letdown", but that's the worst gripe about Aussie star chef, Bill Granger's "chilled", "light and airy" hotspots, rammed particularly for his epic brunches – "interesting, but non-fussy combos" that are superbly "fresh and tasty". Top Menu Tip – "the legendary Granger scrambled eggs on sourdough toast". / Mon-Sat 10 pm, Sun 5pm.

The Grazing Goat W1 £56

6 New Quebec St   020 7724 7243   2–2A

"Handily placed near to Marble Arch", this two-floor pub is "great for Sunday lunch", and with "tasty" cooking generally. "It's nice to sit outside when there's a bit of sunshine as well!" / W1H 7RQ; www.thegrazinggoat.co.uk; @TheGrazingGoat; 10 pm, Sun 9.30 pm.

Great Nepalese NW1 £36

48 Eversholt St   020 7388 6737   9–3C

"Year-in year-out pushing the right buttons" – this subcontinental veteran in a grungy Euston side street is the epitome of a sweet ethnic café, and a very affordable one too. / NW1 1DA; 11.30 pm, Sun 10 pm.

Great Queen Street WC2 £53

32 Great Queen St   020 7242 0622   5–1D

"Sound, straightforward and earthy dishes" – "seasonal British food with fun twists" – still win praise for this "hipster-attracting" gastropub "in the tourist hellhole that is Covent Garden". There are caveats though: its "slightly dismal setting" is "very noisy when full", service is "slightly forgetful", and "standards have slipped" compared to its glory days. / WC2B 5AA; www.greatqueenstreetrestaurant.co.uk; @greatqueenstreet; 10.30 pm, Sun 3.30 pm; closed Sun D; no Amex; set weekday L £32 (FP).

The Greek Larder, Arthouse N1 £50

1 York Way   020 3780 2999   9–3C

"Unusual but successful food combinations" presented tapas-style, make Theodore Kyriakou's "casual and contemporary" yearling both "a lovely addition to the Greek restaurant scene", and "a top place to eat well without breaking the bank near King's Cross". / N1C 4AS; www.thegreeklarder.co.uk; @thegreeklarder; 10.30 pm, Sun 5 pm; closed Sun D.

F S A

Green Cottage NW3 £38 3 2 2
9 New College Pde   020 7722 5305   9–2A
This "long-standing and reliable local" in Swiss Cottage serves "wonderfully tasty", "superbly authentic Chinese food – and it's great value". But "don't go for service or ambience" – "if I lived closer I'd order takeaway". / NW3 5EP; 11 pm; no Amex.

The Green Room, The National Theatre SE1 £44 2 2 2
101 Upper Ground   020 7452 3630   2–3D
The NT's punningly named 'sustainable neighbourhood diner' makes good use of its garden site – and of the props and scenery recycled from productions to use as decoration. The grub's "reasonable but not cheap". / SE1 9PP; www.greenroom.london; @greenroomSE1; 10.30 pm, Sun 7 pm.

Greenberry Café NW1 £50 3 3 3
101 Regent's Park Rd   020 7483 3765   9–2B
"On a roll at the moment!" – this Primrose Hill haunt has "an excellent café atmosphere, ideal for a chat", and serves "great-value" light bites, including top breakfasts. / NW1 8UR; greenberrycafe.co.uk; @Greenberry_Cafe; 10 pm, Mon & Sun 3 pm; closed Mon D & Sun D; no Amex.

The Greenhouse W1 £130 3 4 3
27a Hays Mews   020 7499 3331   3–3B
"Absolute professionalism" characterises Marlon Abela's calm "oasis", "hidden" down a mews in a quiet part of Mayfair, particularly when it comes to chef Arnaud Bignon's "complex" cuisine, or the cellaring of its "amazing wine list" ("arrive an hour early to read it"). Prices are scary however, and although the setting can seem "romantic", it can also appear "stuffy" or "lacking atmosphere". / W1J 5NY; www.greenhouserestaurant.co.uk; 10.30 pm; closed Sat L & Sun; booking max 12 may apply; set weekday L £61 (FP).

Gremio de Brixton, St Matthew's Church SW2 £42 3 2 3
Effra Rd   020 7924 0660   11–2D
"Excellent, basic tapas plus decent and not-overpriced wine" fuels the fun ("loud!") at this atmospheric yearling, in the crypt of St Matthew's Church in Brixton. / SW2 1JF; www.gremiodebrixton.com; @gremiobrixton; 11 pm, Sat 11.30 pm, Sun 10.30 pm; D only.

Ground Coffee Society SW15 £31 3 3 3
79 Lower Richmond Rd   0845 862 9994   11–1B
"Antipodean coffee excellence" is acclaimed at this Putney outfit, which fans say serves some of the best brews in the SWs, alongside baked goodies and light bites. / SW15 1ET; www.groundcoffeesociety.com/grindcoffeebar; 6 pm; no bookings.

Guglee £33 3 2 2
7 New College Pde, NW3   020 7722 8478   9–2A
279 West End Ln, NW6   020 7317 8555   1–1B
"Hot and spicy" street-food-inspired dishes "full of fresh flavours" inspire fans of this "down-to-earth" duo in West Hampstead and Swiss Cottage, which "don't seem to follow a formula" and are "not your average locals". / www.guglee.co.uk; 11 pm.

Guildford Arms SE10 £46 3 3 3
55 Guildford Grove   020 8691 6293   1–3D
One of Greenwich's better eating options – "a great pub", with "tasty bar food", "fine dining upstairs" and a really "delightful spacious garden". / SE10 8JY; www.theguildfordarms.co.uk; Tue-Sat 11.30 pm, Sun 10.30 pm.

The Guinea Grill W1   £75   **4 4 4**
30 Bruton Pl   020 7409 1728   3–3B
"Steak and more steak" is the reason to visit this "old-fashioned" grill room, in a "cute" Mayfair mews: "simply cooked and fabulous". "Close your eyes when receiving the bill" though – it's "terrifyingly expensive!" (for a cheaper eat, sample one of the "legendary pies" in the well-preserved Young's pub, which forms the front of the establishment). / W1J 6NL; www.theguinea.co.uk; @guineagrill; 10.30 pm; closed Sat L & Sun; booking max 8 may apply.

The Gun E14   £62   **3 2 4**
27 Coldharbour   020 7515 5222   12–1C
"A magnificent view" of the Thames and O2 (which you can enjoy from the "heated outside terrace") helps make Tom and Ed Martin's "fantastic, historic gastropub" a popular destination. "It's a fine example of a pub getting the food mix right: from ambitious dishes to bar snacks". / E14 9NS; www.thegundocklands.com; @thegundocklands; 10.30 pm, Sun 9.30 pm.

Gunpowder E1 **NEW**   £44   **4 4 4**
11 Whites Row   020 7426 0542   13–2C
"Pairing Indian ingredients and East London creativity", leads to this "vibrant, if small Spitalfields newcomer", serving "indulgent" and "interesting" Indian tapas from an "ever-evolving menu". / E1 7NF; www.gunpowderlondon.com; @gunpowder_ldn; closed Sun.

Gustoso Ristorante & Enoteca SW1   £45   **3 5 3**
33 Willow Pl   020 7834 5778   2–4B
"A Pimlico treasure"; this newish Italian in the backstreets of Westminster has made a big impact on locals, who feel "pampered by exceptionally friendly staff", who provide "sensibly priced", "carefully prepared" traditional dishes; "take their advice on wine pairings". / SW1P 1JH; ristorantegustoso.co.uk; @GustosoRist; 10.30 pm, Fri & Sat 11 pm, Sun 9.30 pm.

GYMKHANA W1   £66   **5 4 4**
42 Albemarle St   020 3011 5900   3–3C
The Sethi family's "fabulous and exciting" venue, near The Ritz, is London's most talked-about posh Indian nowadays. "Downstairs is an old-style speakeasy with a superb cocktail bar", but the main action is the "gorgeous and clubby" colonial-style restaurant, where staff imbued with "impeccable, old-school manners" provide "a unique twist" on subcontinental dining, "blending regional traditions with fine-dining disciplines". Top Menu Tip – "beautifully spiced grilled meats". / W1S 4JH; www.gymkhanalondon.com; @GymkhanaLondon; 10.30 pm; closed Sun.

Habanera W12   £40   **3 2 3**
280 Uxbridge Rd   020 8001 4887   8–1C
"An interesting take on the Mexi-vibe" helps win fans for this year-old cantina – a bright spark in the still dross-heavy strip, facing Shepherd's Bush Green itself: "fresh and tasty" scoff, including "super taco boards". / W12 7JA; www.habanera.co.uk; @HabaneraW12; 11 pm, Fri & Sat midnight, Sun 10.30 pm; may need 6+ to book.

Haché £35 3 4 4

329-331 Fulham Rd, SW10 020 7823 3515 6–3B
24 Inverness St, NW1 020 7485 9100 9–3B
37 Bedford Hill, SW12 020 8772 9772 11–2C
153 Clapham High St, SW4 020 7738 8760 11–2D
147-149 Curtain Rd, EC2 020 7739 8396 13–1B

"What burgers at Byron hope to be when they grow up: juicy patties, awesome brioche, and fries to die for!" This excellent small group is also "not hostage to the political correctness of so many others who refuse to serve medium-rare meat". / www.hacheburgers.com; 10.30 pm, Fri-Sat 11 pm, Sun 10 pm.

Hakkasan £94 3 2 3

17 Bruton St, W1 020 7907 1888 3–2C
8 Hanway Pl, W1 020 7927 7000 5–1A

For a "classy" night out, these "noisy", "nightclub-style" operations (the seeds of what's now a global brand) have a huge reputation, with their "clever Chinese/pan-Asian" cuisine and "theatrical" Bond-lair styling. "Eye-popping" bills and "up-itself" service have always been hazards here, but accusations that they are "over-hyped and ridiculously over-priced" grew this year. / www.hakkasan.com; midnight, Sun 11 pm.

**Ham Yard Restaurant,
Ham Yard Hotel W1** £61 3 4 4

1 Ham Yd 020 3642 1007 4–3D

"Where better on a summer evening than the piazza tables?" at the "charming" and "chic" Firmdale hotel, whose courtyard "brings the feel of a village into central Soho". Critics do still feel its "looks are deceptive" – with "food no better than fine" and "a substantial bill" – but it has upped its game considerably since the slating it received on opening, and most accounts are of a "most enjoyable" meal. "Exceptional bar" too. Top Tip – "pound for pound, the best value afternoon tea in London". / W1D 7DT; www.firmdalehotels.com; @Ham_Yard; 11.30 pm, Sun 10.30 pm.

The Hampshire Hog W6 £53 3 3 4

227 King St 020 8748 3391 8–2B

There's "plenty of space" at this airy and unusually attractive pub (which has a sizeable garden), near Hammersmith Town Hall. Staff are "always helpful" and the food – though "not exactly cheap" – is "usually tasty". / W6 9JT; www.thehampshirehog.com; @TheHampshireHog; 10.30 pm; closed Sun D.

Hanger SW6 NEW £49

461-465 North End Road 020 7386 9739 6–4A

Opened in summer 2106 – a hangout near Fulham Broadway dedicated to the humble hanger steak (traditionally known as the 'Butcher's Cut') from just £10 a pop. / SW6 1NZ; www.hangersteak.co.uk; @hanger_sw6; 11 pm, Wed & Thu 11.30 pm, Fri & Sat 12.30 am, Sun; closed Mon & Tue L.

The Harcourt W1 NEW £60 4 3 4

32 Harcourt Street 020 3771 8660 7–1D

On the former site of The Harcourt Arms, this Marylebone gastropub reopened in April 2016 with a new menu and a new look. Chef Kimmo Makkonen's (Greenhouse, The Orrery) European menu nods toward Nordic and Scandi cuisine, and – though it's had the odd mixed review in the press – won instant high ratings from reporters for its "high-end restaurant quality food". / W1H 4HX; www.theharcourt.com; @the_harcourt; 11 pm, Fri & Sat 11.30 pm, Sun 10 pm.

Hard Rock Café W1 £60 224
150 Old Park Ln 020 7514 1700 3–4B
"Still rocking" is the considered verdict on the Hyde Park Corner original of what is now, 45 years later, a famous global franchise. *"The atmosphere is electric, loud and proud"*, and it still delivers some *"reliable quality"* burgers, ribs and *"huge nachos"*. / W1K 1QZ; www.hardrock.com/london; @HardRockLondon; 12.30 am, Fri & Sat 1 am, Sun 10.30 pm; may need 20+ to book.

Hardy's Brasserie W1 £49 233
53 Dorset St 020 7935 5929 2–1A
"Unpretentious" *"old-style"* bistro *"tucked away from the tourists in Marylebone"* – the cooking is dependable, and its *"welcoming atmosphere"* makes it very *"handy in the area"*. / W1U 7NH; www.hardysbrasserie.com; @hardys_W1; 10 pm; closed Sun D.

Hare & Tortoise £32 333
11-13 The Brunswick, WC1 020 7278 9799 2–1D
373 Kensington High St, W14 020 7603 8887 8–1D
156 Chiswick High Rd, W4 020 8747 5966 8–2A
38 Haven Grn, W5 020 8810 7066 1–2A
296-298 Upper Richmond Rd, SW15 020 8394 7666 11–2B
90 New Bridge St, EC4 020 7651 0266 10–2A
It's *"pleasantly surprising how good the chow is"*, at these pan-Asian fast food canteens, which are *"always packed"* (with *"queues to contend with"*). *"We eat here at least twice a week and never get tired of the value-for-money sushi, noodles, etc…"* / www.hareandtortoise-restaurants.co.uk; 10.45 pm, Fri & Sat 11.15 pm, EC4 10 pm; W14 no bookings.

Harry Morgan's NW8 £42 222
29-31 St John's Wood High St 020 7722 1869 9–3A
This St John's Wood institution has a loyal following for its Jewish deli classics including *"excellent salt beef"* and *"good chicken soup"*. It's also *"perfect for brunch during a Test match"*, at Lord's cricket ground nearby. / NW8 7NH; www.harryms.co.uk; @morgan_hm; 10 pm.

Harwood Arms SW6 £68 533
Walham Grove 020 7386 1847 6–3A
"Taking pub food to a new level entirely" – this *"gastropub on steroids"* in a quiet Fulham backwater has won fame with its *"superb"*, *"hearty"* cooking, and most particularly its *"interesting game"* (*"especially the deer"*). It's a collaboration between the owners of Berkshire's Pot Kiln, and Ledbury chef, Brett Graham. Top Menu Tip – *"slow-roasted venison is a must-try when in season!"* / SW6 1QR; www.harwoodarms.com; 9.15 pm, Sun 9 pm; closed Mon L; credit card deposit required to book; set always available £40 (FP).

Hashi SW20 £36 443
54 Durham Rd 020 8944 1888 11–2A
This *"not-so-easy-to-find Japanese"* is a *"real surprise to discover tucked away in Raynes Park"*. It's a *"modest venue, but the food has always been really top notch – worthy of a more central location"*: *"very good sushi and sashimi"*, and the prices are *"reasonable"*. / SW20 0TW; www.hashi-restaurant.co.uk; 10.30 pm; closed Mon & Tue L; no Amex.

Hatchetts W1 NEW £58
5 White Horse Street 020 7409 0567 3–4B
More life comes to picturesque Shepherd Market, with the autumn 2016 opening of this bar (ground floor) / (restaurant), serving a modern brasserie menu. / W1J 7LQ; www.hatchetts.london; @hatchettslondon; 10 pm.

The Havelock Tavern W14   £48   3 3 4
57 Masbro Rd   020 7603 5374   8–1C

This Olympia backstreet gastro-boozer isn't the stand-out it once was, but it's still an "eternally reliable" haunt – "an uncomplicated, warming experience" that's "buzzing every week night". A recent refurb "has added table reservations, and the food continues good". Top Menu Tip – "their excellent staple: bavette steak". / W14 0LS; www.havelocktavern.com; @HavelockTavern; 10 pm, Sun 9.30 pm.

The Haven N20   £52   3 4 3
1363-5 High Rd   020 8445 7419   1–1B

"An oasis in the restaurant-desert of Whetstone". The cooking is "reliable" and the staff "always welcoming and helpful" – "we've never had a bad meal here". / N20 9LN; www.haven-bistro.co.uk; 10.30 pm, Sun 10 pm; no shorts; set weekday L £29 (FP).

Hawksmoor   £75   3 3 2
5a, Air St, W1   020 7406 3980   4–4C
11 Langley St, WC2   020 7420 9390   5–2C
3 Yeoman's Row, SW3   020 7590 9290   6–2C
157 Commercial St, E1   020 7426 4850   13–2B
10-12 Basinghall St, EC2   020 7397 8120   10–2C

This cult steakhouse chain (soon to hit NYC) has carved a legendary reputation for its "expert" steaks featuring "brilliant quality" British-bred beef, and "glorious cocktails", and it's also a "go-to choice for a business lunch". However, its ratings continue to slide – especially given the "noisy and unexceptional" ambience at some of the more "dull" locations – supporting those who say "Hawksmoor no longer stands out in a crowded field", while, as ever, the bloated bills can seem "just too much like taking the whatsit". All that said, the business is still on a roll and a new branch near Borough Market is to open in Spring 2017. Top Tip – "the stunning-looking Air Street branch is the best in the empire". / www.thehawksmoor.com; all branches between 10 pm & 11 pm; EC2 closed Sat & Sun; SRA-3 star.

Haz   £37   2 2 2
9 Cutler St, E1   020 7929 7923   10–2D
34 Foster Ln, EC2   020 7600 4172   10–2B
112 Houndsditch, EC3   020 7623 8180   10–2D
6 Mincing Ln, EC3   020 7929 3173   10–3D

These "large" busy Turkish operations across the City provide a solid, affordable, relatively healthy offering. It's "a fuel stop not an occasion" though – the style's a bit "characterless" and the food's "OK so far as it goes, but wouldn't win any prizes". / www.hazrestaurant.co.uk; 11.30 pm; EC3 closed Sun.

Heddon Street Kitchen W1   £61   2 2 2
3-9 Heddon St   020 7592 1212   4–3B

Gordon Ramsay's "laid back" destination just off Regent Street inspires mixed feelings. That it's "very family-friendly, with kids eating free" (if they're 12 or under) earns it the parental vote, but more generally "the food is so-so, not spectacular and a little over-priced". / W1B 4BE; www.gordonramsayrestaurants.com/heddon-street-kitc; @heddonstkitchen; 11 pm, Sun 9 pm.

Hedone W4 £106 `4` `3` `3`

301-303 Chiswick High Rd   020 8747 0377   8–2A

Mikael Jonsson and his "totally committed" team create "an extraordinary culinary experience" behind a "modest" façade in outer-Chiswick (where sitting at the counter watching the preparation is a popular option). It's "one of the best restaurants in the UK", with a "total focus on sourcing the best ingredients and intensifying their flavours" via "adventurous combinations" as part of a "stunning tasting menu", and all complemented by "an exceptional wine list". On the downside, the approach can seem a little "hushed" or "over-anxious", and for a sceptical minority the whole set-up seems "monumentally over-rated and overpriced". / W4 4HH; www.hedonerestaurant.com; @HedoneLondon; 9.30 pm; closed Mon, Tue L, Wed L, Thu L & Sun; credit card deposit required to book.

Heirloom N8 £46 `3` `3` `3`

35 Park Rd   020 8348 3565   1–1C

This "fabulous restaurant in the heart of Crouch End" – supplied from its own farm in Bucks – offers "robust comfort food", and "good value tasting menus with wine pairings". / N8 8TE; www.heirloomn8.co.uk; @HeirloomN8; 11 pm, Sun 7 pm; closed Mon & Tue.

Hélène Darroze,
The Connaught Hotel W1 £130 `3` `4` `3`

Carlos Pl   020 3147 7200   3–3B

This Parisian super-chef won more consistent praise this year for her reign at this "luxurious" dining room, where "helpful and unobsequious" staff provide "brilliantly executed" modern French dishes. It's "unbelievably expensive", but then again, in Mayfair "decadence and pampering don't come cheap". / W1K 2AL; www.the-connaught.co.uk; @TheConnaught; Mon-Sat 10 pm, Sun 9 pm; no trainers; SRA-2 star.

Heliot Steak House WC2 £56 `4` `4` `4`

Cranbourn Street   020 7769 8844   5–3B

The UK's biggest casino – the current occupant of the famous London landmark above Leicester Square tube – boasts a little-known but glam', surprisingly accomplished and reasonably-priced steak house, overlooking the gambling below, from what was the circle of the original theatre. (No entry charge, nor need to wager). Top Tip – great value pre-theatre. / WC2H 7AJ; www.hippodromecasino.com; @HippodromeLDN; Mon-Fri midnight, Sat 1 am, Sun 11 pm.

Hereford Road W2 £49 `4` `4` `3`

3 Hereford Rd   020 7727 1144   7–1B

Tom Pemberton's "authentic, seasonal British food that's always interesting and sometimes unusual" maintains a very loyal following for his "professional" Bayswater venture; "thoughtful wine list" too. Top Tip – "the set lunch is a particularly good deal". / W2 4AB; www.herefordroad.org; @3HerefordRoad; 10.30 pm, Sun 10 pm.

The Heron W2 £32 `5` `3` `1`

1 Norfolk Cr   020 7706 9567   9–4A

"Cheap 'n' cheerful" Thai, in a tiny, no-frills basement beneath a grotty-looking pub built into the foot of a Bayswater block: results are regularly outstanding. / W2 2DN; 11 pm, Sun 10.30 pm.

High Road Brasserie W4 £54 223
162-166 Chiswick High Rd 020 8742 7474 8–2A
This all-day hangout (part of a Soho House club and boutique hotel)
is "ever-popular" and "a good place to take someone if you're in the area"
particularly for brunch on the large outside terrace. But "you can't survive
on name alone – others in Chiswick are surpassing them". / W4 1PR;
highroadbrasserie.co.uk; @HRBrasserie; 11 pm, Fri & Sat midnight, Sun 10 pm.

High Timber EC4 £65 343
8 High Timber 020 7248 1777 10–3B
This "very popular" 'wine-dining' spot has a fab riverside location by the
Wobbly Bridge – owned by a Stellenbosch vineyard, there's a "very good
cellar with the focus on South Africa, plus super French reds". It's "small
inside", so – though business friendly – it's not the place for a confidential
chat. The cooking: "consistently good", with some emphasis on steak.
/ EC4V 3PA; www.hightimber.com; @HTimber; 10 pm; closed Sat & Sun.

Hill & Szrok £42 444
8 East Rd, N1 020 7324 7799 13–1A **NEW**
60 Broadway Mkt, E8 020 7254 8805 14–2B
Just off London Fields, this small butcher's-by-day, perched-on-stools
restaurant by night has rightly carved a name for its high quality meat
(although the cost of sides to accompany dishes can mount). Since January
2016, it's snapped up a grotty former boozer near Old Street,
now transformed into "a lovely pub" serving "great quality steaks" which
fans say "rival the likes of Hawksmoor in my eyes but are served in a fun,
relaxed pub atmosphere". / see web for detail.

Hilliard EC4 £28 443
26a Tudor St 020 7353 8150 10–3A
"Excellent" deli/coffee house "in the midst of legal London", serving
splendid brews, cakes and light bites made from top ingredients. As one
local solicitor notes – "my life changed when this wonderful place opened"
(who says lawyers need to get out more...) / EC4Y 0AY; www.hilliardfood.co.uk;
@hilliardcafe; 5.30 pm; L only, closed Sat & Sun; no bookings.

Hispania EC3 £54 333
72-74 Lombard Street 020 7621 0338 10–3D
"Busy, buzzy Spanish bar/restaurant" in the heart of the City; "as a place
to eat, the bar crowd is often overpowering, which is a shame because the
food and wine are both great". / EC3V 9AY; www.hispanialondon.com;
Mon 9.30 pm, Tue-Fri 10 pm; closed Sat & Sun.

Hix W1 £65 122
66-70 Brewer St 020 7292 3518 4–3C
Mark Hix's "buzzy" Soho venture risks losing its way. It does still have fans
for whom it "delivers the goods", but the food is too often judged "pretty
ordinary", the ambience "flat", and prices "silly" – "I left feeling empty
of soul and wallet!" / W1F 9UP; www.hixsoho.co.uk; @HixRestaurants; 11.30 pm,
Sun 10.30 pm.

Hix Oyster & Chop House EC1 £58 [2][2][2]
36-37 Greenhill Rents, Cowcross St   020 7017 1930   10–1A
Fans of Mark Hix's original solo venue, near Smithfield, applaud its "solid
trencherman's menu" – "one of the few places I can take Americans and
not be embarrassed by the size of the steaks and chops compared with the
US!" Those not on expenses though, can find the food "pricey",
"only just above average", and "a little tired and redundant in a post-
Hawksmoor world". / EC1M 6BN;
www.hixrestaurants.co.uk/restaurant/hix-oyster-cho; @hixchophouse; 11 pm,
Sun 9 pm; closed Sat L.

HKK EC2 £74 [5][4][2]
88 Worship St, Broadgate Quarter   020 3535 1888   13–2B
"Some of the best Chinese food in the UK" is to be had at this "expensive
but brilliant" member of the Hakkasan clan, north of Liverpool Street,
and it "attracts a broad cross-section of diners, from out-and-out foodies,
via bankers to local Hoxtonians". However, reporters are "not so keen
on the room" – "akin to a 4-star hotel in Bangkok", which when empty has
a "ghostly quiet ambience". Top Menu Tip – "the unbelievably tender,
cherry-wood smoked Peking duck is nigh-on a religious experience".
/ EC2A 2BE; www.hkklondon.com; @HKKlondon; 10 pm; closed Sun.

Hoi Polloi, Ace Hotel E1 £57 [2][1][2]
100 Shoreditch High St   020 8880 6100   13–1B
This trendy joint in a Shoreditch hotel can be "fantastic for
breakfast (top pancakes)", but goes downhill later in the day with
"overpriced", "so-so food". In particular, "atrocious service badly lets
it down" – "it's not as hip as it thinks it is". / E1 6JQ, hoi-polloi.co.uk;
@wearehoipolloi; Sun-Wed midnight, Thu-Sat 1 am.

Holborn Dining Room
Rosewood London WC1 £62 [3][3][4]
252 High Holborn   020 3747 8633   2–1D
The "splendid appearance" of this impressive chamber, on the fringe of the
City makes it "perfect for a high-level business discussion" (fuelled perhaps
by a visit to its "fantastic" adjoining Scarfes Bar). "You wouldn't maybe
choose it for a gastronomic experience", but all reports agree "it won't let
you down". / WC1V 7EN; www.holborndiningroom.com; @HolbornDining;
11.15 pm, Sun 10.15 pm.

Homeslice £24 [4][4][4]
52 Wells St, W1   020 3151 7488   2–1B
13 Neal's Yd, WC2   020 7836 4604   5–2C
374-378 Old St, EC1   020 3151 1121   13–1B NEW
"Outstanding pizza" – "unusual flavours but working together really well
and with a wonderful, thin dough base" – win acclaim for these "buzzy
and cheery" pitstops; "have a huge pizza or just a slice" but be prepared
to wait. / see web for detail.

Honest Burgers £30 [4][4][3]
"Simple, perfect burgers… simply the best!" – the survey's top slot,
certainly amongst the bigger burger brands, goes to this "cool" chain,
whose "to-die-for, salty rosemary fries" help inspire addiction; expect
"huge lines", but "their app allowing you to queue virtually is genius". Top
Tip – the original Brixton branch remains a destination in itself.
/ www.honestburgers.co.uk; @honestburgers; 10 pm-11 pm; SW9 closed Mon D.

Honey & Co W1
£48   5 4 2

25a Warren St   020 7388 6175   2–1B

"Unique, modern Israeli cooking" (*"incredible food that you could eat over and over again"*), together with *"the most fantastic welcome"* leaves you *"surprised and smiling"* at this cute café, near Warren Street. Be prepared to *"cosy up"* – it's really *"tiny"*. Top Menu Tip – leave space for the *"outstanding"* cakes (the cheesecake is a *"must-try"*). / W1T 5JZ; www.honeyandco.co.uk; @Honeyandco; Mon-Sat 10.30 pm; closed Sun; no Amex.

Hood SW2
£42   4 3 2

67 Streatham Hill   020 3601 3320   11–2D

"Fantastic local" yearling in Streatham Hill serving *"on-trend brunches with some nice touches"* and at other times an *"excellent"* (if slightly limited) seasonal menu. / SW2 4TX; www.hoodrestaurants.com; @HoodStreatham; 11 pm; closed Mon & Sun D.

Hoppers W1
£29   4 4 4

49 Frith St   no tel   5–2A

"Reminds me of my childhood in South East Asia!" One of the biggest hits of late 2015, the Sethi family's Sri Lankan, street food yearling has stormed into Soho with the *"incredible"* and *"punchy flavours"* of its *"curries, plus crisp dosas and hoppers (rice pancakes) for dipping"*. *"Annoyingly this is another restaurant that doesn't take bookings"*, but most reporters are *"happy to wait"*. Top Menu Tip – *"the bone marrow Varuval is meaty and deep, mopped up perfectly with a roti"*. / W1D 4SG; www.hopperslondon.com; @HoppersLondon; 10.30 pm; closed Sun; no bookings.

The Horseshoe NW3
£48   3 3 4

28 Heath St   020 7431 7206   9–2A

This *"revamped gastropub"* in Hampstead *"delivers on classic but tweaked dishes"* and *"fantastic Sunday roasts"*. There's a *"great beer selection"*, too – the Camden Town Brewery was spawned in the basement before moving into bigger premises, and the whole range is available in the bar. / NW3 6TE; www.thehorseshoehampstead.com; @TheHorseShoeCTB; 10 pm, Fri & Sat 10.30pm, Sun 9.30 pm.

Hot Stuff SW8
£23   3 5 3

23 Wilcox Rd   020 7720 1480   11–1D

"Still the best curry in Vauxhall", this *"lovely little Indian"* BYO (*"tucked away"* on the *"Little Portugal"* stretch) *"isn't the most glam place to eat, but it's usually busy and fun"*, providing *"bright and spicy"* flavours *"at cheap prices"* and *"very friendly"* service. / SW8 2XA; www.welovehotstuff.com; 10 pm, Sun 9.30 pm; closed Mon; no Amex.

The Hour Glass SW3   NEW
£52   3 3 2

279-283 Brompton Rd   020 7581 2497   6–2C

"A basic room above a pub… albeit one in SW3" hosts this new venture run by Brompton Food Market duo Luke Mackay and David Turcan. For fans its deceptively straightforward cooking and *"charming service"* makes it *"almost the perfect neighbourhood pub"*, but the odd critic says *"it's not as good as some have claimed"*. / SW3 2DY; @TheHourGlassSK; 11 pm, Sun 10.30 pm.

House of Ho £58 2 2 2
1 Percy St, W1 020 7323 9130 2–1C
57-59 Old Compton St, W1 020 7287 0770 5–3A
This high-concept 'modern Vietnamese' with Japanese influences has moved from its original Soho address to the prominent Fitzrovia site vacated by Bam-Bou (RIP), with Ian Pengelley now running the kitchen. However, food scores have declined, and while fans still applaud "flavoursome fare with some strong western crossover dishes" critics find the food "lacking" and query "why the hype?" The projected roll-out of a Ho chain has yet to happen. / see web for detail.

House Restaurant, National Theatre SE1 £53 2 3 2
National Theatre, Belvedere Rd 020 7452 3600 2–3D
"Sensible…" "workmanlike…", "good for pre-theatre audiences with a tight turnaround" – such are the benefits of the National Theatre's in-house venue ("try to get a table with a river view"). Food quality is "variable" though. / SE1 9PX; house.nationaltheatre.org.uk; @NT_House; 11 pm; closed Sun D.

Hubbard & Bell, Hoxton Hotel WC1 £57 3 3 3
199-206 High Holborn 020 7661 3030 2–1D
Soho House's all-day diner within their hipster-inspired hotel (for all its groovy name-checking, in drab Holborn) is a useful local amenity: "good for a quick lunch" or coffee. / WC1V 7BD; www.hubbardandbell.com; @HubbardandBell; Mon-Sat midnight, Sun 11 pm.

Humble Grape EC4 NEW £44 3 4 4
1 Saint Bride's Passage 020 7583 0688 10–2A
"A lovely venue in an old crypt of Fleet Street" (under St Bride's, the journalists' church), hosts this new bar/restaurant (which also has an older Battersea sibling). "There's good food to be had here, but it's not really the point – it's the wonderfully diverse and well-priced wine list that will keep you coming back". / EC4Y 8EJ; www.humblegrape.co.uk; @humblegrape; 11 pm, Thu-Sat midnight; closed Sun.

Hunan SW1 £80 5 4 1
51 Pimlico Rd 020 7730 5712 6–2D
"Leave all the ordering to Mr Peng Jr and you won't be disappointed" at this "packed and pedestrian-looking" Pimlico veteran – London's No. 1 Chinese. Expect "a happy adventure" of "course after delectable course" of "tastebud tingling and multi-textured" small dishes "until you can't eat any more… and then the next three courses arrive" (all matched with "excellent, affordable wines"). The "enthusiastic" vibe set up by the "jolly" father and son team who run the place seals the experience. / SW1W 8NE; www.hunanlondon.com; 11 pm; closed Sun.

Hush £68 2 3 3
8 Lancashire Ct, W1 020 7659 1500 3–2B
95-97 High Holborn, WC1 020 7242 4580 2–1D
With a poshly located Mayfair original off Bond Street and handy branches in Holborn and St Paul's, this small group is "great for a business lunch"; there's no sign from reporters of huge excitement about the cooking, but it does the job. / www.hush.co.uk; @Hush_Restaurant; W1 10.45 pm; WC1 10.30 pm, Sun 9.30 pm; WC1 closed Sun.

Hutong, The Shard SE1 £89 3 2 5
31 St Thomas St 020 3011 1257 10–4C
"Exceptional vistas from the 33rd floor" help create a "gorgeous and very romantic" ambience at this "sister to the world-famous Hutong in HK". Seemingly "the view doubles the price" ("astronomical!") for the Chinese cuisine, although on most accounts it's "pretty good too". Less so the so-so service. / SE1 9RY; www.hutong.co.uk; @HutongShard; 11 pm; no shorts.

Ibérica £48 2 2 3
Zig Zag Building, 70 Victoria St, SW1 020 7636 8650 2–4B
195 Great Portland St, W1 020 7636 8650 2–1B
12 Cabot Sq, E14 020 7636 8650 12–1C
89 Turnmill St, EC1 020 7636 8650 10–1A
Fans of these "bustling" modern venues say "they offer a genuine taste of Spain, unrecognisable as part of a chain". And that was probably true once, but with expansion they seem more "hyped" and "impersonal" now, although they can still make "a decent fallback". / 11 pm; W1 closed Sun D.

Ichiryu WC1 NEW £34 4 3 2
84 New Oxford St 020 3405 1254 5–1B
A new "fast food" noodle house in Bloomsbury, courtesy of Shoryu founder Tak Tokumine. Early reports are enthusiastic: "the udon noodles are the standout dish here… exceptional with a truly authentic broth: you will want to go back again and again". / WC1A 1HB; /www.ichiryuudon.com; @IchiryuUdon; 10.30 pm, Sun 9.30 pm; no bookings.

Imli Street W1 £40 2 2 2
167-169 Wardour St 020 7287 4243 4–1C
This large Soho 10-year-old "has a real buzz about it" (aided by its comprehensive cocktail menu), and its Indian street food served by the small plate is "different and enjoyable". / W1F 8WR; www.imlistreet.com; @imlistreet; 11 pm, Sun 10 pm.

Inaho W2 £44 5 3 1
4 Hereford Rd 020 7221 8495 7–1B
"You don't go for the atmosphere" to this quirky, tiny shed, in Bayswater – "the sashimi and authentic, straightforward Japanese are are as good as it gets!" / W2 4AA; 10.30 pm; closed Sat L & Sun; no Amex.

India Club, Strand Continental Hotel WC2 £29 2 2 1
143 Strand 020 7836 4880 2–2D
"You could be in Delhi circa 1960" at this "quirky" veteran near the Indian High Commission in the Strand. Service "can be frantic" and the food is arguably "unexceptional", but "it deserves mention for its great value in a central location". BYO, or grab a pint from the hotel bar. / WC2R 1JA; www.strand-continental.co.uk; 10.50 pm; cash only; booking max 6 may apply.

Indian Moment SW11 £35 3 4 3
47 Northcote Rd 020 7223 6575 11–2C
"Very civilised" Battersea Indian where the curries are "not designed to blow your head off" and there's "never a bad note". "Thalis are a great addition to a menu that is by Indian standards low fat". / SW11 1NZ; www.indianmoment.co.uk; @indianmoment; 11.30 pm, Fri & Sat midnight; closed weekday L

Indian Ocean SW17   £35   3 3 3
214 Trinity Rd   020 8672 7740   11–2C
Long-established Indian near Wandsworth Common with a strong following for its "consistent, superior and interesting dishes". / SW17 7HP; www.indianoceanrestaurant.com; 11.30 pm.

Indian Rasoi N2   £36   4 4 3
7 Denmark Terrace   020 8883 9093   1–1B
"It's always difficult to get a table" at this "very friendly, if rather cramped" Muswell Hill Indian. In part it's "because it's a small place", but mostly it's because "it's miles better than your average curry house", with "original and delicious" dishes. / N2 9HG; www.indian-rasoi.co.uk; 10.30 pm; no Amex.

Indian Zilla SW13   £46   4 2 2
2-3 Rocks Ln   020 8878 3989   11–1A
"Distinctive and original Indian flavours" ("sometimes astounding") make this Barnes sibling to Indian Zing (across the river in Hammersmith) a "standout local curry house". The cooking is back on form after a blip noted by reporters last year. / SW13 0DB; www.indianzilla.co.uk; 11 pm; closed weekday L.

Indian Zing W6   £49   4 3 2
236 King St   020 8748 5959   8–2B
"Better than West End Indians for 2/3 the price" – Manoj Vasaikar's "fabulous, subtle yet punchy" modern cuisine has won a disproportionately huge following for his "busy" venture, especially given its nondescript location, near Ravenscourt Park. "The tables are a little too close together". / W6 0RS; www.indianzing.co.uk; @IndianZing; 11 pm, Sun 10 pm.

Ippudo   £38   3 2 3
Central St Giles Piazza, WC2   020 7240 4469   5–1B
1 Crossrail Pl, E14   020 3326 9485   12–1C
"Fresh" ramen, "gorgeous miso soup", and "helpful staff" are the draws at the London outlets of this global, Japan-based noodle chain with branches near Centre Point and in Canary Wharf, although some would argue that they do suffer from "that 'chain' feel". / @IppudoLondon; see web for detail.

Isarn N1   £45   4 4 2
119 Upper St   020 7424 5153   9–3D
"Authentic, delicate, imaginative and delicious" – the "consistently good" food at this "always busy" Islington fixture, where "courteous" staff help enliven the "narrow, slightly cramped" modern interior. / N1 1QP; www.isarn.co.uk; 11 pm, Sat & Sun 10 pm.

Ishtar W1   £46   3 3 2
10-12 Crawford St   020 7224 2446   2–1A
"Typical Turkish dishes – but done very well", win fans of this Marylebone Anatolian. / W1U 6AZ; www.ishtarrestaurant.com; 11.30 pm, Sun 10.30 pm.

THE IVY WC2 £69   3 4 5
1-5 West St   020 7836 4751   5–3B
*"A lesson in how to improve a legend!" – Richard Caring's "perked up"
Theatreland star has staged an impressive return to form since last year's
revamp: "the old menu classics – bang bang chicken, shepherd's pie,
etc have been spruced up" (they needed to be!), service is "discreet and
professional" and – "even without the buzz of all the c'lebs who are now
upstairs in the adjoining club" – its vibe, romance and glamour have
rediscovered their mojo. That said, there is a large band of refuseniks for
whom it has "lost its verve and originality" – it doesn't help that with spin-
offs sprouting all over town it can now "feel like a high-end franchise"
rather than the unique destination of yesteryear. / WC2H 9NQ;
www.the-ivy.co.uk; @TheIvyWestSt; Mon-Wed 11.30pm, Thu-Sat midnight,
Sun 10.30 pm; no shorts; booking max 6 may apply.*

The Ivy Brasserie, One Tower Bridge SE1 NEW
1 Tower Bridge   awaiting tel   10–4D
*If you don't count the Ivy Cafés, this is the fourth spin-off from Caprice
Holdings' Ivy brand, this time at One Tower Bridge – a new development
next to City Hall and Tower Bridge – set to serve a similar all-day menu
to the Ivy Chelsea Garden. Given the, so far, remorselessly middling
performance of all the spin-offs, next year we will likely treat all the
properties as the single M.O.R. group which seems to be Richard Caring's
aspiration. / SE1.*

The Ivy Café £53   2 2 4
96 Marylebone Ln, W1   020 3301 0400   2–1A
120 St John's Wood High St, NW8   awaiting tel   9–3A NEW
75 High St, SW19   020 3096 9333   11–2B NEW
*"Hooray, Wimbledon now has an Ivy! (in place of an old branch
of Barclays)" – and Marylebone too, has a "busy and bustling" branch
(on the site that was Union Café, RIP) of this spin-off chain. But whereas
many fans do find them "fun" and "attractive", they are also crowded and
"quite expensive", with comfort food that's arguably "not much better than
at Côte" (Richard Caring's other successfully rolled out money-spinner
of recent years). / see web for detail.*

The Ivy Chelsea Garden SW3 £58   2 2 5
197 King's Rd   020 3301 0300   6–3C
*"The garden in summer is perhaps the finest in the capital" and the
interior is "gorgeous" too, at this year-old Chelsea spin-off from the
Theatreland original. Leaving aside the "magical" atmosphere however,
there's less to celebrate – staff are "badly organised", "hubristic" and can
indulge in "pushy table-turning", while the "boring" brasserie fare
underlines the fact that "it's more a place to be seen than to eat".
/ SW3 5ED; www.theivychelseagarden.com; @ivychelsgarden; Mon-Thu 11 pm,
Fri-Sat 11.30 pm, Sun 10.30 pm.*

The Ivy Kensington Brasserie W8 £60   2 2 3
96 Kensington High St   020 3301 0500   6–1A
*"What Kensington High Street has needed for many years", say fans
of Richard Caring's "busy" year-old Ivy spin-off, which brings oodles
of "buzz" (it's "extremely noisy") to the premises that were so dead in their
previous guise (as Pavilion, RIP). But numerous sceptics feel the offer here
is "truly not exciting: the food's very ordinary, takes ages to arrive, and staff
seem uninterested". / W8 4SG; www.theivykensingtonbrasserie.com;
@theivybrasserie; 11 pm Fri & Sat 11.30 pm, Sun 10.30 pm.*

The Ivy Market Grill WC2 £58 ☑☑❸
1 Henrietta St 020 3301 0200 5–3D
"It's a nice-looking and handily-placed brasserie", but this recent Ivy spin-off
is "really not as special as it tries to make itself out to be". Fans say its food
is "very acceptable for Covent Garden" but cynics feel that "they're trading
off the kudos of the brand, without putting the effort in". Top Tip –
"good for a special brunch". / WC2E 8PS; www.theivymarketgrill.com;
@ivymarketgrill; midnight, Sun 11 30 pm

Jackson & Rye £46 ①②②
56 Wardour St, W1 020 7437 8338 4–2D
219-221 Chiswick High Rd, W4 020 8747 1156 8–2A
Hotham House, 1 Heron Sq, TW9 020 8948 6951 1–4A
These smart American-style diners do win some praise for "great
breakfast and brunch", but ratings generally are so-so, particularly when
it comes to "turgid efforts" at the "brilliantly located" riverside Richmond
branch. / @JacksonRye; see web for detail.

Jaffna House SW17 £18 ❺❸②
90 Tooting High St 020 8672 7786 11–2C
"It's bit like eating in someone's back sitting-room" (which is exactly what
it is!), but this "modest" family-run outfit in Tooting provides "great flavours
from some unusual Sri Lankan and South Indian specialities" and
is "very good value for money". / SW17 0RN; www.jaffnahouse.co.uk; 11.30 pm.

Jago, Second Home E1 £49 ❸②②
68-80 Hanbury St 020 3818 3241 13–2C
This "curious, orange-coloured, add-on, covered balcony" adjoining
a Shoreditch tech office space serves "scrumptious, healthy breakfasts",
flat whites, juices and Middle East-inspired "fun tapas". Named after the
area's erstwhile Victorian slums, it "should be hipster heaven, yet feels like
an office canteen... which is exactly what it is, I guess". / E1 5JL;
www.jagorestaurant.com; @jagorestaurant; Mon-Sat 9.30 pm; closed Sat L & Sun.

Jamavar W1 NEW
8 Mount Street 020 7499 1800 3–3B
'Jewel in the crown' of the Leela Palaces Indian hotel chain, Jamavar
London will open in November 2016, under executive chef Rohit Ghai
(Gymkhana, Benares). / W1K 3NF; www.jamavarrestaurants.com;
@jamavarlondon.

Jamie's Italian £44 ①①②
"Just another chain with celeb branding" – Jamie O's Italians can
be "fun for the family" ("kids are very welcome") but go "only if you are
desperate": "it's overly expensive for what's now very mediocre".
/ www.jamiesitalian.com; @JamiesItalianUK; 11.30 pm, Sun 10.30 pm; booking:
min 6.

Jar Kitchen WC2 £49 ❸❸❸
Drury Ln 020 7405 4255 5–1C
"A cute restaurant in a very useful location" this straightforward, year-old
café on the fringes of Covent Garden delivers "unfussy, very tasty food",
plus "lovely service, and an absolutely charming atmosphere". / WC2B 5QF;
www.jarkitchen.com; @JarKitchen; 9 pm; closed Mon & Sun; may need 6+ to book;
SRA-1 star.

Jashan N8 £32 5 4 2
19 Turnpike Ln 020 8340 9880 1–1C

"A slew of dishes not found elsewhere" make this *"hard-to-find restaurant worth the trip to this grubby strip of North London"* (one fan slogs up to Turnpike Lane from SW3, no less). But while the food is *"properly excellent"* – *"in particular the lamb chops"* – there's less acclaim for the *"ropey"* decor. / N8 0EP; www.jashan.co.uk; 10.15 pm, Fri & Sat 10.30 pm; D only, ex Sun open L & D; no Amex; may need 6+ to book.

Jikoni W1 NEW
21 Blandford Street 020 7034 1988 2–1A

Food writer Ravinder Bhogal teamed up with restaurateur Ratnesh Bagdai (previously of Corbin & King, Caprice Holdings and Brindisa) to launch her first restaurant in Marylebone in September 2016. The cuisine reflects the chef-patronne's mixed heritage with flavours from East Africa, the Middle East, Asia and Britain. / W1U 3DJ; www.jikonilondon.com; @JikoniLondon.

Jin Kichi NW3 £44 5 5 3
73 Heath St 020 7794 6158 9–1A

"Some of London's best authentic Japanese cooking" has long made a big hit of this small, *"very basic"* but *"wonderfully reliable"* Hampstead café (and fans say it's getting even better with its *"recently improved interior"*). *"Sitting at the grill bar is the best"*. / NW3 6UG; www.jinkichi.com; 11 pm, Sun 10 pm; closed Mon.

Jinjuu W1 £47 3 3 3
16 Kingly St 020 8181 8887 4–2B

Korean-American Iron Chef star Judy Joo's bar (ground floor, with DJ on some nights) and restaurant (basement) off Regent Street offers a very taste of "something different", with its "delicious authentic Korean fried chicken" – or some more "unusual choices" – plus cocktails and bar snacks. / W1B 5PS; www.jinjuu.com; @JinjuuLDN; Mon-Wed 11.30 pm, Thu-Sat 1 am, Sun 9.30 pm.

Joanna's SE19 £48 3 4 4
56 Westow Hill 020 8670 4052 1–4D

This "fantastic" family-owned local has become a Crystal Palace institution, providing "good and reliable" American-inspired grub and cocktails since 1978. / SE19 1RX; www.joannas.uk.com; @JoannasRest; 10.45 pm, Sun 10.15 pm.

Joe Allen WC2 £54 2 2 4
13 Exeter St 020 7836 0651 5–3D

Still-"vibrant" survivor from the '70s in a Theatreland basement – a "busy American diner" whose Covent Garden location makes it "a great spot for meeting pre-/post-show" and has long been something of a "minor celebrity hangout". That "it hasn't really changed under new ownership" (it's no longer in the same stable as its NYC namesake) is a mixed blessing – fans say "there's a time and place for it and when it's good it's really good", but critics are "not sure how it's still trading, except on a very out-of-date reputation: one friend always suggests meeting there... my heart sinks!" Top Menu Tip – "burgers can be ordered off menu for those in the know". / WC2E 7DT; joeallen.co.uk; @JoeAllenWC2; Mon-Thu 11.30 pm, Fri & Sat 12.30 am, Sun 10.30 pm.

Joe Public SW4 NEW   £14   4|2|3
Former Public Convenience, The Pavement   020 7622 4676   11–1C
*"Genuinely great pizza" – 20-inchers sold whole or by the slice – is the
reward for trying this hip newcomer in a former loo by Clapham Common
station (sibling to nearby WC, also set inside a former public lav). There's
also outside seating, and a hatch for takeaway. / SW4 7AA;
www.joepublicpizza.com; @JoepublicSW4; midnight; no bookings.*

The Joint SW9   £26   5|3|3
87 Brixton Village, Coldharbour Ln   07717 642812   11–1D
*"A brilliant place in trendy Brixton market with amazing BBQ food" –
"it requires a bit of a long wait, but boy is it worth it for the best pulled
pork burgers" and "best ever wings". "It feels great eating in the hustle and
bustle of the market" too, and "all for a very cheap price". / SW9 8PS;
www.the-joint.co; @thefoodjoint; 11 pm; closed Mon.*

Jolly Gardeners SW18   £49   3|2|3
214 Garratt Ln   020 8870 8417   11–2B
*"A cut above your neighbourhood boozer" – MasterChef winner Dhruv
Baker's "excellent local" serves "interesting food with lots of flavour from
a range of influences". Some Earlsfield regulars "would welcome more
change on the menu". / SW18 4EA; www.thejollygardeners.com;
@Jollygardensw15; 9.30 pm; closed Sun D.*

Jones & Sons E8   £55   4|3|4
22-27 Arcola St   020 7241 1211   14–1A
*"You need to grow a beard to blend in properly", but this open kitchen
operation in Dalston studios "gladdens the heart" of reporters: "steaks
which rival Hawksmoor, at half the price" and other "great-tasting and
reasonably priced" British fare. / E8 2DJ; www.jonesandsonsdalston.com;
@JonesSons; 10 pm, Fri & Sat 11 pm.*

The Jones Family Project EC2   £51   3|4|4
78 Great Eastern St   020 7739 1740   13–1B
*This Shoreditch basement beneath a street-level cocktail bar is a "local
gem", with "friendly and efficient" staff; top culinary tips are the "delicious"
steaks and "brilliant truffled macaroni cheese". / EC2A 3JL;
www.jonesfamilyproject.co.uk; @JonesShoreditch; 10.30 pm, Sun 6 pm; closed Sun D.*

José SE1   £47   5|4|5
104 Bermondsey St   020 7403 4902   10–4D
*"A bucket-list experience!" José Pizarro's "hustling and bustling" tapas bar
in Bermondsey is a "must-try!" – "fun, so long as you're happy to perch",
and the "Barcelona-quality" dishes are "so, so good". ("We re-located our
business just so we could be next to it!") / SE1 3UB; www.josepizarro.com;
@Jose_Pizarro; Mon-Sat 10.15 pm; closed Sun D; no bookings.*

José Pizarro EC2   £59   4|3|2
Broadgate Circle   020 7256 5333   13–2B
*"The slightly impersonal location doesn't do any favours" to José P's yearling
in Broadgate Circle, and service can vary too; but on the plus-side his "top-
quality tapas" is "seriously good and authentic"; "arrive early to secure
an outside table on sunny days". / EC2M 2QS;
www.josepizarro.com/Jose-pizarro-broadgate; @JP_Broadgate; 10.45 pm,
Sat 9.45 pm; closed Sun.*

Joy King Lau WC2 £38 **3** **3** **1**
3 Leicester St 020 7437 1132 5–3A
"If you want a safe bet in Chinatown", this "old school" fixture serves
"proper Cantonese" dishes over each of its busy four floors,
and "reasonable prices" make it "amazing value for money" too.
Just "watch out for the queues". / WC2H 7BL; www.joykinglau.com; 11.30 pm,
Sun 10.30 pm.

The Jugged Hare EC1 £66 **3** **2** **3**
49 Chiswell St 020 7614 0134 13–2A
"A very good selection of game" is the surprise feature of this "busy" City-
fringe gastropub, which is "convenient for The Barbican", and also
"serviceable for a quick business lunch". / EC1Y 4SA; www.thejuggedhare.com;
@juggedhare; Mon-Wed 11 pm, Thu-Sat midnight, Sun 10.30 pm.

Julie's W11
135 Portland Rd 020 7229 8331 7–2A
Last year they said it was closed till spring 2016, this year the website says
it's closed till spring 2017. Let's hope the relaunch of this famously
seductive '70s warren in Holland Park does soon see the light of day…
/ W11 4LW; www.juliesrestaurant.com; 11 pm.

Jun Ming Xuan NW9 £42 **4** **4** **2**
28 Heritage Ave 020 8205 6987 1–1A
"A proper Hong Kong experience transplanted" to Colindale's new Beaufort
Park, providing "excellent dim sum, sensibly priced and briskly served".
"At 5pm, a standard Cantonese menu takes over". / NW9 5GE; junming.co.uk;
@jun_ming_xuan; 11 pm.

The Junction Tavern NW5 £48 **3** **3** **3**
101 Fortess Rd 020 7485 9400 9–2B
Fans "always go home on a happy note" from this "pub with good food,
rather than a restaurant disguised as a pub", on the Tufnell Park/Kentish
Town borders. / NW5 1AG; www.junctiontavern.co.uk; @JunctionTavern; 11 pm,
Fri & Sat midnight; Mon-Thu D only, Fri-Sun open L & D; no Amex.

K10 £38 **4** **4** **3**
20 Copthall Ave, EC2 020 7562 8510 10–2C
3 Appold St, EC2 020 7539 9209 13–2B
Minster Ct, Mincing Ln, EC3 020 3019 2510 10–3D
This "conveyor-belt sushi" chain in the City is "tasty, slick, and fun".
"Always fresh and varied", with a "good selection of hot dishes too",
"standards remain high" and it is "hard to find fault" – they're "buzzy even
on a Friday evening". / www.k10.com; Appold 9 pm, Wed-Fri 9.30 pm.

Kaffeine £12 **3** **5** **5**
15 Eastcastle St, W1 020 7580 6755 3–1D
66 Great Titchfield St, W1 020 7580 6755 3–1C
"It feels like you're in Sydney" at this "independent Aussie/Kiwi-owned
coffee shop" in Fitzrovia. "Staff are always smiling, service is fast",
and "standards are exacting when it comes to making a brew"; "delicious",
"deli-style breakfasts, sandwiches and salads" too. / kaffeine.co.uk;
@kaffeinelondon; see web for detail.

Kai Mayfair W1 £98 322

65 South Audley St 020 7493 8988 3–3A
Bernard Yeoh's Mayfair fixture feels too "international and expensive" for some tastes (it's not everywhere you can drink a £7,500 bottle of 1990 Chateau Pétrus with your crispy duck...), but its "Chinese cuisine with a south east Asian twist" (and many other influences besides – there's a selection of Wagyu dishes for example) ranks amongst London's best. / W1K 2QU; www.kaimayfair.co.uk; @kaimayfair; 10.45 pm, Sun 10.15 pm.

Kaifeng NW4 £64 333

51 Church Rd 020 8203 7888 1–1B
"Excellent standards are maintained year after year" at this Hendon stalwart – if you want kosher Chinese cooking, this is the place! / NW4 4DU; www.kaifeng.co.uk; 10 pm; closed Fri & Sat.

Kanada-Ya £19 422

3 Panton St, SW1 020 7930 3511 5–4A **NEW**
64 St Giles High St, WC2 020 7240 0232 5–1B
"Best ramen in London? Quite possibly!" These West End outposts of a Japan-based noodle chain are "nothing fancy" but boil up a "broth so meaty and delicious you have to finish the bowl, even if you feel as if you're about to pop". / see web for detail.

Kaosarn £29 443

110 St Johns Hill, SW11 020 7223 7888 11–2C
Brixton Village, Coldharbour Ln, SW9 020 7095 8922 11–2D
"Fresh, zingy, home-cooked flavours, served quickly" ensure that these Thai cafés in Brixton and Battersea are "always packed and humming". "BYO keeps costs down", too. In SW9, it's "great in the summer when you can eat outside". / SW9 10 pm, Sun 9 pm; SW11 closed Mon L.

Kappacasein SE16 £6 522

1 Voyager Industrial Estate 07837 756852 12–2A
"Taking the cheese toastie to another level (by using three cheeses, plus onion, leek, and shallots in sourdough bread)" – this Borough Market stall is arguably "the nicest way to take in five or six hundred calories" all in one go, even if "the queuing and purchasing tedium aren't the best". / SE16 4RP; www.kappacasein.com; @kappacasein; Thu 5 pm, Fri 6 pm, Sat 5 pm; closed Mon, Tue, Wed & Sun D; cash only.

Karma W14 £40 331

44 Blythe Rd 020 7602 9333 8–1D
A highly satisfactory Indian tucked away on an Olympia corner serving "superb, authentic curries". Ambience-wise however, even its most ardent fan doesn't claim it's a wild scene. / W14 0HA; www.k-a-r-m-a.co.uk; @KarmaKensington; 11 pm; no Amex.

Kaspar's Seafood & Grill,
The Savoy Hotel WC2 £83 233

100 The Strand 020 7836 4343 5–3D
"An interesting menu with hints to the orient" is a feature of the fish and seafood cooking in this "splendid" dining room, known in decades past as The Savoy's River Restaurant. Fans applaud its "breathtaking style and good cuisine" – including sushi, ceviche and laksa – but critics feel "they've ruined one of London's best rooms with poor quality, pub-like food" – "forgivable in a high-street restaurant, but not at The Savoy!" / WC2R 0EU; www.kaspars.co.uk; @KasparsLondon; 11 pm; SRA-3 star.

Kateh W9 £43 3 4 3
5 Warwick Pl   020 7289 3393   9–4A
This "deservedly busy" little spot just off the canal junction in Little Venice provides "enticing" modern Iranian dishes and "a fantastic buzz". / W9 2PX; www.katehrestaurant.co.uk; 11 pm, Sun 9.30 pm; closed weekday L

Kazan £48 3 4 2
77 Wilton Rd, SW1   020 7233 8298   2–4B
93-94 Wilton Rd, SW1   020 7233 7100   2–4B
This "totally reliable neighbourhood Turk never misses a beat" – it's "always crowded" and "rightly so" thanks to its "friendly" style and "delicious" food. "Its younger sibling opposite offers a super selection of mezze" and both are "very good quality, considering the prices". / www.kazan-restaurant.com; 10 pm.

The Keeper's House, Royal Academy W1 £64 2 2 2
Royal Academy Of Arts, Piccadilly   020 7300 5881   3–3D
"Hidden away in the vaults under the Royal Academy", all agree there's promise in this "lovely" spot. But while some reports do find it "very enjoyable", too often "the experience doesn't match up to the prestige of the RA", delivering "mediocre" results that "miss their mark": "could (and certainly should) do better!" / W1J 0BD; www.royalacademy.org.uk/page/the-keepers-house; @KHRestaurant; 9.45 pm; closed Sun.

Ken Lo's Memories SW1 £59 3 4 2
65-69 Ebury St   020 7730 7734   2–4B
Ken Lo's "very old favourite" in Belgravia inspires devotion for its "traditional – indeed, unchanging – menu" and complete reliability: "it's easy to dismiss as old hat, but the cooking remains high quality and the service much better than at most Chinese restaurants, including some which are much more expensive". / SW1W 0NZ; www.memoriesofchina.co.uk; 11 pm, Sun 10.30 pm.

Kennington Tandoori SE11 £45 3 3 3
313 Kennington Rd   020 7735 9247   1–3C
"There's more of a buzz" at this Kennington joint "than at most local Indians" – perhaps because it's "favoured by Conservative Party politicians" from Parliament across the river. It's "much better than you might reasonably expect in the dreariness of Kennington Park Road". / SE11 4QE; www.kenningtontandoori.com; @TheKTLondon; 11 pm; closed weekday L; no Amex.

Kensington Place W8 £62 3 3 2
201-209 Kensington Church St   020 7727 3184   7–2B
"Thanks to all those windows, it's extremely bright" inside this once-famous '90s 'goldfish bowl', off Notting Hill Gate, nowadays enlarged and "re-invented as a fish restaurant to gear up on its excellent adjacent fish shop" (plus "with a popular, pop-up fish 'n' chip shop in the former private dining room"). "Don't expect to hear your dining companions", but the food's "reliable". / W8 7LX; www.kensingtonplace-restaurant.co.uk; @KPRestaurantW8; Mon-Thu 10 pm, Fri-Sat 10.30 pm; closed Mon L & Sun D.

Kensington Square Kitchen W8 £33 3 4 3
9 Kensington Sq   020 7938 2598   6–1A
"OMG I love this place for breakfast" – that's the special strength of this sweet little two-floor café, on one of Kensington's oldest squares, although "the lunches are good too". / W8 5EP; www.kensingtonsquarekitchen.co.uk; @KSKRestaurant; 4.30 pm, Sun 4 pm; L only; no Amex.

The Kensington Wine Rooms W8 £58 2 3 3
127-129 Kensington Church St 020 7727 8142 7–2B
*More than 40 "very different, well-kept wines" are available by the glass
at this Kensington bar (with branches in Fulham and Hammersmith).
A simple food menu is designed to complement the drinks, and staff
"make you feel cherished"! / W8 7LP; www.greatwinesbytheglass.com;
@wine_rooms; 11.30 pm.*

Brew House, Kenwood House NW3 £33 2 2 3
Hampstead Heath 020 8348 4073 9–1A
*Set in the stables of the majestic mansion, this self-service café is hardly
a gastronomic destination, but it has a beautiful garden for tea and a bun,
and makes a good brunch stop-off after a hearty walk on Hampstead
Heath. / NW3 7JR; www.english-heritage.org.uk/visit/places/ke; @EHKenwood; 6 pm
(summer), 4 pm (winter); L only.*

Kerbisher & Malt £25 3 3 2
53 New Broadway, W5 020 8840 4418 1–2A
164 Shepherd's Bush Rd, W6 020 3556 0228 8–1C
170 Upper Richmond Road West, SW14 020 8876 3404 1–4A
50 Abbeville Rd, SW4 020 3417 4350 11–2D
59-61 Rosebery Ave, EC1 020 7833 4434 10–1A
*"Fun and trendy chippies", which are "traditional and yet modern at the
same time" ("if that doesn't make sense you'll have to go and see for
yourself!"). Service is "lovely" (even if it "could be slicker"), and they offer
"really well-cooked, no-nonsense fish 'n' chips". / www.kerbisher.co.uk; 10 pm -
10.30 pm, Sun 9 pm - 9.30 pm; W6 closed Mon; no booking.*

Khan's W2 £23 3 3 3
13-15 Westbourne Grove 020 7727 5420 7–1C
*"It's blasted on for so many years!" This hectic and atmospheric Bayswater
canteen is a "staple" of "reliable", if "basic" Indian scoff. It's 100% halal
too, but there's no alcohol. / W2 4UA; www.khansrestaurant.com;
@KhansRestaurant; 11 pm, Sat & Sun 11.30 pm.*

Kiku W1 £56 3 3 2
17 Half Moon St 020 7499 4208 3–4B
*A "typical old-style Japanese" veteran in Mayfair, all "minimalist and
wooden décor, clean lines and quite formal", so "perfect for business
lunches but maybe not a romantic meal for two". "The food is very good,
if a little pricey". / W1J 7BE; www.kikurestaurant.co.uk; 10.15 pm, Sun 9.45 pm;
closed Sun L.*

Kikuchi W1 £74 4 3 2
14 Hanway St 020 7637 7720 5–1A
*"Outstanding! Could have been back in Japan" – a small izakaya in the
warren of streets near Tottenham Court Road. Caution: even those
awarding it full marks can still find it "overpriced". / W1T 1UD; 10.30 pm,
Sat 9.30 pm; closed Sun.*

Kiln W1 NEW
58 Brewer Street no tel 4–3C
*Ben Chapman, founder of one of London's hottest restaurants of recent
times – Smoking Goat – opened a second Thai venture in September
2016. This Soho venue is described as a 'side-of-the-road-type restaurant',
serving grills and a speciality daily noodle dish. / W1F 9TL.*

Kintan WC1 £44 3 3 3
34-36 High Holborn   020 7242 8076   10–2A
This "great-fun Japanese/Korean barbecue-at-your-table outfit" near
Holborn claims to be one of London's first yakiniku (grilled meat) venues.
"Good for groups and excellent value at lunch". / WC1V 6AE; www.kintan.uk;
@kintanuk; 10.30 pm, Sun 9.30 pm.

Kipferl N1 £46 3 2 2
20 Camden Passage   020 77041 555   9–3D
From the "great dumplings and schnitzel" to "authentic Viennese cakes
and Austrian coffee" (and even wine), this Islington deli-café serves "a good
range of dishes" showing "dedication to the Austrian style and approach".
It's not a Tyrolean kitsch-fest either – in fact the interior is "rather bland".
/ N1 8ED; www.kipferl.co.uk; @KipferlCafe; 9.25 pm; booking weekdays only.

Kiraku W5 £35 4 4 2
8 Station Pde   020 8992 2848   1–3A
"When you need Japanese food without pretension, head here!" – to this
simple café, near Ealing Common tube station, consistently highly rated for
its straightforward but accomplished cuisine. / W5 3LD; www.kiraku.co.uk;
@kirakulondon; 10 pm; closed Mon; no Amex.

Kiru SW3 NEW £54 4 3 3
2 Elystan Street   020 7584 9999   6–2D
A "superb", "friendly and professional" newcomer at Chelsea Green,
serving "Japanese fusion fare" ("Nobu-style, but fresher and better",
featuring "very high-quality sashimi, sushi, and nigiri"), "plus smashing
sake"… "albeit at a price". / SW3; www.kirurestaurant.com; @KiruRestaurant;
10 pm, Fri & Sat 10.30 pm.

Kitchen W8 W8 £71 4 4 2
11-13 Abingdon Road   020 7937 0120   6–1A
"A gastronomic, neighbourhood restaurant" off Kensington High Street
highly lauded for its "casual and sophisticated" approach, "unusually
enthusiastic" service, and "delightful", "seasonal" cuisine (overseen by Phil
Howard). Ratings softened a little this year however – the atmosphere of its
"intimate" interlocking dining spaces is "not electric", and "portion sizes
can be a bit too haute-cuisine style". / W8 6AH; www.kitchenw8.com;
@KitchenW8; 10.30 pm, Sun 9.30 pm.

Kitty Fisher's W1 £64 4 4 4
10 Shepherd's Mkt   020 3302 1661   3–4B
"Entirely deserving of all the hype" is the overwhelming verdict on this
"small, but comfortable and cosy" yearling, by picturesque Shepherd
Market. It's "a real charmer": service is "welcoming and fun", and the
"highly competent cooking" is "big on simplicity and flavour". / W1J 7QF;
www.kittyfishers.com; @kittyfishers; 9.30 pm; closed Sun.

Koffmann's, The Berkeley SW1 £86 4 5 3
The Berkeley, Wilton Pl 020 7107 8844 6–1D
"It's hard to find better French food in London" than Pierre Koffmann's "surprisingly robust" cuisine at his Belgravia basement: "un-concept plates, simply presented with perfect quality, freshness, and flavour".
"The finest service" ("everything runs very smoothly") helps introduce an "intimate" ambience into the slightly "weird and sunken" location – in fact, all-in-all, it arguably "frequently outshines its better-known neighbour" Marcus nowadays. Top Menu Tip – "it's worth the trip for the pistachio soufflé, but the legendary pig's trotter is also tip top".
STOP PRESS: hurry along, because the restaurant is closing in December 2016. / SW1X 7RL; www.pierrekoffmann.co.uk; @theberkeley / @pierrekoffmann; 10.30 pm; jacket & tie required.

Kojawan, Hilton Metropole W2 NEW £65 2 3 4
225 Edgware Rd 020 8088 0111 7–1D
"A fabulous view over London is complemented by crazy-kitsch Asian decor", at this offbeat 23rd floor newcomer at the top of the Hilton Metropole by Edgware Road station, where two, non-Asian, Michelin-friendly chefs (Bjorn Van Der Horst – formerly of Greenhouse – and Omar Romero, a graduate of Rhodes Twenty Four) offer a fusion of KO-rean, JA-panese and Tai-WAN-ese cuisines (geddit?), complemented by a formidable list of drinks. To fans it's a "rooftop gem" – one or two critics though "like the concept, but think they just haven't got it right". / W2; www.kojawan.uk; @kojawan; 2 am; closed weekday L.

Koji SW6 £75 4 4 3
58 New King's Rd 020 7731 2520 11–1B
"Roka-quality food but at more reasonable prices (and great cocktails too!)", win all-round acclaim for Pat & Mark Barnett's "terrific" Japanese-fusion haunt in Parsons Green (which they ran for ages as Mao Tai, long RIP); its swish decor is "great if you're in a group, a bit sparse if you're à deux". / SW6 4LS; www.koji.restaurant; @koji_restaurant; 11.30 pm, Sun 10.30 pm; closed weekday L; no shorts.

Kolossi Grill EC1 £33 3 5 2
56-60 Rosebery Ave 020 7278 5758 10–1A
"You will have to travel a very long way to beat the value for money offered by this eatery off the middle of Exmouth Market" – a 50-year-old survivor that's changed little over the years. The main concern? – "where will I eat if the owner retires!" / EC1R 4RR; www.kolossigrill.com; 10.30 pm; closed Sat L & Sun; set weekday L £15 (FP).

Koya-Bar W1 £34 3 4 4
50 Frith St 020 7434 4463 5–2A
"Takes over where Koya (RIP) left off", this "cramped" but "cool" Soho Japanese is "famous for udon noodles, but their small plates and donburi rice dishes are even better". "The purity of the stocks and sauces is fantastic", so it's "well worth the queue" (you can't book). / W1D 4SQ; www.koyabar.co.uk; @KoyaBar; 10.30 pm, Thu-Sat 11 pm, Sun 10 pm; no Amex; no bookings.

Kricket £44 5 4 3
12 Denman Street, W1 awaiting tel 4–3C NEW
Pop Brixton, 53 Brixton Station Rd, SW9 awaiting tel 11–1D
"A brilliant and totally different, fresh and wonderfully subtle fusion of southern Indian and European food" is "served up with a smile and music in a metal container in Brixton" as part of a "fun" and "funky" community project; a Soho branch is set to open in the autumn of 2016. / see web for detail.

Kulu Kulu £32 **3** 1 1
76 Brewer St, W1   020 7734 7316   4–3C
51-53 Shelton St, WC2   020 7240 5687   5–2C
39 Thurloe Pl, SW7   020 7589 2225   6–2C
"The prices barely seem to have changed in the last 17 years" (similarly the drab decor) at these "grab-a-dish-from-the-belt" cafés, still popular "for a cheap, quick, sushi fix". "The key to an enjoyable meal is to go when it's busy when dishes are at their freshest and hottest". / 10 pm, SW7 10.30 pm; closed Sun; no Amex; no booking.

Kurobuta £56 **5** 2 2
Harvey Nichols, Knightsbridge, SW1   020 7920 6443   6–1D
312 King's Rd, SW3   020 7920 6444   6–3C
17-20 Kendal St, W2   020 7920 6444   7–1D
"Thrilling flavours" from "a wide ranging" Japanese menu again inspire rave reviews for Scott Hallsworth's "hip, modern, trendy, but unpretentious" izakaya-style haunts, which are "a real favourite for a fun night out". They're "not for the hard of hearing" though, and SW3 is "a bit trashy" and "pure Chelsea" for some tastes. / @KurobutaLondon; see web for detail.

The Ladbroke Arms W11 £53 **3** 2 **4**
54 Ladbroke Rd   020 7727 6648   7–2B
"There's always a good crowd, especially on the terrace on a sunny day" at this unusually attractive and "comfortable" pub, at the Holland Park end of Ladbroke Grove. "It's a little chaotic, always fun, bustling and friendly", with "very reliable food". / W11 3NW; www.ladbrokearms.com; @ladbrokearms; 11 pm, Sun 10.30 pm; no booking after 8 pm.

The Lady Ottoline WC1 £50 **3** 2 **3**
11a Northington St   020 7831 0008   2–1D
"Nice little pub" in Bloomsbury – a restored Victorian tavern (part of the upmarket Affinity group) whose comfort food cooking and rather civilised atmosphere are consistently well-rated by reporters. / WC1N 2JF; www.theladyottoline.com; @theladyottoline; 10 pm, Sun 8 pm.

Lahore Karahi SW17 £26 **4** 2 2
1 Tooting High Street, London   020 8767 2477   11–2C
"I keep coming back, week after week, year after year" – so say fans of this "top class Indian / Pakistani" BYO canteen in Tooting, extolling its "sublime food and amazing value". / SW17 0SN; www.lahorekarahirestaurant.co.uk; midnight; no Amex.

Lahore Kebab House £24 **5** 2 2
668 Streatham High Rd, SW16   020 8765 0771   11–2D
2-10 Umberston St, E1   020 7481 9737   12–1A
"The best Pakistani food in London!" This "Whitechapel scrum" is "a true no-nonsense star" – its lamb chops and other grills are "so delicious" but the "curries are very good too" and it's all "so cheap, you almost don't notice paying!" (especially as you can BYO). "Consistently great for over 20 years", old timers "remember when it was just a hole in the wall – nowadays it's a multi-level factory of sorts!" (Fewer reports on the "huge" Streatham outpost, but they say it too is "brilliant" and "a nicer place to eat"). / midnight.

Lamberts SW12 £52 5 5 4
2 Station Pde   020 8675 2233   11–2C
"Lucky Balhamites to have it on their doorstep!" – Joe Lambert's
"consistently excellent" neighbourhood favourite "nibbles at Chez Bruce's
heels" in the affections of SW12 residents. Its "creative, modern and
seasonal British food" is "remarkably good value" and served by "superb"
staff in a "casual" setting. / SW12 9AZ; www.lambertsrestaurant.com;
@lamberts_balham; 10 pm, Sun 5 pm; closed Mon & Sun L; no Amex.

The Landmark, Winter Garden NW1 £78 2 4 5
222 Marylebone Rd   020 7631 8000   9–4A
The "beautiful atrium, with lots of daylight" makes this Marylebone venue
a "very special setting" for an "unbeatable Sunday brunch" (limitless
champagne) or "traditional afternoon tea" ("great ambience with piano
in the background"); it suits business lunchers too. / NW1 6JQ;
www.landmarklondon.co.uk; @landmarklondon; 10.15 pm; no trainers; booking
max 12 may apply.

Langan's Brasserie W1 £68 1 2 4
Stratton St   020 7491 8822   3–3C
"I've been going for 38 years and it still delivers...": a typical
recommendation for this famous brasserie near The Ritz, whose "wonderful
rooms are filled with plenty of character", and which particularly suit
a business occasion. Sceptics, though, can find it even "more old school
than expected" – "very masculine, with lots of boys-only tables,
and comfort food" – and its harshest critics feel its "poor" catering
standards put it "in dire need of a makeover/relaunch". / W1J 8LB;
www.langansrestaurants.co.uk; @langanslondon; 11 pm, Fri & Sat 11.30 pm;
closed Sun.

Palm Court, The Langham W1 £72 3 3 3
1c, Portland Place   020 7965 0195   2–1B
"I think I have done every major afternoon tea in the city and nothing
beats The Langham!" – "most exquisite sweets and yummy savouries",
and "really interesting sandwiches served on a platter rather than left
on the table". (In fact, this "beautiful" space is a handy fall-back
in general). / W1B 1JA; www.palm-court.co.uk; 10:30 pm; no trainers.

Lantana Cafe £35 3 3 3
13-14 Charlotte Pl, W1   020 7323 6601   2–1C
45 Middle Yd, Camden Lock Pl, NW1   020 7428 0421   9–2B
Unit 2, 1 Oliver's Yd, 55 City Rd, EC1   020 7253 5273   13–1A
An "imaginative brunch menu" has made this trio of "atmospheric" Aussie-
style coffee bars worth remembering in Fitzrovia, Camden Lock and
Shoreditch. Be warned, though, they are "very, very busy at times".
/ lantanacafe.co.uk; @lantanacafe; see web for detail.

Lardo £40 3 2 2
158 Sandringham Rd, E8   020 3021 0747   14–1B
197-201 Richmond Rd, E8   020 8533 8229   14–1B
"Very cool" Italian in the Arthaus building near London Fields where
a hipster-heavy crowd hoover up a "fairly limited menu" from the open
kitchen, majoring in charcuterie and pizza. Nearby they've opened Lardo
Bebé – a shop-conversion serving "artisan pizza with original toppings".
/ see web for detail.

Latium W1 £55   4 4 3
21 Berners St   020 7323 9123   3–1D
*"Nothing's 'in yer face', at this discreet and subtle venue", "tucked away"
in Fitzrovia, where new head chef Stefano Motta's seems to be maintaining
its "clean and precise" cooking, "full of strong flavours and interesting
combinations". Thanks to its "charming" and "unobtrusive" service and
"tranquil and well-spaced" (if perhaps "not terribly inspiring") interior, it's a
business favourite too. Top Menu Tip – "the ravioli can be exceptional".
/ W1T 3LP; www.latiumrestaurant.com; @LatiumLondon; 10.30 pm, Sat 11 pm;
closed Sat L & Sun L*

Launceston Place W8 £80   4 5 4
1a Launceston Pl   020 7937 6912   6–1B
*Raphael Francois "has maintained the excellent standards" set by Tim Allen
at this "understated" townhouse in a gorgeous Kensington backwater
(while "taking the menu in a welcome Gallic direction"). It's D&D London's
best all-rounder nowadays: "relaxed yet opulent", with notably "charming"
service and "sound, refined cooking". / W8 5RL;
www.launcestonplace-restaurant.co.uk; @LauncestonPlace; 10 pm, Sun 9.30 pm;
closed Mon & Tue L*

THE LEDBURY W11 £133   5 5 4
127 Ledbury Rd   020 7792 9090   7–1B
*Brett Graham's virtuoso cuisine has established his "special yet unstuffy"
Notting Hill HQ as London's No. 1 gastronomic address (topping this year's
survey nominations as best meal of the year, and losing only narrowly
to The Araki in achieving the highest food rating). "Absence of snob factor"
is key: dishes are "sophisticated and elaborate without being pretentious";
"utterly charming" staff are "much more easy-going than at many
Michelin-starred peers; and the "well-spaced" interior lacks grandiosity
while being "calm and relaxing". / W11 2AQ; www.theledbury.com;
@theledbury; 9.45 pm; closed Mon L & Tue L*

Legs E9 NEW £50
120-122 Morning Lane   020 3441 8765   14–1B
*A new café-cum-wine-bar (the name being a nod to wine-anorak
terminology), not far from Hipster (sorry, we mean Hackney!) Central
station. Beneath the restaurant is a 'makers' basement', where the team
distil vermouth for the bar, cure meats, pickle veg and even mould ceramics
for the tables upstairs [oh good grief, Ed]! It's the brainchild of chef
Magnus Reid (founder of Shoreditch hangout CREAM) and Andy Kanter.
Just one early survey report, but it's mega-enthusiastic, and some early
media reviews likewise give it a big thumbs up. / E9 6LH;
www.legsrestaurant.com; @legsrestaurant; Tue 5 pm, Wed-Sun 11 pm; closed
Mon & Tue D; no bookings at lunch.*

Lemonia NW1 £45   1 3 4
89 Regent's Park Rd   020 7586 7454   9–3B
*"Buzzing with positive energy, seven days a week" – this "phenomenal"
Primrose Hill mega-taverna remains "extraordinarily busy" and
is "like home, only better" for its huge north London fanclub. Even many
fans recognise that "the menu is tired and needs a complete refresh"…
but it's been like that for as long as anyone can remember! / NW1 8UY;
www.lemonia.co.uk; @Lemonia_Greek; 11 pm; closed Sun D; no Amex.*

Leong's Legends W1 £37   3 2 2
3 Macclesfield St   020 7287 0288   5–3A
*"Excellent Shanghai dumplings" (xiao long bao) are the big deal at this
"cramped" Chinatown Taiwanese, which also serves an "abbreviated dim
sum menu realised to an OK-to-good standard". / W1D 6AX;
www.leongslegend.com; 11 pm, Sat 11.30 pm; no bookings.*

Leyton Technical E10 £37 3 2 4
265b High Road   020 8558 4759   1–1D
*Full marks for grandeur to this conversion of Leyton's former town hall into
a prime local. It's perhaps more pub than gastro, but the scoff's
consistently well rated.* / E10 5QN; www.leytontechnical.com; @LeytonTechnical;
10 pm, Sun 7 pm.

The Lido Café, Brockwell Lido SE24 £43 2 2 4
Dulwich Rd   020 7737 8183   11–2D
*No-one doubts this is a "lovely space" beside Brockwell Park's lovingly
preserved Lido in Brixton – a café open from 8am through to dinner. Staff
often "lack oversight" however, and – "tasty" breakfasts aside – the food
can seem "expensive for what it is".* / SE24 0PA; www.thelidocafe.co.uk;
@thelidocafe; 4 pm; closed Sun D; no Amex.

The Light House SW19 £54 3 3 3
75-77 Ridgway   020 8944 6338   11–2B
*Wimbledon's longest-serving contributor to modern gastronomy – a "lovely"
informal fixture that has something of a name for "variable" somewhat "ill-
conceived" dishes. Fans though say "it's gone up a notch in recent times:
no longer does it try and put too much together on a plate or offer too
much variety".* / SW19 4ST; www.lighthousewimbledon.com; 10.30 pm; closed
Sun D.

The Lighterman N1 NEW £52 3 3 4
3 Granary Sq   020 3846 3400   9–3C
*Another resident for King's Cross restaurant hub Granary Square – this new
pub and dining room has "a great location on the banks of Regent's
Canal", and "engaging staff" who provide "reasonably priced, tasty food".
"Attractive if noisy ground floor, quieter first floor".* / N1C 4BH;
www.thelighterman.co.uk; @TheLightermanKX; 10.30 pm, Sun 9.30 pm.

Lima Fitzrovia £66 3 2 1
31 Rathbone Pl, W1   020 3002 2640   2–1C
14 Garrick St, WC2   020 7240 5778   5–3C
*"Elegant renditions of tangy Latino flavours" still win praise for these
modern Peruvians, in Fitzrovia and Covent Garden ('Lima Floral'). Even fans
say they are "expensive" however, not helped by "rather blah" decor,
and harsher critics just feel "they've lost their way".*
/ www.limalondongroup.com; @lima_london; see web for detail.

Lime Orange SW1 £36 3 2 2
312 Vauxhall Bridge Rd   020 8616 0498   2–4B
*"Reliable bibimbap and several other excellent dishes" score praise for this
"good quality cheap 'n' cheerful Korean (with a Japanese slant)"
just by Victoria station. "There's nothing wrong with the ambience, but it's
not the point".* / SW1V; www.limeorange.co.uk; closed Sun.

Lisboa Pâtisserie W10 £10 3 2 4
57 Golborne Rd   020 8968 5242   7–1A
*"Pastéis de nata to die for" are a prime attraction at this lively Portuguese
café – an excellent complement to a trip to nearby Portobello Market.*
/ W10 5NR; 7 pm; L only; no bookings.

LONDON'S HOTTEST NEW RESTAURANTS 2017

CLIPSTONE W1

HOPPERS W1

100 WARDOUR ST W1

DUENDE WC2

SAINT LUKE'S KITCHEN, LIBRARY WC2

PADELLA SE1

ANGLO EC1

RESTAURANT OURS SW7

LEGS E9

OSTERIA, BARBICAN CENTRE EC2

CURIO + TA TA E8

SARDINE N1

SQUIRREL SW7

ENOTECA TURI SW1

PHARMACY 2 SE11

CELESTE, THE LANESBOROUGH SW1

AULIS, FERA AT CLARIDGE'S W1

THE IVY CAFE SW19

THE LIGHTERMAN N1

BAO FITZROVIA W1

FRENCHIE WC2

THE WOODFORD E18

THE FROG E1

CHICK 'N' SOURS WC2

STRUT & CLUCK E1

RANDY'S WING BAR E15

Harden's

LONDON
RESTAURANT
AWARDS 2016

SEPTEMBER 12 2016

Top Gastronomic Experience Award:
Mitsuhiro & Yoko Araki, The Araki

Lifetime Achievement Award:
Bruce Poole, Chez Bruce

The Little Bay NW6 £28
228 Belsize Rd 020 7372 4699 1–2B
"Perfect for a cheap eat", this *"very reliable"* and jolly, theatre-themed bistro is *"very good at catering for large groups, as well as couples in the little balconies here and there"*. The Farringdon branch closed this year (there is still a Croydon 'country cousin'). / NW6 4BT; www.little-bay.co.uk; 11.30 pm; cash only.

Little Georgia Café £40
14 Barnsbury Rd, N1 020 7278 6100 9–3D
87 Goldsmiths Row, E2 020 7739 8154 14–2B
"The best borscht in London" typifies the *"truly interesting"*, *"hearty, warming menu (particularly good in winter)"* at this pair of *"favourite neighbourhood"* cafés in Islington and Hackney, similarly the *"amazing Georgian wine"*. / www.littlegeorgia.co.uk; 10 pm.

Little Social W1 £76
5 Pollen St 020 7870 3730 3–2C
"More relaxed and better than its bigger sister" (over the road) – Jason Atherton's *"home-from-home"* feels *"nicely hidden away like you're not in central London"* and delivers a great *"buzz"*, a menu of *"classic"* dishes, and a *"comprehensive"* wine list. Even fans can quibble though – *"I feel a little mean saying it, it's very good, but just too expensive for somewhere so informal"*. / W1S 1NE; www.littlesocial.co.uk; @_littlesocial; 10.30 pm; closed Sun.

Little Taperia SW17 NEW £34
143 Tooting High St 020 8682 3303 11–2C
"I challenge you to visit and not to spend an evening eating and drinking too much!" – *"a joint project from the owners of Meza and Little Bar"*, this Tooting Spaniard provides *"delicious tapas off a short, imaginative menu"* washed down with cocktails, sherries, ports and cavas. / SW17; www.thelittletaperia.co.uk; @littletaperia; 10 pm, Fri & Sat 11 pm, Sun 9.30 pm; may need 6+ to book.

Lobos Meat & Tapas SE1 £48
14 Borough High St 020 7407 5361 10–4C
"Some of the most inspiring and inspired tapas anywhere" – from a menu featuring *"meat, meat, and more meat"* – is waiting to be discovered in this *"very squished"* year-old dive in Borough Market. It's the creation of alumni from nearby Brindisa, and *"brilliant"*. / SE1 9QG; www.lobostapas.co.uk; @LobosTapas; 11 pm, Sun 10 pm.

Lobster Pot SE11 £62
3 Kennington Ln 020 7582 5556 1–3C
10/10 for the very Gallic, surreal nautical decor (complete with recorded seagull cries) at this 21-year-old, family-run venture, grungily situated in deepest Kennington. At heart, it's a *"fine and traditional"* Breton fish and seafood restaurant. / SE11 4RG; www.lobsterpotrestaurant.co.uk; 10.30 pm; closed Mon & Sun; booking max 8 may apply.

Locanda Locatelli, Hyatt Regency W1 £81
8 Seymour St 020 7935 9088 2–2A
"A wonderful taste of Italy" inspires fans of Giorgio Locatelli's *"dark"*, *"classy"* rather '90s Marylebone HQ. The main man has seemed more in evidence this last year – *"prowling the dining room to ensure all is well"* – and ratings for the *"lovingly crafted food"* and service (mostly *"courteous"*, occasionally *"stand-offish"*) were higher across the board. *"Expensive, but worth it"*. / W1H 7JZ; www.locandalocatelli.com; 11 pm, Thu-Sat 11.30 pm, Sun 10.15 pm; booking max 8 may apply.

Locanda Ottomezzo W8 £67 3 2 3
2-4 Thackeray St 020 7937 2200 6–1B
A "backstreet Italian" near Kensington Square Garden, with "absolutely great ambience, food and wine" – service, though, can be a weak link. / W8 5ET; www.locandaottoemezzo.co.uk; 10.30 pm; closed Mon L, Sat L & Sun.

Loch Fyne £43 2 3 3
"You get what you expect" at this "sensible and reliable" chain: "reasonably priced" fish and seafood that's "basic but OK" in safe, attractive surroundings. / www.lochfyne-restaurants.com; 10 pm, WC2 10.30 pm.

London House SW11 £60 3 3 2
7-9 Battersea Sq 020 7592 8545 11–1C
Gordon Ramsay's "relaxed and friendly" two-year-old in Battersea pleases diners with its "great simple food", and a move to "less formal dining" has been well received. "The menu looks quite limited but the food was really enjoyable". / SW11 3RA; www.gordonramsay.com; @londonhouse; Tue-Fri 10 pm; closed Mon, Tue L & Wed L.

The Lord Northbrook SE12 £42 3 4 4
116 Burnt Ash Rd 020 8318 1127 1–4D
"In an area without huge amounts of choice", this Lea Green boozer provides "a good local gastropub". / SE12 8PU; www.thelordnorthbrook.co.uk; @LordNorthbrook; 9 pm, Fri & Sat 10 pm.

Lorenzo SE19 £44 3 3 3
73 Westow Hill 020 8761 7485 1–4D
This "extremely popular" Italian in Upper Norwood "is still very good value, and the cooking is generous and exemplary". Be warned, though, it's a "lunchtime favourite", so "tables get quite cramped – but it's worth it". / SE19 1TX; www.lorenzo.uk.com; 10.30 pm; no bookings.

Lotus WC2 NEW £59 4 4 3
17 Charing Cross Rd 020 7839 8797 5–4B
This "classy" yearling off Leicester Square serves "elaborate, sophisticated Indian" dishes, "very different from all others in area". There's an "outstanding" range of game and – usefully in the heart of the West End – a "great pre-theatre menu". "I hope it survives". / WC2H 0EP; www.lotus.london; 10.30 pm.

Luce e Limoni WC1 £57 3 5 3
91-93 Gray's Inn Rd 020 7242 3382 10–1A
"Fabrizio is a wonderful host" and his well-appointed Bloomsbury restaurant provides "very kind and polite service" to "make you feel at home", plus "hearty Sicilian cuisine (to be enjoyed by those not accustomed to modern or light Italian food)". "It's opposite ITN so you can always get a cab!" / WC1X 8TX; www.luceelimoni.com; @Luce_e Limoni; 10 pm, Fri - Sat 11 pm.

Luciano's SE12 £42 3 3 3
131 Burnt Ash Rd 020 8852 3186 1–4D
"A fantastic local Italian" in Lee ("which now also has a bar next to the main restaurant" doing "good bar snacks"). "Family owned, it serves fresh pasta and pizza from a proper wood-burning oven". / SE12; lucianoslondon.co.uk; @LucianosLondon; 10.30 pm, Sun 10 pm; closed Mon.

We've turned our ratings system upside down!

As always Harden's will assess:

F – **Food**
S – **Service**
A – **Ambience**

But now <u>high</u> numbers are <u>better</u>...

5 – **Exceptional**

4 – **Very good**

3 – **Good**

2 – **Average**

1 – **Poor**

Lucio SW3　　　　　　　　　£72　　3 3 2
257 Fulham Rd　020 7823 3007　6–3B
"Perfect pasta dishes" are a highlight of the *"simple and tasty"* cooking
at this *"friendly"* (if *"noisy"*) Chelsea trattoria. Top Tip – *"The set lunch
menu is good value and you can see why it's full most lunchtimes"*.
/ SW3 6HY; www.luciorestaurant.com; 10.45 pm.

Lucky Chip E8　NEW　　　　　£42　　3 2 2
25 Ridley Rd　020 7686 9703　14–1A
"Might they be London's best burgers?" query fans of this new foodster-
favourite: the permanent, diner-style home by Dalston's Ridley Road Market
of a pop-up that's been spotted at various Hackney sites. (One or two
other menu options too: steak, chicken parmigiana, and some funky, dude-
ish bites). / E8 2NP; www.luckychip.co.uk/burgers-and-wine; @Lucky_Chip; 11 pm,
Thu-Sat midnight, Sun 10 pm.

Lupita WC2　　　　　　　　　£44　　3 2 2
13-15 Villiers St　020 7930 5355　5–4D
"Authentic" and *"unusual"* Mexican cuisine that's *"good value"* too can
be found at this *"informal"* location, to the side of Charing Cross station.
/ WC2N 6ND; www.lupita.co.uk; @LupitaUK; 11 pm, Fri & Sat 11.30 pm,
Sun 10 pm.

Lure NW5　　　　　　　　　　£40　　4 4 3
56 Chetwynd Rd　020 7267 0163　9–1B
"The new posh fish 'n' chip shop in Dartmouth Park ticks all the boxes" –
"who knew a fish-and-chippy could be this elevated?". Its *"very hands-on
owner"* also wins accolades for his *"home-made pickles"*. / NW5 1DJ;
www.lurefishkitchen.co.uk; @Lurefishkitchen; 10 pm.

Lurra W1　　　　　　　　　　£52　　4 3 3
9 Seymour Pl　020 7724 4545　2–2A
*"The other Spanish food is full of flavour, but the aged Galician steak is the
star"* (some of London's best meat) at this year-old *"Basque BBQ"* near
Marble Arch, a worthy sibling to the illustrious Donostia nearby. With its
"lovely modern interior" and *"friendly"* service it's *"a great night out"*.
/ W1H 5BA; www.lurra.co.uk; @LurraW1.

Lutyens EC4　　　　　　　　　£75　　2 2 2
85 Fleet St　020 7583 8385　10–2A
A smart business-lunch venue on the edge of the City, Sir Terence Conran's
brasserie provides *"reliable food and service"* which cause no grave
complaints. There's *"little adventure beyond the business lunch"* however:
"is this where accountants go for their Christmas meal?" / EC4Y 1AE;
www.lutyens-restaurant.com; 9.45 pm; closed Sat & Sun.

Lyle's E1　　　　　　　　　　£66　　5 4 3
The Tea Building, 56 Shoreditch High St　020 3011 5911　13–1B
"James Lowe and the team continue to inspire" at this *"continually
excellent"*, *"hipster-vibe"* Shoreditch venue, whose menu *"is designed with
simplicity at heart, yet refined with complexity of flavour"*: *"I was a bit
sceptical about the set 5-course dinner but my god, was I proved wrong!
Incredible cooking and great value for money!"* / E1 6JJ; www.lyleslondon.com;
@lyleslondon; 10 pm; closed Sat L & Sun.

M Restaurants £75 2 2 2
Zig Zag Building, Victoria St, SW1   020 3327 7770   2–4B
2-3 Threadneedle Walk, EC2   020 3327 7770   10–2C
"The main restaurant booths are perfect for business", as are the steak and luxurious seafood (sushi, ceviche, etc) selections, and swish bars at these big and brassy entertaining complexes in the City and Victoria. These "hangar-like" spaces can seem soulless however, and "lord above the prices", which leave any mishaps on the cooking front hard to forgive. / see web for detail.

Ma Cuisine TW9 £47 3 2 3
9 Station Approach   020 8332 1923   1–3A
Retro Gallic fare ("a wonderful boudin noir starter" and "coq au vin to die for") matches the gingham tablecloths and Parisian posters of this cute bistro near Kew Gardens station. It can be "pricier than you'd expect" but "who wouldn't want it on their doorstep?" / TW9 3QB; www.macuisinebistrot.co.uk; 10 pm, Fri & Sat 10.30 pm; no Amex.

Ma Goa SW15 £40 4 4 2
242-244 Upper Richmond Rd   020 8780 1767   11–2B
"It's still my favourite, and I keep going back!" – this stalwart Putney south Indian has a hyper-loyal local fanclub. "You are always made to feel special (we almost feel part of the family)" and the cooking is "still authentic, still interesting, and good value for a Sunday buffet". / SW15 6TG; www.ma-goa.com; @magoarestaurant; 10.30 pm, Fri-Sat 11 pm, Sun 10pm; closed Mon.

Mac & Wild W1 £49 4 4 3
65 Great Titchfield St   020 7637 0510   2–1B
"It's good to see this street vendor grow up into a proper restaurant" – Andy Waugh's Fitzrovia yearling offers a "successful riff on Scottish cuisine" majoring in "serious game" (from a "limited menu" focused primarily on venison steaks and burgers), much of it from his family's estate. "There's not a lot of space between tables (you can feel a bit encroached on)", but food (and whisky!) are "first rate" and "reasonably priced". A new Borough opening is planned. / W1; www.macandwild.com; 10.30 pm.

MacellaioRC £53 3 3 3
84 Old Brompton Rd, SW7   020 7589 5834   6–2B NEW
229 Union St, SE1   07467 307 682   10–4B NEW
38-40 Exmouth Market, EC1   020 3696 8220   10–1A NEW
"A must for carnivores!" – These Italian grill-houses, complete with "eccentric" butcher's shop decor, attract adulatory reviews, primarily for their "fantastic range" of "superb" Piedmontese Fassone steaks (although their alternative line in Sardinian bluefin tuna dishes can also be "outstanding"), but also for their "zany" and "charming" service, "excellent, predominantly Italian wines" and "warm and inviting hubbub". And yet… they don't do it for everyone – ratings are undercut by a hardcore band of sceptics who find the whole package a disappointment. The South Kensington original was joined by an Exmouth Market branch in late 2015 (formerly Medcalf's, RIP), and a third branch opens in Southwark's Union Yard arches in autumn 2016. / see web for detail.

Made in Italy £40 **3****2****3**
50 James St, W1 020 7224 0182 3–1A
249 King's Rd, SW3 020 7352 1880 6–3C
141 The Broadway, SW19 020 8540 4330 11–2A
Pizza is sold by the metre at these King's Road, Chelsea and Wimbledon venues, making "a nice change from a regular pizzeria – and the pizzas are superb". "The small space gets very crowded so it's often on the noisy side" – but that's all part of the atmosphere. / www.madeinitalygroup.co.uk; 11 pm, Sun 10 pm; SW3 closed Mon L.

Madhu's UB1 £38 **5****4****3**
39 South Rd 020 8574 1897 1–3A
"Excellent authentic cuisine" and a "bustling fun atmosphere", place this Southall curry legend "on the list of top Asian restaurants in Britain". Over the years it's spawned a major catering empire. / UB1 1SW; www.madhus.co.uk; 11.30 pm; closed Tue, Sat L & Sun L; no bookings.

The Magazine Restaurant,
Serpentine Gallery W2 £58 **2****3****4**
Kensington Gdns 020 7298 7552 7–2D
Zaha Hadid's wonderful "elegant" structure in the centre of Hyde Park elicits surprisingly little feedback despite "surroundings to die for". The lunchtime menu offers 'proper' food (if in a simpler style than when it first opened) but of most interest to reporters is the "tasteful and tasty afternoon tea" (and there are also breakfast and brunch options). / W2 2AR; www.magazine-restaurant.co.uk; @TheMagazineLDN; Tue & Sun 6 pm, Wed-Sat 10.45 pm; closed Mon, Tue D & Sun D.

Magdalen SE1 £54 **3****2****2**
152 Tooley St 020 7403 1342 10–4D
"A welcome beacon over many years" – this "rather formal venue can offer genuine culinary fireworks for its largely business clientele, and really stands out in the poorly served London Bridge area". Its ratings are declining though, with accusations of "increasingly indifferent service", and that it's "going through the motions". / SE1 2TU; www.magdalenrestaurant.co.uk; @Magdalense1; 10 pm; closed Sat L & Sun.

Maggie Jones's W8 £56 **2****2****5**
6 Old Court Pl 020 7937 6462 6–1A
"Eccentric but fun", this enduring "hideaway" near Kensington Palace (named after the pseudonym Princess Margaret used to book under) is "reminiscent of a cluttered farmhouse" and ever-so romantic. "The only thing on the menu which has changed since 1976 are the prices. It's nursery comfort food for maiden aunts (and nothing wrong with that!)" / W8 4PL; www.maggie-jones.co.uk; 11 pm, Sun 10.30 pm.

Maguro W9 £48 **4****4****3**
5 Lanark Pl 020 7289 4353 9–4A
"Spanking-fresh sushi" and other Japanese delicacies draw a loyal following to this "useful hidden local" near Little Venice. Reporters are split between finding it "tiny and friendly" or "cramped, noisy and dark" – but either way, "the food and presentation belie the location". / W9 1BT; www.maguro-restaurant.com; 11 pm, Sun 10.30 pm; no Amex.

Maison Bertaux W1 £16
28 Greek St 020 7437 6007 5–2A
This "unique" Soho treasure opened over 100 years before the current
tea/coffee house craze (est 1871), and "there's nothing else like it". It's
"cramped and not cheap, but serves authentic French pastries and real
tea" – and "the best goodies are still cooked on the premises". / W1D 5DQ;
www.maisonbertaux.com; @Maison_Bertaux; 10.15 pm, Sun 8 pm.

Maison Eric Kayser W1 NEW
8 Baker St no tel 3–1A
This artisan Parisian boulanger opens its first site in London in autumn
2016, with a bakery in Marylebone. Eric Kayser already has a global
empire incorporating Paris, New York, Japan and Hong Kong. / W1H 6AZ;
www.maison-kayser.com/en; @Maison_EK.

Malabar W8 £42 543
27 Uxbridge St 020 7727 8800 7–2B
"A favourite for over 30 years", this Notting Hill Gate Indian manages
to combine longevity with a perennially "fresh and quirky" approach,
"superb ingredients and presentation" and "delicious, high-quality cooking".
"Super-charming, intimate, stylish and lively" – "it just keeps on doing
a great job!" / W8 7TQ; www.malabar-restaurant.co.uk; 11.30 pm.

Malabar Junction WC1 £41 333
107 Gt Russell St 020 7580 5230 2–1C
An attractive "Raj feel and low-stress ambience" help mark out this "good,
long-running South Indian" near the British Museum. "Ignore the
unassuming entrance and cavernous dining room which is like a business
hotel lobby – the food is very tasty and well prepared!" / WC1B 3NA;
www.malabarjunction.com; 11 pm.

Mamie's WC2 NEW
19 Catherine Street 020 7836 7216 5–2D
Covent Garden's new three-floor crêperie opened in summer 2016 with the
added bonus of a cider bar. La Cidrothèque will serve French ciders from
Normandy and Brittany, as well as other brews from Britain and beyond.
/ WC2B 5JS; www.mamies.co.uk; @MAMIESLondon.

Mamma Dough £28 344
76-78 Honor Oak Pk, SE23 020 8699 5196 1–4D
354 Coldharbour Ln, SW9 020 7095 1491 11–1D
This growing South London group (Honor Oak Park, Brixton and Peckham)
serves "interesting but not too wacky" sourdough pizza in a "relaxed,
cheerful atmosphere". Local craft beers and coffee roasted in Shoreditch
complete the picture. / see web for detail.

Mandarin Kitchen W2 £41 411
14-16 Queensway 020 7727 9012 7–2C
"Still the go-to place for lobster noodles" – this busy, crowded Bayswater
operation has long been one of the capital's most notable spots for Chinese
seafood. "Both service and ambience detract from the experience"
however. / W2 3RX; 11.15 pm.

Mangal 1 E8 £28 543
10 Arcola St 020 7275 8981 14–1A
"Exceptional meat from the charcoal and fresh salads" draw fans from
across town to Dalston to this "perfect Turkish grill" – "I go every week"
and it "never fails to impress"! It's also cheap as chips, plus "you can BYO".
/ E8 2DJ; www.mangal1.com; @Mangalone; midnight, Sat & Sun 1 am; cash only.

Mangal 1.1 EC2 NEW   £30
68 Rivington Street   020 7275 8981   13–1B
*It's taken them 25 years, but finally the owners of the mega popular
Dalston ocakbasi have announced a second location, taking over the
former site of Jubo in Shoreditch – too little feedback for a rating as yet.
/ EC2A 3AY; midnight; closed Sun.*

Manicomio   £66   2 2 3
85 Duke of York Sq, SW3   020 7730 3366   6–2D
6 Gutter Ln, EC2   020 7726 5010   10–2B
*The Chelsea branch of this Italian duo is "such a nice spot to sit out on a
sunny day", and EC2 provides "a peaceful escape from the City" –
both are "pleasant", with "unfussy" cooking. / www.manicomio.co.uk;
SW3 10.30 pm, Sun 10 pm; EC2 10 pm; EC2 closed Sat & Sun.*

Manna NW3   £52   3 2 2
4 Erskine Rd   020 7722 8028   9–3B
*The UK's oldest veggie has put in an up-and-down performance for the
history of our guide, but reports do still mostly praise it for its "highly
imaginative vegetarian cooking". / NW3 3AJ; www.mannav.com; @mannacuisine;
10 pm; closed Mon.*

The Manor SW4   £58   4 3 3
148 Clapham Manor St   020 7720 4662   11–2D
*"A food revelation!", say fans of this year-old sibling to nearby Dairy,
who hail "food artistry, with novel and exciting textures and flavours that
explode in the mouth". Even fans can find the place too "clinically
industrial" however, not everyone likes "the tendency to slip offal into
dishes, sometimes unannounced", and sceptics find the overall performance
"interesting, but trying a bit too hard". / SW4 6BS;
www.themanorclapham.co.uk; 10 pm, Sun 4pm.*

Manuka Kitchen SW6   £48   3 2 3
510 Fulham Rd   020 7736 7588   6–4A
*"A limited but interesting and well-prepared menu" wins ongoing praise for
this "lovely" New Zealand-inspired bistro in Fulham, as does its "great gin
bar downstairs". / SW6 5NJ; www.manukakitchen.com; @manukakitchen; 11 pm,
Sun 5 pm.*

Mar I Terra SE1   £31   2 4 2
14 Gambia St   020 7928 7628   10–4A
*This Southwark pub-turned-tapas bar "looks a bit rough but the staff,
food and wine are fantastic", making it "a real favourite". "Perfect for
a pre-theatre meal" if you're heading for the Old or Young Vic, the National
or Shakespeare's Globe. / SE1 0XH; www.mariterra.co.uk; 11 pm; closed
Sat L & Sun.*

Marcus, The Berkeley SW1   £118   3 2 3
Wilton Pl   020 7235 1200   6–1D
*Reports of "stunning" cuisine, and heightened approval for the "elegant",
revamped interior helped restore ratings this year for Marcus Wareing's
famous Knightsbridge flagship. Not all is rosy though – the approach can
still feel "over-formal", service in particular can "fall way short
of expectations", and many of the worst reviews are from long-term fans
who feel by comparison with its glory years, the cooking is "vastly
expensive" and "not worth the bother": "Marcus, you can do better than
this!" / SW1X 7RL; www.marcuswareing.com; @marcuswareing; 10.45 pm; closed
Sun; no jeans; booking max 8 may apply.*

Margot WC2 NEW
45 Great Queen Street   020 3409 4777   5–2D
*Bar Boulud Maitre d' Paulo de Tarso leaves Knightsbridge to open this new
Italian restaurant, in Covent Garden in October 2016 alongside
restaurateur Nicolas Jaouën. / WC2B 5AA; www.margotrestaurant.com;
@MargotLDN.*

Mari Vanna SW1
£71   2 2 **4**
116 Knightsbridge   020 7225 3122   6–1D
*"Certainly the genuine Russian experience" is to be had at this beautifully
decorated Knightsbridge haunt. Unsurprisingly, it's not the greatest value-
wise – "basically simple Russian cooking at top London prices" –
but compensation is to be found in the huge range of vodkas. / SW1X 7PJ;
www.marivanna.co.uk; @marivannalondon; 11.30 pm.*

Marianne W2
£128   **4 3 4**
104 Chepstow Rd   020 3675 7750   7–1B
*"Exceptional in so many ways" – Marianne Lumb's "tiny space for 12"
is "like eating in someone's front room, but with better food", and with the
"small kitchen (a vision of calm efficiency) entirely on view". "It is rare that
a tasting menu is all hits: this is" and "some of her creations are
breathtaking". "Truly welcoming staff" manage the confines of the space
well, and it's an experience many find "romantic". / W2 5QS;
www.mariannerestaurant.com; @Marianne_W2; 11 pm; closed Mon; set weekday L
£95 (FP).*

Market NW1
£51   **3 4** 2
43 Parkway   020 7267 9700   9–3B
*"Always buzzing" – this "great little place" in Camden Town features
"consistently good and interesting food from a subtly changing menu",
prepared with "locally sourced ingredients"; "strongly recommended".
/ NW1 7PN; www.marketrestaurant.co.uk; @MarketCamden; 10.30 pm.*

The Marksman E2
£50   **3** 2 **3**
254 Hackney Rd   020 7739 7393   14–2A
*"The kitchen has a fine pedigree and has garnered excellent reviews" for
this "achingly trendy" year-old, relaunched Hackney pub. Our reporters are
very polarised though: to fans it's "part pub, part gastro, with absolutely
brilliantly fresh, interesting as well as classic combinations, accurately
cooked" – to foes it's "a case study of how the rise of East London can
go really wrong – massively overpriced with bland dishes at stupid prices".
/ E2 7SJ; www.marksmanpub.com; @marksman_pub; midnight, Sun 11 pm.*

Maroush
£54   **3** 2 2
I) 21 Edgware Rd, W2   020 7723 0773   7–1D
II) 38 Beauchamp Pl, SW3   020 7581 5434   6–1C
V) 3-4 Vere St, W1   020 7493 5050   3–1B
VI) 68 Edgware Rd, W2   020 7224 9339   7–1D
'Garden') 1 Connaught St, W2   020 7262 0222   7–1D
*"Some of the best places for Lebanese food and open all hours" – this well-
known chain provides wraps and "exceptional mezze" in its café sections
(part of I and II) and "well-executed" more substantial fare in its
restaurants. "The decor is a bit naff, but it's all part of the charm".
/ www.maroush.com; most branches close between 12.30 am-5 am.*

Martha Ortiz W1 NEW

InterContinental London Park Lane, Park Lane   no tel   3–4A
Martha Ortiz, of Mexico City's acclaimed Dulce Patria, will open her first London venture alongside Theo Randall at The Intercontinental Park Lane. The new dining room, designed by David Collins Studio, will serve the chef's take on Mexican cuisine and is expected to open in early 2017. / W1J 7QY.

Masala Grill SW10   £58   3 4 4

535 King's Rd   020 7351 7788   6–4B
This relaunched Indian near Lot's Road – "with the same layout as Chutney Mary but a new interior" – divides regulars. Fans say "I thought I'd really miss CM, but this is just as good, with aromatic food that's not cheap, but worth it". Others are more cautious: "average food at posh prices – I like it but is it worth the money?" / SW10 0SZ; www.masalagrill.co; @masalagrill_; 10.30 pm.

Masala Zone   £32   3 3 3

"Surprisingly good for a chain" – these "fun" and "fast" street-food Indians provide a "genuine, varied and healthy" pit stop, with "good value thalis" a popular bet. The handy Covent Garden branch is particularly worth remembering. / www.realindianfood.com; 11 pm, Sun 10.30 pm; no Amex; booking: min 10.

MASH Steakhouse W1   £84   2 3 3

77 Brewer St   020 7734 2608   4–3C
Despite its prime location (off Piccadilly Circus), "lovely" gilded interior and "great bar", this huge subterranean steakhouse (next to Brasserie Zédel) has never really made waves and – though it avoids harsh critiques and is well-rated by those who patronise it – attracts few reports. It can't be doing so badly though – its Dutch owners are said to be looking at sites in both the City and Mayfair. / W1F 9ZN; www.mashsteak.co.uk; 11.30 pm, Sun 11 pm; closed Sun L.

Massimo, Corinthia Hotel WC2   £76   2 2 3

10 Northumberland Ave   020 7998 0555   2–3D
Given its splendour, this Italian dining room of a luxury hotel off Trafalgar Square still inspires remarkably little feedback. All reports are positive though, and for a business meal it has evident attractions. / WC2N 5AE; www.massimo-restaurant.co.uk; @massimorest; 10.45 pm; closed Sun.

Masters Super Fish SE1   £25   3 2 2

191 Waterloo Rd   020 7928 6924   10–4A
"Fish and chip heaven – as generations of black cab drivers can attest" ensure that this Waterloo chippie remains "deservedly popular", even as "the bar is being raised across London". "Large portions, first-rate chips". / SE1 8UX; 10.30 pm; closed Sun; no Amex; no booking Fri D.

Matsuba TW9   £46   3 3 2

10 Red Lion St   020 8605 3513   1–4A
"It's not the most scenic location in Richmond", and this small Korean-run, Japanese café "lacks atmosphere". "Excellent sushi and service make up" for any deficiencies, however. / TW9 1RW; www.matsuba-restaurant.com; @matsuba; 10.30 pm; closed Sun.

Matsuri SW1 £85 3 3 1
15 Bury St 020 7839 1101 3–3D
"The teppanyaki hotplate grill with small sushi bar" at this low-key St James's basement "could not be more authentically Japanese". Food and service are generally praised, especially the "fixed-price lunch menu", but a sizeable minority complain that it's "overpriced for what it is". / SW1Y 6AL; www.matsuri-restaurant.com; 10.30 pm, Sun 10 pm.

Max's Sandwich Shop N4 £20 4 3 3
19 Crouch Hill awaiting tel 1–1C
Decidedly not for office workers: Max Halley's Crouch Hill shop sells meal-sized home-baked focaccia stuffed with hot fillings alongside beer, wine and cocktails, evenings and weekends only. "Great sarnies, great booze and great service from Max and co". / N4 4AP; @lunchluncheon; 11 pm, Sun 6 pm.

May The Fifteenth SW4 £55 3 3 3
47 Abbeville Rd 020 8772 1110 11–2D
Formerly Abbeville Kitchen – this "local gem" in Clapham underwent "a makeover following a part change of ownership, but chef and core team remain". The reformat seemingly "has burnished this already solid local bistro – the cooking's as good as ever, and there's a new focus on wine". / SW4 9JX; www.maythe15th.com; 11 pm, Sun 9.30 pm; closed Mon.

Mayfair Pizza Company W1 £47 3 4 3
4 Lancashire Ct 020 7629 2889 3–2B
A "fantastic location" in a "lovely mews" off Bond Street combines with "un-Mayfair prices" to make this pizzeria a "great standby for the area". The staff are notably "cheerful and friendly" (and "their pizza-making course is lots of fun!") / W1S 1EY; www.mayfairpizzaco.com; @mayfairpizzaco; 11 pm.

maze W1 £84 2 2 2
10-13 Grosvenor Sq 020 7107 0000 3–2A
A decade ago, with Jason Atherton running the kitchen, Gordon Ramsay's Mayfair outfit produced some of the most exciting meals in London. Nowadays feedback is much more limited, scores are relatively low across the board, and a significant number of reporters find the level of cooking "unacceptable". / W1K 6JP; www.gordonramsayrestaurants.com; @mazerestaurant; 11 pm.

maze Grill W1 £76 1 2 2
10-13 Grosvenor Sq 020 7495 2211 3–2A
"Wouldn't bother again" is a typical reaction to Gordon Ramsay's "overpriced" Mayfair grill, where even the most positive report says "there's better meat to be had elsewhere". Having once been one of the hottest tickets in town, this is a prime example of 'how have the mighty fallen'... / W1K 6JP; www.gordonramsay.com; @mazegrill; 11 pm; no shorts.

maze Grill SW10 £75 3 3 3
11 Park Wk 020 7255 9299 6–3B
Surprisingly little feedback on Gordon Ramsay's year-old offshoot of his maze brand on the chichi Chelsea sidestreet where he first won renown – such as there is praises its "sophisticated interior and immaculately treated meat with oodles of flavour". / SW10 0AJ; www.gordonramsay.com/mazegrill/park-walk; 11 pm.

Mazi W8 £62 4 4 4
12-14 Hillgate St 020 7229 3794 7–2B
"Wonderful and interesting" versions of Greek classic dishes inspire fans
of this contemporary taverna, off Notting Hill Gate (which – formerly
Costas, long RIP – has been the site of tavernas since the war). "Delightful
garden for summer evenings". / W8 7SR; www.mazi.co.uk; @mazinottinghill;
10.30 pm; closed Mon L & Tue L.

Meat Mission N1 £33 3 3 4
14-15 Hoxton Mkt 020 7739 8212 13–1B
"For juice-up-to-your-elbows eating" this "fun and noisy" Hoxton Square
outpost of the 'Meat' franchise is just the job: melting burgers of course,
plus "superb monkey fingers", "heavenly chilli cheese fries", and "excellent
cocktails". / N1 6HG; www.meatmission.com; @MEATmission; midnight,
Sun 10 pm.

MEATLiquor £38 3 3 4
74 Welbeck St, W1 020 7224 4239 3–1B
133b Upper St, N1 020 3711 0104 9–3D
37 Lordship Lane, SE22 020 3066 0008 1–4D **NEW**
"Delicious, dirty burgers" have won fame and fortune for these "dark and
loud" grunge-fests, but – given the noise, hustle, and hard chairs – "they're
not a place to linger". / meatliquor.com; @MEATLiquor; see web for detail.

MEATmarket WC2 £28 4 2 2
Jubilee Market Hall, 1 Tavistock Ct 020 7836 2139 5–3D
"Sloppy and full of flavour" – the keypoints on the 'dirty' burgers at this
well-known Covent Garden grungefest ("the Dead Hippie is especially
great"). The rum cocktails slip down a treat too. / WC2E 8BD;
www.themeatmarket.co.uk; midnight, Sun 10 pm; no Amex.

MeatUp SW18 **NEW**
350 Old York Road 020 8425 0017 11–2B
The name says it all about this new, summer 2016 opening – a bar/BBQ
in Wandsworth Town serving up steak, burgers and rotisserie chicken
(to name a few) as well as an extensive prosecco list and cocktails.
/ SW18 1SS; www.meatupgrill.com; @meatupuk.

Mediterraneo W11 £62 3 2 3
37 Kensington Park Rd 020 7792 3131 7–1A
"A lively traditional Italian in the heart of Notting Hill" that's been
a linchpin of the area for the last quarter century. / W11 2EU;
www.mediterraneo-restaurant.co.uk; 11.30 pm, Sun 10.30 pm; booking max 10 may
apply.

MEDLAR SW10 £70 4 4 3
438 King's Rd 020 7349 1900 6–3B
"The location's not great" and "signage needs improving", but this
"welcome refuge" near World's End – run by alumni of Chez Bruce –
"exceeds expectations", and has won a huge following. "It's a comfortable,
quiet space" pepped up by "professional" staff who "try extra hard",
and the "masterfully executed" food is "seasonal, understated, big on
flavour", and accompanied by an "outstanding" wine list. That Michelin
took its star away is a screw-up on their part. Top Tip – "incredible value
lunch menu". / SW10 0LJ; www.medlarrestaurant.co.uk; @MedlarChelsea;
10.30 pm, sun 9.30pm; set weekday L £28 (FP), set Sun L £35 (FP), set dinner
£46 (FP).

Megan's Delicatessen SW6 £45 2 3 5
571 Kings Rd 020 7371 7837 6–4A
"Love, love, love the garden" at this *"charming oasis"* on the King's Road –
brunch goes down particularly well, but *"it's a lovely local catering to all
needs"*. (The St John's Wood branch is no more.) / SW6 2EB;
www.megansrestaurant.com; @meganscafe; Mon-Thu 10 pm, Fri & Sat 10.30 pm,
Sun 5 pm; closed Sun D; no Amex.

Melange N8 £50 3 3 3
45 Topsfield Parade, Tottenham Lane 020 8341 1681 1–1C
"Just right for a local restaurant" – *"a lively and cheerful bistro in Crouch
End"* serving an *"interesting mixture of French and Italian dishes, all well-
cooked with helpful service"*. / N8 8PT; www.melangerestaurant.co.uk;
@malange_malange; 11 pm, Sat & Sun midnight.

Mele e Pere W1 £51 3 3 2
46 Brewer St 020 7096 2096 4–3C
"Accomplished Italian cooking" at *"amazing prices"* makes this Soho bar-
trattoria a useful West End hangout. Adding *"fantastic cocktails"*,
an *"interesting wine list"* and even their own vermouths leaves only one
drawback: *"it's so noisy, you end up hoarse after a night out!"* / W1F 9TF;
www.meleepere.co.uk; @meleEpere; 11 pm.

Melody at St Paul's W14 £56 2 3 3
153 Hammersmith Road 020 8846 9119 8–2C
A very grand, Gothic Victorian building creates a slightly *"strange"* but
rather *"lovely"* setting for this newish hotel, by a small park on the
Hammersmith/Olympia borders. The dining room itself is *"calm"* and
serves straightforward fare that's *"well prepared"* and *"well presented"*.
/ W14 0QL; www.themelodyrestaurant.co.uk.

Menier Chocolate Factory SE1 £53 2 2 3
51-53 Southwark St 020 7234 9610 10–4B
The kitchen at this small theatre in a listed Victorian chocolate factory
in Borough *"does its job if you're going to a play"*. But *"you wouldn't go out
of your way to dine here"* (as a standalone attraction, the fare can seem
"boring, and poorly executed"). / SE1 1RU; www.menierchocolatefactory.com;
@MenChocFactory; 11 pm; closed Mon & Sun D.

The Mercer EC2 £62 2 2 2
34 Threadneedle St 020 7628 0001 10–2C
Good-enough *"old and modern British dishes at sensible prices"* help draw
a City crowd to this dining room in a converted Square Mile banking hall.
It's ideal for business: *"they understand that people need to be served,
but not rushed, and then get back to work"*. / EC2R 8AY; www.themercer.co.uk;
@TheMercerLondon; 9.30 pm; closed Sat & Sun.

Merchants Tavern EC2 £62 3 4 4
36 Charlotte Rd 020 7060 5335 13–1B
"Just outside the price bubble of the City", Angela Hartnett's *"large pub"*
with open kitchen is *"not just an afterthought to her flashier
establishments"* – the cooking *"goes from strength to strength"*, service
is *"slick"* and the interior feels *"dark and Shoreditch-y"*. Tasty bar bites too.
/ EC2A 3PG; www.merchantstavern.co.uk; @merchantstavern; 11 pm, Sun 9 pm.

Le Mercury N1 £33 2 2 4
154-155 Upper St 020 7354 4088 9–2D
This "very cute", ancient Islington bistro has "classic" status 1) for its
"efficient and consistent" provision of "good cheap French food" for as long
as anyone can remember ("better than expected" at the price); and 2) the
"Parisian-style, romantic candlelit atmosphere – perfect for a date".
/ N1 1QY; www.lemercury.co.uk; midnight, Sun 11 pm; Mon-Thu D only, Fri-Sun open
L & D.

Mere W1 NEW
74 Charlotte St no tel 2–1B
Long-time right hand woman of Michel Roux Jr and 'MasterChef: The
Professionals' judge, Monica Galetti, has revealed plans for her first solo
venture. Incorporating a small ground-floor bar and basement restaurant,
it's set to open in January 2017. / W1.

Meson don Felipe SE1 £39 2 3 4
53 The Cut 020 7928 3237 10–4A
"Olé! Why go to Spain?!" – This "plainly decorated" Hispanic veteran
"just down from the Old Vic" has a "great buzz" fuelled by its "very good
wine list" and sherry selection. The tapas selection is is "all the usual stuff
you expect" ("simpler items are often best"), but "for a snack and a good
glass of vino" this is a "top place near the South Bank". / SE1 8LF;
www.mesondonfelipe.com; 11 pm; closed Sun; no Amex; no booking after 8 pm.

Mews of Mayfair W1 £68 3 3 3
10 Lancashire Ct, New Bond St 020 7518 9388 3–2B
This clubbable bistro and cocktail bar (owned by Roger Moore's son) in a
super-cute yard off Bond Street knows how to keep Mayfair punters happy,
with its "impressive set lunch offer" and "pleasant, busy and casual" vibe.
/ W1S 1EY; www.mewsofmayfair.com; @mewsofmayfair; 10.45 pm; closed Sun D;
SRA-3 star.

Meza £30 4 4 3
34 Trinity Rd, SW17 0772 211 1299 11–2C
70 Mitcham Rd, SW17 020 8672 2131 11–2C
"Absolutely wonderful Lebanese/Middle Eastern dishes" – "a never-
changing menu" of "very fresh bright tastes" – means this pair of "tiny"
and "utilitarian" Tooting cafés tend to be "heaving"; "genuinely hospitable"
and "prompt" service too. / www.mezarestaurant.co.uk; @MezaRestaurants; see
web for detail.

Michael Nadra £58 4 4 2
6-8 Elliott Rd, W4 020 8742 0766 8–2A
42 Gloucester Ave, NW1 020 7722 2800 9–2C
"Top notch" modern French cuisine that "outperforms many more famous
names" maintains high satisfaction with Michael Nadra's duo of local
restaurants, in Chiswick (the better known original) and Camden Town
("juxtapositioned between Regents Park and Camden Town just near the
canal"), even if both venues share in different ways a somewhat "difficult
layout". Top Menu Tip – "always good fish" is the highlight with
"an interesting twist on old favourite dishes".
/ www.restaurant-michaelnadra.co.uk; @michaelnadra; W4 10 pm, Fri-Sat 10.30 pm,
NW1 10.30 pm, Sun 9 pm; NW1 closed Mon, W4 closed Sun.

Mien Tay £31 4 2 2
180 Lavender Hill, SW11   020 7350 0721   11–1C
122 Kingsland Rd, E2   020 7729 3074   13–1B
*"The goat and galangal is one of the tastiest Asian dishes in London",
at these busy Vietnamese joints in Battersea, Fulham and Shoreditch;
they're "fantastically consistent" as well as "extremely good value". / 11 pm,
Fri & Sat 11.30 pm, Sun 10.30 pm; cash only.*

Mildreds W1 £43 3 3 3
45 Lexington St   020 7494 1634   4–2C
*"Brilliant – and I don't even like veggie food!" is a typically ringing
endorsement for this Soho institution that is many people's favourite for
meat-free scoffing. "Shame about the wait times, as they don't take
bookings". / W1F 9AN; www.mildreds.co.uk; @mildredslondon; 10.45 pm; closed
Sun; no Amex; no bookings.*

Milk SW12 £14 4 3 3
20 Bedford Hill   020 8772 9085   11–2C
*"Hands-down the best breakfast in SW London" ("you need to get there
early because this is no secret") is to be found at this kickass Antipodean
joint in Balham, which (recently expanding) now has "an alcohol license
and plans for evening openings". "Amazing flat whites" and other coffee
too, but "avoid the yummy mummy post-school-drop-off rush". Top Menu
Tip – the Convict and Young Betty. / SW12 9RG; www.milk.london.*

Min Jiang, The Royal Garden Hotel W8 £77 4 3 5
2-24 Kensington High St   020 7361 1988   6–1A
*"Sensational views" set the scene at this "very plush" 8th-floor dining room,
bordering Kensington Gardens, which – with its "fantastically fragrant and
subtle" Chinese cuisine – offers one of the capital's best all-round
experiences. Top Menu Tip – "the absolutely delicious, wood-fired Beijing
duck is a must!" / W8 4PT; www.minjiang.co.uk; @minjianglondon; 10 pm.*

Mint Leaf £65 3 3 4
Suffolk Pl, Haymarket, SW1   020 7930 9020   2–2C
Angel Ct, Lothbury, EC2   020 7600 0992   10–2C
*"Delicious pimped-up Indian food" is served in a "cool and slick", "night-
club-vibe" setting at this conveniently sited duo, with locations just off
Trafalgar Square and Bank: "not cheap but value for money".
/ www.mintleafrestaurant.com; SW1 11 pm, Sun 10.30 pm – EC2 10.30 pm;
SW1 closed Sat & Sun L, EC2 closed Sat & Sun.*

Mirch Masala SW17 £26 5 2 1
213 Upper Tooting Rd   020 8767 8638   11–2D
*This "no-frills (and no licence)" Pakistani canteen in Tooting offers
"fantastic flavours at amazing prices". The food is "excellent, spicy and
authentic", with the "weekend slow-cooked meat specials especially good".
Service is fast, but it "can be noisy and crowded". / SW17 7TG;
www.mirchmasalarestaurant.co.uk; midnight; cash only.*

Mister Lasagna W1 NEW £37
53 Rupert Street   020 7734 0064   4–2D
*A summer 2016 Soho opening serving nothing but lasagne (in no less than
21 different varieties). It's open all day, offering pastries and coffee in the
mornings, communal seating and takeaway, plus Italian liqueurs in the
evening. / W1D 7PG; www.misterlasagna.co.uk; @misterlasagna; 11 pm, Fri & Sat
midnight, Sun 10.30 pm; no bookings.*

MNKY HSE W1 NEW
10 Dover Street   020 3870 4880   3–3C
On the former site of Mayfair's long-departed Dover Street Wine Bar (RIP), this late-night dining and drinking venue is set to open in October 2016. The PR info tells us to expect 'contemporary Latin American food and drink, alongside live music and DJ performances'. No advice yet about how to pronounce the name... / W1S 4LQ; www.mnky-hse.com; @mnky_hse.

The Modern Pantry   £59   222
47-48 St Johns Sq, EC1   020 7553 9210   10–1A
14 Finsbury Sq, EC2   020 3696 6565   13–2A
For "an innovative brunch", many tip Aussie chef, Anna Hansen's "chilled" ("somewhat stark") ventures, in Clerkenwell, and now also in Finsbury Square too. For other meal times, fans extol her "great spin on traditional ideas" generally, but ratings are dragged down by critics of "needlessly complex" fusion "for its own sake", and "poor ambience at the new Moorgate branch". / www.themodernpantry.co.uk, see web for detail.

MOMMI SW4   £46   233
44 Clapham High St   020 3814 1818   11–2D
"Buzzy Japanese/Peruvian fusion" yearling that splits opinion – to fans it's a "great addition to Clapham High Street" with "plenty of choice", but critics find it "expensive" and "disappointingly formulaic". / SW4 7UR; www.wearemommi.com; @wearemommi; 11 pm ; closed weekday L; cancellation charge for larger bookings.

Momo W1   £69   334
25 Heddon St   020 7434 4040   4–3B
Mourad Mamouz's "noisy" souk-style party-Moroccan, off Regent Street maintains its dark, "romantic" allure (particularly if you kick off with a drink in the superb basement bar). Although the Moroccan cuisine is arguably incidental, it's not bad. / W1B 4BH; www.momoresto.com; @momoresto; 11.30 pm, Sun 11 pm; credit card deposit required to book; set weekday L £40 (FP).

Mon Plaisir WC2   £59   244
19-21 Monmouth St   020 7836 7243   5–2B
"A firm favourite for over 20 years!" This "old-fashioned", Covent Garden 70-year-old – much-expanded over the decades – is supremely "idiosyncratic, with lots of quaint, little hidey-holes". Its "traditional Gallic staples" are "not the best in town, but you know you'll be well fed without spending crazy prices", especially if you go for the super-popular pre-theatre and lunch deals. / WC2H 9DD; www.monplaisir.co.uk; @MonPlaisir4; 11 pm; closed Sun.

Mona Lisa SW10   £30   332
417 King's Rd   020 7376 5447   6–3B
"Builders for breakfast, out-of-work creatives for lunch and cheap-date couples for dinner" – that's just part of the line-up at this veteran Italian greasy spoon, near World's End, whose bargain evening 3-course deal for £10 has long epitomised its "cheap 'n' cheerful" charms. / SW10 0LR; monalisarestaurant.co.uk/new-page.html; 11 pm, Sun 5.30 pm; closed Sun D; no Amex; set weekday L £16 (FP), set dinner £17 (FP).

Monmouth Coffee Company £6 5 5 4
27 Monmouth St, WC2   020 7232 3010   5–2B
2 Park St, SE1   020 7232 3010   10–4C
"The queues can be ridiculous" for these "shrines to coffee" but "the sheer quality of their beans makes it a first choice" and "service is five-star even when they are manically busy" (i.e. mostly). The famous Borough Market shop suffers "an annoying number of hipsters outside" but otherwise "makes a wonderful place to watch the world go by", and enjoy "delicious bread and jam" too. All branches serve "a few yummy pastries".
/ www.monmouthcoffee.co.uk; 6 pm-6.30 pm, SE16 midnight; closed Sun; SE16 open Sat only; no Amex; no booking.

Morada Brindisa Asador W1 £48 2 2 2
18-20 Rupert St   020 7478 8758   5–3A
A "surprise find up a side street" off Shaftesbury Avenue, this ambitious Spanish yearling from the Brindisa group showcases Castilian-style asador wood-fire roasts. Fans hail both "style and substance", but there are complaints of "incompetent" staff and "high prices". / W1D 6DE; www.brindisatapaskitchens.com/morada; @Brindisa.

The Morgan Arms E3 £50 4 3 3
43 Morgan St   020 8980 6389   14–2C
"Fab Sunday roast" is typical of the "very good food" at this "pleasant (if loud)" Mile End gastropub. / E3 5AA; www.morganarmsbow.com; @TheMorganArms; 10 pm.

Morito £37 4 4 4
195 Hackney Road, E2   020 7613 0754   14–2A **NEW**
32 Exmouth Mkt, EC1   020 7278 7007   10–1A
"Constantly astounding food, despite always being frenetically busy" means this Spanish/North African tapas spot in Exmouth Market is "just as good as big sister Moro next door" – some even "prefer it". Good ratings too for its new Hoxton sibling, just a stone's throw from Columbia Road Flower Market. / see web for detail.

MORO EC1 £58 5 4 3
34-36 Exmouth Mkt   020 7833 8336   10–1A
"Gosh, it's impressive when a restaurant can stay on form in this way!" – Samuel and Samantha Clark's Exmouth Market favourite holds "many special memories" for legions of reporters. The "beautifully judged" Moorish/Iberian dishes deliver "wonderful flavours" as does the "unique selection of Iberian wines and superlative range of sherries". There is a 'but' however – ratings did ease off a smidgeon this year, with incidents of "chaotic" service and the remorseless noise-levels of this deafening, hard-edged room denting the "happy vibe". / EC1R 4QE; www.moro.co.uk; 10.30 pm; closed Sun D.

Motcombs SW1 £57 2 3 3
26 Motcomb St   020 7235 6382   6–1D
"If you want a discreet conversation", this stalwart wine bar (upstairs) and restaurant (downstairs) is something of a Belgravia "old favourite", with cooking that's "always dependable, if not exceptional". / SW1X 8JU; www.motcombs.co.uk; @Motcombs; 10 pm; closed Sun.

Mr Bao SE15 NEW £34 322
293 Rye Ln 020 7635 0325 1–4D
"A real, new gem in the crown of Peckham's up-and-coming food scene!" –
this "local Taiwanese café" may be "packed in" and "hectic", but it's also
"friendly", "fun" and "affordable". "I'm not sure how authentic the food
is but it's delicious!" (lots of "interesting", "snack-sized bites"). / SE15 4UA;
www.mrbao.co.uk; @MrBaoUK; 11 pm; closed Mon; no bookings.

Mr Chow SW1 £87 222
151 Knightsbridge 020 7589 7347 6–1D
A Knightsbridge institution since 1968, its upscale Beijing cuisine still
attracts diners; complaints too however as usual that it's "massively
overpriced for what's essentially average Chinese food". / SW1X 7PA;
www.mrchow.com; @mrchow; midnight; closed Mon L.

Murakami WC2 £45 333
63-66 St Martin's Ln 020 3417 6966 5–3B
Feedback remains limited on this large, glossy Japanese canteen in Covent
Garden (owned by a Ukranian restaurant group) – results from its wide
robata-to-sushi menu are decently rated, however. / WC2N 4JS;
www.murakami-london.co.uk; @hello_murakami; 10.30 pm.

Murano W1 £99 443
20-22 Queen St 020 7495 1127 3–3B
"Not a restaurant for those who want fireworks… just very good!" Angela
Hartnett's "smooth-running" Mayfair haven is low-key stylewise, but it's
a "comfortable" place "exuding warmth", thanks to its "first-class" yet
"unpompous" staff. Chef Pip Lacey has upped the ante, when it comes
to the Italianate food – "superb" – and the flexible "build your own menu"
approach is a "simple yet brilliant idea". / W1J 5PP; www.muranolondon.com;
@muranolondon; 11 pm; closed Sun.

Mustard W6 NEW £44 354
98-100 Shepherd's Bush Rd 020 3019 1175 8–1C
"A great neighbourhood newcomer" – from the same owners as Covent
Garden's famous Joe Allen – on a nondescript highway north of Brook
Green. It's everything the Café Rouge it replaced was not, with affordable
British fare, unusually professional service and a swish refit. / W6 7PD;
www.mustardrestaurants.co.uk; @mustarddining; 11 pm, Sun 10 pm.

Namaaste Kitchen NW1 £44 342
64 Parkway 020 7485 5977 9–3B
Advocates of this Camden Town cuzza hail it as a "completely unexpected
delight" and would even rate it as "north London's best Indian". But this
culinary ambition also prompts detractors: "not bad, but it tries to be
a fine-dining restaurant with fine dining prices when it isn't one".
/ NW1 7AH; www.namaastekitchen.co.uk; 11 pm.

Nanban SW9 NEW £43 432
Coldharbour Ln 020 7346 0098 11–2D
"Terrific Brixton fusion place from former MasterChef winner Tim
Anderson", whose "Japanese soul food" ("blending flavours from Japan
with more local staples") wins "extra points for originality" – "so unlikely
this: spectacularly good Japanese carbonara of spaghetti!" "I was sceptical,
but what a bangin' place!" / SW9; www.nanban.co.uk; @NanbanLondon; 11 pm,
Sun 10 pm.

The Narrow E14 £56
44 Narrow St 020 7592 7950 12–1B
Gordon Ramsay's potentially wonderful waterfront Limehouse pub has never found its mojo, but it avoided the usual drubbing from diners this year and achieved OK ratings, despite still sometimes seeming "expensive" and "disappointing". / E14 8DP; www.gordonramsay.com; @thenarrow; 10.30 pm, Sun 8 pm.

Native WC2 NEW £44
3 Neal's Yd 020 3638 8214 5–2C
"A hard working couple who care" ("the really welcoming feel from the owner made the meal") are carving a good reputation for this sweet, foraging-focused Covent Garden newcomer ("very small upstairs, larger downstairs" in the "very pleasant basement"). Even cynics who say "it doesn't really need its silly 'local food' gimmick" say "the food varies between good and excellent". / WC2H 9DP; www.eatnative.co.uk; @eatnativeuk; 10 pm; closed Mon L.

Naughty Piglets SW2 £54
28 Brixton Water Ln 020 7274 7796 11–2D
"You can watch the food being cooked by the husband and served by the wife" at Margaux Aubry and Joe Sharratt's "very laid back" yearling – "another fantastic addition to the Brixton scene" – which delivers "exceptional bistro food" and "awesome service"; "interesting natural wine list" too (La Patronne used to work at Terroirs). / SW2 1PE; www.naughtypiglets.co.uk; 10 pm, Sun 3 pm.

Nautilus NW6 £41
27-29 Fortune Green Rd 020 7435 2532 1–1B
"Still the best fish 'n' chips in North London", this "exceptional" West Hampstead chippy has been known for decades for "excellent, very fresh fish which is coated in matzo meal and then fried". Interior decor – 'nul points!' / NW6 1DU; 10 pm; closed Sun; no Amex.

Needoo E1 £28
87 New Rd 020 7247 0648 13–2D
"Grilled meats to die for" – not least "top lamb chops, no question" – inspire rave reviews for this East End Pakistani, which fans find "preferable to the over-hyped Tayyab's" (its much better-known near-neighbour); the ambience? – it's "dire". / E1 1HH; www.needoogrill.co.uk; @NeedooGrill; 11.30 pm.

New Mayflower W1 £42
68-70 Shaftesbury Ave 020 7734 9207 5–3A
"The food, especially the seafood, is good as usual" at this long-established Cantonese stalwart on the fringe of Chinatown – particularly worth discovering if you want some proper food in the wee hours. / W1D 6LY; www.newmayflowerlondon.com; 4 am; D only; no Amex; set dinner £25 (FP).

New World W1 £38
1 Gerrard Place 020 7734 0677 5–3A
Still a favourite for some reporters – this massive Chinatown fixture is one of the very few still to serve dim sum from circulating trolleys ("but only on weekends"). / W1D 5PA; www.newworldlondon.com; 10.30 pm; set dinner £20 (FP).

The Newman Arms W1 £46

23 Rathbone Street 020 3643 6285 5–1A

"Part of the Cornwall Project sourcing fresh ingredients from small producers (in Cornwall, obviously)" – Matt Chatfield's "quaint" Fitzrovia boozer inspires enthusiastic feedback on its "fantastically flavoursome and earthy dishes", "charming service and intimate style". / W1T 1NG; www.newmanarmspub.com; @NewmanArmsPub; 10 pm, Sun 6 pm; closed Sat.

The Ninth W1 NEW £62

22 Charlotte St 020 3019 0880 2–1C

Jun Tanaka's Fitzrovia newcomer wins praise both for his "exceptional" cooking and some "exceedingly pleasant service". Some reporters gripe that "decor is lacking" though, or feel that "tables are too small for the sharing plates format". / W1T 2NB; www.theninthlondon.com; @theninthlondon; 10.30 pm; closed Sun.

Nirvana Kitchen W1 NEW £66

61 Upper Berkeley Street 020 7958 3222 2–2A

A summer 2016 Indian newcomer adjoining a hotel north of Marble Arch, with a glossy interior and a menu of some ambition. / W1H 7PP; www.nirvana.restaurant; @KitchensNirvana; 10.45 pm; closed Sun.

Nissi N13 £40

62 Aldermans Hill 020 8882 3170 1–1C

"The ambience is modern, open and family friendly" at this refreshing Greek/Cypriot venture in Palmers Green serving "superior, fresh Greek mezze, cooked in a contemporary style". / N13; www.nissirestaurant.co.uk; @NissiRestaurant; 10.30 pm, Fri & Sat 11.30 pm, Sun 9 pm; closed Mon.

No 197 Chiswick Fire Station W4 NEW £50

199 Chiswick High Road 020 3857 4669 8–2A

"Extremely buzzy and atmospheric", neighbourhood bar from chain Darwin & Wallace (in the white-walled and airy setting of a converted old fire station) that's "a great addition to the Chiswick scene" – much of the appeal is the cocktails and craft beers, but early reports say the Antipodean-influenced scoff can also be "surprisingly good". / W4 2DR; www.no197chiswickfirestation.com; @No197Chiswick; midnight, Fri & Sat 1 am, Sun 11 pm; booking max 9 may apply.

Noble Rot WC1 NEW £58

51 Lamb's Conduit St 020 7242 8963 2–1D

"Paradise for wine lovers"; Mark Andrew and Daniel Keeling's Bloomsbury newcomer (they also run the cult wine mag' of the same name) offers the "unbeatably interesting" list you might hope for "with lots of intriguing vintages" (including "many mature wines") from in-the-know vineyards, "served in a wide variety by the glass in sizes as low as 75ml". Its location is the "lovely" old-school '70s wine bar premises that were formerly VATs (RIP), which provide "the perfect place to come and find your new favourite tipple". On most accounts, the "uncomplicated" cooking – with input from afar by acclaimed Sportsman chef, Stephen Harris – is "uncommonly good" too, but ratings are undercut by a minority who say it's "not as good as claimed in the newspaper reviews". / WC1N 3NB; www.noblerot.co.uk; @noblerotbar; 9.30 pm; closed Sun.

Nobu, Metropolitan Hotel W1 £99

19 Old Park Ln   020 7447 4747   3–4A

"The black cod is legendary" at this once path-breaking Japanese-fusion icon overlooking Park Lane, and for some long-term fans *"it can never be beaten"*. That this erstwhile paparazzi favourite is *"horrendously overpriced"* and has *"mediocre service"* has always gone with the territory, but its culinary performance seems ever-more *"tired"*. / W1K 1LB; www.noburestaurants.com; @NobuOldParkLane; 10.15 pm, Fri & Sat 11 pm, Sun 10 pm.

Nobu Berkeley W1 £99

15 Berkeley St   020 7290 9222   3–3C

"Amazingly delicate" Japanese/South American fusion fare *"made with precision"* and *"packed with flavour"* ensures Mayfair's second branch of this global franchise is *"always popular and sometimes very busy"*. But numerous sceptics feel it *"trades on its reputation and celebrity status"* – *"despite the work that goes into the food, and the fancy schmancy location, prices are insane"*, especially as *"the dining room is quite rowdy, and service perfunctory"*. / W1J 8DY; www.noburestaurants.com; 11 pm, Thu-Sat midnight, Sun 9.45 pm; closed Sun L.

Noor Jahan £40

2a Bina Gdns, SW5   020 7373 6522   6–2B
26 Sussex Pl, W2   020 7402 2332   7–1D

"A consistent pleasure for over 20 years!" – this *"old-fashioned Indian"* in Earl's Court is *"a bit crowded and expensive but reliably good"* and *"always attracts a well-heeled clientele"* for whom it's a big old-favourite. (*"Dependable"* but much lesser known Bayswater spin-off too). / 11.30 pm, Sun 10 pm.

Nopi W1 £71

21-22 Warwick St   020 7494 9584   4–3B

"Creativity, enticing variety, vitality, sensuality and style" are combined in Yotam Ottolenghi's *"very thoughtful and alternative"* cuisine, and many reporters seem to leave his *"guilt-free"* Middle Eastern-inspired spot off Regent Street *"feeling more healthy than when they arrived"*. Even some who rate it highly, though, say *"it's not for me, given the dieter-sized portions at big prices"*. / W1B 5NE; www.nopi-restaurant.com; @ottolenghi; 10.30 pm, Sun 4 pm; closed Sun D; set pre-theatre £37 (FP), set dinner £47 (FP), set always available £54 (FP).

Nordic Bakery £15

14a Golden Sq, W1   020 3230 1077   4–3C
37b New Cavendish St, W1   020 7935 3590   2–1A
48 Dorset St, W1   020 7487 5877   2–1A

"The best coffee and cinnamon buns" make this Scandi trio in Soho and Marylebone go-to destinations for *"Nordic sweet treats"*; *"good for people-watching, too"*. / Golden Square 8 pm, Sat 7 pm, Sun 7 pm, Cavendish Street & Dorset Street 6 pm.

The Norfolk Arms WC1 £44

28 Leigh St   020 7388 3937   9–4C

This *"convivial"*, *"efficient and reasonably priced"* King's Cross gastropub doubles as a tapas bar – *"all with a twist and generally very high quality"* – a combination that results in a *"lovely neighbourhood bar/restaurant"*. / WC1H 9EP; www.norfolkarms.co.uk; 11pm, Sun 10.30 pm; no Amex.

North China W3   £42   3 3 3
305 Uxbridge Rd   020 8992 9183   8–1A
"Consistently good and welcoming" family-run Chinese, which remains one of Acton's few contributions to London gastronomy. / W3 9QU; www.northchina.co.uk; 11 pm, Fri & Sat 11.30 pm.

North Sea Fish WC1   £38   3 3 2
7-8 Leigh St   020 7387 5892   9–4C
"Excellent fish, and particularly good chips" are the hallmarks of this "grand little chippie" in Bloomsbury ("with old-fashioned home-made puds if you have the stamina"). Once "so dated it was almost charming", regulars are now split over whether the recent refurb has "smartened it up" or "lost some of its former character". / WC1H 9EW; www.northseafishrestaurant.co.uk; 10.30 pm; closed Sun; no Amex.

The Northall, Corinthia Hotel WC2   £85   3 3 4
10a Northumberland Ave   020 7321 3100   2–3C
This "beautifully appointed venue oozes class and luxury" and not only is its "great location near Whitehall ideal for working lunches and client dinners" but is "big enough to maintain a peaceful, relaxed atmosphere, however much business is being conducted". The cooking? – it has "a fair amount of flair". / WC2N 5AE; www.thenorthall.co.uk; @CorinthiaLondon; 10.45 pm; set pre theatre £55 (FP).

Northbank EC4   £58   2 2 3
Millennium Bridge   020 7329 9299   10–3B
Views across the river of Tate Modern and the Shard take precedence at this bar-restaurant beside the Wobbly Bridge. But marks are wobbling across the board here – perhaps, as one critic suggests, "they need more staff". / EC4V 3QH; www.northbankrestaurant.co.uk; @NorthbankLondon; 11 pm; closed Sun; set weekday L £38 (FP).

Novikov (Asian restaurant) W1   £94   2 1 2
50a Berkeley St   020 7399 4330   3–3C
"It's flash, gaudy, and the crowd is very Mayfair", but "if you overlook the nightclub style" of this Russian-owned scene near Berkeley Square, "the pan-Asian food is actually exceptional – the best ingredients prepared very well… just at cripplingly expensive prices". / W1J 8HA; www.novikovrestaurant.co.uk; 11.15 pm; set weekday L £43 (FP).

Novikov (Italian restaurant) W1   £106   1 1 2
50a Berkeley St   020 7399 4330   3–3C
The "peaceful-at-lunch, steadily-louder-in-the-evening" Italian chamber of this Russian-owned Mayfair glam-palace is an attractive space. The food though is "nothing special, however the insane prices: OMG!! How do they get away with it? And it's rammed! I just don't get it…" / W1J 8HA; www.novikovrestaurant.co.uk; 11.15 pm, Sun 10 pm.

Numero Uno SW11   £54   3 3 3
139 Northcote Rd   020 7978 5837   11–2C
"Always lovely food" with "friendly service" form the recipe for a "great local" Italian on the borders of Battersea's Nappy Valley. "Not much changes: I could choose from the menu with a blindfold on, but that is the charm of this buzzy but not raucous place". / SW11 6PX; 11.30 pm; no Amex.

Nuovi Sapori SW6 £48 3 4 2
295 New King's Rd 020 7736 3363 11–1B
"Ultra-friendly" local near Parsons Green, which serves "consistently good" dishes. "Staff used to keep an eye on our sleeping baby when he was in his carry-cot – now they feed him proper Italian food (no nuggets or chips) and treat him like a valued guest!" / SW6 4RE; www.nuovisaporilondon.co.uk; 11 pm; closed Sun.

Oak £50 4 3 4
243 Goldhawk Rd, W12 020 8741 7700 8–1B
137 Westbourne Park Rd, W2 020 7221 3355 7–1B
"Perfect crispy-based pizza" – "so light that normal pizza-associated guilt is forgotten" – as usual wins high praise for this pub-conversion duo. The newish Shepherd's Bush branch is "very comfy, with a large bar", while the very "buzzy" original is a Notting Hill classic for "a fun night out". / W12 Mon-Sat 10.30 pm, Sun 9.30 pm – W2 Mon-Thu 10.30 pm, Fri-Sat 11pm, Sun 10 pm.

Obicà £52 3 3 2
11 Charlotte St, W1 020 7637 7153 2–1C
19-20 Poland St, W1 020 3327 7070 4–1C
96 Draycott Ave, SW3 020 7581 5208 6–2C
1 West Wintergarden, 35 Bank St, E14 awaiting Tel 12–1C **NEW**
4 Limeburners Lane, EC4 020 3327 0984 10–2A **NEW**
Once called Obika, these 'Mozzarella bars' – part of an international chain – are "much better than many in the pizza and pasta market", and are tipped for "grabbing a glass of wine with enjoyable small bites". / www.obica.com; 10 pm-11 pm; E14 Closed Sun.

Oblix SE1 £88 2 1 5
Level 32, The Shard, 31 St Thomas Street 020 7268 6700 10–4C
"The location has definite 'wow' factor" at this 32nd-floor dining lounge in the Shard – "unbeatable for romance at night time (if you can get a window table for the views)". "Rude service" is a hazard however, as is "average" food, all "at prices to match the altitude". / SE1 9RY; www.oblixrestaurant.com; @OblixRestaurant; 11 pm.

Odette's NW1 £63 4 4 4
130 Regent's Park Rd 020 7586 8569 9–3B
Bryn Williams "seems to be on top of his game" currently at his "intimate" north London old favourite in Primrose Hill, with even stronger ratings this year for his "clever" and "beautifully presented" cuisine (particularly the "astonishing tasting menu") and "exemplary" service. / NW1 8XL; www.odettesprimrosehill.com; @Odettes_rest; 10 pm, Sat 10.30 pm, Sun 9.30 pm; closed Mon & Tue L; no Amex; set weekday L £36 (FP), set Sun L £42 (FP).

Ognisko Restaurant SW7 £52 3 4 4
55 Prince's Gate, Exhibition Rd 020 7589 0101 6–1C
"The really lovely, ornate interior" – "with period features, candles and tasteful decoration" – underpins the "romantic" appeal of this quirky émigrés club dining room, near the Science Museum. Since Jan Woroniecki took it over, its "hearty" Polish fare has become more varied, and there's "a massive range of vodkas". Top Tip – at the rear there's "a wonderful, tented outside terrace". / SW7 2PN; www.ogniskorestaurant.co.uk; @OgniskoRest; 11 pm; no trainers.

Oka £47 **4** **3** **2**

Kingly Court, I Kingly Court, WI 020 7734 3556 4–2B
71 Regents Park Rd, NWI 020 7483 2072 9–3B
"Amazing, inventive sushi" and "Asian-fusion cooking" at "great value"
prices ensure that the three small venues in this group – in Primrose Hill,
Soho's Kingly Court and Chelsea – are "always packed". / see web for detail.

Oklava EC2 NEW £56 **4** **4** **3**

74 Luke St 020 7729 3032 13–1B
"An excellent Turkish newcomer with a modern twist" – Selin Kiazim's
"ambitious flavour combinations" ("innovative" kebabs, flatbreads and
mezze) inspire good vibes for this tile-and-brick Shoreditch venture with
open kitchen, as does its "welcoming" attitude. / EC2A 4PY; www.oklava.co.uk;
@oklava_ldn; 10.30 pm, Sun 4 pm; closed Mon & Sun D.

Oldroyd N I £42 **4** **3** **2**

344 Upper Street 020 8617 9010 9–3D
"A really exciting addition to Upper Street in terms of innovative cooking" –
Tom Oldroyd's "tiny kitchen" creates "wonderful" tapas-style dishes. Shame
his Islington yearling is way "too cramped" though – "it detracts from
a meal". / N1 0PD; www.oldroydlondon.com; @oldroydlondon; Mon-Thu 10.30 pm,
Fri 11 pm, Sun 9 pm; set weekday L £18 (FP).

Oliver Maki W I NEW £69

33 Dean St 020 7734 0408 5–2A
The first London outpost of a flash Middle Eastern-owned sushi group
(with branches in Kuwait and Bahrain) comes to Soho, in these two-floor
premises, with former Nobu Las Vegas head chef Louis Kenji Huang
heading up the kitchen. It's induced little feedback so far, however.
/ W1D 4PP; www.olivermaki.co.uk; @OliverMakiUK; 10.30 pm, Fri & Sat 11 pm,
Sun 9.30 pm.

Oliveto SW I £63 **3** **2** **1**

49 Elizabeth St 020 7730 0074 2–4A
"Always rammed", this Sardinian pizza and pasta specialist is "predictably
good". "On weekends, it seems like all of Belgravia descends,
with screaming children a-plenty" – "sometimes it's hard to tell if it's over-
noisy, or jumping with energy". / SW1W 9PP; www.olivorestaurants.com;
10.30 pm, Sun 10 pm; booking max 7 may apply.

Olivo SW I £65 **3** **3** **2**

21 Eccleston St 020 7730 2505 2–4B
This squished Belgravia Sardinian has a "fabulous menu" and its very
competent cooking is very consistently highly rated; it's perennially pricey
though – even fans can feel costs are "pushed up to unaffordable levels for
what is in essence a neighbourhood restaurant". / SW1 9LX;
www.olivorestaurants.com; 10.30 pm; closed Sat L & Sun L

Olivocarne SW I £61 **3** **3** **2**

61 Elizabeth St 020 7730 7997 2–4A
"Traditional cooking with a sophisticated touch", along with
"the neatest of wine lists" are big draws to this slightly "oddly configured"
and "very crowded" Belgravia Sardinian (stablemate to Olivo, Oliveto etc.).
/ SW1W 9PP; www.olivorestaurants.com; 11 pm, Sun 10.30 pm.

Olivomare SW1   £61   4 3 2
10 Lower Belgrave St   020 7730 9022   2–4B
*"Low-key sophistication" is the hallmark of the "sensationally good"
Sardinian seafood cooking of Mauro Sanna's well-established Belgravian.
The "odd decor" ("Alice in Wonderland with an austere look") is thought
"very cool" by its fans, but the consensus is that it's "soulless". / SW1W 0LJ;
www.olivorestaurants.com; 11 pm, Sun 10.30 pm; booking max 10 may apply.*

Olympic, Olympic Studios SW13   £52   2 2 4
117-123 Church Rd   020 8912 5161   11–1A
*"Fast becoming an SW13 institution", the all-day café/brasserie at the
independent Olympic Studios cinema in Barnes (formerly a recording
studio) is a very agreeably "buzzy" venue. "Service can be slow" and the
food's a tad complacent, but they do a "really good breakfast/brunch".
/ SW13 9HL; www.olympiccinema.co.uk; @Olympic_Cinema; 11 pm, Sun 10 pm.*

Olympus Fish N3   £35   4 5 2
140-144 Ballards Ln   020 8371 8666   1–1B
*"Amazing charcoal-grilled fish", in addition to the more conventional deep-
fried version, "is always succulent and never greasy" at this popular
Finchley fixture, which is "better than the (well-known) local competition
by a country mile". / N3 2PA; 11 pm; set weekday L £17 (FP).*

On The Bab   £36   3 3 2
39 Marylebone Ln, W1   020 7935 2000   2–1A
36 Wellington St, WC2   020 7240 8825   5–3D
305 Old St, EC1   020 7683 0361   13–1B
9 Ludgate Broadway, EC4   020 7248 8777   10–2A **NEW**
*"Everything is very tasty" ("the fried chicken is amazing!") at these
"packed" Korean street-food joints, with their "no frills" industrial interiors,
where "there's no booking, and often queueing out the door".
/ onthebab.co.uk; @onthebab; see web for detail.*

One Canada Square E14   £58   2 3 3
1 Canada Square   020 7559 5199   12–1C
*In the lobby of Canary Wharf's main 'scraper, this prominently situated
establishment provides a convenient business rendezvous, but is also
praised for its "amazing bottomless weekend brunch". / E14 5AB;
www.onecanadasquarerestaurant.com; @OneCanadaSquare; 10.45 pm; closed Sun;
set pre theatre £34 (FP).*

100 Wardour Street W1 **NEW**   £64   2 2 3
100 Wardour St   020 7314 4000   4–2D
*D&D London's latest venture on this huge Soho site that's seen their
Mezzo, Meza and Floridita brands come and go (and in aeons past was
The Marquee Club) inspires similarly mixed reports for its plus-ça-change
formula mixing Asian/European cuisine, cocktails, live music and dancing.
/ W1F 0TN; /www.100wardourst.com; @100WardourSt; 2 am, Thu-Sat 3 am,
Sun 5 pm; closed Mon & Sun D.*

1 Lombard Street EC3   £74   2 2 2
1 Lombard St   020 7929 6611   10–3C
*"Location, location and location" help explain the ongoing appeal
to dealmakers of Soren Jessen's "City stalwart" in the heart of the Square
Mile ("don't go for a secret meeting, as you're bound to bump into
someone you know!"). The formula of this large ex-banking hall "doesn't
move on" – the food's "accomplished but not an event" and "nowhere near
as good as it should be for the price". / EC3V 9AA; www.1lombardstreet.com;
10 pm; closed Sat & Sun; booking max 6 may apply.*

One Sixty Smokehouse £53 `4` `3` `4`
291 West End Ln, NW6 020 7794 9786 1–1B
9 Stoney Ln, E1 020 7283 8367 10–2D
"Consistently brilliant BBQ at prices that keep it friendly" –
in "big portions", and with "a great selection of craft beers" – win fans for
David Moore and Sean Martin's "fantastically buzzy" American-inspired
operations in West Hampstead, and the City. STOP PRESS – NW6 closed
as we went to press. / www.one-sixty.co.uk; @onesixtylondon; see web for detail.

One-O-One,
Park Tower Knightsbridge SW1 £98 `4` `2` `1`
101 Knightsbridge 020 7290 7101 6–1D
"Pascal Proyart continues to be the 'King of Fish' in London", say fans of his
Knightsbridge dining room, which despite its "totally depressing", "hotel-
foyer-style" ambience, has built a formidable reputation for "stunning"
seafood and fish dishes. Its ratings came off the boil this year though,
with some reports of "very good, certainly inventive food, but not quite the
wizardry some people have described". / SW1X 7RN;
www.oneoonerestaurant.com; @OneOOneLondon; 10 pm; closed Mon & Sun;
booking max 6 may apply.

Les 110 de Taillevent W1 £65 `3` `3` `3`
16 Cavendish Sq 020 3141 6016 3–1B
"110 wines by the glass with suggested matches for each dish in a range
of prices" (and including 70ml options) is a "lovely, simple and tempting
concept" that wins much praise for this "slightly stark and rectilinear"
Parisian yearling, on the square behind Oxford Street's John Lewis. Still,
"with a famous name like Taillevent, expectations are bound to be high"
and while the food is "interesting", critics feel it's "not exceptional" and can
seem a mite "pricey". / W1G 9DD; www.les-110-taillevent-london.com/en;
@110London; D only, closed Sun.

Opera Tavern WC2 £51 `4` `4` `3`
23 Catherine St 020 7836 3680 5–3D
Some of "the capital's smartest modern tapas" are served at this
"very pleasant" (if sometimes cacophonous) Dehesa sibling – a two-floor
Covent Garden pub-conversion, where "results can be hit and miss, but are
mostly hit". Top Menu Tip – "sinful mini Iberico pork and foie gras
burgers". / WC2B 5JS; www.operatavern.co.uk; @saltyardgroup; 11.15 pm,
Sun 9.45 pm.

Opso W1 £44 `3` `2` `3`
10 Paddington St 020 7487 5088 2–1A
"The food is amazing" ("my beetroot and green bean salad was to die
for!") at this modern Greek two-year-old in Marylebone... "even if the set
lunch is pretty expensive, and the portions teeny-tiny". / W1U 5QL;
www.opso.co.uk; @OPSO_london; 10 pm, Fri & Sat 10.30 pm; closed Sun D.

The Orange SW1 £59 `3` `4` `4`
37 Pimlico Rd 020 7881 9844 6–2D
"For a fun lunch with friends", this Pimlico gastropub provides both a bar
and "charming first-floor dining room" – on the menu, wood-fired pizza
and other well-prepared dishes. / SW1W 8NE; www.theorange.co.uk;
@theorangesw1; 10 pm, Sun 9.30 pm.

Orange Pekoe SW13 £26 344
3 White Hart Ln 020 8876 6070 11–1A
Busy Barnes tea room with pavement tables that's a "lovely place to go for a cup of something and some cake". It's "not your deluxe afternoon tea of central London hotels", but "the range of teas served is amazing" and "the kitchen turns out delicious scones and cakes" as well as breakfasts and light lunches. / SW13 0PX; www.orangepekoeteas.com; 5 pm; L only.

Orée SW10 NEW £13 423
275-277 Fulham Rd 020 3813 9724 6–3B
'A taste of rural France' and its freshly baked viennoiserie, artisan bread and fine patisserie are promised by this new Chelsea café, also offering breakfasts and light lunches (tartines, salads, etc). Early reports applaud its "delicious food and charming staff". / SW10; www.oree.co.uk; @oreeboulangerie; 7 pm, Sun 6 pm; no bookings.

Ormer Mayfair,
Flemings Mayfair Hotel W1 NEW
Half Moon St 020 7016 5601 3–4B
Star Jersey chef, Shaun Rankin, has oversight of the 85-cover dining room at this Mayfair hotel, following its recent £14m revamp – it opened in mid-summer 2016. / W1J 7BH; www.ormermayfair.com; @ormermayfair; closed Sun; no shorts.

Orrery W1 £80 333
55 Marylebone High St 020 7616 8000 2–1A
Above Marylebone's Conran Shop, this "classic" D&D London venture provides a "calm, stress-free environment" for business or romance (with "a nice al fresco terrace when the weather is fine"). "Well-drilled staff" provide modern French cuisine that's "not cheap" but "of a consistently high standard". / W1U 5RB; www.orreryrestaurant.co.uk; @orrery; 10 pm, Fri & Sat 10.30 pm, Sun 10 pm; set weekday L £47 (FP), set Sun L £50 (FP).

Orso WC2 £55 232
27 Wellington St 020 7240 5269 5–3D
"Extremely convenient for the opera or theatre" – this long-established basement in Covent Garden remains a favourite for many reporters, for its "varied Italian fare", "restrained interior" and "attentive and informal" service. However, numerous old-timers (perhaps remembering its late '80s glory days) are harsher, finding it "underwhelming" and "tired". Top Tip – "top value pre-show deal". / WC2E 7DB; www.orsorestaurant.co.uk; @Orso_Restaurant; 11.30 pm, Sun 10 pm; set weekday L £33 (FP).

Oscar Wilde Bar At Cafe Royal W1 £55 244
68 Regent Street 020 7406 3333 4–4C
"Just amazing! The theatre of the whole thing". This "most beautiful room" – dating back to 1865 and formerly known as the Café Royal Grill – nowadays operates as a bar within what, in latter years, has become an über-swanky hotel. Most of the feedback it attracts relates to the afternoon tea – "more of a full meal!" but "wonderful". / W1B; www.hotelcaferoyal.com; @HotelCafeRoyal.

Oslo Court NW8 £64

Charlbert St, off Prince Albert Rd 020 7722 8795 9–3A

"Whether you're 70, 80 or 90 years old: the place to party!" This priceless veteran, quirkily tucked away at the foot of a Regent's Park apartment block, is "a top choice for senior citizens" across north London, "who want to take out 2-3 generations of their family for a celebratory dinner". "It's a total time warp", but "very good at what it does": "sturdy, classic '70s food" is served in "generous portions" ("you'll never leave hungry!") by "unfailing" staff of the old school, in a "wonderfully camp", "plush, pink and comfortable" (if "cramped") setting. Special marks go to the "long-serving and extremely enthusiastic dessert waiter" ("OTT but fun") who "always 'saves the last one just for you!'". Top Tip – "birthday cakes can be pre-ordered free for parties of 4+, and the singing's not bad either!" / NW8 7EN; 11 pm; closed Sun; no jeans.

Osteria, Barbican Centre EC2 NEW £54

Level 2 Silk St 020 7588 3008 10–1B

Anthony Demetre (of Soho's Arbutus, and Urban Coterie in Shoreditch) has teamed up with Searcys once again, this time to jazz up the food offering at the Barbican Centre brasserie with this new Italian, which opened to mixed feedback – it's well rated in some accounts, but to sceptics merely "the usual woeful catering at the Barbican". As ever, nice views here from the window tables. / EC2Y 8DS; www.osteriabarbican.co.uk; @osterialondon; 11 pm.

Osteria 60 SW7 NEW £77

60 Hyde Park Gate 020 7937 8886 6–1B

The new incarnation of the dining room of Kensington's luxurious Baglioni hotel – initial feedback, admittedly limited, suggests it may struggle to defy the overpriced and indifferent DNA of the site (formerly Brunello, RIP). / SW7 5BB; www.osteria60.com; @osteria_60; 10.30 pm.

Osteria Antica Bologna SW11 £43

23 Northcote Rd 020 7978 4771 11–2C

A "little, cheap 'n' cheerful gem" near Clapham Junction long known locally and beyond for its "good value Northern Italian cuisine, whether sitting out on the pavement on a sunny day, or tucking into wild boar stew on a wintry Sunday". / SW11 1NG; www.osteria.co.uk; @OsteriaAntica; 10.30 pm, Sun 10 pm.

Osteria Basilico W11 £58

29 Kensington Park Rd 020 7727 9957 7–1A

The "best authentic Italian pizza in town" plus "delicious home-made pasta and seasonal specials" ensure that this long-running Notting Hill local is "always full". / W11 2EU; www.osteriabasilico.co.uk; 11.30 pm, Sun 10.30 pm; no booking, Sat L.

Osteria Tufo N4 £47

67 Fonthill Rd 020 7272 2911 9–1D

"Enticing aromas hit you as you enter" this superb "find" in Finsbury Park – a "wonderfully friendly" operation, serving a "good selection of interesting Italian specialities" in "bohemian surroundings". "I had no idea it even existed, but now I'll be going back all the time!" / N4 3HZ; www.osteriatufo.co.uk; 10.30 pm, Sun 9.30 pm; closed Mon, Tue-Sat D only, Sun open L & D; no Amex.

Ostuni £49 3 3 3
1 Hampstead Lane, N6   020 7624 8035   9–1B NEW
43-45 Lonsdale Rd, NW6   020 7624 8035   1–2B
"Authentic Puglian cuisine to an excellent standard" has won quite
a following for this spacious three-year-old, in *"distinctly middle-of-the-road
Queen's Park"*. The odd sceptic fears that *"it's more hit and miss than
when it first opened"*, but they must be doing something right as June
2016 saw the opening of a Highgate sibling, similarly with an open kitchen.
/ see web for detail.

Otto's WC1 £67 4 5 3
182 Grays Inn Rd   020 7713 0107   2–1D
*How did this "oasis of traditional and consistently superb Gallic cooking"
end up in a nondescript corner of Bloomsbury? Its overall approach
is "pleasantly old-fashioned" but "not stuffy and always with a humorous
twist"* thanks to the *"very personal"* attention of *"effervescent"* patron Otto
(who also provides *"helpful advice on the impressive wine list"*). Top Menu
Tip – *"the Canard à la Presse helped me find god!"* / WC1X 8EW;
www.ottos-restaurant.com; 9.45 pm; closed Sat L & Sun.

Ottolenghi £55 3 2 2
13 Motcomb St, SW1   020 7823 2707   6–1D
63 Ledbury Rd, W11   020 7727 1121   7–1B
1 Holland St, W8   020 7937 0003   6–1A
287 Upper St, N1   020 7288 1454   9–2D
50 Artillery Pas, E1   020 7247 1999   10–2D
"Zingy fresh flavours dance in the mouth", at Yotam Ottolenghi's *"funky"*
communal cafés, known for their *"inspired"* salads and *"scrumptious"*
cakes. *"Cramped conditions"* are a pain however, and while even fans
"do wonder how a small meal can cost quite so much", critics fear they risk
"disappearing up their own fundaments". / www.ottolenghi.co.uk; N1 10.15 pm,
W8 & W11 8 pm, Sat 7 pm, Sun 6 pm; N1 closed Sun D; Holland St takeaway only;
W11 & SW1 no booking, N1 booking for D only.

Restaurant Ours SW3 NEW £68 2 4 4
264 Brompton Rd   020 7100 2200   6–2C
"Who is the target market for this strangely mixed experience?" Über-chef
Tom Sellers's ambitious South Kensington newcomer – mixing *"blingy,
nightclub style"* with funky culinary aspirations – hasn't yet found its mark.
The site comes complete with indoor trees, open kitchen, and the catwalk-
style, narrow, glass-floored entrance-walkway it inherited from The
Collection (long RIP). However *"despite the amazing interior and friendly,
solicitous service, it's marred by some very clumsy and overpriced cooking"*,
which *"despite Mr Sellers at the helm, is not sharp enough for serious
eaters"*. And *"while it's attracting some tall, very thin, very well-dressed
young women and their minders, that crowd gets sooo bored sooo quickly"*.
/ SW3 2AS; www.restaurant-ours.com; @restaurant_ours; 10 pm, Thu-Sat 11 pm;
no bookings at lunch.

Outlaw's at The Capital SW3 £86 4 4 2
22-24 Basil St   020 7591 1202   6–1D
"Stunning" fish and seafood *"presented with panache"* win huge acclaim
for this *"hidden gem, so close to the brassiness of Harrods"*. The ambience
of the *"small"* room is not to all tastes though – what is *"quiet and
dignified"* to fans is to critics *"staid"* and *"too formal"*. Top Tip – BYO with
no corkage on Thursdays. / SW3 1AT; www.capitalhotel.co.uk;
@OUTLAWSinLondon; 10 pm; closed Sun; set weekday L £51 (FP).

Oxo Tower, Restaurant SE1 £85 111

Barge House St   020 7803 3888   10–3A

"Urrggh!" – "Why can't they get it right?" at this South Bank landmark.
It has "exceptional views over the Thames" and "feels special outside
in summer", but "dreadful" standards make it the survey's perennial
No. 1 disappointment. / SE1 9PH; www.harveynichols.com/restaurants;
@OxoTowerWharf; 11 pm, Sun 10 pm; set weekday L & dinner £47
(FP); SRA-3 star.

Oxo Tower, Brasserie SE1 £72 112

Barge House St   020 7803 3888   10–3A

Cheaper than the adjoining restaurant, the brasserie of this South Bank
landmark is likewise "one for the view rather than the food" and "should
be so much better". / SE1 9PH;
www.harveynichols.com/restaurants/oxo-tower-london; 11 pm, Sun 10 pm; may need
2+ to book; set weekday L & dinner £47 (FP).

P Franco E5 £35

107 Lower Clapton Road   020 8533 4660   14–1B

More reports please on this cool little wine bar in Clapton, where you sit
at a long table in the evenings and enjoy a daily-changing menu alongside
superb plonk. / E5 0NP; www.pfranco.co.uk; @pfranco_e5; 9 pm, Thu 11 pm,
Fri & Sat 11 pm, Sun 9pm; closed Mon, Tue-Fri D only, Sat & Sun open L & D;
no Amex.

Pachamama W1 £63 312

18 Thayer St   020 7935 9393   2–1A

"Peruvian fusion without the high prices" is to be found at this Marylebone
two-year-old, which delivers "brilliant tapas and good Pisco cocktails" in a
"fun and buzzy" – but "too noisy" – setting. Service "doesn't quite live
up to the rest (lack of training, I suspect)". / W1U 3JY;
www.pachamamalondon.com; @pachamama_ldn; 10.45 pm, Sun 10 pm; closed
Mon L; set brunch £35 (FP).

Padella SE1 NEW £28 443

6 Southwark St   no tel   10–4C

"Arrive early: the queue can be a killer", but this "simple, easy and
unfussy" new Italian near Borough Market (from the team behind Trullo)
is "one of the few places worth enduring them" – "amazing, freshly made
pasta, and so wonderfully cheap" is the highlight of the "short menu".
/ SE1 1TQ; www.padella.co; @padella_pasta; 10 pm, Sun 5 pm; no bookings.

The Painted Heron SW10 £56 542

112 Cheyne Walk   020 7351 5232   6–3B

"Indian food on steroids, but without being pretentious" ("familiar enough
to be comforting, different enough to be exciting") wins the customary
hymn of praise to this "hidden gem", off the Chelsea Embankment – "I still
don't think it has the reputation it deserves!" / SW10 0DJ;
www.thepaintedheron.com; @thepaintedheron; 10.30 pm; set weekday L & Sun L
£15 (FP).

The Palmerston SE22 £55 333

91 Lordship Ln   020 8693 1629   1–4D

"Good and sometimes exceptional cooking" with a modern British slant
distinguishes this former boozer – nowadays a well-established fixture
of East Dulwich. / SE22 8EP; www.thepalmerston.co.uk; @thepalmerston; 10 pm,
Sun 9.30 pm; no Amex.

The Palomar W1 £51 5 5 4
34 Rupert St 020 7439 8777 5–3A
"If you can't visit their original restaurant, Machneyuda in Israel" this *"piece of trendy Tel Aviv in London"* is *"the next best thing"*. *"Cramped, noisy and pulsating with life"*, you can book for the side room, but the place to be is the *"buzzy, free-style"* bar *"rubbing elbows with your neighbours"*. Service is *"friendly"* and *"as it comes"*, and the *"adventurous Levantine food"* is *"ultra-fresh"* and *"anything but dull!"* / W1D 6DN; www.thepalomar.co.uk; 11 pm, Sun 9 pm.

Pappa Ciccia £34 3 4 3
105 Munster Rd, SW6 020 7384 1884 11–1B
41 Fulham High St, SW6 020 7736 0900 11–1B
This popular group cooks *"by far the best pizza"* in Fulham and Putney – they're even *"great reheated the next day"*. An *"exceptionally good tagliatelle nero con vongole"* also wins plaudits, while the BYO policy keeps bills in check. / www.pappaciccia.com; 11 pm, Sat & Sun 11.30 pm; Munster Rd no credit cards.

Parabola W8 NEW
224-238 Kensington High Street 020 3862 5900 6–1A
Named for the shape of its roof, Parabola is Sir Terence Conran's and Peter Prescott's latest brainchild inside the re-located Design Museum, which opens by Holland Park in late November 2016. The restaurant will be open all day, then plans to host guest chefs for dinner, with private dining in a members' room. / W8 6AG; designmuseum.org.

Paradise by Way of Kensal Green W10 £50 3 3 5
19 Kilburn Ln 020 8969 0098 1–2B
"An absolute gem of a restaurant" – part of a massive shabby-chic Kensal Green tavern that's long been a magnet for hip creative industry types, with gardens, roof-terraces and bars galore. / W10 4AE; www.theparadise.co.uk; @weloveparadise; 10.30 pm, Fri & Sat 11 pm, Sun 9 pm; closed weekday L; no Amex.

Paradise Garage E2 £45 4 4 3
254 Paradise Row 020 7613 1502 13–1D
"The flavours and presentation are superb" at chef Robin Gill's (The Manor and Dairy in Clapham) *"so-trendy"* yearling under a Bethnal Green railway arch. It's *"good value considering the fantastic quality of the inventive food"*, *"although with the small plates, the cost can easily mount"*. / E2 9LE; www.paradise254.com; @ParadiseRow254; 10 pm; closed Mon, Tue L & Sun D; set weekday L £25 (FP).

Paradise Hampstead NW3 £33 4 5 4
49 South End Rd 020 7794 6314 9–2A
A *"wonderful front of house"* further boosts the *"highly convivial"* style of this *"excellent, traditional Indian"* of nearly a half-century's standing, near Hampstead Heath station. It's *"madly busy"*, *"so booking is recommended"* – the food's *"not the most adventurous, but done exceptionally well"*. / NW3 2QB; www.paradisehampstead.co.uk; 10.45 pm.

El Parador NW1 £38 4 4 3
245 Eversholt St 020 7387 2789 9–3C
A strong option near Mornington Crescent – this *"great little Hispanic spot"* offers *"quality"*, *"reasonably priced tapas"*. *"Unstuffy"*, *"efficient"* service and a *"great garden for sunny days"* complete the deal, but *"it gets busy and slightly congested, so don't tell anyone…"* / NW1 1BA; www.elparadorlondon.com; 11 pm, Fri & Sat 11.30 pm, Sun 9.30 pm; closed Sat L & Sun L; no Amex.

Park Chinois W1 NEW £94   2 5 4
17 Berkeley St   020 3327 8888   3–3C
"A night out in 1920's Shanghai, with live music and dancing" is the aim at Alan Yau's barmily "opulent" Mayfair newcomer (on the site that was Automat, RIP). Service is "amazing", but the luxurious cuisine (Peking Duck, caviar, dim sum) is "bone-crunchingly expensive" yet "nothing spectacular". / W1S 4NF; www.parkchinois.com; 11 pm, Sun 10.15 pm; no jeans.

Parlour Kensal NW10 £49   4 4 4
5 Regent St   020 8969 2184   1–2B
"No ordinary gastropub" – Jesse Dunford Wood's "quirky" Kensal Rise pub conversion features a "fabulous chef's table" amongst its dining options. Top Menu Tip – the "enormous cow pie". / NW10 5LG; www.parlourkensal.com; @ParlourUK; 10 pm; closed Mon.

El Pastór SE1 NEW
7a Stoney Street   awaiting tel   10–4C
Having conquered Spanish cuisine, Barrafina bros Sam & Eddie Hart are setting their sights on the Latino market with this November 2016 Mexican opening, by Borough Market. The venue will primarily be a taqueria, specialising in tacos. To drink there's to be mezcal, tequila, cocktails and Mexican beers. / SE1 9AA; @Tacos_El_Pastor.

Patara £61   3 4 4
15 Greek St, W1   020 7437 1071   5–2A
5 Berners St, W1   020 8874 6503   3–1D
7 Maddox St, W1   020 7499 6008   4–2A
181 Fulham Rd, SW3   020 7351 5692   6–2C
9 Beauchamp Pl, SW3   020 7581 8820   6–1C
"An excellent Thai chain", which "reinvents itself from time to time". "Service is amazing, and with a smile", the "always buzzing" branches are very civilised, and "the food is of a consistently high quality". / www.pataralondon.com; 10.30 pm; Greek St closed Sun L.

Paternoster Chop House EC4 £55   2 1 1
1 Warwick Court   020 7029 9400   10–2B
"With a location like this they should try harder", but D&D London's steakhouse – with its al fresco tables and magnificent pavement-side views of St Paul's – is too busy making money from its captive be-suited market: it's "overpriced and the food's not that good". / EC4M 7DX; www.paternosterchophouse.co.uk; @paternoster1; 10.30 pm; closed Sat L & Sun D.

Patio W12 £35   3 5 5
5 Goldhawk Rd   020 8743 5194   8–1C
The "delightful" and "gloriously eccentric" Polish hospitality at this family-run Shepherd's Bush veteran "never lets you down". With its "wide range of flavoured vodkas" and "old-fashioned décor", it's perfect for a "cheap 'n' cheerful" get-together. / W12 8QQ; www.patiolondon.com; 11 pm, Sat & Sun 11.30 pm; closed Sat L & Sun L.

Patogh W1 £22   4 3 3
8 Crawford Pl   020 7262 4015   7–1D
"Ignore the shabby decor, just savour the outstanding Persian food" ("grilled meat and bread is the order of the day"), at this long-established "hustling and bustling" shopfront cafe off the Edgware Road, where "waiters do their best with manic crowd control". "Don't come in a big group, there just isn't room!" (NB it's BYO, with "Waitrose round the corner for the wine"). / W1H 5NE; n/a; 11 pm; cash only; booking max may apply.

Patron NW5 £49 3 4 4
26 Fortress Road   020 7813 2540   9–2C
*"Good French cooking in an intimate atmosphere" has made this cute little
year old 'Cave à Manger' a "brilliant addition to the Kentish Town food
scene". It's "romantic" for a date, too ("even though we ate dinner at the
bar!") / NW5 2HB; www.patronlondon.com; 11 pm, Sun 10 pm; closed Mon,
Tue-Thu D only,Fri-Sun open L & D.*

Patty and Bun £23 4 3 2
18 Old Compton St, W1   020 7287 1818   5–2A NEW
54 James St, W1   020 7487 3188   3–1A
36 Redchurch Street, E2   020 7613 3335   13–1B NEW
397 Mentmore Terrace, E8   020 8510 0252   14–1B
22-23 Liverpool St, EC2   020 7621 1331   10–2D
*"To-die-for", "messy" burgers – amongst "the best in London?" – are to
be had at these "super hip" pitstops. "Count yourself lucky if you get
a table at the James Street original!" / www.pattyandbun.co.uk; Mon - Wed
10pm, Thu - Fri 11 pm, Sat 9 pm, Sun 6 pm.*

The Pear Tree W6 £44 3 3 4
14 Margravine Rd   020 7381 1787   8–2C
*"A lovely romantic atmosphere" is the most distinctive feature of this
"amazing", small Victorian pub hideaway, behind the Charing Cross
Hospital, but its cooking is "very competent" too. / W6 8HJ;
www.thepeartreefulham.com; 9.30 pm, Fri-Sun 9 pm; Mon-Thu D only, Fri-Sun open
L & D.*

Pear Tree Cafe SW11 NEW
Lakeside Cafe, Battersea Park   no tel   6–4D
*At last someone tries to do something with this gorgeously located park
café, by Battersea Park's boating lake. The autumn 2016 opening
by Annabel Partridge, formerly at Petersham Nurseries, and Will Burrett,
previously at Spring, provides an outdoor terrace, all-day dining and
weekend brunch. / SW11 4NJ; www.peartreecafe.co.uk.*

Pearl Liang W2 £48 4 4 3
8 Sheldon Square   020 7289 7000   7–1C
*"Always excellent dim sum" tops the list of "genuine Cantonese food"
at this big basement, tucked-away in Paddington Basin. Service is "brisk but
attentive", while "the room is loud enough to drown out any noise from the
kids". / W2 6EZ; www.pearlliang.co.uk; 11 pm.*

Peckham Bazaar SE15 £49 5 3 4
119 Consort Rd   020 7732 2525   1–4D
*"Rare but smart regional food" from the Balkans via Greece to the Middle
East makes for an "exciting and imaginative" eating experience at this
"honest" Peckham venue. Wines, including from the Greek islands,
come "at very fair mark-ups". / SE15 3RU; www.peckhambazaar.com; 10 pm,
Sun 8 pm; closed Mon, Tue-Fri D only, Sat & Sun open L & D; no Amex.*

Peckham Refreshment Rooms SE15 £41 3 2 2
12-16 Blenheim Grove   020 7639 1106   1–4D
*Chilled, affordable Peckham hangout, again well-rated for a casual bite:
"we found it hard to find (they don't seem to believe in signage), difficult
to order (staff didn't seem clear what was 'on'), difficult to sit (the stools
are super uncomfortable), but the food was delicious!" / SE15 4QL;
www.peckhamrefreshment.com; midnight; closed Sun D.*

Pedler SE15 £38 3 4 4
58 Peckham Rye   020 3030 1515   1–4D
"A kitchen with real judgement and lightness of touch" helps win praise for
this trendy, packed Peckham bistro-yearling, as does its above-average
weekend brunch. / SE15 4JR; www.thebeautifulpizzaboy.london;
@pizzaboylondon1; 10.45 pm; closed Mon, Tue L, Wed L, Thu L, Fri L & Sun D.

Pellicano Restaurant SW3 £59 3 4 2
19-21 Elystan St   020 7589 3718   6–2C
"Reopened after redecoration, and re-relocation and back on top form".
This "attentive and friendly" Chelsea old-favourite is back on its original site
and maintains a loyal, small fanclub for its "limited" but "excellent menu
of Sardinian specialities and wines". "The physical ambiente is a little
forlorn when there isn't a full house". / SW3 3NT;
www.pellicanorestaurant.co.uk; 11 pm, Sun 9.30 pm.

E Pellicci E2 £16 3 4 5
332 Bethnal Green Rd   020 7739 4873   13–1D
"Still the most fun breakfast in the East End" – this trad' caff has
"been here for generations" and boasts wonderful Art Deco quarters
("you'll have seen the wood- panelled interior in many TV dramas").
A "warm welcome's guaranteed", with "fry-ups cooked to perfection" –
all in "huge portions". / E2 0AG; 4 pm; L only, closed Sun; cash only.

Pentolina W14 £48 4 5 4
71 Blythe Rd   020 3010 0091   8–1C
This "smart" and "charming" Italian in the backstreets of Olympia
is "just what a local restaurant should be": "a great all-round experience",
with "quality at decent prices" and "interesting" cooking (although
"the menu doesn't change very frequently"). / W14 0HP;
www.pentolinarestaurant.co.uk; 10 pm; closed Mon & Sun; no Amex.

The Pepper Tree SW4 £33 3 3 3
19 Clapham Common South Side   020 7622 1758   11–2D
"Sharing tables makes for a fun and buzzy experience" at this "cheap 'n'
cheerful", "old favourite" Thai canteen in Clapham – "great value and
perfect for a bite before the movies". / SW4 7AB; www.thepeppertree.co.uk;
10.45 pm, Sun & Mon 10.15 pm; no bookings.

Percy & Founders W1 £55 4 3 2
1 Pearson Square, Fitzroy Place   020 3761 0200   2–1B
"Huge" year-old pub, dining room and bar occupying the spacious ground
floor of a Fitzrovia development on the site of the old Middlesex Hospital.
All reports approve its menu of grills and brasserie fare, but "it feels very
new" and can seem a tad "artificial and clinical". / W1T 3BF;
www.percyandfounders.co.uk; @PercyFounders; 10.30 pm; closed Sun D.

Perilla N16 NEW
1-3 Green Lanes   074 67067393   1–1C
Following their stylish pop-ups across London, Ben Marks and Matt
Emmerson are set to open Perilla in a permanent Newington Green
location in November, with backing from Philip Howard, among others.
/ N16 9BS; www.perilladining.co.uk; closed Mon, Tue L, Wed L, Thu L & Sun D.

The Perry Vale SE23 £46 3 4 3
31 Perry Vale   020 8291 0432   1–4D
From the team behind Camberwell's crowd-pleasing Crooked Well comes
a simple, modern bistro/brasserie yearling in up-and-coming Forest Hill –
fans say it's proving "a wonderful addition to the SE23 scene!" / SE23 2AR;
www.theperryvale.com; @theperryvale.

Petersham Hotel TW10 £65 3 3 5

Nightingale Ln   020 8939 1084   1–4A

This "beautifully situated hotel on Richmond Hill" is a little "old-fashioned" and "conservative" and generally appeals to an older crowd. It offers "magnificent views (especially at lunch)", the food is "better than you might expect from a hotel", and overall it's a "delightful experience". / TW10 6UZ; www.petershamhotel.co.uk; @thepetersham; 9.45 pm, Sun 8.45 pm.

Petersham Nurseries Cafe TW10 £69 2 1 3

Church Lane (signposted 'St Peter's Church')   020 8940 5230   1–4A

"Such a romantic venue" – "a lovely glasshouse" that's "perfect for a summer day" – along with ambitious cuisine has earnt a huge reputation for this shabby-chic garden centre café, near Richmond Park. But while it has always been "massively overpriced" ("queuing for the loo with the garden centre customers, and paying £100 per head does not feel right"), since Skye Gyngell moved on "the food is nothing like it was", and to critics it feels like "it's totally lost the plot": "laughable" to charge "elite central London prices" for "a garden shed" with "indifferent service and interspersed with a few silly antiques!" / TW10 7AG; www.petershamnurseries.com; L only, closed Mon.

Petit Pois Bistro N1 NEW £47

9 Hoxton Square   020 7613 3689   13–1B

In a corner of hip Hoxton Square (with terrace), a new (summer 2016) French bistro serving fave raves like steak frites, moules marinière and croque madame. Its chocolate mousse has been described by Jay Rayner as 'the best three minutes you can have in London for a fiver right now'. / N1 6NU; www.petitpoisbistro.com; @petitpoisbistro; 10.30 pm, Sun 4 pm; closed Sun D.

The Petite Coree NW6 £39 4 5 2

98 West End Lane   020 7624 9209   1–1B

"A lovely and refreshing local run by a couple (husband downstairs cooking and wife serving). They deserve real support in their effort to bring French food with a Korean twist in every dish to West Hampstead!" / NW6 2LU; www.thepetitecoree.com; @thepetitecoree; Tue-Thu 10 pm, Fri & Sat 10.30 pm, Sun 10 pm; closed Mon, Tue-Thu D only, Fri-Sun open L & D; set dinner £24 (FP).

La Petite Maison W1 £83 5 4 5

54 Brook's Mews   020 7495 4774   3–2B

"The wonderful flavours of Southern Europe" ("sharing plates, that are not your typical French food: much lighter and fresher", prepared to "an incredibly high standard" and with "everything tasting of its ingredients and the sun!") – plus a "fantastic", Côte d'Azure atmosphere to match, inspire "simply outstanding" feedback on Arjun Waney's "busy and noisy" Mayfair haunt… even if "prices are flabbergasting" and "it's something of a hedge fund canteen". / W1K 4EG; www.lpmlondon.co.uk; @lpmlondon; 10.45 pm, Sun 9.45 pm.

Pétrus SW1 £111 3 3 2

1 Kinnerton St   020 7592 1609   6–1D

"It takes a week to review the wine list!" at Gordon Ramsay's plush Belgravian, whose centrepiece is a floor-to-ceiling, cylindrical, glass wine vault. On many accounts the "wonderful" cuisine lives up to it too, but enthusiasm for the "hushed" ("like a doctor's waiting room") and "spacious" interior is more muted, and even fans can feel prices are "crazy". Top Tip – "make the most of the lunch deal". / SW1X 8EA; www.gordonramsayrestaurants.com; @petrus; 10.15 pm; closed Sun; no trainers; set weekday L £42 (FP), set dinner £84 (FP).

Peyote W1 £74 3 3 2
13 Cork St   020 7409 1300   4–4A
By the yardstick of his other ventures, Arjun Waney's Mayfair Latino three-year-old has made few waves, and attracts thin feedback. Fans say the "different" cooking ('consulted on' by Mexico City legend, Eduardo Garcia) can be "surprisingly good" – certainly in comparison with the dire press reviews the place has attracted – but even they can feel that high prices and "the overt focus on the commercial side (table time limits, advance credit card guarantees) take the shine off the experience". / W1S 3NS; www.peyoterestaurant.com; Mon-Thu 1 am, Fri & Sat 2 am; closed Sat L & Sun; set weekday L & pre-theatre £27 (FP).

Peyotito W11 NEW £53
31 Kensington Park Road   020 7043 1400   7–1A
In the heart of Notting Hill, a new Mexican serving Mezcal cocktails and sharing plates such as ceviche, moles, crudos and maza until late, as well as weekend brunch. / W11 2EU; www.peyotitorestaurant.com; @peyotitolondon; midnight, Fri & Sat 1 am.

Pham Sushi EC1 £36 5 3 1
159 Whitecross St   020 7251 6336   13–2A
Don't go for the ambience (it's "cramped and noisy"), but some of "the best-value Japanese in London" is found at this simple, "off-the-beaten-track" Barbican fixture – "consistently excellent sushi (of which crunchy tuna and flying dragon are highlights)", all "at a fraction of West End prices". / EC1Y 8JL, www.phamsushi.co.uk; @phamsushi; 10 pm; closed Sat L & Sun.

Pharmacy 2,
Newport Street Gallery SE11 NEW £54 3 3 3
Newport St   020 3141 9333   2–4D
As with the original Pharmacy (back in the day, on Notting Hill Gate) "there is a chalk-and-cheese clash between the sterile decor and warming food" at this new venture, "tucked away on a Lambeth backstreet". But initially at least, more people find the effect "fun" and "love it" than find it "too bright for relaxation and enjoyment". The food – "no particular stand out, but all competently done" – likewise is mostly well received, and only the odd cynic feels that "Mark Hix's cooking is as predictable as Damien Hirst's art". / SE11 6AJ; www.pharmacyrestaurant.com; @Ph2restaurant; midnight, Sun 6 pm; closed Mon & Sun D.

Pho £35 2 3 3
"Very fresh and genuine tastes" have driven the success of these Vietnamese street-food cafés – "great for a cheap bowl of noodles" (but nowadays "fine, but nothing more"). / www.phocafe.co.uk; EC1 10 pm, Fri & Sat 10.30 pm, W1 10.30 pm, W12 9 pm, Sat 7 pm, Sun 6 pm; EC1 closed Sat L & Sun, W1 closed Sun; no Amex; no booking.

The Phoenix SW3 £51 2 2 4
23 Smith St   020 7730 9182   6–2D
With its "neighbourhood feel" and "relaxed atmosphere", this Chelsea backstreet pub "exudes genuine happiness". "Great food (not just the usual pub grub)", that suits "the whole family". / SW3 4EE; www.geronimo-inns.co.uk; @ThePhoenixSW3; 10 pm.

Phoenix Palace NW1   £56   3 2 2
5-9 Glentworth St   020 7486 3515   2–1A
"Divine, juicy, well-stuffed, fresh mouthfuls of pure joy!" – that's the "delicious dim sum" at this "large", well-established Chinese venue, near Baker Street, "frequented by lots of Chinese". Its ratings suffered, though, from a couple of disappointing reports this year. / NW1 5PG; www.phoenixpalace.co.uk; 11.30 pm, Sun 10.30 pm.

Picture   £48   4 4 3
110 Great Portland St, W1   020 7637 7892   2–1B
19 New Cavendish Street, W1   020 7935 0058   2–1A NEW
"A bare dining room and small tasting plates – not everyone's idea of a satisfying formula but to my taste well prepared and interesting!" This low-key but accomplished venture near Broadcasting House can be enjoyed via its tasting menu – "a steal (and marvellous)" – or "two of their small plates is perfect for a quick light bite with friends or for business". It has a new Marylebone sibling too – one early report says it's "a really good addition north of Oxford Street". / see web for detail.

Pidgin E8 NEW   £62   5 5 4
52 Wilton Way   020 7254 8311   1–2D
"A great little addition to the London dining scene" – this "small, cramped-but-magical" room with about 26 covers behind a "tiny Hackney shopfront" offers "an ever-changing, weekly set menu". "The absence of choice is abated by the spectacularly good cooking" from chef Elizabeth Allen – "truly innovative" ("we were reaching for Wikipedia to understand the ingredients") but "well thought-out", "surprising and delightful". / E8 1BG; @PidginLondon; 9.45 pm, Sun 9 pm; closed Mon, Tue-Fri D only, Sat & Sun open L & D.

Piebury Corner N7   £19   3 4 3
209-211 Holloway Rd   020 7700 5441   9–2D
"Pies rammed to the brim with fillings" and "fabulous gravy" draw Gunners fans and foodies to this small, "very friendly" deli near the Emirates; "good selection of craft beers" too. / N7 8DL; www.pieburycorner.com; @PieburyCorner; closed Mon, Tue, Wed & Sun; no bookings.

PIED À TERRE W1   £112   4 4 3
34 Charlotte St   020 7636 1178   2–1C
"In spite of another chef change, it goes from strength to strength!" – David Moore's "intimate" Fitzrovia townhouse is one of the capital's most enduring havens of gastronomy, with "very precise, fine attention to every detail". "Staff are charming from start to finish" and Andy McFadden's "assured" cuisine can be "extraordinary" ("he makes the food burst into life!") There's "one of the best cellars in London" too, presided over by the "helpful and hugely knowledgeable sommelier", Mathieu Germond. / W1T 2NH; www.pied-a-terre.co.uk; @PiedaTerreUK; 10.45 pm; closed Sat L & Sun; booking max 7 may apply.

Pig & Butcher N1   £51   4 4 4
80 Liverpool Road   020 7226 8304   9–3D
"Very strong all round" – this Islington hostelry provides "professional and caring" service of an "inventive and stylish, though meaty, menu" ("amazing roasts") and all reporters "have never had a poor meal". "The upstairs room is a great venue for a big party, downstairs a more traditional gastropub". / N1 0QD; www.thepigandbutcher.co.uk; @pigandbutcher; 10 pm, Sun 9 pm; Mon-Thu D only, Fri-Sun open L & D.

Pilpel £11 442

38 Brushfield Street, London, E1 020 7247 0146 13–2B
Old Spitalfields Mkt, E1 020 7375 2282 13–2B
146 Fleet St, EC4 020 7583 2030 10–2A
Paternoster Sq, EC4 020 7248 9281 10–2B

No wonder there are usually queues at this small Middle Eastern chain, where "great, piping-hot falafel with wonderful fresh fillings are crammed into pitta in about 45 seconds". They make a "really tasty vegetarian lunch – so much better than it needs to be". / www.pilpel.co.uk; 4 pm-9 pm; some branches closed Sat & Sun.

Pique Nique SE1 NEW

32 Tanner Street awaiting tel 10–4D

What aims to be a proper, French rotisserie from the people who brought us Bermondsey's Casse-Croute – just over the road; this 40-seater café is to revolve around the AOC breed, Poulet de Bresse, and set to open in autumn 2016. / SE1 3LD; @piquenique32.

El Pirata W1 £40 344

5-6 Down St 020 7491 3810 3–4B

"If you're in Mayfair and want a low key and relatively inexpensive meal" this "hectic" little tapas spot is "perfect" (even if "the tables are so small they old hold about two dishes at once"). / W1J 7AQ; www.elpirata.co.uk; @elpirataw1; 11.30 pm; closed Sat L & Sun.

Pitt Cue Co EC2 £49 544

1 The Ave, Devonshire Sq 020 7324 7770 10–2D

"A meat Mecca and no mistake" – this epic US-style BBQ has "transitioned beautifully" from Soho to its "stunning new home" in Devonshire Square, and its dishes are "off-the-charts good", if "not for the faint hearted" ("pig's head scrumpet? Yes please!"). "Service tries hard" – "these guys clearly love their meat, treat it with respect" and "have tremendous knowledge of the breeds of animals and the cuts". "Excellent bar too". / EC2; www.pittcue.co.uk; @PittCueCo; 10.30 pm; closed Sat & Sun.

Pizarro SE1 £56 333

194 Bermondsey St 020 7256 5333 10–4D

"The bigger brother of José, nearby" – this "more traditional Spanish restaurant" in Bermondsey wins praise for its "friendly welcome", and "delicious individual or sharing plates". Some of José P's fans feel it's a turn off though – "the extraordinary just became ordinary, over-extended and over-priced". / SE1 3TQ; www.josepizarro.com; @Jose_Pizarro; 10.45 pm, Sun 9.45 pm.

Pizza East £52 334

310 Portobello Rd, W10 020 8969 4500 7–1A
79 Highgate Rd, NW5 020 3310 2000 9–1B
56 Shoreditch High St, E1 020 7729 1888 13–1B

"Channel your inner hipster, and cruise along" to these grungily-glam, industrial-style Soho House-owned haunts ("you have to be under 30 really to appreciate them fully"). They seemed a little more "over-stretched" this year, but for somewhere so "achingly trendy", service is surprisingly "amiable" and while the pizza is "inauthentic", it wins lots of praise for its "unusual toppings and fantastic, thin crispy bases". / www.pizzaeast.com; @PizzaEast; E1 Sun-Wed 11 pm, Thu 12 am, Fri-Sat 1am; W10 Mon-Thu 11.30 pm, Fri-Sat 12 am, Sun 10.30 pm.

Pizza Metro £43 3 2 2
147-149 Notting Hill Gate, W11   020 7727 8877   7–2B
64 Battersea Rise, SW11   020 7228 3812   11–2C
"Genuine pizza" – "enormous oblong offerings" – still win fans for this
"noisy" Battersea stalwart (with a Notting Hill sibling) which introduced
pizza-sold-by-the-metre to London. The service is "friendly" but "can be
a bit hit-and-miss". / pizzametropizza.com; @pizzametropizza; see web for detail.

Pizza Pilgrims £33 4 3 4
102 Berwick St, W1   0778 066 7258   4–1D
11-12 Dean St, W1   020 7287 8964   4–1D
Kingly Ct, Carnaby St, W1   020 7287 2200   4–2B
23 Garrick Street, WC2   020 3019 1881   5–3C **NEW**
15 Exmouth Mkt, EC1   020 7287 8964   10–1A **NEW**
"Way better than the mainstream chains!" – the Elliot brothers' trendy pitstops "do nothing fussy or exotic, just genuinely good pizza" with "just the
right balance between toppings and crust". / Mon-Sat 10.30 pm, Sun 9.30 pm.

PizzaExpress £41 2 2 2
"All outlets deliver great grub and a cheery ambience" – for as long
as we've produced this guide, that's been the most common view on this
"amazingly consistent" 50-year-old, chain, also renowned as "a super place
for kids" ("basically a crèche serving OK food!"). Is that changing since
Hony Capital took over last year though? Critics have found it more
"money driven" of late, and the atmosphere in particular seems far less
sunny than it did. / www.pizzaexpress.co.uk; 11.30 pm-midnight; most City
branches closed all or part of weekend; no booking at most branches.

Pizzeria Oregano N1 £42 3 4 3
18-19 St Albans Pl   020 7288 1123   9–3D
"Consistently good thin-crust pizza" makes it worth remembering this cute,
family-friendly Italian, hidden off Upper Street. / N1 0NX;
www.pizzaoregano.co.uk; @PizzeriaOregano; 11 pm, Fri & Sun 11.30 pm; closed
weekday L.

Pizzeria Pappagone N4 £36 3 4 4
131 Stroud Green Rd   020 7263 2114   9–1D
"A proper, Italian, noisy trattoria" in Finsbury Park that's "a go-to family
pick" for many locals, thanks to its "bustling pace with speedy service" and
"exquisite pizza – we can't pass up the house special, Pizza Max
no matter how hard we try!" / N4 3PX; www.pizzeriapappagone.co.uk; midnight.

Pizzeria Pellone SE24 £23 4 3 2
Herne Hill, 153a Dulwich Road   020 8001 7652   11–2D
"A cracking new pizzeria in Herne Hill": "a traditional oven turns out
uncomplicated, tasty pizzas with satisfyingly chewy-yet-crispy crusts plus
a good, short list of toppings. Service is fine, staff friendly, vibe good".
/ SE24; www.pizzeriapellone.co.uk; @PizzeriaPellone; 11 pm, Sun 10 pm.

Pizzeria Rustica TW9 £42 3 3 2
32 The Quadrant   020 8332 6262   1–4A
"Much nicer than the chains!" – this "cheap 'n' cheerful" indie
is "extremely convenient, being just by Richmond Tube" and produces
"consistently excellent pizzas". / TW9 1DN; www.pizzeriarustica.co.uk; Mon-Sat
11 pm, Sun 10 pm; no Amex.

Pizzicotto W8   £40   4 4 3

267 Kensington High Street   020 7602 6777   8–1D

"An offshoot of the ever-busy Il Portico" – this "slightly downmarket, but truly excellent-value version of its parent" provides "terrific pizza", "with unusually good ingredient sourcing", and using black dough (healthier so they say). / W8 6NA; www.pizzicotto.co.uk; @pizzicottow8; 10.30 pm, Sun 9.30 pm; closed Mon.

Plateau E14   £74   2 2 3

4th Floor   020 7715 7100   12–1C

With its prime Canary Wharf perch offering splendid views of Docklands, this D&D London operation is first-and-foremost "a great place to take clients", if not an especially inspired one. After hours, look out for special evening offers. / E14 5ER; www.plateau-restaurant.co.uk; @plateaulondon; 10.30 pm; closed Sat L & Sun; set weekday L £53 (FP), set dinner £61 (FP).

The Plough SW14   £45   3 4 5

42 Christ Church Rd   020 8876 7833   11–2A

A perfect pitstop after a walk in Richmond Park, a few minutes away – this "kid and dog-friendly" pub in a quiet East Sheen lane boasts a wonderful outside terrace as well as an extremely atmospheric interior. All this plus "quality" cooking and "the nicest staff". / SW14 7AF; www.theplough.com; Mon-Thu 9.30 pm, Fri & Sat 10 pm, Sun 9 pm; no Amex.

Plum + Spilt Milk,
Great Northern Hotel N1   £69   2 3 4

Great Northern Hotel   020 3388 0818   9–3C

This "beautiful dining room" has a "top location" – if you're travelling through King's Cross station anyhow – and it's a particularly handy option on business. Fans say it's "better value than its neighbour, The Gilbert Scott", although like its rival, the food can seem "lacklustre". / N1C 4TB; www.gnhlondon.com; @PlumSpiltMilk; 11 pm, Sun 10 pm.

Poco E2 NEW   £45

129a Prichards Rd, Broadway Mkt   020 7739 3042   14–2B

A new opening from a successful Bristol venture aiming to storm Hackney's Broadway Market with its eco-friendly tapas – early reports are of good food, especially for brunch, but that it's "not the most relaxing" spot at busy times. / E2 9AP; www.eatpoco.com; @eatpoco; 11 pm, Sat & Sun 10 pm; SRA-3 star.

POLLEN STREET SOCIAL W1   £101   2 2 3

8-10 Pollen St   020 7290 7600   3–2C

"Maybe a victim of its own success?" – Jason Atherton's first solo venture in Mayfair remains one of London's most popular destinations, but "seems to have lost its way a bit". To fans, the "dreamy" and "creative cuisine" is a "perfect indulgence"; and even if the "cool" decor has a challenging acoustic ("for Social, read noisy") they applaud a "refreshingly relaxed approach to fine dining" that's "not too fussy and formal". Doubters, however, have had meals here that "lack any wow-factor" and choke on prices that are now "the wrong side of excruciating". / W1S 1NQ; www.pollenstreetsocial.com; @PollenStSocial; 10.45 pm; closed Sun; set weekday L £69 (FP).

Polpetto W1 £48 2 3 3
11 Berwick St 020 7439 8627 4–2D
*Fans of Russell Norman's Soho 'bacaro' say it's "so much better" than any
of his other Venetian-via-New York 'cichetti' bars. Its ratings aren't that
great though, because too many reporters feel it's "overpriced and boring",
especially since Florence Knight gave up the stoves. / W1F 0PL;
www.polpo.co.uk; 11 pm, Sun 10.30 pm; no bookings.*

Polpo £40 2 2 2
Harvey Nichols, SW1 020 7201 8625 6–1D NEW
41 Beak St, W1 020 7734 4479 4–2B
142 Shaftesbury Ave, WC2 020 7836 3119 5–2B
6 Maiden Ln, WC2 020 7836 8448 5–3D
Duke Of York Sq, SW3 020 7730 8900 6–2D
126-128 Notting Hill Gate, W11 020 7229 3283 7–2B
2-3 Cowcross St, EC1 020 7250 0034 10–1A
*"Can't see what the hype is (was) about?" Russell Norman's "frenetic",
Venetian cichetti cafés are, at their best, "a fun option for a quick bite,
with an appealing choice of small plates" but they are "slipping" fast –
the food is "losing its edge", service is "very rushed", and "there's not
enough space between tables". / www.polpo.co.uk; W1 & EC1 11 pm;
WC2 11 pm, Sun 10.30 pm; W1 & EC1 closed D Sun.*

Le Pont de la Tour SE1 £78 2 2 4
36d Shad Thames 020 7403 8403 10–4D
*"There's something about having Tower Bridge in the background that sets
the mood just right..." at this D&D London Thames-side landmark (where
Tony Blair once hosted dinner with Bill Clinton). But, despite a "beautiful
restoration" this year, its Gallic cuisine remains "very mediocre for the
price", and the "huge and complex wine list" likewise comes with
"huge mark ups". / SE1 2YE; www.lepontdelatour.co.uk; @lepontdelatour;
10.30 pm, Sun 9.30 pm; no trainers; set weekday L £45 (FP).*

Popeseye £47 3 2 2
108 Blythe Rd, W14 020 7610 4578 8–1C
36 Highgate Hill, N19 020 3601 3830 9–1B
277 Upper Richmond Rd, SW15 020 8788 7733 11–2A
*"Super steaks" from 28-day-hung Aberdeen Angus served with "good chips,
green salad and really good wine that's not expensive" is the raison d'être
of this trio in Olympia (est 1994), Putney and Highgate; the last of these
was new in 2015, and puts in "a huge effort on service in a tough
location". There's the odd disappointment recorded, but fans are adamant:
"for all the talk of Hawksmoor and Goodman I still prefer Popeseye, so to
hell with the new boys!" / www.popeseye.com; 10.30 pm; D only, closed Sun;
no credit cards.*

Poppies £29 3 3 3
59 Old Compton Street, W1 020 7482 2977 5–3A NEW
30 Hawley Cr, NW1 020 7267 0440 9–2B
6-8 Hanbury St, E1 020 7247 0892 13–2C
*Fans applaud the "very good chips" and "great-tasting fresh fish" at these
chippies in Spitalfields, Camden Town and now Covent Garden,
all decorated with post-war memorabilia (founder Pat "Pop" Newland
entered the trade aged 11 in 1952). A dissenting minority complain that
they've become "overpriced tourist traps". / see web for detail.*

La Porchetta Pizzeria £34 233

33 Boswell St, WCI   020 7242 2434   2–1D
141-142 Upper St, N1   020 7288 2488   9–2D
147 Stroud Green Rd, N4   020 7281 2892   9–1D
74-77 Chalk Farm Rd, NW1   020 7267 6822   9–2B
84-86 Rosebery Ave, EC1   020 7837 6060   10–1A

"No-nonsense Italian comfort food in very generous helpings" maintains the buzz at these four family-owned north London standbys – most notably "huge, crisp, fresh pizzas". / www.laporchetta.net; Mon-Sat 11 pm, Sun 10 pm; WC1 closed Sat L & Sun; N1,EC1 & NW1 closed Mon-Fri L; N4 closed weekday L; no Amex.

La Porte des Indes W1 £79 335

32 Bryanston St   020 7224 0055   2–2A

"Travel in time and space to Pondicherry" at this exotic venue in a converted subterranean Edwardian ballroom off Marble Arch. "Inside, it's vast, like a tropical forest", and with "fine", rather unusual Franco-Indian cuisine, it adds up to "a real experience": "expensive, but understandably so". / W1H 7EG; www.laportedesindes.com; @LaPorteDesIndes; 11.30 pm, Sun 10.30 pm; no Amex; set weekday L £41 (FP), set Sun L £53 (FP).

Il Portico W8 £55 354

277 Kensington High St   020 7602 6262   8–1D

"Don't be put off by the bland exterior in an unremarkable parade of shops", say fans of this "family-owned stalwart in Kensington", which has been operated by the same family for 50 years. The dated ambience is "very warm" and they serve "wonderful northern Italian (Emilia-Romagna) cuisine, lovingly prepared". / W8 6NA; www.ilportico.co.uk; 11 pm; closed Sun.

Portland W1 £67 543

113 Great Portland St   020 7436 3261   2–1B

"Immaculately prepared", thoughtful dishes delivered "with great enthusiasm" by "youthful and charming" staff create "an air of calm contentment" at this "unassuming" Fitzrovia yearling – one of the best foodie arrivals of recent years. In looks, it's a tad "IKEA-esque". / W1W 6QQ; www.portlandrestaurant.co.uk; 9.45 pm; closed Sun.

Portobello Ristorante W11 £53 343

7 Ladbroke Rd   020 7221 1373   7–2B

"There's a great atmosphere outside when busy... which is often", at this "fun" Italian, just off Notting Hill Gate (by comparison, the indoor decor is a tad "dull"). "Charming" staff provide "reliably enjoyable" Sicilian dishes, and "great pizza". / W11 3PA; www.portobellolondon.co.uk; 10 pm, Fri-Sat 11 pm, Sun 10 pm.

The Portrait,
National Portrait Gallery WC2 £65 234

St Martin's Pl   020 7312 2490   5–4B

"A new arrival is faced head-on with an amazing panorama of Nelson, Big Ben, Whitehall and Trafalgar Square", at this roof-top dining room, above the gallery. "The food is seasonal, British, tasty, and a bit unimaginative", but – even if "prices reflect the unique surroundings" – generally "better than you might expect". / WC2H 0HE; www.npg.org.uk/visit/shop-eat-drink.php; Thu-Sat 8.30 pm; closed Mon D, Tue D, Wed D & Sun D; set pre theatre £40 (FP).

Potli W6 £42 5 4 3
319-321 King St 020 8741 4328 8–2B
"Better than Indian Zing!" (nearby). This "exceptional and stylish" Hammersmith venue ("crowded and filled with artefacts from India") offers cooking that's "a great deal more accomplished than the street food it bills itself as" – "everything excites the palate, from the cocktail blending basil, cardamom and limoncello with gin, to the last scraping of the gloriously decadent mango shrikhand". / W6 9NH; www.potli.co.uk; @Potlirestaurant; 10.15 pm, Fri & Sat 10:30 pm, Sun 10 pm.

LA POULE AU POT SW1 £63 2 2 5
231 Ebury St 020 7730 7763 6–2D
"Romance is in the air" of this "extravagantly French" Pimlico veteran, especially "after dark in the magical candlelight" of its "secluded and dim-lit dining spots" (and also "on the pavement, under umbrellas in summer"). Foodwise, its stolid, "rustic" classics are "OK, but nothing special", and delivered – "with a Gallic shrug" – by service that's "haphazard" but generally "friendly, colourful and accommodating". / SW1W 8UT; www.pouleaupot.co.uk; 11 pm, Sun 10 pm.

Prawn On The Lawn N1 £49 4 3 3
220 St Paul's Rd 020 3302 8668 9–2D
"Absolutely fresh fish, beautifully cooked" is the major selling-point of this "very hipster" fishmonger and restaurant near Highbury & Islington tube. It can get "very cramped – but so what?" / N1 2LY; prawnonthelawn.com; @PrawnOnTheLawn; 11 pm; closed Mon & Sun; no Amex.

Primeur N5 £48 4 3 4
116 Petherton Rd 020 7226 5271 1–1C
"A great recent find", this Highbury local with communal seating serves "fantastic" sharing plates from an "ever-changing" hand-written menu, plus 'low intervention' wines – "knowledgeable staff help you pair them with the food". "Sit at the bar for the best view of the kitchen – I wanted to order everything!" / N5 2RT; www.primeurn5.co.uk; @Primeurs1; 10.30 pm, Sun 5 pm; closed Mon, Tue L, Wed L, Thu L & Sun D.

Princess of Shoreditch EC2 £55 3 3 3
76 Paul St 020 7729 9270 13–1B
This well-established gastropub revival of a traditional old watering hole – one of the original hip venues on the Shoreditch-City border – still pulls in a "lively and trendy clientele" with "top food" both in the bar and up the spiral stairs in a more formal dining room. / EC2A 4NE; www.theprincessofshoreditch.com; @princessofs; 10.30 pm, Sun 9 pm; no Amex.

Princess Victoria W12 £46 3 3 3
217 Uxbridge Rd 020 8749 5886 8–1B
"A beautiful old gin palace" on a busy highway in deepest Shepherd's Bush; the food is "variable" – at best "sensational", at worst just "fine" – but a consistent draw is the "fabulous wine list" (NB "great deal on Mondays, with wine sold at retail prices"). / W12 9DH; www.princessvictoria.co.uk; @pvwestlondon; 10.30 pm, Sun 9.30 pm; no Amex.

Princi W1 £34 3 3 4
135 Wardour St 020 7478 8888 4–1D
"Fast and furious" smart bakery in Soho with a "great buzz"; "cheap 'n' cheerful with plenty of choice" – "delicious Milanese pizza" wins top billing and "the cakes aren't half bad either". / W1F 0UT; www.princi.com; midnight, Sun 10 pm; no bookings.

Prix Fixe W1 £42 3 3 2
39 Dean St 020 7734 5976 5–2A
"Who does food at these prices in Soho these days?" "Well-executed
French classics" ("the menu won't surprise you") ensure this "reliable" and
"exceptional value" bistro is "always busy". It's "very handy for pre- and
post-theatre dining", and – as the name suggests – "the prix fixe is not
restricted to those hours". / W1D 4PU; www.prixfixe.net; @prixfixelondon;
11.30 pm.

The Promenade at The Dorchester W1 £120 2 4 4
The Dorchester Hotel, 53 Park Lane 020 7629 8888 3–3A
"A rare treat nowadays, but over half a century it's always been
a particular pleasure!" This ultra-plush and "beautiful" lounge provides
a picturebook setting for a light bite, but most particularly afternoon tea:
"absolutely delicious with simply masses of yummy treats!" / W1K 1QA;
10.30 pm; no shorts.

Provender E11 £39 3 4 3
17 High St 020 8530 3050 1–1D
This "authentic French bistro" in Wanstead is the latest venture from
seasoned restaurateur Max Renzland. It is "deservedly popular" for the
"excellence" of its cuisine and a "good-value set lunch" – "the côte
de boeuf for two is epic". / E11 2AA; www.provenderlondon.co.uk;
@ProvenderBistro; Sun 9 pm, Mon-Thu 10 pm, Fri 10.30 pm, Sat 11.30 pm.

The Providores & Tapa Room W1 £75 3 2 2
109 Marylebone High St 020 7935 6175 2–1A
"Peter Gordon's genius still works its magic" at his long-established pan-
Pacific HQ. The upstairs room is "small, crowded, dark and noisy", but the
"fusion dishes are wondrous – simple tastes combine to make something
unique and totally delicious". "Great and interesting breakfast" too.
/ W1U 4RX; www.theprovidores.co.uk; @theprovidores; 10 pm, Sun 9.45 pm;
SRA-2 star.

Prufrock Coffee EC1 £13 3 2 4
23-25 Leather Ln 07852 243 470 10–2A
"Coffee just as it should be – like being back on Bondi beach!" – is found
at this haven for caffeine addicts near Chancery Lane, along with "super
tasty healthy and slightly different lunch options". / EC1N 7TE;
www.prufrockcoffee.com; @PrufrockCoffee; L only; no Amex.

Pulia SE1 £38 3 4 3
36 Stoney St 020 7407 8766 10–4C
"Authentic food and interesting wine from Puglia" win approval for this
invitingly chichi, "friendly and airy" deli/café (the first outside Italy in the
group), a short walk from happening Borough Market. / SE1 9AD;
www.pulia.com/london; @Puliauk; 9 pm.

The Punchbowl W1 £48 4 4 4
41 Farm St 020 7493 6841 3–3A
"I went in for a bar snack and got something so much better!" –
This attractive Mayfair pub (once owned by Madonna-ex, Guy Ritchie)
is something of a "surprise", serving some "really inspired dishes, cooked
from the heart". / W1J 5RP; www.punchbowllondon.com; @ThePunchBowlLDN;
11 pm, Sun 10.30 pm; closed Sun D.

Punjab WC2 £33 3 2 3
80 Neal St 020 7836 9787 5–2C
One of London's longest-serving Indians in a handy Covent Garden location,
this traditional curry house is still managing to record some very decent
food scores. / WC2H 9PA; www.punjab.co.uk; 11 pm, Sun 10.30 pm.

Pure Indian Cooking SW6   £48

67 Fulham High Street   020 7736 2521   11–1B

*For a curry fix north of Putney Bridge, this straightforward contemporary
Indian is worth remembering – more reports please. / SW6 3JJ;
www.pureindiancooking.com; @PureCooking; closed Sat L & Sun L*

Quaglino's SW1   £72   1 1 3

16 Bury St   020 7930 6767   3–3D

*Fans "love the glimmering glamour" of this big D&D-group basement
in St James's – "make sure you dress up!" As it hots up though, the noise
can be "overwhelming", and prices are scary for food that's so "average".
/ SW1Y 6AJ; www.quaglinos-restaurant.co.uk; @quaglinos; 10.30 pm, Fri & Sat
11 pm; closed Sun; no trainers; set weekday L & dinner £43 (FP).*

The Quality Chop House EC1   £48   3 4 3

94 Farringdon Rd   020 7278 1452   10–1A

*"Evocative", restored Victorian 'Working Class Caterer', near Exmouth
Market, whose "authentic wooden booths" have infamously "uncomfortable
benches". At its best currently, it's an all-round success with "enthusiastic"
service and "superb quality" British-sourced fare ("meat especially") but it's
not consistent – bad days feature "staff all over the place" and
"unremarkable", "expensive" dishes. An "exceptionally well-chosen" wine
list is the pluspoint you might expect of somewhere part-owned by Jancis
Robinson's son. Top Menu Tip – "confit potato to die for". / EC1R 3EA;
www.thequalitychophouse.com; @QualityChop; 10.30 pm; closed Sun; SRA-1 star.*

Quantus W4   £48   4 5 4

38 Devonshire Rd   020 8994 0488   8–2A

*"Fabulous service defines this place" – a "Chiswick neighbourhood gem"
that serves a Latino-influenced modern European menu including "great
steaks and fish". "Leo, the owner and maître d', is a great character and
cements the charm". / W4 2HD; www.quantus-london.com; 10 pm; closed Mon L,
Tue L & Sun.*

Quattro Passi W1   £96   3 3 2

34 Dover St   020 3096 1444   3–3C

*The two-year-old Mayfair outpost of Antonio Mellino's noted Amalfi venue
showcases the cuisine of Campania. Ratings are solid, but the vertiginous
prices – particularly when it comes to the vino – somewhat restricts
appreciation to a business clientele. / W1S 4NG; www.quattropassi.co.uk;
@quattropassiuk; 10.30 pm; closed Sun D.*

Le Querce SE23   £39   3 4 3

66-68 Brockley Rise   020 8690 3761   1–4D

*"It looks just like a café outside", but this "very friendly" family run
restaurant in Brockley is known for its "superb value" Italian cooking,
with the best choices from the specials board – "an impressive array" that's
"particularly interesting". Its ratings have dipped however, and while
reports are all upbeat, the most cautious says "it's good, but not as top
notch as it used to be". Top Menu Tip – "Three scoops of a
vast assortment of esoteric ice cream flavours for less than a fiver!"
/ SE23 1LN; www.lequerce.co.uk; 9.30 pm, Fri & Sat 9.45 pm, Sun 20.30 pm; closed
Mon & Tue L.*

Quilon SW1 £71 442
41 Buckingham Gate 020 7821 1899 2–4B
"Sophisticated and beautifully presented" Keralan cuisine has won much foodie acclaim for the Taj Group's luxurious Indian, near Buckingham Palace, whose plush modern decor teeters between bland and stylish. It's a practical choice too – "is this the only Michelin Star restaurant ever that understands and delivers a perfect working lunch?" / SW1E 6AF; www.quilon.co.uk; @thequilon; 11 pm, Sun 10.30 pm.

Quirinale SW1 £61 442
North Ct, 1 Gt Peter St 020 7222 7080 2–4C
"A great venue for parliamentarian-spotting – it's easy to understand why lobbyists wine and dine MPs here", when you consider the "exceptional" Italian cuisine ("consistently excellent without being overly fussy") at this "high-quality" basement near Westminster. Also, "it's a quiet room you can easily have a conversation in, and there's an extensive list of Italian wines – what more could you ask for?" / SW1P 3LL; www.quirinale.co.uk; @quirinaleresto; 10.30 pm; closed Sat & Sun.

Quo Vadis W1 £56
26-29 Dean St 020 7437 9585 5–2A
Just as it was hitting a "really special" stride, it's all change at the Hart Bros' Soho veteran (hence we've left it un-rated). From autumn 2016, much of the ground floor is set to become a branch of their Barrafina brand. The remainder of the ground floor, the ex-bar, will continue as Quo Vadis, while with echoes of The Ivy, chef Jeremy Lee will refocus more of his efforts on a new dining room within the Quo Vadis members' club (which occupies the floors above). / W1D 3LL; www.quovadissoho.co.uk; 11 pm; closed Sun.

Rabbit SW3 £49 443
172 King's Rd 020 3750 0172 6–3C
"Finally a decent restaurant at the heart of the Kings Road!" – this offbeat "organic, farm-to-table" sibling to Notting Hill's Shed remains an unexpected hit in an area where brainless mediocrity is the prevailing norm. Despite a "cramped space" with "wonky tables and excruciatingly uncomfy seats designed to add to the rustic vibe" the style is "fun" and "there is real originality in many of the tapas-y dishes (even if they are expensive for their small size)". / SW3 4UP; www.rabbit-restaurant.com; @RabbitResto; midnight, Mon 11 pm, Sun 6 pm; closed Mon L & Sun D.

Rabot 1745 SE1 £60 322
2-4 Bedale St 020 7378 8226 10–4C
This choccy-themed bar-with-dining in Borough Market, named after a 250-year-old St Lucia cocoa estate, is a "great chocolatey experience" with interesting food and drink pairings. Plus, of course, "hot chocolate to die for – seriously rich, smooth, luxurious and with deep, deep flavours". / SE1 9AL; www.rabot1745.com; @rabot1745; 9.30 pm; closed Mon.

Ragam W1 £28 431
57 Cleveland St 020 7636 9098 2–1B
"Though not the greatest looker" (and that's after the refurb!) this stalwart Indian near the Telecom Tower remains "first choice for genuine Keralan food" for many reporters, with "the crowning glory being when the bill arrives – £20 a head for grub this good should be impossible!" But its ratings were hit by some unusually downbeat reports this year, saying it was "notably not as good"... "OK but no longer outstanding or destinational". / W1T 4JN; www.ragam.co.uk; 11 pm.

Rail House Café SW1 NEW
Nova, Victoria Street   no tel   2–4B
From Adam White (the man behind Fitzrovia's popular brunch spot Riding House Café and trendy Village East in Bermondsey) comes a vast new café in Victoria's monumental Nova development. The 330-cover venue is spread over two floors with a raised private dining room and outdoor seating area with al-fresco bar. It's set to open just as our print guide goes to press (in September 2016). / SW1H 0HW.

Rainforest Café W1   £61   2 3 3
20-24 Shaftesbury Ave   020 7434 3111   4–3D
"Eating in the Amazon rainforest! Kids love it!", "gorillas/ elephants/ thunder storms…" and all at this theatrical Piccadilly Circus experience – "it's not the greatest food, but it never fails to deliver in the entertainment stakes". / W1V 7EU; www.therainforestcafe.co.uk; @RainforestCafe; 9.30 pm, Sat 10 pm; credit card deposit required to book.

Randall & Aubin W1   £60   3 4 4
14-16 Brewer St   020 7287 4447   4–2D
"There's just something about sitting on one of the stools" ("they even replaced the old uncomfortable ones!"), and "watching the world go by", at this "fun-and-frisky" Soho haven (a characterful, tiled ex butcher's shop). "Charming" and "flamboyant" staff provide "so-fresh" seafood and "excellent rôtisserie chicken". / W1F 0SG; www.randallandaubin.com; @randallandaubin; 11 pm, Fri & Sat 11.30 pm, Sun 9.30 pm; booking lunch only.

Randy's Wing Bar E15 NEW   £30
Here East, 28 East Bay Lane   020 8555 5971   14–1C
A summer 2016 newcomer – this chicken wing specialist at Hackney Wick's Here East development serves everything from their signature American buffalo wings to the Bombay Indian spice and Vietnamese Hanoi Tuk Tuk varieties. / E15 2GW; www.randyswingbar.co.uk; @randyswingbar; 11 pm, Thu-Sun 11.30 pm; closed Mon L.

Rani N3   £30   3 2 2
7 Long Ln   020 8349 4386   1–1B
This "always dependable" Gujarati veggie veteran in Finchley is "now under new ownership but still up to scratch" – the buffet is "very good and very cheap", even if the "clean and bright" ambience "could be jollier". / N3 2PR; www.raniuk.com; 10.30 pm.

Raoul's Café   £46   2 2 3
105-107 Talbot Rd, W11   020 7229 2400   7–1B
13 Clifton Rd, W9   020 7289 7313   9–4A
"The best eggs Benedict in London" and "French toast to die for" make these "busy" Maida Vale ("particularly nice when you can sit outside") and Notting Hill cafés favourites for brunch. The "retro Sixties décor" goes down well, but they're "not family-friendly". / www.raoulsgourmet.com; 10.15 pm, W11 6.15 pm; booking after 5 pm only.

Rasa £38
6 Dering St, W1   020 7629 1346   3–2B
Holiday Inn Hotel, 1 Kings Cross, WC1   020 7833 9787   9–3D
55 Stoke Newington Church St, N16   020 7249 0344   1–1C
56 Stoke Newington Church St, N16   020 7249 1340   1–1C
*"Remarkable value and delicious South Indian food" still dazzles at the
Stoke Newington original of this small Keralan chain (the "decent and very
convenient" branch near Oxford Circus is the next most popular).
"The overall formula hasn't evolved over the years" however, and ratings
generally have declined – "please Rasa, mix it up!" / www.rasarestaurants.com;
10.45 pm; WC1 & W1 closed Sun.*

Ravi Shankar NW1 £32
132-135 Drummond St   020 7388 6458   9–4C
*The "wonderful lunchtime buffet is incredible value", at this stalwart café,
like many of its rivals in the Little India "just around the corner from Euston
Station". / NW1 2HL; 10.30 pm.*

Red Fort W1 £66
77 Dean St   020 7437 2525   5–2A
*This "Soho classic" (which underwent a contemporary revamp some years
ago) was more consistently highly rated this year for its "refined Indian
cuisine" from a menu "which gets away from the normal well-trodden
footpaths". Even fans though still concede that it remains "pricey".
/ W1D 3SH; redfort.co.uk; @redfortlondon; 10.30 pm; closed Sat L & Sun; no shorts;
set weekday L & pre-theatre £42 (FP).*

Red Lion & Sun N6 £52
25 North Road   020 8340 1780   9–1B
*"A lovely location in the heights of Highgate" and "interesting" menu win
all-round praise for this "perfect", "old-established" hostelry. / N6;
www.theredlionandsun.com; @redlionandsun; 10 pm, Sun 9 pm.*

The Red Pepper W9 £48
8 Formosa St   020 7266 2708   9–4A
*This "cramped but surprisingly good" Italian local in Maida Vale does
"great wood-fired pizza (if not much else)" – "fresh, high quality and
remarkably consistent given the size of the kitchen!" / W9 1EE;
www.theredpepperrestaurant.co.uk; Sat 11 pm, Sun 10 pm; Mon-Thu D only, Fri-Sun
open L & D; no Amex.*

Le Relais de Venise L'Entrecôte £46
120 Marylebone Ln, W1   020 7486 0878   2–1A
18-20 Mackenzie Walk, E14   020 3475 3331   12–1C
5 Throgmorton St, EC2   020 7638 6325   10–2C
*"Addictive steak, secret sauce and fries" (and no other menu options) is the
winning formula of this "busy" Gallic grill-house chain, whose "efficient but
perfunctory", "bums-on-seats" approach adds little to the ambience.
"Annoying no-reservations policy" – expect a queue. / www.relaisdevenise.com;
W1 11 pm, Sun 10.30 pm; EC2 10 pm; EC2 closed Sat & Sun; no booking.*

Le Restaurant de Paul £38
29-30 Bedford St, WC2   020 7836 3304   5–3C
Tower 42, Old Broad St, EC2   020 7562 5599   10–2C
*Fans of the Covent Garden HQ of the well-known pâtisserie chain say that,
away from the bakery counters, its civilised, traditional dining room
"deserves to be taken seriously" as a Theatreland destination in its own
right, for an "authentically Gallic" light bite or afternoon tea. There is also
a year-old, much more contemporary-style outpost in the City's Tower 42.
/ @PAUL_BAKERY; see web for detail.*

Reubens W1 £56

79 Baker St   020 7486 0035   2–1A
Long-established kosher deli (ground floor) / restaurant (basement)
in Marylebone whose "salt beef on rye bread is still the benchmark"
according to fans. Sceptics say it's "indifferent and expensive"… as they
have been doing for the last 20 years. / W1U 6RG;
www.reubensrestaurant.co.uk; 10 pm; closed Fri D & Sat; no Amex.

The Rib Man E1 £12

Brick Lane, Brick Lane Market   no tel   13–2C
"A fantastic bloke with a concept and passion that others can only admire":
Mark Gevaux is "one of the few pulled-pork purveyors in London to take
real care over what he's doing" and sells "massive rolls piled high with meat
and his trademark Holy F##k hot sauce". "Lovely piggy goodness!"
/ E1 6HR; www.theribman.co.uk; @theribman.

Rib Room,
Jumeirah Carlton Tower Hotel SW1 £103

Cadogan Pl   020 7858 7250   6–1D
This luxurious Belgravia haunt has its fans – "such a special treat" –
but the appeal is qualified: "the eponymous rib of beef is splendid but not
really backed up by other items", and "to price it at the same level as the
Ledbury and Ritz is considerably too high". / SW1X 9PY; www.theribroom.co.uk;
@RibRoomSW1; 11 pm, weekends 10.30 pm; set weekday L & dinner £52 (FP).

Riccardo's SW3 £43

126 Fulham Rd   020 7370 6656   6–3B
"Always lively, always good", insist fans of this "popular local Italian"
in Chelsea applauding its "great welcome from fantastic staff" and
"options to satisfy the fussiest eater" ("spelt, wheat-free pasta, etc"). But
a sizeable minority still complain that "they're content to rest on their hind
legs" here, and find "the overall experience is disappointing". / SW3 6HU;
www.riccardos.it; @ricardoslondon; 11.30 pm, Sun 10.30 pm.

The Richmond E8 £53

316 Queensbridge Rd   020 7241 1638   14–1A
"Fabulous oysters" at £1 each during happy hour set the tone at Brett
Redman's "smartened up" Hackney pub conversion "with a brilliant raw
bar attached". Fish dishes including "superb monkfish" also impress.
/ E8 3NH; www.therichmondhackney.com; @TheRichmond_; midnight, Sun 5 pm;
closed Sun D.

Riding House Café W1 £57

43-51 Great Titchfield St   020 7927 0840   3–1C
"Quirky decoration lends an interesting and buzzy atmosphere" to this
"always lively and bustling" Fitzrovia venue. It's useful for business
or breakfast (or both) – for the latter "you can be healthy or sinful
according to your mood". / W1W 7PQ; www.ridinghousecafe.co.uk; 10.30 pm,
Sun 9.30 pm.

The Rising Sun NW7 £48

137 Marsh Ln, Highwood Hill   020 8959 1357   1–1B
This "lively and picturesque pub" in Mill Hill serves "the best food in the
area" – a "varied menu of British and Italian dishes" now "back to its high
standard" with the return of chef Paolo Mortali. / NW7 4EY;
www.therisingsunmillhill.co.uk; @therisingsunpub; 9.30 pm, Sun 8.30 pm; closed
Mon L.

Ristorante Frescobaldi W1   £78   **3 3 2**
15 New Burlington Pl   020 3693 3435   4–2A
*After a year in operation, this ambitious Mayfair Italian (first UK venture
of a 700-year-old Italian wine dynasty) wins praise for its "more-ish menu"
and of course "great wines". However, there's a "feeling that this is a
missed opportunity" – the room "looks lovely" but "doesn't quite work";
and "prices are high, even for Mayfair" yet "portions are small".
/ W1S 5HX; www.frescobaldirestaurants.com; @frescobaldi_uk; 11 pm;
set weekday L £42 (FP).*

The Ritz, Palm Court W1   £77   **2 3 5**
150 Piccadilly   020 7493 8181   3–4C
*"The gold standard for afternoon tea" – this "splendid and iconic" room
wins praise as "a quintessential English experience with melt-in-the-mouth
petit fours, sandwiches and cakes" and even if it's "tooooooo expensive"
most reporters feel it's "worth it" to "feel a little bit special". / W1J 9BR;
www.theritzlondon.com; 7.30 pm; jacket & tie required; set always available £52
(FP); SRA-2 star.*

The Ritz Restaurant, The Ritz W1   £134   **3 4 5**
150 Piccadilly   020 7493 8181   3–4C
*"London's most beautiful dining room" (decorated in the style of Louis XVI)
"never fails to work its magic" (and you can also "eat out on the terrace
overlooking Green Park for a lovely treat"). Historically the "exemplary"
service has tended to outshine the "traditional" British cuisine here,
but most reports this year found it "exceptionally good in every way". Top
Tip – "the dinner-dance on Friday and Saturday is a top experience".
/ W1J 9BR; www.theritzlondon.com; @theritzlondon; 10 pm; jacket & tie required;
set weekday L £74 (FP); SRA-2 star.*

Riva SW13   £64   **4 4 2**
169 Church Rd   020 8748 0434   11–1A
*"The best authentic north Italian food in London" is a credible claim for
Andrea Riva's intimate Barnes fixture – a long-fêted favourite of the
fooderati. It is un-changing over the years: it's "a bit expensive", the "drab"
decor "needs an update" and "it's rather like a club: either you are
recognised by the proprietor as a regular, or he ignores you". / SW13 9HR;
10.30 pm, Sun 9 pm; closed Sat L.*

Rivea, Bulgari Hotel SW7   £71   **3 3 2**
171 Knightsbridge   020 7151 1025   6–1C
*The second London outlet of French superchef Alain Ducasse, this "blingy"
Knightsbridge basement serves up "wonderfully creative" cuisine: "small
dishes of exceptionally high quality that sing of the Mediterranean". Even
fans, though, can feel it's "a bit wasted on its hotel-guest clientele".
/ SW7 1DW; www.bulgarihotels.com; 10.30 pm.*

THE RIVER CAFÉ W6 £102 **3** **2** **4**
Thames Wharf, Rainville Rd 020 7386 4200 8–2C
*"So special, but also so nose-bleedingly expensive" – that's the perennial
trade-off at Ruth Rogers's world-famous café, whose celebrity is totally
at odds with its backstreet Hammersmith location, in a Thames-side wharf
shared with hubbie Lord Richard Roger's architectural practice (till the latter
moved this year). For its many advocates, it's "the holy grail of restaurants"
featuring "phenomenal ingredients" (a "true definition of provenance and
quality") on "an ever-changing menu" displaying both "simplicity and
complexity"; and all this delivered in a "light and buzzing",
"minimalist warehouse-style dining room" next to a riverside terrace that's
"stunning on a sunny day". On the downside, service can be "smug",
and even those sold on its virtues often leave feeling the prices make
it "a glaring con": "it's good, but with this price point attached, it's such
a poor representation of the heart, passion and grass roots of Italian
cooking, and when you get the bill, you just feel nothing is worth this
much!" (Plans for a new Mayfair branch are currently on hold.)* / W6 9HA;
www.rivercafe.co.uk; @RiverCafeLondon; 9 pm, Sat 9.15 pm; closed Sun D;
set weekday L £51 (FP).

Rivington Grill £53 **2** **2** **2**
178 Greenwich High Rd, SE10 020 8293 9270 1–3D
28-30 Rivington St, EC2 020 7729 7053 13–1B
*These "relaxed", "straightforward" grills in Shoreditch and Greenwich –
owned by Richard Caring's Caprice Group – delight some reporters with
their "lively buzz" and "all-round menu". They can also appear "dull"
or "ordinary" however, and invite comparisons with "more edgy
competition".* / www.rivingtongrill.co.uk; 11 pm, Sun 10 pm; SE10 closed Mon,
Tue L & Wed L.

Roast SE1 £70 **2** **2** **3**
Stoney St 0845 034 7300 10–4C
*"A beautiful, light-filled interior" boosts the draw (particularly to business
diners) of this "upscale" fixture over Borough Market, which specialises
in the cooking of traditional British meat dishes. Aside from the
"unbeatable" breakfasts however, the cuisine is no better than "pleasant",
especially at prices critics feel are "scandalous".* / SE1 1TL;
www.roast-restaurant.com; 10.45 pm; closed Sun D.

Rocca Di Papa £37 **2** **2** **3**
73 Old Brompton Rd, SW7 020 7225 3413 6–2B
75-79 Dulwich Village, SE21 020 8299 6333 1–4D
*"Good solid traditional Italian fare" helps fuel the "lively" and "extremely
friendly" atmosphere at these South Kensington and Dulwich Village locals,
whose "big selling point for parents is that they like children who eat
properly (so anything from the main menu is approx. half price)". "Pizza
is not only better than PizzaExpress across the road, but cheaper".* / SW7
11.30 pm; SE21 11 pm.

Rochelle Canteen E2 £51 **3** **2** **4**
Arnold Circus 020 7729 5677 13–1C
*"On a sunny day you feel you have discovered the perfect escape" on the
terrace of this "offbeat and vibey", "hidden-London" venue – converted
bikesheds of a former school near Spitalfields. Run by Melanie Arnold and
Margot Henderson (wife of St John's Fergus), it "creates great flavours from
seasonal ingredients" in a "bright, airy canteen setting", and is "one of the
few top-quality BYOs".* / E2 7ES; www.arnoldandhenderson.com; L only, closed
Sat & Sun; no Amex.

Rocket £46 `3` `3` `3`

2 Churchill Pl, E14 020 3200 2022 12–1C
201 Bishopsgate, EC2 020 7377 8863 13–2B
6 Adams Ct, EC2 020 7628 0808 10–2C

For a "decent" lunchtime or post-work pizza, salad or steak, these "cheap 'n' cheerful" cafés around the City and Canary Wharf receive a number of recommendations. / 10.30 pm, Sun 9.30 pm; W1 closed Sun; EC2 closed Sat & Sun; SW15 Mon-Wed D only, Bishopsgate closed Sun D, E14.

Rök £42 `4` `2` `2`

149 Upper Street, N1 no tel 9–3D `NEW`
26 Curtain Rd, EC2 020 7377 2152 13–2B

"Outstanding smoked goods and pickled everything" inspire fans of the "brilliant Nordic-inspired food" at this white-walled Scandi-look yearling (which since mid-2016 now has an Islington sibling too). "Tables are squashed" however, and sceptics – who scent "hype" – claim "all the dishes taste the same". / see web for detail.

Roka £80 `4` `3` `3`

30 North Audley St, W1 020 7305 5644 3–2A
37 Charlotte St, W1 020 7580 6464 2–1C
Aldwych House, 71-91 Aldwych, WC2 020 7294 7636 2–2D
Unit 4, Park Pavilion, 40 Canada Sq, E14 020 7636 5228 12–1C

"Exquisite" dishes "bursting with flavour" – be they "sumptuous sushi and sashimi" or "wonderful robata-yaki style BBQ" – are the hallmark of these "cool and vibrant" Japanese-fusion operations. The Charlotte Street original is still the best: "sit at the bar made of slabs of tree trunk and watch the chefs' delicate preparations!" / www.rokarestaurant.com; 11.15 pm, Sun 10.30 pm; booking: max 8.

Romulo Café W8 `NEW` £50 `3` `3` `3`

343 Kensington High Street 020 3141 6390 6–1A

The first international branch (in Kensington) of a restaurant group from the Philippines (owned by the grandchildren of General Carlos Romulo) showcasing Filipino cuisine. Lorenzo Maderas (formerly of Latin American/Japanese fusion spot Sushisamba) oversees the kitchen – early reports say the place is "trying hard", and "worth a second visit". / W8 6NW; www.romulocafe.co.uk; @romulolondon; midnight, Sun 11.30 pm.

Rosa's £35 `3` `3` `2`

5 Gillingham Street, SW1 020 3813 6773 2–4C `NEW`
23a Ganton St, W1 020 7287 9617 4–2B
48 Dean St, W1 020 7494 1638 5–3A
246 Fulham Rd, SW10 020 7583 9021 6–3B
Atlantic Road, SW9 no tel 11–2D `NEW`
Westfield Stratford City, E15 020 8519 1302 14–1D
12 Hanbury St, E1 020 7247 1093 13–2C

"Does what it says on the tin!" – these "reliable" cafés are a trusty source of "tasty, unpretentious Thai food", with the "heart-of-Soho" branch by far the best known. / www.rosaslondon.com; 10.30 pm, Fri & Sat 11 pm, Ganton St Sun 10 pm; some booking restrictions apply.

Rossopomodoro £43 3 2 2

John Lewis, 300 Oxford St, W1 020 7495 8409 3–2A **NEW**
50-52 Monmouth St, WC2 020 7240 9095 5–3B
214 Fulham Rd, SW10 020 7352 7677 6–3B
1 Rufus St, N1 020 7739 1899 13–1B
10 Jamestown Rd, NW1 020 7424 9900 9–3B
46 Garrett Ln, SW18 020 8877 9903 11–2B

"Surprisingly good pizza" – "really fresh and authentic" with "crispy bases"
and "fresh mozzarella and other ingredients imported from Italy" –
wins praise for this Naples-based chain. Service can be "disorganised"
however, and depending on your tastes, the ambience is either "pleasantly
frenetic" or "chaotic and noisy". / www.rossopomodoro.co.uk; 11.30 pm,
WC2 Sun 11.30 pm.

Roti Chai W1 £46 4 3 4

3 Portman Mews South 020 7408 0101 3–1A

"Good Indian street food is hard to come by... even in India!", but this
upbeat two-floor venue near Selfridges (no-booking ground floor,
more formal basement) "brilliantly captures the charm and tastes
of railway station vendors of yore" with its "varied dishes, amazing flavours,
and great value for money". / W1H 6HS; www.rotichai.com; @rotichai;
10.30 pm.

Roti King, Ian Hamilton House NW1 £22 5 2 1

40 Doric Way 07966 093467 9–3C

"Boy, it gets crowded" in this "friendly but chaotic" Euston basement caff
("there's no real chance of avoiding queueing or being cheek-by-jowl at a
shared table"). Why? – "the best freshly made rotis outside of Malaysia"
(plus "very tasty" noodle dishes) at bargain prices. / NW1 1LH.

Rotorino E8 £48 2 3 3

434 Kingsland Rd 020 7249 9081 14–1A

Stevie Parle's low-lit, Italian-inspired kitchen in Dalston again inspired
somewhat mixed feelings: most reporters applaud "interesting,
yet ungimmicky" culinary creations plus "charming" staff, but to
a significant minority the food seems "over-priced", and "lacks the flair
associated with a big-name chef". / E8 4AA; www.rotorino.com; @Rotorino;
11 pm.

**Rotunda Bar & Restaurant,
Kings Place N1** £55 3 4 3

90 York Way 020 7014 2840 9–3C

"Amazing views over the canal" from the outside terrace, are a highlight
of this "very relaxing" arts centre brasserie. Service is "first class" too,
and the food is "very respectably cooked". / N1 9AG;
www.rotundabarandrestaurant.co.uk; @rotundalondon; 10.30 pm; set weekday L
£34 (FP).

**Roux at Parliament Square,
RICS SW1** £88 5 5 3

12 Great George St 020 7334 3737 2–3C

"Faultless cuisine" (better than MPs deserve) distinguishes the Roux family's
formal Parliament Square outlet, where MasterChef winner Steve Groves
thrills diners "every time". Critics say the setting is "dull" but we agree with
those who find it 'stately'. / SW1P 3AD; www.rouxatparliamentsquare.co.uk;
10 pm; closed Sat & Sun; set weekday L £52 (FP).

Roux at the Landau, The Langham W1   £94   3 4 4

1c Portland Pl   020 7965 0165   2–1B

"The room will make your date swoon", at this "oasis", over the road from Broadcasting House, whose spaciousness and serenity also mark it out as being "great for a business lunch". "Classic cuisine is beautifully presented, and immaculately served". / W1B 1JA; www.rouxatthelandau.com; @Langham_Hotel; 10.30 pm; closed Sat L & Sun; no trainers.

Rowley's SW1   £70   2 2 2

113 Jermyn St   020 7930 2707   4–4D

This St James's veteran occupies the original Wall's sausages and ice cream premises. Some swear by the Chateaubriand steak and "endless fries", but others say its grills are "not special" and "overpriced for what you get" ("they have to pay for that real estate somehow"). / SW1Y 6HJ; www.rowleys.co.uk; @rowleys_steak; 10.30 pm.

Rox Burger SE13   £26   4 3 3

82 Lee High Rd   020 3372 4631   1–4D

"Amazing burgers" mean this Lewisham joint is "so popular you can't always get a table" – in fact, "the only criticism is that it's too small!" ("although they do a takeaway service now, too"). The veggie burgers and craft beers are excellent, "and the freshly made lemonade is out of this world". / SE13 5PT; www.roxburger.com; @RoxburgerUK; 10 pm, Fri & Sat 11 pm.

Royal China W1   £48   3 1 2

24-26 Baker St, W1   020 7487 4688   2–1A
805 Fulham Rd, SW6   020 7731 0081   11–1B
13 Queensway, W2   020 7221 2535   7–2C
30 Westferry Circus, E14   020 7719 0888   12–1B

Legions of fans still hail "the best dim sum outside of Hong Kong" at these "always buzzing" Cantonese stalwarts. Some reporters feel they are "starting to live on their reputation" however, but one constant is the "brusque service – like a downmarket airline!" / www.royalchinagroup.co.uk; 10.45 pm, Fri & Sat 11.15 pm, Sun 9.45 pm; no booking Sat & Sun L.

Royal China Club W1   £75   4 3 3

40-42 Baker St   020 7486 3898   2–1A

"Even better than Hong Kong" is the wild claim made by fans of the dim sum at this Marylebone flagship for the China Club group – it's "pricier than the rest, but a cut above, so worth it". And don't arrive late for your booking: "they limit your time to 1.5 hours because they're always packed at the weekend". / W1U 7AJ; www.royalchinagroup.co.uk; 11 pm, Sun 10.30 pm.

The Royal Exchange Grand Café,
The Royal Exchange EC3   £56   2 2 4

The Royal Exchange Bank   020 7618 2480   10–2C

The grandeur of its majestic covered courtyard setting, and its heart-of-the-City location makes this seafood café a "constant, convenient rendezvous" for business, despite "lackadaisical service and pricey uninspired fare". / EC3V 3LR; www.royalexchange-grandcafe.co.uk; @rexlondon; 10 pm; closed Sat & Sun.

RSJ SE1   £51   3 3 2

33 Coin St   020 7928 4554   10–4A

"A real stalwart!" – Nigel Wilkinson's South Bank fixture, by the National Theatre, is an exemplar of "consistently solid, French-bourgeois food at fair prices". 'Nul points' for the '80s interior decor, but the wine list is "amazing" – "probably the best Loire selection in the world". / SE1 9NR; www.rsj.uk.com; @RSJWaterloo; 11 pm; closed Sat L & Sun; set weekday L & dinner £25 (FP).

Rubedo N16 NEW   £43   4 4 3
35 Stoke Newington Church St   020 7254 0364   1–1C
"Food from the heart!" Culinary results can be "exceptional" – and are
matched with "organic, non-filtered wines from a temperature-controlled
wine cellar", plus "friendly and knowledgeable" service – at this simple new
bistro, on Stokie's main drag. / N16 0NX; www.rubedolondon.com;
@rubedolondon; 10 pm, Fri & Sat 10.30 pm; closed Mon & Sun D.

Rucoletta EC2   £47   2 2 1
6 Foster Lane   020 7600 7776   10–2C
"The food's honest, not flashy", and "decent value" at this handy Italian
"in the heart of the City (near St Paul's)" – "extremely popular
at lunchtime" (including with business lunchers), when "the little
conservatory at the back is one of the nicer places to sit in the area".
/ EC2V 6HH; www.rucoletta.co.uk; @RucolettaLondon; 9.30 pm, Thu-Sat 10 pm;
closed Sat D & Sun; no Amex.

Rugoletta   £38   4 3 3
308 Ballards Ln, N12   020 8445 6742   1–1B
59 Church Ln, N2   020 8815 1743   1–1B
"You feel like you're in Italy" at these traditional Barnet and East Finchley
locals, which are family-run "and it shows". "It's very Lady and the Tramp,
the spaghetti-sharing scene – AND the spaghetti is exceptionally good!"
/ see web for detail.

Rules WC2   £78   4 3 5
35 Maiden Ln   020 7836 5314   5–3D
"History oozes out of the walls" of London's oldest restaurant (established
1798) – still one of its most "iconic", whose "olde-worlde, panelled
interior" has a "priceless warmth and depth". Many a Londoner still
considers it "a reliable old favourite" for "traditional British roasts, games,
pies and oysters", but it has seemed more and more "overpriced" in recent
times – any more, and it will achieve the Covent Garden tourist-trap status
it's heretofore miraculously avoided. / WC2E 7LB; www.rules.co.uk; 11.30 pm,
Sun 10.30 pm; no shorts.

Le Sacré-Coeur N1   £36   4 4 4
18 Theberton St   020 7354 2618   9–3D
"Step in from Theberton Street and you're in a little bit of France"…
(in reality a veteran bistro, just north of Angel). "Good simple, rustic
traditional French fare with good size portions and a well-priced wine
offer". / N1 0QX; www.lesacrecoeur.co.uk; @LeSacreCoeurUK; 11 pm, Fri & Sat
11.30 pm, Sun 10.30 pm; set weekday L £22 (FP).

Sacro Cuore NW10   £36   4 3 3
45 Chamberlayne Rd   020 8960 8558   1–2B
"A serious contender for best pizza in London", this Kensal Rise 4-year-old
has now been joined by a branch in Crouch End that's "even better". The
Neapolitan-style pizza is "soft, light and airy" ("just the right internal
bounce with crisp searing and delicious flavour"), and topped with
"ludicrously good tomato sauce" and "super-fresh mozzarella di buffala".
/ NW10 3NB; www.sacrocuore.co.uk/menu.html; @SacroCuorePizza; 10.30 pm,
Fri & Sat 11 pm; no Amex.

Sagar £36
17a Percy St, W1 020 7631 3319 3–2B
31 Catherine St, WC2 020 7836 6377 5–3D
157 King St, W6 020 8741 8563 8–2C
*The South Indian vegetarian fare at this small chain (Covent Garden,
Tottenham Court Road, Hammersmith and Harrow) "is consistently good
and great value for money". "The excellent thali and dosa make up for the
decor – you're here for the food". / www.sagarveg.co.uk; Sun-Thu 10.45 pm,
Fri & Sat 11.30 pm.*

Sagardi EC2 NEW
Cordy House, 87-95 Curtain Road awaiting tel 13–1B
*A Basque-inspired international group – with operations from Barcelona
to Buenos Aires – which opened its first London outpost in Shoreditch
in late summer 2016. Galician (Txuleton) beef cooked on a charcoal grill
is a mainstay of both menu and decor, and there's a pintxos bar serving
Basque ciders, as well as wine and beer. / EC2A 3AH; @Sagardi_UK.*

Sager + Wilde E2 £38 2 4 4
193 Hackney Rd 020 8127 7330 13–1C
*"It's not about the food" at this "Brooklyn meets Hackney" haunt –
"the highlight is definitely the amazing wines by the glass" ("many with real
bottle age, without paying the earth"). This said, its cheese toasties ("great
smell") and charcuterie are "well considered and well prepared". / E2 8JP;
www.sagerandwilde.com; @snw_paradiserow; 10 pm; closed weekday L.*

Sager + Wilde Restaurant E2 £56 3 3 4
250 Paradise Row 020 7613 0478 13–1D
*"A wine-lover's haven, and the food's good as well" at this "fantastic"
Bethnal Green railway arch venue, by the couple behind the popular
Hackney Road wine bar of the same name. "All the staff are so helpful
and knowledgeable" – "not to mention the great wines available by the
glass", and "hearty, well-crafted British fare". / E2 9LE;
www.sagerandwilde.com; @sagerandwilde; midnight.*

Saigon Saigon W6 £39 3 3 3
313-317 King St 020 8748 6887 8–2B
*"Authentic" Vietnamese flavours, a "friendly atmosphere" and
"good prices" ensure that this long-serving local in Hammersmith is often
busy – so it's worth booking. / W6 9NH; www.saigon-saigon.co.uk;
@saigonsaigonuk; 11 pm, Sat & Mon 10 pm.*

St John EC1 £65 5 4 3
26 St John St 020 7251 0848 10–1B
*"A pioneer of British food" – Fergus Henderson & Trevor Gulliver's
"austere" but "staunch" Smithfield ex-smokehouse remains an "amazingly
consistent, ever-quirky" source of "honest" enjoyment. "Staff are
so accommodating, the atmosphere is relaxed and constantly buzzing",
and the focus is on the "incredible" dishes: be it "outlandish stuff (all the
bits of the animal that you didn't know about that you then think you could
maybe eat); or something traditional done impressively well." Top Tip –
regulars go to the "atmospheric" adjacent bar, with its "simple but
perfectly adequate menu". / EC1M 4AY; www.stjohngroup.uk.com;
@SJRestaurant; Mon -Sun 11 pm; closed Sat L & Sun D.*

St John Bread & Wine E1   £56   5 3 2
94-96 Commercial St   020 7251 0848   13–2C
This "stark (very St John)" white-walled canteen near Spitalfields
is arguably "reminiscent of a public convenience", but it's "always a treat
to go there". The often "wacky" and offal-centric British dishes are
"exceptional" – "mouth-wateringly good" – and "they always seem to have
a wine that you've never tried before, and it's always first class". Top Tip –
breakfast comprises "bacon sandwich heaven". / E1 6LZ;
www.stjohngroup.uk.com/spitalfields; @StJBW; Mon 8 pm, 10.30 pm.

St Johns N19   £46   3 3 5
91 Junction Rd   020 7272 1587   9–1C
A "favourite local gastropub" in Archway, where the refurb of the front bar
and gorgeous old rear dining room (built as a ballroom) is now complete.
Despite the gentrification, "it still has great beer" and "food that pleases
everyone". / N19 5QU; www.stjohnstavern.com; @stjohnstavern; Mon 10 pm,
11 pm, Sun 9 pm; closed Mon L; no Amex; booking max 12 may apply.

**Saint Luke's Kitchen,
Library WC2 NEW**   £56
112 Saint Martin's Lane   020 3302 7912   5–4C
Near the Coliseum, a boutique-guesthouse 'Library', which launched a new
restaurant in late spring 2016, whose menu is to rotate every 6-8 weeks
in accordance with a new guest chef with a forthcoming cook book launch
to plug! No feedback yet on this splendid concept, but it's certainly
a handsomely designed and very convenient venue. / WC2N 4BD;
www.lib-rary.com/restaurant; @LibraryLondon; 1 am; closed Sun.

St Moritz W1   £54   4 3 3
161 Wardour St   020 7734 3324   4–1C
"Sharing a delicious fondue is always romantic" and where better than this
"wonderful, olde worlde" chalet-style stalwart in the heart of Soho, which
"feels just like you are in Switzerland!" – "not the lightest of meals" but
surprisingly good. "There's nothing else like it in London" – long may
it survive! / W1F 8WJ; www.stmoritz-restaurant.co.uk; Mon-Sat 11.30 pm,
Sun 10.30 pm.

Sakagura W1 NEW
8 Heddon Street   no tel   4–3B
From the group behind Shoryu ramen and The Japan Centre – an autumn
2016 opening in the Crown Estates development just off Regent Street.
A theatrical robata grill will contribute dishes to a menu including udon,
soba noodles and sushi, alongside a wide range of sake, from leading brand
Gekkeikan. / W1B 4BU; www.sakaguralondon.com; @sakaguraldn.

Sake No Hana SW1   £76   3 1 2
23 St James's St   020 7925 8988   3–4C
This offbeat, potentially impressive Japanese-inspired outfit has an unusual
'60s setting next to The Economist in St James's, and its "trendy" but
soulless decor was the result of a refit (overseen by Alan Yau) several years
ago. Its modern Asian cuisine can be "incredible", but is too often "only OK
at the top-end prices" making the "patchy" service all the harder to bear.
/ SW1A 1HA; www.sakenohana.com; @sakenonhana; 11 pm, Fri & Sat 11.30 pm;
closed Sun.

Salaam Namaste WC1 £36 3 4 3
68 Millman St 020 7405 3697 2–1D
"An Indian with a real difference", this little place "off the beaten track
in Bloomsbury" serves up an "interesting menu of carefully spiced dishes" –
"and it's good value for central London". / WC1N 3EF;
www.salaam-namaste.co.uk; @SalaamNamasteUK; 11.30 pm, Sun 11 pm.

Sale e Pepe SW1 £68 3 4 4
9-15 Pavilion Road 020 7235 0098 6–1D
"Always very welcoming staff" ("completely nuts!") help drive the "fun"
atmosphere at this "genuine" ("cramped" and "noisy") trattoria, hidden
away near Harrods, which is "unchanged in over two decades" –
"a fantastic all-round experience" with "a wide choice of tasty dishes".
/ SW1X 0HD; www.saleepepe.co.uk.

Salloos SW1 £55 4 3 2
62-64 Kinnerton St 020 7235 4444 6–1D
This age-old survivor in a Belgravia mews is known for its "very good old-
fashioned Pakistani cuisine", in particular "brilliant lamb chops". Over the
years however, perhaps "due to a seemingly high proportion of Gulf
clientele, prices have sky-rocketed". / SW1X 8ER; www.salloos.co.uk; 11 pm;
closed Sun; may need 5+ to book.

Salmontini SW1 £72 2 2 3
1 Pont St 020 7118 1999 6–1D
Mixed feedback on this Belgravia yearling some still recall as Drones
(long RIP) and nowadays a plush Beirut-backed operation. Foes say it's
"a good location wasted" – "all show, no substance" – but fans applaud
"a great variation" on its predecessors, with very good cooking
(with smoked fish and sushi the speciality). / SW1X 9EJ; www.salmontini.com;
@Salmontini_Uk; 10.45 pm, Fri & Sat 11.15 pm, Sun 10.30 pm.

Salon Brixton SW9 £46 4 3 3
18 Market Row 020 7501 9152 11–2D
"A tiny upstairs restaurant in the atmospheric and hip Brixton market,
whose crammed-together tables only add to the atmosphere". It serves
"very good, adventurous small plates" and there's also an ever-changing,
no-choice set menu. / SW9 8LD; www.salonbrixton.co.uk; @Salon_Brixton; 10 pm;
closed Mon & Sun D.

Le Salon Privé TW1 £46 4 4 4
43 Crown Rd 020 8892 0602 1–4A
"You can't fault the food" at this classic French bistro, which has "hit its
stride" since taking over the St Margarets site of the former Brula (RIP).
"It's very good now – actually, excellent!" / TW1 3EJ; lesalonprive.net;
@lesalon_tweet; 10.30 pm; closed Mon & Sun D.

Salt & Honey W2 £47 3 4 2
28 Sussex Pl 020 7706 7900 7–1D
This "tiny bistro" serving "imaginative home cooking" is a "welcome new
local in the restaurant desert near Paddington station", set up by the Kiwi
duo behind Fulham's Manuka Kitchen. / W2 2TH; www.saltandhoneybistro.com;
@SaltHoneyBistro; 10 pm, Sun 9 pm; closed Mon; set weekday L £26 (FP).

Salt Yard W1   £49   3 3 3
54 Goodge St   020 7637 0657   2–1B
*"Upmarket Italian/Spanish tapas", ("some genuinely exciting standouts")
served by "knowledgeable but not over-bearing" staff in an "informal"
setting earn enduring popularity for this well-known Fitzrovia haunt
(the original of Simon Mullins's small group), even if it no longer appears
as cutting edge as it once did. / W1T 4NA; www.saltyard.co.uk; @SaltYardGroup;
10.45 pm, Sun 9.45 pm.*

Salut N1 NEW   £50   4 4 3
412 Essex Rd   020 3441 8808   9–3D
*"A gem of a place situated inauspiciously at the wrong end of Essex Road"
– a new Islington opening on the site of 3 Course (RIP), whose "location
can be overlooked" thanks to its "taste-bud tickling" modern European
fare, with interesting Nordic and German touches. / N1 3PJ;
www.salut-london.co.uk; @Salut_London; 11 pm, Sun 10 pm.*

Salvation In Noodles   £34   3 2 2
122 Balls Pond Rd, N1   020 7254 4534   14–1A
2 Blackstock Rd, N4   020 7254 4534   9–1D
*"Still a fave for pho" – a "cheap 'n' cheerful" Dalston Vietnamese, which
also has a lower-profile, year-old sibling in Finsbury Park.
/ www.salvationinnoodles.co.uk; see web for detail.*

Samarkand W1 NEW
33 Charlotte Street   020 3871 4969   2–1C
*Vodka has replaced sherry at this Fitzrovia basement, where the Hart Bros'
tapas-spot Fino (RIP) has been usurped by this Uzbeki venture – named for
the famous city on the Silk Road – which opened in late summer 2016.
Plov (or pilaf) is the best-known central Asian dish. / W1T 1RR;
www.samarkand.london; @SamarkandLondon.*

San Carlo Cicchetti   £51   3 3 4
215 Piccadilly, W1   020 7494 9435   4–4C
30 Wellington St, WC2   020 7240 6339   5–3D
*"If the Tardis had been done up with a wealth of gold and mirrors" it would
be akin to the "deceptively small-looking" Covent Garden branch of this
northern-owned Venetian tapas chain, which is a "quieter and calmer"
choice than its "really buzzy" sibling, "conveniently located a few steps
from Piccadilly Circus tube". Critics accuse them of "slightly aggressive
pricing", but most reports praise the "extensive, something-for-everyone
menu" of "fairly authentic" small plates. / www.sancarlocicchetti.co.uk; see web
for detail.*

San Daniele del Friuli N5   £44   3 4 3
72 Highbury Park   020 7226 1609   9–1D
*This "traditional" family-run Italian is "a good place for a quiet night out"
in Highbury Park. Its kitchen sends out food that's "always good and
sometimes very good". / N5 2XE; www.sandanielehighbury.co.uk; 10.30 pm;
closed Mon L, Tue L, Wed L & Sun; no Amex.*

The Sands End SW6   £51   2 3 3
135 Stephendale Rd   020 7731 7823   11–1B
*Fans of this deepest Fulham gastroboozer still say it's "great fun", but there
were a couple of reports this year over "very basic service and food issues",
including the odd "shocking" dish. / SW6 2PR; www.thesandsend.co.uk;
@thesandsend; 10 pm, Sun 9 pm.*

Santa Maria £33 5 4 3
92-94 Waterford Road, SW6 020 7384 2844 6–4A **NEW**
15 St Mary's Rd, W5 020 8579 1462 1–3A
"Superlative pizzas" – "up there with the best in Naples" – served
by "warm and welcoming staff" have made the "tiny and squashed"
W5 original one of the biggest things ever to happen to Ealing. Its new
"well-designed" Fulham sibling is going down well too – "a great addition
to SW6"… you can even book! / see web for detail.

Santini SW1 £79 2 3 3
29 Ebury St 020 7730 4094 2–4B
This "upmarket" stalwart Belgravia Italian (an A-lister favourite in days
of yore) with a "lovely terrace for summer" wins pretty solid praise for its
overall appeal. "It's on the pricey side however" and its harshest critics feel
"the food's not up to scratch". / SW1W 0NZ; www.santini-restaurant.com;
10 pm, Sat 11 pm.

Santore EC1 £46 4 3 3
59-61 Exmouth Mkt 020 7812 1488 10–1A
This "very genuine" Exmouth Market venue serves up "excellent"
Neapolitan fare including pizza, all in notably "large portions". "A little
piece of Italy in London", it's "family-friendly" and a good choice for Sunday
lunch. / EC1R 4QL; www.santorerestaurant.london; @Santore_london; 11 pm;
set weekday L £29 (FP).

Sapori Sardi SW6 £48 3 2 2
786 Fulham Rd 020 7731 0755 11–1B
"A home-from-home!" – fans continue to laud the "interesting, simple
Sardinian food" and "friendly staff" at this "splendid place" in Fulham.
/ SW6 5SL; www.saporisardi.co.uk; @saporisardi; 11 pm; no Amex.

Sardine N1 **NEW**
15 Micawber Street 020 7490 0144 13–1A
Former Rotorino head chef Alex Jackson cooks much of the French-centric
cuisine over a charcoal grill in Stevie Parle's simple, packed-in newcomer,
between Angel and Old Street, which opened in September 2016. / N1 7TB;
www.sardine.london; @sardinelondon.

Sardo W1 £58 3 2 2
45 Grafton Way 020 7387 2521 2–1B
This "authentic Sardinian" in Fitzrovia serves "consistently excellent food"
and the "fish is always good and fresh". But it's "a little cramped", and one
former fan fears it may be "living on its past reputation" somewhat
nowadays. / W1T 5DQ; www.sardo-restaurant.com; 11 pm; closed Sat L & Sun.

Sarracino NW6 £45 4 2 2
186 Broadhurst Gdns 020 7372 5889 1–1B
West Hampstead trattoria "stalwart" serving "traditional Italian dishes at a
reasonable price" – "it's known for its pizzas", but "pastas and mains are
equally good". / NW6 3AY; www.sarracinorestaurant.com; 11 pm; closed
weekday L.

Sartoria W1 £71 2 3 3
20 Savile Row 020 7534 7000 4–3A
Fans do say D&D London's "upmarket" expense-accounter favourite
in Mayfair is "much-improved" since it was re-launched in late 2015 with
Francesco Mazzei at the stoves. But his arrival has done little to shake the
overall consensus on this "so comfortable" but "somewhat impersonal"
Italian: "unexciting and pricey". / W1S 3PR; www.sartoria-restaurant.co.uk;
@SartoriaRest; 10.45 pm; closed Sun; set weekday L £37 (FP).

Satay House W2 £35 **3**|2|2
13 Sale Pl 020 7723 6763 7–1D
*"Lip smacking" (if sometimes slightly 'rough-edged') Malaysian food
continues to maintain the appeal of this "friendly" stalwart (est 1973) –
a two-floor operation, in a quiet street off Edgware Road. / W2 1PX;
www.satay-house.co.uk; 11 pm.*

Sauterelle, Royal Exchange EC3 £62 **3**|**3**|**4**
Bank 020 7618 2483 10–2C
*"Stunning views over the interior of the delightful Royal Exchange",
a "comfortable ambience, reliable food and an excellent wine list" make
this D&D London mezzanine "a great place to enjoy a decent dinner in the
heart of the City". On the debit side, "you certainly pay for it". / EC3V 3LR;
www.sauterelle-restaurant.co.uk; 9.30 pm; closed Sat & Sun; no trainers; set weekday
L & dinner £35 (FP).*

Savini at Criterion W1 NEW £86 1|1|2
224 Piccadilly 020 7930 1459 4–4D
*"Another dud" – this "extraordinary neo-Byzantine dining room" ("possibly
the most jaw-dropping space in the West End") – is so "disappointing
when one considers just how great it could be." With the previous
incumbent going into administration, this new Milanese régime is not only
"eyewateringly expensive" but too often provides "shocking food and
inattentive service". / W1J 9HP; www.saviniatcriterion.co.uk; @SaviniMilano;
midnight.*

Savoir Faire WC1 £39 **3**|**3**|**3**
42 New Oxford St 020 7436 0707 5–1C
*Budget, two-floor Gallic bistro decorated with posters from West End
productions, handy for the British Museum – "very good" classics
at affordable prices. / WC1A 1EP; www.savoir.co.uk; 10.30 pm, Sun 10 pm.*

The Savoy Hotel, Savoy Grill WC2 £89 2|**3**|**3**
Strand 020 7592 1600 5–3D
*This "elegant" panelled grill room has for decades been a "prestigious"
destination. Under Gordon Ramsay's reign, the "heftily priced" British
cooking can seem a little "short of its ambitions", but most reports are
upbeat, and the place remains a popular rendezvous, particularly for
"a discreet business lunch". / WC2R 0EU; www.gordonramsayrestaurants.com;
@savoygrill; 11 pm, Sun 10.30 pm; set weekday L & pre-theatre £51 (FP).*

The Savoy Hotel, Thames Foyer WC2 £79 2|**3**|**5**
The Savoy, The Strand 020 7420 2111 5–3D
*"The afternoon tea of dreams" – "a wonderful range of teas" coupled with
"absolutely fantastic pâtisserie" – is regularly reported in the "lavish,
comfortable and enthralling" central lounge of this London landmark:
service in particular "helps make for a delightful experience". / WC2R;
www.fairmont.com/savoy-london; @fairmonthotels; 11 pm.*

Scalini SW3 £76 **3**|2|**3**
1-3 Walton St 020 7225 2301 6–2C
*"Being always full and a bit cramped only adds to the atmosphere" of this
"old-fashioned" Italian on the fringes of Knightsbridge. Arguably this
is "safety first" cooking and there's no doubting the "sky-high prices",
but "you'll eat well" and it's "great fun". / SW3 2JD; www.scalinilondon.co.uk;
11.30 pm; no shorts.*

Scandinavian Kitchen W1 £14 **3** **3** **3**
61 Great Titchfield St 020 7580 7161 2–1B
"The coffee is good and the smorgasbord offerings are excellent" –
"especially the open sandwiches" – *at this Nordic café/grocer in Fitzrovia.
"You can also stock up on your favourite Scandi store-cupboard goodies".*
/ W1W 7PP; www.scandikitchen.co.uk; @scanditwitchen; 7 pm, Sat 6 pm, Sun 4 pm;
L only; no bookings.

SCOTT'S W1 £80 **4** **5** **5**
20 Mount St 020 7495 7309 3–3A
"Impossibly glamorous" and *"oozing class"* – Richard Caring's *"sumptuous"*
Mayfair star-magnet *"always creates a sense of occasion". "Effortlessly
polished"* service provides *"impeccable"* fish and seafood (*"so fresh
it practically swims onto your plate!"*) in an *"understated"* setting full
of *"old world charm".* / W1K 2HE; www.scotts-restaurant.com; 10.30 pm,
Sun 10 pm; booking max 6 may apply.

Sea Containers, Mondrian London SE1 £68 **2** **2** **4**
20 Upper Ground 0808 234 9523 10–3A
The "nautical-themed setting" and *"splendid Thames views"* of this
American-owned hotel dining room on the South Bank *"do justice to the
former shipping-line building's heritage".* Instances of food that's *"nothing
exciting or special"* however, lead to numerous gripes about the
"unwarranted price tag". / SE1 9PD; www.mondrianlondon.com; @MondrianLDN;
11 pm.

Seafresh SW1 £38 **3** **4** **2**
80-81 Wilton Rd 020 7828 0747 2–4B
This "brill fish and seafood resto" in Pimlico has for many years attracted
"millionaires, MPs and taxi drivers" with its *"delicious fresh fish 'n' chips"* –
"and the Greek salad's good, too". / SW1V 1DL; www.seafresh-dining.com;
10.30 pm; closed Sun.

The Sea Shell NW1 £44 **3** **3** **2**
49 Lisson Grove 020 7224 9000 9–4A
*One of London's best-established chippies is, say fans, "still difficult to beat"
and "a great stop-off for fresh fish 'n' chips". Aficionados feel that
"the restaurant section lags behind its standout takeout".* / NW1 6UH;
www.seashellrestaurant.co.uk; @SeashellRestaur; 10.30 pm; closed Sun.

Season Kitchen N4 £42 **3** **3** **2**
53 Stroud Green Rd 020 7263 5500 9–1D
*Fabulous-for-Finsbury Park local with an "uncompromising short menu"
of seasonal specials: critics may find the choice "limited", but on
most accounts it's "all the better for it" given the "interesting" cooking.*
/ N4 3EF; www.seasonkitchen.co.uk; @seasonkitchen; 10.30 pm, Sun 8 pm; D only.

Señor Ceviche W1 £42 **3** **3** **4**
Kingly Ct 020 7842 8540 4–2B
The "amazing range of Peruvian street food" served at this *"vibrant"*
hangout in Soho's Kingly Court gastro hub is *"a cut above most ceviche
operations",* and with *"decor that's very cool by the standards of this
slightly lame restaurant mall".* / W1B 5PW; www.senor-ceviche.com;
@SenorCevicheLDN; 11.30 pm, Sun 10.15 pm; set weekday L £26 (FP).

Seven Park Place SW1 £93 4️⃣4️⃣4️⃣
7-8 Park Pl 020 7316 1615 3–4C
This "gorgeous", "very small, but comfortable and cosy dining room"
is "so private" within a luxurious St James's hotel. It deserves to be better
known thanks to its "genuinely kind, helpful and passionate" staff and –
last but not least – William Drabble's "first rate cuisine". / SW1A 1LS;
www.stjameshotelandclub.com; @SevenParkPlace; 10 pm; closed Mon & Sun.

Seven Stars WC2 £34 2️⃣3️⃣3️⃣
53 Carey St 020 7242 8521 2–2D
"This tiny, charismatic pub" behind the Royal Courts of Justice – run by
landlady Roxy Beaujolais – "offers traditional ales and quirky food at very
good value prices". / WC2A 2JB; 9 pm.

Sexy Fish W1 £82 2️⃣1️⃣2️⃣
1-4 Berkeley Sq 020 3764 2000 3–3B
"Bling and blondes abound" at this "latest multi-million £££ venture from
Richard Caring" which is "arguably better suited to Vegas than to Mayfair".
A minority do swoon over the "stunning decor" and "beautifully presented"
sushi, robata, and Asian seafood dishes, but for the majority of reporters
it's just a "big", "brash" and "ridiculous" glitter ball, serving "uninspiring,
knock-off fusion dishes" to "D-list celebs and ecstatic wannabes taking
selfies"; and – given the "inattentive" service and humungous price tag –
"utterly disappointing". / W1J 6BR; www.sexyfish.com; @sexyfishlondon.

Shackfuyu W1 £48 5️⃣4️⃣4️⃣
14a, Old Compton St 020 7734 7492 5–2B
"Power-packed", taste combinations of "wonderful Japanese-Western
hybrid dishes" are served by "laid back" but "very knowledgeable" staff
at this "hip" Bone Daddies sibling, near Cambridge Circus: "creative,
unusual" and "amazing value for money". / W1D 4TH; www.bonedaddies.com;
@shackfuyu; 11 pm, Mon & Tue 10 pm, Sun 9 pm.

Shake Shack £24 3️⃣2️⃣2️⃣
Nova, Buckingham Palace Rd, SW1 no tel 2–4C NEW
80 New Oxford St, WC1 01925 555 171 5–1B
24 The Market, WC2 020 3598 1360 5–3D
The Street, Westfield Stratford, E20 awaiting tel 14–1D
"Accurately cooked, with good char", but "a bit small for the price" –
such are the pros and cons of the "quality burgers (and hot dogs)"
at Danny Meyer's American-style operations. / see web for detail.

Shampers W1 £49 2️⃣4️⃣5️⃣
4 Kingly St 020 7437 1692 4–2B
"Like an old friend" – this "bustling", '70s-survivor wine bar in Soho
is "always full of fun, as owner Simon presides over the very clubby
atmosphere" ("it's seemingly perpetually full of chartered surveyors!").
"Even if the menu does seem a little trapped in time", the food is "varied,
well prepared and always good value", and "the selection of wine
is amazing". / W1B 5PE; www.shampers.net; @shampers_soho; 10.30 pm;
closed Sun.

The Shed W8 £48 3️⃣2️⃣4️⃣
122 Palace Gardens Ter 020 7229 4024 7–2B
"Bigger than it first seems from the outside", this quirky, farm-to-table
venture in Notting Hill "lives up to its name" decorwise, and "it's a fun
place" (if with "hideously uncomfortable seats and tables that are too
small"). Its "seasonal British tapas" is "interesting and different" but expect
"a high bill". / W8 4RT; www.theshed-restaurant.com; @theshed_resto; 11 pm;
closed Mon L & Sun; SRA-3 star.

J SHEEKEY WC2 £75

28-34 St Martin's Ct   020 7240 2565   5–3B

"The kind of place that makes London special!" – Richard Caring's "so-classy" institution (est 1896) is tucked away down a Dickensian alley "in the heart of Theatreland" and remains not only the survey's most talked-about destination, but also its No. 1 for fish and seafood (narrowly trumping its stablemate Scott's in nominations as London's best). Beyond the doorman and intriguing, etched-glass façade, "congenial" staff are "amazingly well-drilled", and the "warm and inviting" interior is "almost like an exclusive club, divided into small, oak-panelled areas", and decorated with "black and white stills of famous actors". Mind you, it's "noisy", and "you pack in like sardines!" Top Menu Tip – fish pie. / WC2N 4AL; www.j-sheekey.co.uk; @JSheekeyRest; 11.30 pm, Sun 10 pm; booking max 6 may apply; set weekday L £46 (FP).

J Sheekey Atlantic Bar WC2 £76 ▣▣▣

28-34 St Martin's Ct   020 7240 2565   5–3B

"Nothing makes me happier than sitting up at this beautiful bar, and having a range of oysters and a glass of champagne!" – This "indulgent" Theatreland rendezvous "combines a relaxed tone with a fizzing vibe" and provides "a hard-to-beat selection of shellfish". The recent rebranding and launch under a new name rightly underlines its distinctive appeal to the adjacent main restaurant. / WC2N 4AL; www.j-sheekey.co.uk; @JSheekeyRest; 11.30 pm, Sun 10.30 pm; booking max 3 may apply.

Shepherd Market Wine House W1 NEW £54

21-23 Shepherd Market   020 7499 8555   3–4B

In the middle of super-cute Shepherd Market, a cute, old-fashioned-looking wine shop, offering quality vinos plus small plates, which opened in summer 2016 – only 18 covers but a fun perch. / W1J 7PN; www.shepherdmarketwinehouse.co.uk; @ShepMarketWine; 11 pm, Sun 10.30 pm.

Shepherd's SW1 £54 ▣▣▣

Marsham Ct, Marsham St   020 7834 9552   2–4C

"It's back, and doing a good job for the lobbyists!" This traditional Westminster stalwart – a well-known politico haunt – re-opened last year, and "retains its excellent ambience with booths and well-spaced tables, plus very good food and service. Top Menu Tip – The shepherd's pie (of course!) is recommended…" / SW1P 4LA; www.shepherdsrestaurant.co.uk; @shepherdsLondon; 10.30 pm; closed Mon L, Sat & Sun.

Shikumen, Dorsett Hotel W12 £39 ▣▣▣

58 Shepherd's Bush Grn   020 8749 9978   8–1C

Mixed feedback this year on this Chinese luminary, whose "upmarket" style in an "impressive" new hotel is slightly at odds with its location on still-grungy Shepherd's Bush Green. Fans again extol its "consistently delicious" cooking – particularly "fantastic dim sum" – but it has also seemed "unmemorable" at times this year, and the "cavernous" room strikes many as "attractive", but can also give an impression that's "subdued". / W12 5AA; www.shikumen.co.uk; @ShikumenUK; 10 pm.

Shilpa W6 £31 ▣▣▣

206 King St   020 8741 3127   8–2B

"From the outside it looks like an average Indian café/takeaway restaurant" but this "fantastic", if unassuming South Indian outfit "serves very good honest Keralan food at unbelievably low prices". "You don't go for the great ambience" though. / W6 0RA; www.shilparestaurant.co.uk; 11 pm, Thu-Sat midnight.

Shoryu Ramen £42 3 2 2
9 Regent St, SW1   no tel   4–2B
3 Denman St, W1   no tel   4–3C
5 Kingly Ct, W1   no tel   4–4D
Broadgate Circle, EC2   no tel   13–2B
*For fans of these "crowded and cramped" Japanese, they are a "go-to,
quick cheap eat with steaming bowls of ramen"; overall though, ratings
were more M.O.R. this year. / Regent St 11.30 pm, Sun 10.30 pm –
Soho midnight, Sun 10.30 pm; no booking (except Kingly Ct).*

Shotgun W1 £50 2 2 2
26 Kingly St   020 3137 7252   4–2B
*Mississippi-born Brad McDonald opened his "lively" Soho BBQ to much
fanfare last year, but reporter feedback is mixed. Fans say its "combination
plates make for a great evening", but sceptics "don't get the love for this
place": "slowly it dawned on people that it's really not so amazing and the
portions-price ratio is somewhat larcenous". / W1B 5QD;
www.shotgunbbq.com; @ShotgunBBQ; 11 pm.*

Shuang Shuang W1 NEW £41 3 3 3
64 Shaftesbury Ave   020 7734 5416   5–3A
*"Fun, healthy and cheap" new venture from Thai restaurateur Fah
Sundravorakul, on Chinatown's northern border, seeking to differentiate
itself from the competition by establishing a trend for Chinese DIY hot pot
– you cook the meal yourself using implements provided, grabbing
ingredients as necessary from a central conveyor belt. / W1D 6LU;
www.shuangshuang.co.uk; @HotPotShuang; 11 pm, Fri & Sat 11.30 pm; may need
4+ to book.*

The Sichuan EC1 £46 4 2 2
14 City Road   020 7588 5489   9–3D
*"Superb", "very authentic", "spicy" Sichuan cooking has won instant
acclaim for this "no-nonsense" City-fringe newcomer, near the Honourable
Artillery Company, despite sometimes "perfunctory service" and "a lack
of thought in the decor". / EC1Y 2AA; www.thesichuan.co.uk; 11 pm.*

Sichuan Folk E1 £44 4 4 2
32 Hanbury St   020 7247 4735   13–2C
*Fans say you find "probably London's best Sichuan cooking" at this small
East End spot, off Brick Lane – it's "amazing value for money". / E1 6QR;
www.sichuan-folk.co.uk; 10.30 pm; no Amex.*

The Sign of The Don Bar & Bistro EC4 £54 2 3 4
21 St Swithin's Ln   020 7626 2606   10–3C
*"In the basement of the more formal Don (next door) – a relatively relaxed
venue for a business lunch" that's "quite inexpensive for the area". These
converted cellars feel more "enjoyable" than their grander neighbour,
with "very dependable" brasserie fare, and "a great wine list" and selection
of sherries. / EC4N 8AD; www.thesignofthedon.com; @signofthedon; 10 pm; closed
Sat & Sun.*

Signor Sassi SW1 £69 3 3 4
14 Knightsbridge Grn   020 7584 2277   6–1D
*"Lively and fun", this traditional Knightsbridge trattoria has "great Italian-
family-restaurant values", making it both child-friendly and romantic: "ideal
for a date, with just the right amount of fuss made of your
guest to impress". / SW1X 7QL; www.signorsassi.co.uk; @SignorSassi; 11.30 pm,
Sun 10.30 pm.*

Silk Road SE5 £24 5️⃣2️⃣2️⃣
49 Camberwell Church St 020 7703 4832 1–3C
"Everyone crams in on benches at bare tables" at this "vibrant, no-frills
canteen-style eatery in Camberwell". Why? – "Wonderful, spicy food from
Xianjing province" that's "amazingly cheap" ("I'd happily pay double, it's so
interesting"); "as a Chinese person, I can tell you this is authentic cooking
at best!!" / SE5 8TR; 10.30 pm; closed weekday L; cash only.

Simpson's Tavern EC3 £40 2️⃣3️⃣5️⃣
38 1/2 Ball Ct, Cornhill 020 7626 9985 10–2C
This "old-school inn and chophouse" in a Dickensian City alleyway has
a history that stretches back to 1757, and still serves up "top-notch grub
at very sensible prices". "Fantastic staff" add to the appeal, and it's
"brilliant for a breakfast meeting". / EC3V 9DR; www.simpsonstavern.co.uk;
@SimpsonsTavern; 3 pm; L only, closed Sat & Sun.

Simpsons-in-the-Strand WC2 £76 1️⃣1️⃣1️⃣
100 Strand 020 7836 9112 5–3D
This "lovely period dining room" is renowned as a bastion of the
best British cuisine (most famously Roast Beef) but its performance can
seem "sad" nowadays. For "the best breakfast" it does win praise
("for business or pure indulgence") but more generally it seems "old-
fashioned" and lacklustre – "a once-famous, busy and respected restaurant
that's been devastated and left to a handful of tourists". / WC2R 0EW;
www.simpsonsinthestrand.co.uk, 10.30 pm, Sun 9 pm; no trainers; set weekday L &
dinner £53 (FP).

Singapore Garden NW6 £43 3️⃣3️⃣2️⃣
83a Fairfax Rd 020 7624 8233 9–2A
"Can't fault it over the years!" – this "always buzzing and noisy" north
London favourite, tucked away in a parade of shops in Swiss Cottage,
boasts a large and loyal fanclub thanks to its "reliable" realisation of an
"eclectic" menu mixing Chinese, Malaysian and Singaporean dishes.
/ NW6 4DY; www.singaporegarden.co.uk; @SingaporeGarden; 11 pm, Fri & Sat
11.30 pm.

Six Portland Road W11 NEW £53 4️⃣4️⃣3️⃣
6 Portland Road 020 7229 3130 7–2A
"At last we have a terrific local" – Holland Park types are cock-a-hoop with
this "buzzy and busy" indie newcomer (just 40 seats) from an ex-Terroirs
duo. Service is "impeccable" ("no pomposity or smugness here"),
the modern British dishes are "lovely, fresh and beautifully cooked" and
there's a well-selected wine list. / W11 4LA; www.sixportlandroad.com; 11 pm,
Sun 5 pm; closed Mon & Sun D.

Sketch, Lecture Room W1 £134 3️⃣3️⃣5️⃣
9 Conduit St 020 7659 4500 4–2A
"You may feel you've taken a sip of something psychedelic!" as you take
in the "fabulously camp" decor of this "spectacular" Mayfair dining room,
overseen by superstar chef, Pierre Gagnaire. The idiosyncratic cuisine can
be "fantastic" too, but the "complicated" combinations can also seem
"too clever by half". Hallucinogens may be advisable on arrival of the bill…
/ W1S 2XG; www.sketch.uk.com; @sketchlondon; 10.30 pm; closed Mon,
Sat L & Sun; no trainers; booking max 8 may apply.

Sketch, Gallery W1 £80 2 3 4
9 Conduit St 020 7659 4500 4–2A

"The must-visit loos" are traditionally a more consistent attraction than the perennially pricey and gimmicky cuisine at this Mayfair fashionista-favourite, given a romantic but mad, rhapsody-in-pink makeover a couple of years ago (with art from designer/director David Shrigley). It avoided harsh feedback this year however, and for afternoon tea in particular it's worth a whirl – "(over) indulgence with a lightness of touch". / W1S 2XG; www.sketch.uk.com; @sketchlondon; 1 am, Sun Midnight; booking max 10 may apply.

Skylon, South Bank Centre SE1 £76 1 1 2
Belvedere Rd 020 7654 7800 2–3D

"The bar is good and the views of the Thames unparalleled" at this vast but "anodyne" cultural-centre dining room. That's the end of the good news: "the food is nothing to write home about", "service is inconsistent" and bills can be "shocking". ("I felt extremely bad for my companions, who were visiting London and really deserved better.") See also Skylon Grill. / SE1 8XX; www.skylon-restaurant.co.uk; @skylonsouthbank; 10.30 pm; closed Sun D; no trainers; set Sun L £45 (FP), set weekday L & pre-theatre £47 (FP).

Skylon Grill SE1 £74 2 2 3
Belvedere Rd 020 7654 7800 2–3D

"The best view in London", overlooking the Thames from the "iconic Royal Festival Hall", could make this huge D&D London venue the perfect place "to impress". But while most reviews are more positive than at the adjacent restaurant, a few are similarly downbeat: "left feeling hungry and a little cheated price-wise". / SE1 8XX; www.skylon-restaurant.co.uk; @skylonsouthbank; 11 pm; closed Sun D; set weekday L & pre-theatre £39 (FP).

Smith & Wollensky WC2 £102 1 1 2
The Adelphi Building, 1- 11 John Adam St 020 7321 6007 5–4D

"Overpriced, overhyped"… and over here! This year-old outpost of the famous NYC steakhouse brand – part of the Adelphi, just off the Strand – inspires very mixed feedback. Its business appeal is evident: it's "very spacious", "very well furnished (if you like that 'prestigious' US steakhouse furnishings and decor thing)", and provides "a 500+ bin wine list featuring some esoteric US vintages". Service though is not only "American-Yank style" ("I'm your waiter this evening, etc"), but also surprisingly "hit and miss"; the interior can seem "loud and booming"; and though many reports acknowledge that this is some of the best meat in London, the price/quality trade-off is much better elsewhere. / WC2N 6HT; www.smithandwollensky.co.uk; @sandwollenskyuk; 11 pm; closed Sun D; set weekday L & pre-theatre £47 (FP).

Smith's Wapping E1 £58 4 3 4
22 Wapping High St 020 7488 3456 12–1A

"A fantastic location with brilliant views over towards Tower Bridge", isn't the only reason this Wapping venue is "always busy": its fish and seafood is "always superb" too. Sibling to a well-established Ongar venture, it's "generally filled with Essex likely lads and their molls". / E1W 1NJ; www.smithsrestaurants.com; @smithswapping; 10 pm; closed Sun D; no trainers.

Smiths of Smithfield, Top Floor EC1 £79 2 2 2
67-77 Charterhouse St 020 7251 7950 10–1A

"Great rooftop views" over the City make this an attractive location for business entertaining, with steak the appropriate focus for the Smithfield meat market setting. The catch? – it's "expensive for what it is". / EC1M 6HJ; www.smithsofsmithfield.co.uk; @thisissmiths; 10.45 pm; closed Sat L & Sun D; booking max 10 may apply.

Smiths of Smithfield, Dining Room EC1   £56   2 2 1

67-77 Charterhouse St   020 7251 7950   10–1A

"For a run-of-the-mill brasserie, this first floor overlooking Smithfield meat market (hence the beef-heavy menu) is absolutely fine" even if the cooking is no better than "acceptable". Fans say it's "fun", but its acoustics mean it's "very noisy" to the extent it can seem "pretty unpleasant". / EC1M 6HJ; www.smithsofsmithfield.co.uk; @thisismiths; 10.45 pm; closed Sat L & Sun; booking max 12 may apply.

Smiths of Smithfield, Ground Floor EC1   £32   2 2 3

67-77 Charterhouse St   020 7251 7950   10–1A

Once one of London's ultimate brunch hotspots, this big and buzzy Smithfield hangout is "still a favourite place for breakfast" for some reporters. / EC1M 6HJ; www.smithsofsmithfield.co.uk; @thisismiths; 5 pm; L only; no bookings.

Smoke & Salt N1 NEW   £56

The Chapel Bar, 29 Penton Street   07421 327 556   9–3D

A year-long residency in Angel's Chapel Bar (launched in May 2016), offering a set five-course dinner alongside cocktails and a small wine list, brought to us by chefs Remi Williams and Aaron Webster who met working at The Shed in Notting Hill; Sunday brunch too. / N1 9PX; www.smokeandsalt.com; @smokeandsaltldn; 10 pm; closed Mon L, Tue L, Wed L, Thu L, Fri, Sat & Sun L.

Smokehouse Chiswick W4   £50   3 3 3

12 Sutton Lane North   020 7354 1144   8–2A

"A reminder of how great pulled pork can be" – this tucked-away, year-old outpost of Smokehouse Islington has been "a good addition to W4". Other attractions? – a cute garden and an "outstanding whisky selection". / W4 4LD; www.smokehousechiswick.co.uk; 10 pm, Sun 9 pm; Mon-Thu D only, Fri-Sun open L & D.

The Smokehouse Islington N1   £54   4 4 4

63-69 Canonbury Rd   020 7354 1144   9–2D

This Canonbury gastro-boozer boasts "all the charm and hospitality of your local pub, but with extra good food". Smoked or roast meat dishes are its forte, but there are "veggie options which have lured carnivores away from the obvious choices". There's a sister pub in Chiswick. / N1 2RG; www.smokehouseislington.co.uk; @smokehouseN1; 10 pm, Sun 9 pm; closed weekday L.

Smokestak   £14   5 3 –

11 Sclater Street, E1   13–2C NEW

Dinerama, EC2   no tel

"Once tasted no other BBQ will do!" So say fans of the results from David Carter's 4.5 tonne, custom-built smoker from Texas. Top Menu Tip – "the beef brisket is the thing of dreams!" STOP PRESS – now he's going permanent too with a new 75-cover Shoreditch site to open in November 2016 and centred on a 2m charcoal grill. / see web for detail.

Smoking Goat WC2   £44   4 3 2

7 Denmark St   no tel   5–1B

"Noisy hipsters; small, rickety tables and a small, dark room" set the scene at Ben Chapman's no-bookings Soho phenomenon. "Plates may be small, but they carry big, big flavours" – "deep", "well-judged", "meat-heavy" and "unusual" Thai dishes, many from the BBQ. / WC2H 8LZ; www.smokinggoatsoho.com; @smokinggoatsoho; 10 pm, Sun 8.30 pm.

Snaps & Rye W10   £40   4 5 3
93 Golborne Rd   020 8964 3004   7–1A
"Delicious, well-executed dishes with a Danish twist" and "natural, highly attentive service" (plus the house-infused Akvavit) are pluspoints of this Scandi dining room in North Kensington. "Great for brunch that's a bit out-of-the-ordinary". / W10 5NL; www.snapsandrye.com; @snapsandrye; 10 pm; closed Mon, Tue D, Wed D & Sun D.

Social Eating House W1   £73   4 3 3
58-59 Poland St   020 7993 3251   4–1C
Jason Atherton's Soho three-year-old "hits all the right buttons" for most reporters, with its "proper comfort eating", "hip" service and "lively (but not over-loud) atmosphere". "The 'Blind Pig' bar upstairs is super cool for an aperitif too". / W1F 7NR; www.socialeatinghouse.com; @socialeathouse; 10 pm; closed Sun; set weekday L £42 (FP).

Social Wine & Tapas W1   £44   3 2 3
39 James St   020 7993 3257   3–1A
With its "tempting, well thought-out and unusual wine selection", Jason Atherton's Marylebone yearling particularly wins praise for its "casual" buzz. Even fans of its "superb" tapas concede it's "not cheap" however, and critics say it's "not up to the standard of the other Socials", not helped by "blaring" music and an interior that can feel "too crowded" and "self-conscious". / W1U 1EB; www.socialwineandtapas.com; @socialwinetapas; 10.30 pm; closed Sun; credit card deposit required to book.

Soif SW11   £56   3 3 3
27 Battersea Rise   020 7223 1112   11–2C
With its "fascinating list of natural wines", this "authentically French" bistro in Battersea bears the hallmarks of its better-known sibling Terroirs – a "little gem" whose "gutsy" menu is "full of robust flavours" and "top-quality seasonal fare done nicely". So "go for the wine and fall in love with the food…" / SW11 1HG; www.soif.co; @Soif_SW11; 10 pm; closed Mon L & Sun D.

Som Saa E1 NEW   £47   5 2 3
43a Commercial St   020 7324 7790   13–2C
"The food is like good drugs!" at the new "Spitalfields forever-home" of this epic Thai ("which has perhaps lost some of its ramshackle charm in the move from Hackney railway arches"). "It's a real eye-opener for what Thai food can be" – "raw authentic flavours", "great taste combinations" and "some dishes that could blow your head off!" – "I'm addicted!" / E1 6BD; www.somsaa.com; @somsaa_london; 11.30 pm, Sat midnight, Sun 10.30 pm; D only; may need 4+ to book.

Sông Quê E2   £31   3 2 2
134 Kingsland Rd   020 7613 3222   13–1B
"It's Spartan and hurried", but this Shoreditch canteen with sharing tables does provide "delicious" Vietnamese grub: "the pho's the thing here, but other dishes are worth trying, too". / E2 8DY; www.songque.co.uk; 11 pm, Sun 10.30 pm; no Amex.

Sonny's Kitchen SW13   £56   2 2 3
94 Church Rd   020 8748 0393   11–1A
"Perhaps not quite as special as it used to be", this "local staple" retains the loyalty of its Barnes following despite a "pleasant but unexciting" performance in recent times. Still it's "sensibly priced", and by-and-large "what a local should be". / SW13 0DQ; www.sonnyskitchen.co.uk; @sonnyskitchen; Fri-Sat 11 pm, Sun 9.30 pm; set weekday L & dinner £35 (FP).

Sophie's Steakhouse   £58   2 4 3
29-31 Wellington St, WC2   020 7836 8836   5–3D
311-313 Fulham Rd, SW10   020 7352 0088   6–3B
*Well-established steakhouses in Covent Garden and Fulham; reports are
generally of "good quality" meals, but they equally owe their popularity
to their "accommodating" staff and "fun", family-friendly atmosphere.
/ www.sophiessteakhouse.com; SW10 11.45 pm, Sun 11.15 pm; WC2 12.45 am,
Sun 11 pm; no booking.*

Sosharu, Turnmill Building EC1   £79   2 3 2
63 Clerkenwell Rd   020 3805 2304   10–1A
*So far, the wait hasn't been worth it for the opening of Jason Atherton's
long-anticipated Japanese on the big Clerkenwell site that was Turnmills
nightclub. Some fans do hail his "modern twist on izakaya food", but even
they can find it expensive, while to critics it's "incredibly overpriced" given
the "heavy-handed" cooking – "the chefs seem to have no understanding
of Japanese cuisine and how to balance flavours". / EC1M 5NP;
www.sosharulondon.com; @SocialCompany; 10 pm, Fri & Sat 10.30 pm; closed Sun;
credit card deposit required to book.*

Spring Restaurant WC2   £88   3 3 4
New Wing, Lancaster Pl   020 3011 0115   2–2D
*"The spectacular, light-filled space" – "one of the most elegant rooms"
in town, in gracious Somerset House – provides a "beautiful"
("too perfect?") setting for Skye Gyngell's "serene" two-year-old. Her
"somewhat esoteric", "delicate" cuisine using "the very best seasonal
ingredients" is "quietly delicious" too, but even fans concede it's
"not cheap" (and critics say "it's priced only for business"). / WC2R 1LA;
www.springrestaurant.co.uk; @Spring_Rest; 10.30 pm; closed Sun D; credit card
deposit required to book; set weekday L & pre-theatre £51 (FP).*

Spring Workshop W1 NEW   £25
19 Brooks Mews   020 7493 5367   3–2B
*In the well-heeled environs of Mayfair, this Ikea-style café is worth knowing
about it: 1) it's a modestly priced all-day option in a pricey area; and 2) it's
a not-for-profit café supporting social mobility. If service lags, remember it's
in a good cause… / W1 4DX; www.springworkshop.co.uk; @Spring_Workshop;
5.30 pm; closed Sat & Sun.*

Spuntino W1   £44   3 3 3
61 Rupert St   020 7734 4479   4–2D
*Russell Norman's "very cool" Italian-American bar in Soho – "27 stools and
one popcorn machine" – serves "really interesting small plates". "I go again
and again, but have realised that it's best to visit out of busy hours"; "after
the theatre is perfect". / W1D 7PW; www.spuntino.co.uk; @Spuntino; 11.30 pm,
Sun 10.30 pm; no bookings.*

The Square W1   £130
6-10 Bruton St   020 7495 7100   3–2C
*This "classy" gastronomic temple in Mayfair was sold by its creators Phil
Howard and Nigel Platts-Martin in Spring 2016 (just before this year's
survey). With its "very formal" ("dull"), style – underpinned by a "bible of a
wine list" – it's a shoe-in for the portfolio of new owner, Marlon Abela,
who seems sure to maintain its business friendly appeal. Whether the
cuisine will hold up is less certain – hence we've left it un-rated – but one
early report says it's "still Fabulous with a capital F". STOP PRESS –
in September 2016 Yu Sugimoto was named the new executive chef.
/ W1J 6PU; www.squarerestaurant.com; @square_rest; 9.45 pm, Sat 10.15 pm,
Sun 9.30 pm; closed Sun L; booking max 8 may apply; set weekday L £68 (FP).*

Squirrel SW7 NEW
11 Harrington Road   020 7095 0377   6–2B
From the owners of Bunga Bunga, this virtuous summer 2016 newcomer south of Gloucester Road tube is a big departure from its louche-living stablemate. A cutely decked out, simple café (acorn lights, acorn bowls, etc) – here the focus is on salads, grain bowls and porridge pots – no alcohol, so expect water infusions, matcha lattes… / SW7 3ES; www.wearesquirrel.com; @wearesquirrel.

Sree Krishna SW17 £27   4 3 2
192-194 Tooting High St   020 8672 4250   11–2C
"Unchanging, as ever", this "long-established South Indian" on Tooting's curry strip serves "mouth-watering" fish and chicken dishes along with "especially good Keralan starters – dosas, dahi vada, etc". "There's a lot of competition here and this is a little further from the Tube, but it's worth the walk!" / SW17 0SF; www.sreekrishna.co.uk; @SreeKrishnaUk; 10.45 pm, Thurs 12.45pm, Fri & Sat 11.30 pm.

The Stable E1 NEW £34   2 2 3
16-18 Whitechapel Road   020 7377 1133   13–2D
First London outpost of a 13-site British chain, specialising in pizza, pies and featuring 80 craft ciders, which opened in Whitechapel in April 2016. All early ratings say the food's not bad, but there are some gripes: "a 4-chilli rated pizza had ZERO heat. It didn't have balls!" / E1 1EW; www.stablepizza.com; @stablepizza; 10 pm; may need 8+ to book.

Star of India SW5 £55   4 2 3
154 Old Brompton Rd   020 7373 2901   6–2B
One of post-war London's original curry houses, on the Kensington edge of Earl's Court, this classic veteran still produces "interesting" cooking. The once famously camp interior "is a little tired these days, but that doesn't detract from the main event". / SW5 0BE; www.starofindia.eu; 11.45 pm, Sun 11.15 pm.

Stick & Bowl W8 £24   4 3 1
31 Kensington High Street   020 7937 2778   6–1A
"Been there for years, and always full" – this tiny, "everyday" High Street Ken canteen ladles out "yummy Singapore noodles, mouth-watering wonton soup, succulent pork belly and rice" as you perch on stools (defo "not a place to linger!") / W8 5NP; 10.45 pm; cash only; no bookings.

Sticks'n'Sushi £48   4 4 4
11 Henrietta St, WC2   020 3141 8810   5–3D
Nelson Rd, SE10   020 3141 8220   1–3D
58 Wimbledon Hill Rd, SW19   020 3141 8800   11–2B
Crossrail Pl, E14   020 3141 8230   12–1C
"A strange but pleasant mix of Denmark and Japan" – this "fun and buzzy" Danish chain puts a Scandi twist on sushi and yakitori and results from the "bewilderingly long menu" are "beautifully presented and delicious" (if "not cheap"). The original, "aircraft-hangar-sized" branch near Wimbledon Tube remains the best known. / www.sticksnsushi.com; Sun-Tue 10 pm, Wed-Sat 11 pm; SRA-1 star.

STORY SE1 £132 3|3|3
199 Tooley St 020 7183 2117 10–4D
The "diversity of the dishes…", "the incredible work that goes into them…", the "massively seasonal ingredients…" – Tom Sellers's "mind-blowing" multi-course epics still win huge acclaim for his "edgy, modernist, Scandi-chic temple", near Tower Bridge. But ratings dipped here palpably this year. Is it higher prices? Is it the pressure of opening Restaurant Ours? Whatever reason, a disgruntled minority found their meals "gimmicky", or "ill-conceived". / SE1 2UE; www.restaurantstory.co.uk; @Rest_Story; 9.15 pm; closed Mon & Sun.

Strut & Cluck E1 NEW £42
151-153 Commercial Street 020 7078 0770 13–2B
Having popped up in Shoreditch House, this restaurant dedicated to the wonders of turkey opened in good time for Christmas in summer 2016 in Shoreditch. Dishes are often charcoal-grilled and come with a Middle Eastern twist. / E1 6BJ; www.strutandcluck.com; 10:30 pm.

Sukho Fine Thai Cuisine SW6 £56 5|4|3
855 Fulham Rd 020 7371 7600 11–1B
Celebrated by many as "the best Thai in London" – this "crowded" Fulham shop-conversion is "justifiably packed most nights" thanks to its "superb service" and "beautifully presented food with great depth of flavour". / SW6 5HJ; www.sukhogroups.com; 11 pm.

Suksan SW10 £49 4|3|2
7 Park Walk 020 7351 9881 6–3B
"Exceptionally good Thai cuisine – delicate when necessary but packing a punch when it should" – makes it worth remembering this Chelsea corner café: sibling to Fulham's esteemed 'Sukho Fine Thai Cuisine'. / SW10 0AJ; www.sukhogroups.com/suksan.html; 10.45 pm.

The Summerhouse W9 £56 2|3|5
60 Blomfield Rd 020 7286 6752 9–4A
The "lovely waterside location" on a Little Venice canal is the 'crown jewel' feature ("unbeatable on a summer evening… if you can get in") of this "relaxed", little outfit in Maida Vale. On most accounts the fish and seafood cooking is another strength, but the view persists in some quarters that it's merely "average". / W9 2PA; www.thesummerhouse.co; @FRGSummerhouse; 10.30 pm, Sun 10 pm; no Amex.

Sumosan W1 £78
26b Albemarle St 020 7495 5999 6–1D
This Russian-owned rival to Nobu is relocating after nearly 15 years – leaving Mayfair for a new Sloane Street home, where it will also (like others in their international chain) now provide Italian cuisine. Opening is planned for October 2016. / W1S 4HY; www.sumosan.com; @sumosan_; 11.30 pm, Sun 10.30 pm; closed Sat L & Sun L.

Super Tuscan E1 £51 4|4|3
8a, Artillery Passage 020 7247 8717 13–2B
"Very small" ("so book") and "initially tricky-to-find" Italian – in an alley on the fringe of the Square Mile: a "family-owned gem set up by brothers in 2012" offering "exceptional wines" and food "sourced direct from Italy". "The menu changes daily, and the specials are the dishes to go for". / E1 7LJ; www.supertuscan.co.uk; 10 pm.

Sushi Bar Makoto W4 £46 3 3 4
57 Turnham Green Terrace   020 8987 3180   8–2A
"Lovely and simple" Japanese cafe in Chiswick, newly moved to the busy strip by Turnham Green Tube from humbler premises on nearby Devonshire Road. Most reports applaud "truly excellent sushi, etc" but one or two caution that "it looks like a bargain, but is actually quite expensive". / W4 1RP; 10 pm, Sun 9 pm.

Sushi Masa NW2 NEW £41
33b Walm Lane   020 8459 2971   1–1A
Sushi Say (RIP) is a very tough act to follow, and its successor attracts limited and downbeat feedback (hence no rating) – on this year's survey, it would be hard to recommend the trip to distant Willesden Green. / NW2 5SH; 10 pm.

Sushi Tetsu EC1 £59 5 5 4
12 Jerusalem Pas   020 3217 0090   10–1A
"Having eaten in the fish market in Tokyo I know how authentic this restaurant is. Amazing!" – Harumi and Toru Takahashi are "charming hosts" and their "very intimate" Clerkenwell 7-seater serves "astonishing" sushi and other fare – "a mix of traditional and experimental dishes with perfect quality as the unifying factor". It invites some comparison with The Araki, although "here you can enjoy Japanese-style seasonality without splashing quite so much cash". "Booking is taken in one morning, two weeks in advance. It's a race. Follow the Twitter account for a chance to get a last-minute seat". / EC1V 4JP; www.sushitetsu.co.uk; @SushiTetsuUK; 7.45 pm, Thu-Fri 8 pm, Sat 7 pm; closed Mon, Thu L, Fri L, Sat L & Sun; booking essential.

Sushisamba £90 3 3 5
The Piazza, WC2   no tel   5–3D NEW
Heron Tower, 110 Bishopsgate, EC2   020 3640 7330   10–2D
"How can the view not create atmosphere – you're in the atmosphere!" Reached by one of Europe's fastest lifts, this "simply amazing", 39th-floor eyrie – complete with a movie-set bar, and "lovely outdoor spaces" – is hard to beat for sheer glam. The mesospheric prices "go with the height" though, and even those applauding the "beautifully tasty" Japanese/South American fusion bites "would question the price tag that goes with them!" Coming soon in 2017 – a sibling in the gorgeous, but perennially disappointing space above Covent Garden Market, overlooking the back of the Royal Opera House. / see web for detail.

Sutton And Sons £32 4 3 3
90 Stoke Newington High St, N16   020 7249 6444   1–1C NEW
356 Essex Rd, N1   020 7359 1210   14–1A
240 Graham Road, E8   020 3643 2017   14–1B NEW
"All chippies should be like this!" – these "upmarket" cafés have "a twist on the original look" and supply "top-quality fish 'n' chips" and also "other variants such as lobster rolls or grills for the more discerning palate". "The first branch in N16 is well worth the trip", and there's a new branch too in Hipster Central. / see web for detail.

The Swan W4 £49 3 3 5
1 Evershed Walk, 119 Acton Ln   020 8994 8262   8–1A
"A tucked-away location between Chiswick and Acton" lends a "rustic" atmosphere to this "hidden gem" of a pub, with "surprisingly sophisticated" food, plus "a good wine list, and changing list of cask beers". "It's a pub for all seasons: in the cool/freezing months, with wood panelling, open fires, and sofas… in the summer, the enormous garden and the mature trees make you feel like you're 100 miles from London". / W4 5HH; www.theswanchiswick.co.uk; @SwanPubChiswick; 10 pm, Fri & Sat 10.30 pm, Sun 10 pm; closed weekday L.

The Swan at the Globe SE1 £60 2 2 3
21 New Globe Walk   020 7928 9444   10–3B
"Fabulous views of the Thames and London skyline" make this first-floor venue at Shakespeare's Globe "much more than just a pre-theatre restaurant". But while fans say it's a "wonderful" all-rounder, reports of "slow service" and "ordinary food" are persistent complaints. / SE1 9DT; www.swanlondon.co.uk; @swanabout; 10.30 pm, Sun 9 pm.

Sweet Thursday N1 £40 3 2 3
95 Southgate Rd   020 7226 1727   1–2C
"Very good neighbourhood pizzeria" and wine shop ("plus a good beer selection too") in "a lovely bit of De Beauvoir" – "reliable", "kid-friendly", with a "chilled-out vibe". / N1 3JS; www.sweetthursday.co.uk; @Pizza_and_Wine; 10 pm, Fri-Sat 10.30 pm, Sun 9 pm.

Sweetings EC4 £75 2 2 4
39 Queen Victoria St   020 7248 3062   10–3B
"Untrammelled by fads and fashion" – this "quirky old restaurant, with its cramped tables and bar seating" has been an "unchanging staple" of City life since Victorian times. "Fun but fearsomely expensive", you get "great fish done the old-fashioned way" ("ie nothing is overly mucked around with") and alongside wines and champagnes, "Black Velvet in tankards" is another tradition. Arrive early if you want a seat. / EC4N 4SA; www.sweetingsrestaurant.co.uk; 3 pm; L only, closed Sat & Sun; no bookings.

Taberna do Mercado E1 £44 5 4 3
Spitalfields Mkt   020 7375 0649   13–2B
"You can feel Nuno Medes's passion for the food" at his "casual taberna-style" yearling in Spitalfields Market, which is "equally suited to a drop in for a pastel de nata and a coffee, as for a full meal". The "unfussy" and "nostalgic" Portuguese dishes "use lots of obscure ingredients", but are "brilliantly successful", while "friendly, well-informed staff are keen to assist with selections". Top Menu Tip – "fish in a tin is the highlight". / E1 6EW; www.tabernamercado.co.uk; @tabernamercado; 9.30 pm, Sun 7.30 pm.

Taberna Etrusca EC4 £55 2 3 3
9 -11 Bow Churchyard   020 7248 5552   10–2C
This "good value" Italian is "still one of the most relaxing restaurants in the City": "well run, pleasant, efficient, helpful and upmarket", while "the al fresco patio is great in warm weather". Critics, though, feel it sells itself short: "somehow my heart never quite sings, even though nothing is missed and it's always a pleasure". / EC4M 9DQ; www.etruscarestaurants.com; 9.30 pm; closed Sat & Sun.

The Table SE1   £38   **3** **2** **2**
83 Southwark St   020 7401 2760   10–4B
*A top spot for brekkie and lunch near Tate Modern, this "communal
(essentially functional)" canteen offers "decent quality, simple dishes".
"It gets busier every week – but it's worth tackling the pushchairs for the
pancakes!" / SE1 0HX; www.thetablecafe.com; @thetablecafe; 10.30 pm; closed
Mon D, Sat D & Sun D.*

Tabun Kitchen W1 NEW   £37
77 Berwick Street   020 7437 8568   4–1C
*A summer 2016 modern Israeli newcomer promising 'Jerusalem street
food' and 'Palestinian pizza' in the heart of Soho, from breakfast on.
/ W1F 8TH; www.tabunkitchen.com; @TabunKitchen; midnight, Sun 11 pm.*

Taiwan Village SW6   £35   **4** **5** **3**
85 Lillie Rd   020 7381 2900   6–3A
*"It's all too easy to walk past" this "hidden gem" just off the North End
Road, which is "as good as many of the leading Chinese restaurants
in London, and much cheaper". "Pick the chef's Leave It To Us menu" and
"dish after dish arrives at your table", all of them "convincing" and some
"insanely good". / SW6 1UD; www.taiwanvillage.com; 11 pm, Sun 10.30 pm;
D only, closed Mon; booking max 20 may apply.*

Takahashi SW19 NEW   £44   **5** **3** **3**
228 Merton Rd   020 8540 3041   11–2A
*"Unbelievable Japanese-European fusion food" including stellar sushi
(from a "lovely ex-Nobu chef" and his wife) is a "stunning" find at this
pleasant, but totally unremarkable looking, new shop-conversion in a
parade near South Wimbledon tube. / SW19; www.takahashi-restaurant.co.uk;
@takahashi_sw19; 10 pm, Fri & Sat 10.30 pm, Sun 9 pm; closed Mon, Tue, Wed L,
Thu L & Fri L.*

Talli Joe WC2 NEW   £41
152-156 Shaftesbury Avenue   020 7836 5400   5–2B
*Good vibes surround this new Indian tapas/cocktails hangout in the heart
of Theatreland, with the former devised by ex-Benares executive chef
Sameer Taneja. It opened in late spring 2016. / WC2H 8HL; www.tallijoe.com;
@tallijoe; 11.30 pm; closed Sun.*

Tamarind W1   £75   **5** **4** **2**
20 Queen St   020 7629 3561   3–3B
*"A class act!" This stalwart Mayfair basement put in a particularly strong
showing this year, with many reports of "truly outstanding" cuisine. The
location? – "pleasant but underwhelming", it's "time for a makeover".
/ W1J 5PR; www.tamarindrestaurant.com; @TamarindMayfair; 10.45 pm,
Sun 10.30 pm; closed Sat L; no trainers; set weekday L £59 (FP), set pre-theatre
£60 (FP).*

Tamp Coffee W4   £40   **3** **3** **3**
1 Devonshire Road   no tel   8–2A
*"A great Argentinian-themed coffee stop" in Chiswick with "really good Joe"
and simple fare, including "addictive empandas". Weekend evenings,
there's more substantial tapas and wine. / W4; www.tampcoffee.co.uk;
@tampcoffee; 5.30 pm, Thur-Sat 10 pm, Sun 6 pm.*

Tangerine Dream,
Chelsea Physic Garden SW3   £30   3 2 4
66 Royal Hospital Road   020 7352 5646   6–3D
"The gardens are quite wonderful" at this very Chelsea destination,
for which these airy tea rooms provide refreshments. To fans it's a "sublime
secret" – "everything is home produced" and "the cakes are exceptionally
good" . However the "ordering system is chaotic and stressful" – "if only
they could reduce the queuing time, it would indeed be nirvana".
/ SW3 4HS; www.chelseaphysicgarden.co.uk; Tue-Fri 5 pm, Sun 5 pm; closed
Mon & Sat.

Tapas Brindisa   £45   2 2 2
18-20 Rupert St, W1   020 7478 8758   5–3A
46 Broadwick St, W1   020 7534 1690   4–2B
18-20 Southwark St, SE1   020 7357 8880   10–4C
41-43 Atlantic Rd, SW9   020 7733 0634   11–2D
You're "lucky to get a table at peak times" at these "busy tapas
restaurants" – especially at the Borough Market original. "Prices mount
quickly" though, for the "small but densely flavoured plates", and while
most reporters applaud their "excellent quality", critics – particularly those
encountering "terrible service" – find them "extremely overpriced".
/ 10.45 pm, Sun 10 pm; W1 booking: max 10.

Taqueria W11   £35   4 4 3
141-145 Westbourne Grove   020 7229 4734   7–1B
"An authentic Mexican" – a tightly packed cantina on the Notting
Hill/Bayswater borders, focused on tacos, cocktails and beer – "fresh and
tasty, real street flavours, and also very friendly". / W11 2RS;
www.taqueria.co.uk; @TaqueriaUK; 11 pm, Fri & Sat 11.30 pm, Sun 10.30 pm;
no Amex.

Taro   £36   3 3 2
10 Old Compton St, W1   020 7439 2275   5–2B
61 Brewer St, W1   020 7734 5826   4–3C
Mr Taro's "busy", "no-frills Japanese" canteens are among the "few really
cheap eateries still remaining in Soho" – "food arrives quickly so it's ideal
for a fast lunch or snack". "You may have to share a large table with
others". / www.tarorestaurants.co.uk; 10.30 pm, Sun 9.30 pm; no Amex; Brewer
St only small bookings.

Tartufo SW3   £58   3 3 2
11 Cadogan Gdns   020 7730 6383   6–2D
"Squirrelled away in the basement of a lovely little hotel in a mansion block
not far from Sloane Square", Alexis Gauthier's "tucked-away Italian" earnt
a mixed rep this year. On most accounts, it's "a hidden gem" with "subtle
and sophisticated" cooking (not least "the eponymous and hugely satisfying
truffle menu") and a "romantic" ambience. Sceptics though, say it "used to
be good" but feels "gloomy" nowadays, and "is not a patch on Gauthier
itself". / SW3 2RJ; www.tartufolondon.co.uk; 10 pm; closed Mon & Sun D.

Tas   £37   1 2 3
Its mezze-based menu is "nothing special", but – despite its low food score
– these "buzzy" and "packed" Turks are still a popular "cheap 'n'
cheerful" option for reporters, especially for "a quick pre- or post- theatre
bite". / www.tasrestaurant.com; 11.30 pm, Sun 10.30 pm; EC4 Closed Sun.

Tas Pide SE1 £40

20-22 New Globe Walk 020 7928 3300 10–3B

"A very convenient location" – by Shakespeare's Globe – adds to the lustre of this "cavernous" but "nicely buzzy" branch of the "reliable Tas chain". There's a "good-value sharing menu" with "very decent mezze" and filling pide – "a Turkish take on pizza" (although "it's quite clear why it's the Italian version that's conquered the world!") / SE1 9DR; www.tasrestaurant.com/tas_pide; @TasRestaurants; 11.30 pm, Sun 10.30 pm.

Tate Britain, Whistler Restaurant SW1 £55

Millbank 020 7887 8825 2–4C

As well as the famous Whistler murals, "it is the wine list which steals the show" at this gracious-looking museum café – a famously "innovative world list at reasonable prices" (curated by Hamish Anderson) "with some exceptional value clarets and burgundies" thrown in. The food is "reliable" but is not the reason to detour. / SW1 4RG; www.tate.org.uk; @Tate; 3 pm, afternoon tea Sat-Sun 5 pm; L only; booking lunch only.

Tate Modern Restaurant, Switch House SE1 NEW

Level 9, Switch House, Bankside 020 7887 8888 10–3B

All the clichés about architect-designed restaurants are true at this 9th-floor dining room, where only the staff can enjoy the magnificent vistas (whose idea was it to put the windows at head height?). On early press feedback this is a re-run of the Level 6 restaurant, with admirable emphasis on British sourced food, but little culinary follow-through. At least across the way you can see the Thames. / SE1 9TG; www.tate.org.uk/visit/tate-modern/switch-ho; 6 pm, Fri & Sat 10 pm; no bookings.

Tate Modern, Restaurant, Level 6 SE1 £59

Bankside 020 7887 8888 10–3B

The "wonderful view" of St Paul's and the river is the most reliable attraction at this airy, rather Spartan dining room – as a showcase for British food and drink, it puts in a more mixed performance, and service is perennially so-so. / SE1 9TG; www.tate.org.uk; @TateFood; 9 pm; closed Mon D, Tue D, Wed D, Thu D & Sun D.

Taylor St Baristas £11

"A welcome change from monotonous high-street chains" – these "hipster-friendly" outfits provide "exceptional coffee" as well as OK cakes and salads. Staff are "dedicated" – if your order is slow it's "worth it, because it takes time to brew". / www.taylor-st.com; all branches 5 pm; Old Broad ST, Clifton St, W1, E14 closed Sat & Sun; New St closed Sat; TW9 closed Sun.

Tayyabs E1 £31

83 Fieldgate St 020 7247 6400 10–2D

"If you can deal with the chaos and the mayhem" (and the "enormous queue"), this "cavernous" East End Pakistani is "worth it" for its "to-die-for" tandoori lamb chops, kebabs and curries – "they're a world apart from the sorry food culture of nearby Brick Lane". / E1 1JU; www.tayyabs.co.uk; @itayyabs; 11.30 pm.

temper W1 NEW

25 Broadwick Street no tel 4–1C

Opening on Bonfire Night 2016, a new 'whole animal barbecue' concept – complete with 4.5m open fire pit – from Neil Rankin, of Pitt Cue Co and Smokehouse fame. / W1F 0DF; www.temperrestaurant.com; @temperldn.

The 10 Cases WC2 £55 2 1 3
16 Endell St 020 7836 6801 5–2C
"An innovative and really interesting wine list" underpins the "super idea and concept" ("there are only ten, ever-changing choices", hence the name) of this "great little spot" in Covent Garden, where "knowledgeable staff really help the enjoyment of the vino". Soak it up with "simple but tasty" fare – it's not why you go, but "better than you might expect". / WC2H 9BD; www.the10cases.co.uk; @10cases; 11 pm; closed Sun.

10 Greek Street W1 £56 4 4 3
10 Greek St 020 7734 4677 5–2A
"The rough 'n' ready appearance of this small joint belies the highly competent kitchen which is open at the far end of this converted Soho shop". Yes it's "a bit cramped" and "too noisy", but staff are "laid back and friendly", and its "no-frills but faultless quality" dishes are packed with "lovely, simple flavours". "Naturally they don't accept reservations, but you can't have it all…" / W1D 4DH; www.10greekstreet.com; @10GreekStreet; 10.45 pm; closed Sun; booking lunch only.

Tendido Cero SW5 £52 2 3 3
174 Old Brompton Rd 020 7370 3685 6–2B
"You feel you are in Barcelona" at this "buzzy tapas bar" in South Kensington – except when it comes to the bill! "I love this place, but have stopped going because it's so ridiculously priced. Such a pity, they're so nice and the food is good". / SW5 0BA; www.cambiodetercio.co.uk; @CambiodTercio; 11 pm.

Tendido Cuatro SW6 £50 2 2 2
108-110 New King's Rd 020 7371 5147 11–1B
This "noisy" Parsons Green tapas bar (an offshoot of Cambio de Tercio in Earl's Court) serves "really authentic food" and Spanish wines, but at prices sceptics find "unbelievable". / SW6 4LY; www.cambiodetercio.co.uk; @CambiodTercio; 11 pm, Sun & Mon 10.30 pm.

Terroirs WC2 £49 3 2 4
5 William IV St 020 7036 0660 5–4C
"The kind of spot you'd get excited about if you chanced on it in Paris!" – this "buzzing", subterranean bistro near Charing Cross station remains a well-known pioneer both of "honestly Gallic", "rustic" dishes (with much charcuterie and cheese) and also "weird and wonderful biodynamique wines from owners Caves de Pyrene" – "organic, unfiltered, and with a heavy French accent… like the staff!" / WC2N 4DW; www.terroirswinebar.com; @TerroirsWineBar; 11 pm; closed Sun.

Texture W1 £102 4 3 3
34 Portman St 020 7224 0028 2–2A
"It somehow misses out on the acclaim it deserves", say fans of this "spacious" dining room – part of a hotel, near Selfridges. Agnar Sverrisson's "excitingly original" Icelandic cuisine is "light, clever and delicious", service is "pleasant and precise" and there's an "exceptional wine list" too. / W1H 7BY; www.texture-restaurant.co.uk; @TextureLondon; 10.30 pm; closed Mon, Tue L & Sun; set weekday L £69 (FP).

Thali SW5 £48 4 3 3
166 Old Brompton Rd 020 7373 2626 6–2B
Bollywood classic posters add character to this contemporary Indian in South Kensington – a "pleasant and reliable" option, whose "menu is made unique by following regional and family recipes of the owners". / SW5 0BA; www.thali.uk.com; @ThaliLondon; 11.30 pm, Sun 10.30 pm.

F S A

Theo Randall, W1   £91   3 3 1
1 Hamilton Pl   020 7318 8747   3–4A
*"Magnifico!", say fans of this ex-River Café chef's Hyde Park Corner HQ,
who hail it as "London's best Italian". Despite a major refurb in early 2016
however, its windowless quarters still feel very much "like a hotel
restaurant", and more cautious reporters feel it's "better than average,
but very overpriced". / W1J 7QY; www.theorandall.com; @theorandall; 11 pm;
closed Sat L & Sun; set dinner £55 (FP).*

Theo's SE5 NEW   £38   4 3 3
2 Grove Ln   020 3026 4224   1–3C
*"A great addition to the Camberwell foodie scene" – "welcome newcomer"
serving "wonderful wood-fired pizza" from "the excellent toppings to the
flavoursome bases, without too much of the frippery or hype of better-
known joints". / SE5; @theospizzaldn; 10.30 pm, Fri & Sat 11 pm, Sun 10 pm
; no Amex.*

Theo's Simple Italian SW5 NEW   £64
34–44 Barkston Gardens   020 7370 9130   6–2A
*Pasta-prodigy Theo Randall dips his toe into casual dining with an all-day
cicchetti and pasta spot in a pleasant, but very anonymous west London
hotel. Too little survey feedback for a rating – reading the runes online and
in the press, it's a handy Earl's Court standby rather than a destination.
/ SW5 0EW; www.theossimpleitalian.co.uk; @TRSimpleItalian; 10.30 pm.*

34 Mayfair W1   £79   2 2 2
34 Grosvenor Sq   020 3350 3434   3–3A
*As "a discreet and well-spaced venue to take clients and would-be clients",
Richard Caring's "upmarket steakhouse" near the old American Embassy
has "the right balance of formality and a relaxed approach". Those paying
their own way tend to judge it more harshly however, saying it's
"very average" and "woeful value for money". / W1K 2HD;
www.34-restaurant.co.uk; 11 pm, Sun 10 pm.*

The Thomas Cubitt SW1   £61   3 4 4
44 Elizabeth St   020 7730 6060   2–4A
*"Busy, exuberant and seriously popular" – this "fun" Belgravia pub
becomes "very noisy" in its downstairs bar (where pub grub is served) but
is calmer in its upstairs dining room, serving more ambitious fare.
/ SW1W 9PA; www.thethomascubitt.co.uk; 10 pm, Sun 9.30 pm.*

3 South Place, South Place Hotel EC2   £66   3 3 3
3 South Pl   020 3503 0000   13–2A
*For a "sound" business breakfast or lunch near Liverpool Street,
D&D group's "modern and trendy" ground floor bar/restaurant provides
a "solid menu and professional service". (See also Angler upstairs, for a
more 'gastro' experience). / EC2M 2AF; www.southplacehotel.com;
@southplacehotel; 10.30 pm.*

tibits W1   £35   2 2 3
12-14 Heddon St   020 7758 4110   4–3B
*"Unusual self-service vegan operation (where you pay by plate-weight)",
which makes a handy veggie pit stop near Piccadilly Circus. The setting
is "much nicer than the cafeteria style you might expect", and the "varied
selection" of dishes offers "a great choice"… if "at central London prices".
/ W1B 4DA; www.tibits.co.uk; @tibits_uk; Sun-Wed 10 pm, Thu-Sat 10.30 pm;
no Amex.*

Ting,
Shangri-La Hotel at the Shard SE1   £98   2 2 **3**
Level 35, 31 St Thomas St   020 7234 8000   10–4C
"What a vista (even from the gents!)" at this swanky 35th-floor chamber,
which added a 'Chef's Market Table' this year to celebrate the arrival
of new chef, Gareth Bowen (from the Marriott County Hall) to oversee its
Asian-influenced modern British cuisine. No change yet to reporters' verdict
that "you are overpaying for the view" but one bright spark: afternoon tea
is widely thought to be "worth it" for the "sense of occasion". / SE1 9RY;
www.ting-shangri-la.com; @ShangriLaShard; 11.30 pm; no trainers; credit card
deposit required to book; set weekday L £59 (FP).

Toff's N10   £40   **3** 2 2
38 Muswell Hill Broadway   020 8883 8656   1–1B
"One of the best chippies around" – this acclaimed Muswell Hill institution
inspires proper loyalty in the locality: "you get large portions of fine nosh
that feels like you've had value for money". / N10 3RT; www.toffsfish.co.uk;
@toffsfish; 10 pm; closed Sun.

Tokimeite W1 NEW   £79   **4 4 3**
23 Conduit St   020 3826 4411   3–2C
"Superb Japanese cuisine using the highest quality ingredients" is what
you'd expect from Yoshihiro Murata's Mayfair newcomer (on the former site
of Sakura, RIP) – not just because he himself has many Michelin gongs,
but because his backer is Japan's largest agricultural co-operative ("you can
try a true Japanese Wagyu here"). It's "expensive" naturally, but while
press and food-cognoscenti reviews have been restrained, all reporters are
wowed by "fabulous tastes" and "dishes that are good for breaking the ice,
as they look amazing!" / W1S 2XS; www.tokimeite.com; @tokimeitelondon;
10.30 pm; closed Sun.

Tokyo Diner WC2   £26   **3 4 3**
2 Newport Place   020 7287 8777   5–3B
"Rock-bottom prices" make this stalwart Japanese café a very competitive
option, even in Chinatown. Its sushi, noodles and curries are "neither fancy
nor expensive, but honest, tasty, wholesome and top value". / WC2H 7JJ;
www.tokyodiner.com; 11.30 pm; closed Mon; no Amex; no booking, Fri & Sat;
set weekday L £16 (FP).

Tokyo Sukiyaki-Tei & Bar SW3   £52
85 Sloane Ave   020 3583 3797   6–2C
A Chelsea hideaway serving an eclectic range of Japanese dishes –
from Wagyu beef to sushi, sashimi and shabu-shabu (hot pot); reports are
still too few for a rating, but very upbeat. / SW3 3DX;
www.tokyosukiyakitei.com; @TokyoSukiyakiT; online bookings only, Fri & Sat.

Tom's Kitchen   £63   2 2 2
Somerset House, 150 Strand, WC2   020 7845 4646   2–2D
27 Cale St, SW3   020 7349 0202   6–2C
11 Westferry Circus, E14   020 3011 1555   12–1C
1 Commodity Quay, E1   020 3011 5433   10–3D
"For a serious weekend breakfast", fans do tip Tom Aikens's casual bistros
(particularly the backstreet Chelsea original), but overall they give
an impression that's decidedly "average". / 10 pm-10.45 pm; WC2 closed
Sun D.

Tommi's Burger Joint £20 4 4 4
30 Thayer St, W1 020 7224 3828 3–1A
37 Berwick Street, W1 awaiting tel 4–2D NEW
342 Kings Rd, SW3 020 7349 0691 6–3C
"Burgers are to die for, and service is slick and fast" at these "easy and
effective" pitstops, where "some of it is self-service" ("you queue up for
ordering and paying"). "Loud music and dim lighting" helps make them
"cool and trendy" too. / 9 pm.

The Tommy Tucker SW6 £54 3 3 4
22 Waterford Rd 020 7736 1023 6–4A
"Forget jokes about singing for your supper – this is a very good gastropub"
in Fulham, with food by Claude Compton of nearby Claude's Kitchen,
and "delicious wines and ales". "Don't go when Chelsea are playing
at home". / SW6 2DR; www.thetommytucker.com; @tommytuckerpub; Mon-Sat
10 pm, Sun 9 pm.

Tomoe SW15 £40 4 3 2
292 Upper Richmond Road 020 3730 7884 11–2B
A new team transplanted from Marylebone have taken over this Putney
site, formerly called Cho-San (RIP: that is the restaurant not the man,
he's just retired!) The "small" premises retain their "very traditional",
"genuine Tokyo feel" and still provide "authentic sushi" and other
"excellent" fare. / SW15; closed Mon.

Tonkotsu £32 2 3 3
Selfridges, 400 Oxford St, W1 020 7437 0071 3–1A
63 Dean St, W1 020 7437 0071 5–2A
7 Blenheim Cr, W11 020 7221 8300 7–1A NEW
4 Canvey St, SE1 020 7928 2228 10–4B
382 Mare St, E8 020 8533 1840 14–1B
Arch 334 1a Dunston St, E8 020 7254 2478 14–2A
"Deservedly popular for a good slurp", say fans of these "cramped and
buzzy" noodle stops, who praise "broths that are things of beauty". Critics
on the other hand "don't understand the hype" – they feel it's "passable
when hungry" but "nothing more". / see web for detail.

Tosa W6 £38 3 3 2
332 King St 020 8748 0002 8–2B
"There are always several Japanese customers (a great sign!)" at this
yakitori (charcoal-grilled chicken skewers) specialist in Stamford Brook. It's
"excellent value, especially the sushi and sashimi", with a "great lunch
deal". / W6 0RR; www.tosauk.com; 10.30 pm.

Toto's SW3 £88 2 3 4
Walton Hs, Lennox Gardens Mews 020 7589 2062 6–2C
Despite a revamp a couple of years ago, this "stunning" Knightsbridge
Italian (with a lovely courtyard in summer) remains resolutely of the
"old school", and even fans of its "consistent, high-quality cuisine and
service" concede it "can be expensive" (while foes just leave "unsatisfied
and poorer"). / SW3 2JH; www.totosrestaurant.com; @TotosRestaurant; 11 pm;
set weekday L £33 (FP).

Tozi SW1 £47 3 3 3
8 Gillingham St 020 7769 9771 2–4B
This cicchetti (Venetian small plates) specialist is a "neighbourhood go-to"
near Victoria station, with "charming service, fine cooking and gentle
prices". It's "attached to a hotel, although not obviously", but that doesn't
prevent "a great buzz" – and it's "a brilliant place to take children".
/ SW1V 1HN; www.tozirestaurant.co.uk; @ToziRestaurant; 10 pm.

The Trading House EC2 £45 **3 4 4**

89-91 Gresham St   020 7600 5050   10–1A

Year-old City gastropub already making "old friends" with its "great staff", "excellent kebabs (fun too, hanging on a rack!)", and "impressive range of bottled and cask beers". "Sadly, it's not open on the weekends". / EC2V 7NQ; www.thetradinghouse.uk.com; @tradinghouse; 10 pm; closed Sat L & Sun; no Amex.

The Tramshed EC2 £56 **2 3 4**

32 Rivington St   020 7749 0478   13–1B

"Cool, dead-cow decor" (Damien Hirst's well-known formaldehyde tank artwork) adds lustre to the "sunny ambience" of Mark Hix's spacious Shoreditch shed. Sceptics feel its straightforward cooking (primarily chicken or steak-based) "has lost its mojo", but fans do applaud "simple food well done". Top Tip – "kids' deals and the special treatment they get makes it a great family lunch choice". / EC2A 3LX; www.hixrestaurants.co.uk / www.chickenandsteak.co.; @the_tramshed; Mon & Tue 11 pm, Wed-Sat 12.00 am, Sun 9.30 pm.

Trangallan N16 £44 **5 4 4**

61 Newington Grn   020 7359 4988   1–1C

"Brilliant Galician food and a very intriguing list of Spanish wines" ensure this Stoke Newington Hispanic is a hit. "Service is attentive and staff well informed", but "some tables for two are too small". Top Menu Tip – "The chocolate ganache with sea salt and olive oil is a dish everyone should try before they die". / N16 9PX; www.trangallan.com; 10.30 pm; closed Mon; no Amex; no trainers.

Tredwell's WC2 £61 **2 2 2**

4 Upper St Martin's Ln   020 3764 0840   5–3B

Right in the heart of the West End, Marcus Wareing's casual, multi-floor diner is still struggling to make its mark with our reporters (feedback is thin for a venture by such a big name). It does have a fanbase who really dig it – they "love, love, love the very innovative dishes, and yummy cocktails, and the super-cool ambience". Many others though are "very disappointed" – they find the brasserie-with-an-haute-twist cooking "variable" and "too expensive for what it is", and are nonplussed by its styling. / WC2H 9NY; www.tredwells.com; @tredwells; 10 pm, Fri - Sat 11 pm; closed Sun D.

Tried & True SW15 £15 **3 3 3**

279 Upper Richmond Rd   020 8789 0410   11–2A

Another "great addition to the Putney breakfast/brunch scene" – an "airy", "New Zealander-run" café "a little bit off the main drag", serving "wonderfully original breakfasts (with homemade just about everything) and light lunches", plus "excellent coffee". Needless to say, "it can get a bit overrun by yummy mummies". / SW15; www.triedandtruecafe.co.uk; @tried_true_cafe; 4 pm, Sat & Sun 4.30 pm.

Trinity SW4 £71 5 5 4
4 The Polygon 020 7622 1199 11–2D

"Since the refurb last year, Adam Byatt is at the top of his game", and his "classy" Clapham ten-year-old – "so much more than a neighbourhood local!" – rivals nearby Chez Bruce as the area's top gastronomic destination. His "clever" cuisine is "exciting AND completely satisfying" and there's a "wide-ranging and superb" wine selection available by the glass, all delivered by "well-informed and un-pompous" staff. ("The addition of upstairs at Trinity is working well" too – an "interesting and appealing", but cheaper option to the ground floor – formula price £43). Mr Michelin Man – "a star must be due surely?" STOP PRESS – Michelin finally provided the much-overdue star in October 2016. / SW4 0JG; www.trinityrestaurant.co.uk; @TrinityLondon; 10 pm, Sun 9 pm.

Trishna W1 £76 5 3 3
15-17 Blandford St 020 7935 5624 2–1A

"Exciting, well-crafted, deft... balanced in terms of spicing and heat" – such are the "assured culinary delights" featuring "extremely unusual ingredients" at the Sethi family's original Marylebone venture, that made it London's No. 1 nouvelle Indian this year. When busy, it can seem "noisy" and "cramped", and service "slightly rushed". / W1U 3DG; www.trishnalondon.com; @TrishnaLondon; 10.30 pm, Sun 9.45 pm.

LA TROMPETTE W4 £75 5 4 3
5-7 Devonshire Rd 020 8747 1836 8–2A

"You can't fail to have a good meal" at this "West End-style operation" off Chiswick's main drag, whose "very accomplished cuisine" and "polished" service ("insightful wine advice" in particular) create an experience almost "on a par with Chez Bruce" (its stablemate). "Worth the schlep across town"... says a fan from E18! / W4 2EU; www.latrompette.co.uk; @LaTrompetteUK; 10.30 pm, Sun 9.30 pm.

Trullo N1 £59 4 3 3
300-302 St Paul's Rd 020 7226 2733 9–2D

"High-quality ingredients are left to speak for themselves", at this "noisy" and "crowded", "little bit of Puglia", on "the wrong side of the Highbury roundabout" – an ongoing hit, with a "stunning Italian-heavy wine list". / N1 2LH; www.trullorestaurant.com; @Trullo_LDN; 10.15 pm; closed Sun D; no Amex.

Tsunami £46 5 2 3
93 Charlotte St, W1 020 7637 0050 2–1C
5-7 Voltaire Rd, SW4 020 7978 1610 11–1D

"Sensational", Nobu-esque Japanese-fusion dishes have long made this "darkly-lit" Clapham venture an "exciting" culinary destination; in fact "both branches are good", but the Fitzrovia outlet is less well known and not quite as highly rated. / www.tsunamirestaurant.co.uk; @Tsunamirest; SW4 10.30 pm, Fri & Sat 11 pm, Sun 9.30 pm; W1 11 pm; SW4 closed Mon - Fri L, W1 closed Sat L and Sun; no Amex.

Tulse Hill Hotel SE24 £46 3 2 3
150 Norwood Rd 020 8671 7499 1–4D

"A high standard of food from a versatile menu, an amazing garden with summer BBQs, a welcome with a smile, and a great selection of real ales" have won hipster acclaim for this "hidden south London gem", between Brixton and Dulwich. / SE24 9AY; www.tulsehillhotel.com; @TulseHillHotel; 10 pm, Sun 9 pm.

28-50 £54 **2 3 4**

15 Maddox St, W1 020 7495 1505 4–2A

15-17 Marylebone Ln, W1 020 7486 7922 3–1A

140 Fetter Ln, EC4 020 7242 8877 10–2A

The "exceptional wine list with sensible mark-ups" (available "in a wide range of glass sizes") is key to the appeal of this very popular bar/bistro chain – supporting features are the "very pleasant staff" ("happy to discuss without being in your face"), and "simple", "reliable" cooking. / www.2850.co.uk; EC4 9.30 pm, W1 Mon-Wed 10 pm, Thu-Sat 10.30 pm, Sun 9.30 pm; EC4 closed Sat & Sun.

Twist W1 £59 **4 4 4**

42 Crawford St 020 7723 3377 2–1A

"There's so much passion and creativity" in Eduardo Tuccillo's "enjoyable and brilliantly cooked" Italo-Spanish tapas, at this Marylebone yearling, which fans say is "something special". / W1H 1JW; www.twistkitchen.co.uk; @twistkitchen; 11 pm, Fri & Sat 11.30 pm; closed Sun.

Two Brothers N3 £33 **3 2 2**

297-303 Regent's Park Rd 020 8346 0469 1–1B

"Really authentic, old-fashioned fish 'n' chips" have long been the raison d'être of this Finsbury "old favourite". There's a wide range of dishes, portions are "huge, fresh and hot" – and "even the fried chicken is good". / N3 1DP; www.twobrothers.co.uk; 10 pm; closed Mon; set weekday L £20 (FP).

2 Veneti W1 £52 **3 4 3**

10 Wigmore St 020 7637 0789 3–1B

This "friendly" outfit close to the Wigmore Hall serves an "authentic, high quality Venetian menu" – "not the standard Italian dishes" – and shows "depth in the list of Italian wines and grappas". / W1U 2RD; www.2veneti.com; @2Veneti; 10.30 pm, Sat 11 pm; closed Sat L & Sun.

Typing Room, Town Hall Hotel E2 £86 **4 5 3**

Patriot Square 020 7871 0461 14–2B

A minority find it "over-fussy", but Lee Westcott's "brilliantly executed" cuisine wins ecstatic reviews from most reporters, who say its "flair and creativity" are "well worth the trip to deepest Bethnal Green" (and that "it's crazy it doesn't have a Michelin Star!"). An open kitchen adds life to the "clean and elegant" dining room – the corner of "a boutique hotel created from the old town hall" – as does the "terrific" service. / E2 9NF; www.typingroom.com; @TypingRoom; 10 pm; closed Mon & Tue L; set weekday L £50 (FP).

Uli W11 **NEW**

5 Ladbroke Road 020 3141 5878 7–2B

Previously tucked away in nearby All Saints Road, this neighbourhood pan-Asian restaurant – formerly one of the west London's better local hideaways – was resurrected, after a couple of years' closure, in summer 2016 in a new location on Ladbroke Road. The ebullient Michael is back too – looking forward to next year's survey reports. / W11 3PA; www.ulilondon.com; 10.30 pm; D only, closed Sun; no Amex.

Umu W1 £118 **3 3 2**

14-16 Bruton Pl 020 7499 8881 3–2C

If you can get over the "insane prices", Marlon Abela's Kyoto-style fixture in a cute Mayfair mews provides "superb and beautifully presented Kaiseki-cuisine" – even those griping about the "dizzying expense" say "it's worth it for the sensational sushi" and other fare from chef Yoshinori Ishii. / W1J 6LX; www.umurestaurant.com; 10.30 pm; closed Sat L & Sun; no trainers; booking max 14 may apply.

Union Street Café SE1 £58 2 3 2
47-51 Great Suffolk St 020 7592 7977 10–4B
Gordon Ramsay's bare-walled casual Italian, with ingredients from nearby Borough Market, inspires some praise for its "relaxed" style, "fabulous" wines and dependable food. Overall however, the verdict is "nice but uninspiring" (and "not cheap"). / SE1 0BS; www.gordonramsayrestaurants.com/union-street-cafe; @unionstreetcafe; Mon-Sat 10.45 pm; closed Sun D.

Upstairs at John the Unicorn SE15 NEW £39
Rye Lane 020 7732 8483 1–4D
Yet-to-be-rated small-plates-focused dining room above a newly opened Antic pub near Peckham Rye station. Ex-Opera Tavern chef Ben Mulock heads up the kitchen. / SE15 4TL; www.johntheunicorn.com; @JohnTUnicorn; 10 pm, Sun 5 pm; closed Mon, Tue L, Wed L, Thu L, Fri L & Sun D.

Urban Coterie,
M By Montcalm EC1 NEW £61
17th-floor, 151-157 City Rd 020 3837 3000 13–1A
You get some "great views" from the 17th-floor dining room of this eye-catchingly angular building, just north of Old Street roundabout. A collaboration between Searcys, chef Anthony Demetre, and the hotel – limited feedback as yet, but very positive. / EC1V 1JH; www.mbymontcalm.co.uk/urban-coterie-at-m-by-montca; @UrbanCoterie; 10 pm, Fri & Sat 10.30 pm; closed Mon; no trainers.

Le Vacherin W4 £63 3 2 2
76-77 South Pde 020 8742 2121 8–1A
Malcolm John's authentically Gallic bistro beside Acton Green has become a well-known local fixture thanks to its "reliable" traditional French cuisine. Top Tip – particularly "good-value deals at lunchtime". / W4 5LF; www.levacherin.co.uk; @Le_Vacherin; 9.45 pm, Fri & Sat 10.15 pm, Sun 8.30 pm; closed Mon L.

Vanilla Black EC4 £61 4 2 2
17-18 Tooks Ct 020 7242 2622 10–2A
"Seductive and tasty vegetarian food" from an "impressive and expansive menu" at this modern Chancery Lane establishment make it "great, even if you aren't a veggie": "I went with a meat-eater, and it's one of their favourite places!" / EC4A 1LB; www.vanillablack.co.uk; @vanillablack1; 10 pm; closed Sun; no Amex.

Vapiano £30 3 2 3
19-21 Great Portland St, W1 020 7268 0080 3–1C
90b Southwark St, SE1 020 7593 2010 10–4B
"Love the concept but it can be a scrum at the counters!" This global Italian fast-food franchise, (founded in Hamburg, with UK branches in Soho, Southwark and Fitzrovia) offers a food court format with salads, pizza or pasta prepared in front of you. It can be a bit of a bun-fight, but it's cheap, and "the food quality is generally good". / www.vapiano.co.uk; Mon-Thu 11 pm, SE1 Fri & Sat 10.30 pm, W1 Fri & Sat 11.30 pm.

Vasco & Piero's Pavilion W1 £60 3 4 3
15 Poland St 020 7437 8774 4–1C
This "old-style" Soho veteran is easily overlooked but worth discovering, in particular for its "attentive, funny and charming service" ("father and son have been together for over 40 years and they're training the grandson too"). The "traditional" cooking can seem "fairly standard" – go for the Umbrian specialities. / W1F 8QE; www.vascosfood.com; @Vasco_and_Piero; 9.30 pm; closed Sat L & Sun; set dinner £39 (FP).

Veeraswamy W1 £77 3 3 3
Victory Hs, 99-101 Regent St 020 7734 1401 4–4B
*"A veteran that's still delivering the goods!" – London's oldest Indian
(est 1926), near Piccadilly Circus remains "a favourite upscale
subcontinental", with "up-to-date" contemporary decor, "attentive" staff,
and "very special, interesting and delicate cooking"; predictably, it's not
especially cheap. / W1B 4RS; www.veeraswamy.com; @theveeraswamy; 10.30 pm,
Sun 10 pm; booking max 12 may apply.*

Veneta SW1 NEW
St James's Market no tel 4–3D
*From the Salt Yard Group (Opera Tavern, Salt Yard, Dehesa, Ember Yard)
a new autumn-2016 Venetian-inspired restaurant in Haymarket's
St James's Market development. (It will open alongside a second Duck
& Waffle outpost and the London version of Aquavit). / SW1Y 4SB;
www.veneta-stjames.co.uk; midnight.*

Verdi's E1 £44 3 3 3
237 Mile End Rd 020 7423 9563 14–2B
*"A very welcome change from the chicken shops of Whitechapel" –
this East End trattoria specialises in the regional cuisine of Emilia-Romagna.
Scores have dropped a little since it opened last year, but most reporters
still rate it as very good. / E1 4AA; www.gverdi.uk; @verdislondon.*

El Vergel SE1 £30 4 3 4
132 Webber St 020 7401 2308 10–4B
*"A great South American place", near Borough tube – this "cheap 'n'
cheerful", lively canteen serves a wide range of zesty Latino fare, including
empanadas and steak sarnies; recommended for brunch. / SE1 0QL;
www.elvergel.co.uk; @ElVergel_London; 3 pm Mon-Fri, Sat-Sun 4 pm; L only;
no Amex.*

Vico WC2 £58 2 2 1
140a Shaftesbury Ave 020 7379 0303 5–2B
*"No wow factor" on any front came as a surprise at the Bocca di Lupo
team's Italian street food and gelati yearling, right on Cambridge Circus.
A mid-year shake-up seems to be working though: "how this has improved
now they have changed the furniture and have some front-of-house staff.
I'm a Bocco di Lupo fan and was so disappointed on my first visit last year
– only went back by chance and had a so much better experience: a very
good lunch at reasonable price". / WC2H 8PA; www.eatvico.com; @eatvico.*

Il Vicolo SW1 £49 3 3 3
3-4 Crown Passage 020 7839 3960 3–4D
*"Tucked away" in a St James's passage, this "good-value family-run Italian"
comes as a nice surprise in what can be a forbiddingly expensive district.
"The owner and staff are engaging" and it scores well for its daily specials.
/ SW1Y 6PP; 10 pm; closed Sat L & Sun.*

The Victoria SW14 £51 2 3 4
10 West Temple Sheen 020 8876 4238 11–2A
*A short walk from Richmond Park, Paul Merrett's "super local gastropub"
deep in residential Sheen is unusually stylish, and boasts a huge dining
conservatory plus "a garden with a play area for children" ("sometimes
it feels a bit too family-friendly, a bit like dining in a crèche"). Foodwise
"perhaps it doesn't have the culinary flair it once did", but most reporters
still find the menu has "something for everyone". / SW14 7RT;
www.thevictoria.net; @TheVictoria_Pub; 10 pm, Sun 9 pm; no Amex.*

Viet Food W1 NEW   £31   3 3 3
34-36 Wardour St   020 7494 4555   5–3A
*"Very good Vietnamese food" – with "tasty, clean flavours" and
at "excellent prices" ("especially for Chinatown") is building a following for
Jeff Tan's consistent newcomer – "a bit of a clattery place", but with
attractive (if slightly "rustic") styling. / W1D 6QT; www.vietnamfood.co.uk;
10.30 pm, Fri & Sat 11 pm.*

Viet Grill E2   £44   3 2 2
58 Kingsland Rd   020 7739 6686   13–1B
*Critics diss it as "poor, dismal and studenty", but most reports acclaim this
cafe on Kingsland Road, Shoreditch – aka "pho mile" – lauding "terrific
fresh food, consistent quality and excellent customer service", and say it's
"a great introduction to Vietnamese food". / E2 8DP;
www.vietnamesekitchen.co.uk; @CayTreVietGrill; 11 pm, Fri & Sat 11.30 pm,
Sun 10.30 pm.*

View 94 SW18 NEW
Prospect Quay, 94 Point Pleasant   020 8425 9870   11–2B
*A fine position – with a Thames-side terrace – is a highpoint at this
bar/restaurant near Wandsworth Park: too limited feedback yet on its
ambitious modern European cooking for a rating. / SW18 1PP; view94.com;
@view94_sw18; closed Sat L & Sun; no shorts.*

Vijay NW6   £33   3 2 1
49 Willesden Ln   020 7328 1087   1–1B
*"Unfussy, unfussed, unhurried and happily obscure" – this long-running
(since 1964), slightly decrepit South Indian fixture in Kilburn can
be "excellent, including for vegetarians". / NW6 7RF; www.vijayrestaurant.co.uk;
10.45 pm, Fri & Sat 11.45 pm; no bookings.*

Villa Bianca NW3   £58   2 2 2
1 Perrins Ct   020 7435 3131   9–2A
*"This Hampstead veteran continues to churn out classic Italian fare" –
"great pasta, fish and steaks/veal" – in a "proper, unpretentious setting"
replete with "1970s Capri-style elegance". Even fans, though, can find the
cooking a tad "uninspired" ("tasty, but the usual Italian panache
is absent"). / NW3 1QS; www.villabiancanw3.com; @VillaBiancaNW3; 11.30 pm,
Sun 10.30 pm.*

Villa Di Geggiano W4   £64   2 2 2
66-68 Chiswick High Rd   020 3384 9442   8–2B
*The "high-end" Tuscan cuisine and "wine from their own vineyard" at this
Chiswick-fringe establishment do inspire some rave reviews. Its
"high prices" are a major sticking point however, and for its harshest critics
it's "noisy, unappealing and rather gaudy". / W4 1SY; www.villadigeggiano.co.uk;
@villadigeggiano; 10 pm; closed Mon.*

Village East SE1   £58   2 2 3
171-173 Bermondsey St   020 7357 6082   10–4D
*The food – brunch and European brasserie fare – and cocktails are
"always great, and there's a brilliant atmosphere" at this Bermondsey joint.
On the downside, it can be so busy that "you feel squashed in" and
"service gets a bit hit-and-miss". / SE1 3UW; www.villageeast.co.uk;
@VillageEastSE1; 10 pm, Sun 9.30 pm.*

Villandry £56 1 1 2

11-12 Waterloo Pl, SW1 020 7930 3305 2–3C
170 Gt Portland St, W1 020 7631 3131 2–1B

These "elegant and rather peaceful" cafes with smart St James's and
Marylebone addresses are potentially "useful", "versatile" rendezvous,
but "sadly, the cooking lets them down"; breakfast though is "good value".
/ www.villandry.com; see web for detail.

**The Vincent Rooms,
Westminster Kingsway College SW1** £38 3 3 3

76 Vincent Sq 020 7802 8391 2–4C

This training-ground for young chefs – part of a catering college in a
tranquil and leafy corner of Westminster – is worth a try: you get "large
portions" and "excellent value for money". "Serving staff can be erratic,
but they're learning!" / SW1P 2PD; www.wcstking.ac.uk; @thevincentrooms; 7 pm;
closed Mon D, Tue D, Fri D, Sat & Sun; no Amex.

Vineet Bhatia SW3 £99 3 2 3

10 Lincoln St 020 7225 1881 6–2D

Formerly called Rasoi (RIP), Vineet Bhatia's "very quiet and peaceful"
townhouse in Chelsea re-opened in October 2016 after a complete refit. In
its previous guise (price given, and ratings awarded) it won praise for its
"phenomenal", "cross-over" Indian cuisine "on a level no-one else can
compete with", if you can "get over the 'second-mortgage' prices". It looks
like it will become even more expensive now: menus start from £105.
/ SW3 2TS; www.vineetbhatia.com; awaiting details.

Vinoteca £51 2 2 3

15 Seymour Pl, W1 020 7724 7288 2–2A
55 Beak St, W1 020 3544 7411 4–2B
18 Devonshire Rd, W4 020 3701 8822 8–2A
One Pancras Sq, N1 020 3793 7210 9–3C
7 St John St, EC1 020 7253 8786 10–1B

"One of the best and most unusual wine selections in London" underpins
the high popularity of these "appealing" modern haunts (whose "smart"
King's Cross branch attracts most mention). The "unfussy" food? – "nothing
too thrilling, but competent". / www.vinoteca.co.uk.

Vintage Salt £44 3 4 3

189 Upper St, N1 020 3227 0979 9–2D
69 Old Broad St, EC2 020 7920 9103 10–2C

"Marvellous" fish 'n' chips (plain or grilled if you prefer) are on the menu
at this Islington prototype and Liverpool Street spin-off for a planned chain
of "posh", "modern chippie/diners". (Old-timers see echoes of former
concepts that have come and gone nearby: "If Alan and Olga – of the
original Upper Street Fish Shop – were still around, I think they would
approve!") / @vintagesaltldn; see web for detail.

Vivat Bacchus £53 3 3 3

4 Hay's Ln, SE1 020 7234 0891 10–4C
47 Farringdon St, EC4 020 7353 2648 10–2A

"An all-round winner" – this busy operation in Farringdon (there's a second
venue in Bankside) majors on South African wines, steaks and cheeses.
"They take real care of their customers" – "and I loved the cheese room"
(you can visit to make your choice). / www.vivatbacchus.co.uk; 10.30 pm;
EC4 closed Sat & Sun, SE1 closed Sat L & Sun.

VQ £46 2 4 3
St Giles Hotel, Great Russell St, WC1 020 7636 5888 5–1A
325 Fulham Rd, SW10 020 7376 7224 6–3B
24 Pembridge Road, W11 020 3745 7224 7–2B NEW
"Smoked salmon and scrambled eggs"… "great veggie fry-ups" – that's
the kind of all-day breakfast food that's "always reliable" at these 24/7
diners. The ancient SW10 branch is the best known, while the new Notting
Hill branch isn't actually open the whole 24 hours (but is still handy if you
fancy a full English in W11 at 2am). / www.vingtquatre.co.uk; open 24 hours.

Vrisaki N22 £37 3 3 2
73 Middleton Rd 020 8889 8760 1–1C
Last year this ancient Bounds Green Greek "underwent a modern refit and
a big change from its traditional taverna-style setting". But even those who
feel the "atmosphere is now depleted" say the "food is still OK" – including
the massive mezze special, which it has been a challenge to finish since
time immemorial. / N22 8LZ; www.vrisaki.uk.com; @vrisakiuk; 11.30 pm,
Sun 9 pm; closed Mon; no Amex.

Wagamama £39 2 4 3
"The UK's rising standard of Asian cuisine has outpaced these well-
established noodle canteens", but – for a "fresh and reasonably healthy"
bite, with "generous portions and reasonable prices" – armies of fans still
say it's "a great format", and "a staple with kids". / www.wagamama.com;
10 pm-11 pm; EC4 & EC2 closed Sat & Sun; no booking.

Wahaca £33 3 3 3
"Bustling and so fun!"; Thomasina Miers's "easygoing" Mexican chain
offers a "constantly refreshed" menu of zesty dishes, which – "even if
consistency can vary – are usually good, filling and amazing value". Service
is "accommodating too", but "that branches get so rammed can impact
wait times", and queues to enter "are a pain" too. / www.wahaca.com;
10 pm-11 pm; no booking; SRA-3 star.

The Wallace,
The Wallace Collection W1 £55 2 1 5
Hertford Hs, Manchester Sq 020 7563 9505 3–1A
"A beautiful glass-ceilinged atrium" creates a "wonderful bright and open"
atmosphere at this café adjoining the famous 18th-century palazzo and
gallery. In other respects this Peyton & Byrne operation is a mixed bag –
the food's just about OK (stick to coffee and simpler items), while service
is "a bit crap". / W1U 3BN; www.peytonandbyrne.co.uk; Fri & Sat 9.30 pm; closed
Mon D, Tue D, Wed D, Thu D & Sun D; no Amex.

Walter & Monty EC3 NEW £26
6 Bury Street 020 7283 6666 10–2D
Yet another street food trader puts down permanent roots – this time
in the City with this small, carnivorous café/takeaway by the Gherkin,
majoring in charcoal-grilled meats. / EC3A 7BA; www.walterandmonty.com;
@walterandmonty; 2.30 pm; L only, closed Sat & Sun; no bookings.

Waterloo Bar & Kitchen SE1 £51 2 1 2
131 Waterloo Rd 020 7928 5086 10–4A
This "great-value brasserie" near Waterloo is often packed, perhaps
because it's "the perfect place to eat when going to the Old Vic". / SE1 8UR;
www.barandkitchen.co.uk; @BarKitchen; 10.30 pm.

The Waterway W9 £53 ②②④
54 Formosa St 020 7266 3557 9–4A
Well-named canal-side bar/restaurant on the fringe of Little Venice – sibling to the nearby Summerhouse – lovely in summer and serving "a reasonable menu". / W9 2JU; www.thewaterway.co.uk; @thewaterway_; 11 pm, Sun 10.30 pm.

Wazen WC1 NEW £55 ④④②
2 Acton St 020 3632 1069 9–3D
South of King's Cross, this "rather sparse" Japanese newcomer occupies a tough site (once home to Konstam at The Prince Albert, long RIP). "It needs your help" and will repay it with "charming service", and "exceptional quality sushi and sashimi" and other "innovative fare without the pomp", prepared by an ex-Matsuri head chef. / WC1X 9NA; www.wazen-restaurant.co.uk; @wazenlondon; 11 pm; closed Mon & Sun.

The Wells NW3 £51 ②②③
30 Well Walk 020 7794 3785 9–1A
"The dog comes too", with many regulars at Hampstead's most popular pub, about 100m from the Heath: a top choice for a Sunday roast, either in the bar, or the "light and airy upstairs room". The food – "classics and also some grills, such as steak" – is "variable, but usually pretty dependable". / NW3 1BX; www.thewellshampstead.co.uk; @WellsHampstead; 10 pm, Sun 9.30 pm.

West Thirty Six W10 £60 ②②③
36 Golborne Rd 020 3752 0530 7–1A
Very mixed reports on this ambitious three-story yearling (with grill, lounge, bar, terrace and BBQ) in the shadow of north Kensington's Trellick Tower. Fans applaud "the best burger in a while" and a "cosy upstairs" – critics say that "hype doesn't match reality" with "variable food and high prices". / W10 5PR; www.westthirtysix.co.uk; @westthirtysix; 10 pm.

The Wet Fish Café NW6 £50 ③②③
242 West End Ln 020 7443 9222 1–1B
This all-day café in West Hampstead is named after the "original fish shop, whose (Art Deco) wall tiles make the whole experience something special". An "inventive menu which always delivers" combines with "friendly service" to make it a "dream local" (especially for brunch). / NW6 1LG; www.thewetfishcafe.co.uk; @thewetfishcafe; 10 pm; no Amex; booking evening only.

The White Onion SW19 £60 ③②②
67 High St 020 8947 8278 11–2B
"This really could be it for Wimbledon finally cracking fine dining!" – Eric and Sarah Guignard's ambitious yearling is, say fans, "just as good as its Surbiton sibling" (the well-known French Table) and brings "classic French cuisine plus a few surprise choices" to this perennially underserved 'burb. On the downside, "service is friendly but can be unfocused, the place can lack a little buzz" and the cooking strikes sceptics as "OK, but too fussy and overcomplicated". Top Tip – "impressive set lunch". / SW19 5EE; www.thewhiteonion.co.uk; @thewhiteonionSW; 10.30 pm; closed Mon, Tue-Thu D only,Fri-Sun open L & D.

The White Swan EC4 £62 ③③②
108 Fetter Ln 020 7242 9696 10–2A
Look out for the "frequent 50% discount offer" if you want "value for money" in the "thankfully quiet" dining room on the top floor of this "loud" pub off Fleet Street, where the cooking can be surprisingly ambitious. / EC4A 1ES; www.thewhiteswanlondon.com; @thewhiteswanEC4; 10 pm; closed Sat & Sun.

Wild Honey W1 £79 **3** **3** **3**
12 St George St 020 7758 9160 3–2C
Back on form this year: Will Smith and Anthony Demetre's club-like (and business-friendly) fixture provides meaty fare and an "excellent array of wines by the glass", and "understated and professional service". It's "well-priced" for Mayfair too ("I often go for the fixed-price lunch, but happily pay my bill when I go à la carte"). / W1S 2FB; www.wildhoneyrestaurant.co.uk; @whrestaurant; 10.30 pm; closed Sun.

Wiltons SW1 £95 **3** **4** **4**
55 Jermyn St 020 7629 9955 3–3C
"The equivalent of the best of St James's clubs"; this "bastion of traditional British cuisine" (est 1742, here since 1984) offers a "truly magnificent", "old-school" experience majoring in "wonderful fish" ("the best-ever sole meunière") and "great game" ("it's the only place I've ever had the chance to eat snipe, then woodcock!"). "Long may it survive, even if prices are crazy!" / SW1Y 6LX; www.wiltons.co.uk; @wiltons1742; 10.15 pm; closed Sat L & Sun; jacket required.

The Windmill W1 £48 **3** **2** **3**
6-8 Mill St 020 7491 8050 4–2A
"Excellent pies!" – steak 'n' kidney particularly recommended – put this Mayfair boozer in a class of its own. "What a joy to go to a real pub as against a tarted-up wine bar, with more people drinking beer than lager". / W1S 2AZ; www.windmillmayfair.co.uk; @tweetiepie_w1; 10 pm, Sat 5 pm.

The Wine Library EC3 £34 **1** **3** **5**
43 Trinity Sq 020 7481 0415 10–3D
"Many a happy afternoon can be lost" at this extremely atmospheric, ancient cellar near Tower Hill – a "fabulous selection of bottles" are available at shop prices plus corkage, accompanied by a "cold smorgasbord" of nibbles ("love the rillettes"). / EC3N 4DJ; www.winelibrary.co.uk; Mon 6 pm, 7.30 pm; closed Mon D, Sat & Sun.

Wolfe's Bar & Grill WC2 £49 **3** **2** **2**
30 Gt Queen St 020 7831 4442 5–1D
An early-wave surfer of the burger craze – the one in the 1970s that is (when it was on Park Lane) – this Covent Garden family diner still serves "consistently good" burgers, plus other decent, retro-ish fare. / WC2B 5BB; www.wolfes-grill.net; @wolfesbargrill; 9.30 pm, Fri & Sat 10.30 pm; no bookings.

THE WOLSELEY W1 £62 **2** **3** **5**
160 Piccadilly 020 7499 6996 3–3C
From "the perfect power breakfast" ("like a Who's Who of the FTSE100!") to "celeb-spotting" over lunch or dinner, Corbin & King's "cosmopolitan and Continental feeling" Grand Café by The Ritz is "always full of fizz", even if the "bistro-style" Mittel-European fare has always been decidedly "formulaic". A few accuse it of laurel-resting though? – in particular service (typically "very professional") was patchier this year. Top Tip – "one of the few grand afternoon teas in central London that isn't a total rip-off". / W1J 9EB; www.thewolseley.com; @TheWolseleyRest; midnight, Sun 11 pm.

Wong Kei W1 £33 **2** **2** **2**
41-43 Wardour St 020 7437 8408 5–3A
For a "cheap if not so cheerful" chow in Chinatown, this "solid and consistent" multi-storey canteen of decades standing "is the daddy of them all". But while it's known for its "famously abrupt" staff, reporters feel they've lightened up under the new management of the last couple of years. / W1D 6PY; www.wongkeilondon.com; Mon-Sat 11.15 pm, Sun 10.30 pm; cash only.

The Woodford E18 NEW   £77   **3** **4** **4**
159 High Rd   020 8504 5952   1–1D
"A star on the outskirts of London" – Pierre Koffmann protégé (and former
Young Chef of the Year) Ben Murphy – just 25 – was backed by Essex
restaurateur Steve Andrews to open this "ambitious" (one or two critics
would say "over-ambitious") and very plushly "comfortable" new 100-cover
restaurant in South Woodford (complete with Churchill Lounge bar). It's
"a fabulous addition to an area which surprisingly lacks an upmarket
establishment" and "shows great promise", even if some of the classic
cuisine is "still finding its feet". STOP PRESS – after 10 months Ben Murphy
and his team announced they were off in mid-October 2016. / E18 2PA;
www.thewoodford.co.uk; @TheWoodford_; 9.30 pm, Sun 6 pm; closed Mon & Tue.

Workshop Coffee   £45   **3** **3** **4**
80a Mortimer St, W1   020 7253 5754   3–1C
St Christopher's Place, W1   020 7253 5754   3–1A
27 Clerkenwell Rd, EC1   020 7253 5754   10–1A
60a Holborn Viaduct, EC1   no tel   10–2A
'Source, Roast, Brew' is the motto of this "casual" chain, nominated by its
many fans for its brilliant, in-house-roasted brews (it opened a new Bethnal
Green roastery this year). The five-year-old Clerkenwell original (price
shown) has the only significant food operation, and is particularly tipped for
"great breakfast options". / workshopcoffee.com; @workshopcoffee; see web for
detail.

Wormwood W11   £65   **4** **3** **2**
16 All Saints Rd   020 7854 1808   7–1B
"Successful experimentation" in combining North African and
Mediterranean flavours to produce shared plates win praise for this
"boho hangout" in deepest Notting Hill – "beautifully presented and they
taste delicious!" / W11 1HH; www.wormwoodnottinghill.com; 9.30 pm, Fri & Sat
10 pm; closed Mon, Tue, Wed L, Thu L, Fri L, Sat L & Sun L.

Wright Brothers   £63   **4** **3** **3**
13 Kingly St, W1   020 7434 3611   4–2B
56 Old Brompton Rd, SW7   020 7581 0131   6–2B
11 Stoney St, SE1   020 7403 9554   10–4C
8 Lamb St, E1   020 7377 8706   10–2D
"A terrific oyster selection"… "fabulous dressed crab"… "superb mussels"
– such are the "fuss-free" delicacies at these extremely popular, "friendly"
and "always buzzing" seafood specialists. / 10.30 pm, Sun 9 pm; booking:
max 8.

Xi'an Impression N7 NEW   £21   **4** **4** **2**
117 Benwell Rd   020 3441 0191   9–2D
"A little gem, tucked away in the shadows of the Emirates stadium", whose
"incredible, homemade noodles are a thing of wonder". "With its slick
service and top street-food, you forget the basic chairs and Formica tables".
/ N7; www.xianimpression.co.uk; @xianimpression; 10 pm.

Yalla Yalla   £39   **3** **2** **3**
1 Green's Ct, W1   020 7287 7663   4–2D
12 Winsley St, W1   020 7637 4748   3–1C
Greenwich Peninsula Sq, SE10   0772 584 1372   9–3C
"Cheap, cheerful, plentiful and so very tasty" – the "zingy" mezze at these
"down-to-earth" ("tiny and cramped") Lebanese cafés, where "it's easy
to get carried away and order too much". Top Menu Tip – "never
go without having the chicken livers". / www.yalla-yalla.co.uk; Green's Court
11 pm, Sun 10 pm – Winsley Street 11.30 pm, Sat 11 pm; W1 Sun.

Yama Momo SE22 £56 4 2 3

72 Lordship Ln 020 8299 1007 1–4D

"There's superb sushi and sashimi, but also a Pacific-fusion element to the main dishes" at this outpost of Clapham's long-running Tsunami which has "come to Lordship Lane and conquered!", despite service that can be "a bit slapdash". "Tasty cocktails" help fuel "something of a nightclub atmosphere": "it's buzzy for the suburbs on a weekday night!" / SE22 8HF; www.yamamomo.co.uk; @YamamomoRest; 10 pm, Fri & Sat 10.30 pm, Sun 9.30 pm; closed weekday L.

Yard Sale Pizza £30 4 3 2

54 Blackstock Road, N4 020 7226 2651 9–1D **NEW**
105 Lower Clapton Rd, E5 020 3602 9090 14–1B

"Inventive pizza in hipster-land" is the promise at this "too-cool-for-school" Clapton haunt, which now also has a trendy outpost in Finsbury Park too. / see web for detail.

Yashin W8 £79 3 2 2

1a Argyll Rd 020 7938 1536 6–1A

This pioneering modern Japanese haunt in Kensington ranks "among the best sushi in London", but scores have taken a tumble in the past year. For some critics, "delicious food" is balanced by "diabolical service: incompetent and snooty". Others complain that it is "overpriced" and "overrated". (Very limited feedback on its lesser-known 'Ocean' branch, on the Old Brompton Road). / W8 7DB; www.yashinsushi.com; @Yashinsushi; 10 pm.

Yauatcha £77 4 3 3

Broadwick Hs, 15-17 Broadwick St, W1 020 7494 8888 4–1C
Broadgate Circle, EC2 020 3817 9888 13–2B

"A happy combo of exquisite dim sum and glamorous settings" creates massive popularity for these "staple" but still "on-trend" pan-Asians. Fans of the Soho original dispute the virtues of the basement ("dark" and "clubby") and the ground floor ("lovely openness"), while the "bright and light branch above Broadgate Circle" is proving "a great addition to the City". / see web for detail.

The Yellow House SE16 £45 3 3 2

126 Lower Rd 020 7231 8777 12–2A

A neighbourhood bar/restaurant right next to Surrey Quays station – pizza is the most popular culinary pick but more substantial fare is also available. / SE16 2UE; www.theyellowhouse.eu; @theyellowhousejazz; 10 pm, Sun 8 pm; closed Mon, Tue-Sat D only, Sun open L & D.

Yi-Ban E16 £45 3 3 3

London Regatta Centre, Royal Albert Dock 020 7473 6699 12–1D

"An interesting waterside location near City Airport helps justify the trek to this obscure Chinese in deepest Docklands", where "watching the planes take off opposite" provides a moving backdrop to a meal. A "spacious and convivial" venue, it offers "solidly good (without being quite top-drawer and fusion-y) dim sum" at "very reasonable prices". / E16 2QT; www.yi-ban.co.uk; 11 pm, Sun 10.30 pm.

Yipin China N1 £43 3 2 1

70-72 Liverpool Rd 020 7354 3388 9–3D

"It's not for the faint-hearted" ("heavy use of chilli", and "a heavy hand on the oil"), but for an "authentic taste" of "China in N1", this "brusque" and "basic" Hunanese/Sichuan operation has a certain "utilitarian" charm, and the best results are "sensational". / N1 0QD; www.yipinchina.co.uk; 11 pm.

Yming W1 £42 **3** **4** **3**

35-36 Greek St   020 7734 2721   5–2A

"So different from Chinatown a hundred yards south!" –
this "unpretentious" but "welcoming" Soho "refuge" maintains a big
following thanks to its "smiling staff" (overseen by "convivial host,
William") and food that's been "steadfastly good" over many years (if a tad
"predictable"). / W1D 5DL; www.yminglondon.com; 11.45 pm; closed Sun.

York & Albany NW1 £59 **2** **2** **2**

127-129 Parkway   020 7592 1227   9–3B

Gordon Ramsay's "roomy" and rambling old tavern on the edge of Regent's
Park is a "pleasant old building". No great culinary fireworks though –
more upbeat reports say it's "good, plain food". / NW1 7PS;
www.gordonramsayrestaurants.com/york-and-a; @yorkandalbany; 11 pm, Sun 9 pm.

Yoshi Sushi W6 £39 **3** **4** **2**

210 King St   020 8748 5058   8–2B

"Fine Japanese/Korean food at very reasonable prices plus super-friendly
staff" maintain the appeal of this traditional stalwart, in a nondescript run
of cafés near Ravenscourt Park tube. It's a favourite of many food-writers,
including Toby Young and Simon Parker Bowles. / W6 0RA; 11 pm,
Sun 10.30 pm; closed Sun L.

Yoshino W1 £44 **4** **4** **3**

3 Piccadilly Pl   020 7287 6622   4–4C

"Tucked away in an alley off Piccadilly", this quirky café-style venue
is "as near as you can get to genuine Japanese food" in London. Opinions
differ on whether it is nicer downstairs or in the small upstairs area,
but "sitting at the counter is a great option for the solo diner". / W1J 0DB;
www.yoshino.net; @Yoshino_London; 10 pm; closed Sun.

Yum Bun EC2 £14 **5** **3** –

Dinerama, 19 Great Eastern St   07919 408 221   13–1A

Lisa Meyer's Taiwanese-style steamed buns are "great fun street food that
pack flavour and texture", and "deserve the respect of being eaten slowly".
You can find stalls at various food events in East London. / EC2A 3EJ;
www.yumbun.co.uk; @yum_bun; 10 pm; closed Mon D, Tue D, Wed D, Sat L & Sun.

Yum Yum N16 £43 **3** **2** **2**

187 Stoke Newington High St   020 7254 6751   1–1D

"It looks wonderful from the outside" – a Georgian building "with fairy
lights galore and Thai statues" – once inside this Stoke Newington stalwart
the "absolutely massive" space feels a tad "barn-like", but the affordable
cooking remains good value. / N16 0LH; www.yumyum.co.uk; @yumyum; 11 pm,
Fri & Sat midnight; set weekday L £17 (FP).

Yumi Izakaya W1 NEW £40

The Piccadilly West End hotel, 67 Shaftesbury Ave   no tel   5–3A

A collaboration between Tom & Ed Martin of the ETM Group (The Gun,
The Botanist et al) and Caspar von Hofmannsthal (ex-Quo Vadis and
Rotorino) has brought this izakaya to a Theatreland hotel. An early report
is upbeat: "a very friendly spot with wonderful skewers and other Japanese
classics – the smoky interior adds to the experience". / W1D 6EX;
www.yumirestaurants.com; @yumi_izakaya; 12.30 am; no bookings.

Zafferano SW1 £81 2 2 2

15 Lowndes St   020 7235 5800   6–1D

"Having once been amongst the best Italian restaurants in London the cuisine has become more ordinary" at this well-known Belgravian, which is widely seen as "resting on its laurels", and to its harshest critics is "awful". It's not without support though: even some who feel it's "overpriced, staid and could do better" say "it's still worth a visit for the bible-like wine list and classic cooking". / SW1X 9EY; www.zafferanorestaurant.com; 11.30 pm, Sun 11 pm; set weekday L £42 (FP).

Zaffrani N1 £46 3 2 2

47 Cross St   020 7226 5522   9–3D

"Upmarket" Indian off Islington's main drag, with "a menu that's markedly different from the average"; to the odd reporter results are "nothing special", but on most accounts a meal here is "seriously good". / N1 2BB; www.zaffrani.co.uk; 10.30 pm.

Zaibatsu SE10 £35 4 5 2

96 Trafalgar Rd   020 8858 9317   1–3D

Both staff and prices are "very friendly" at this tiny Japanese BYO café in Greenwich, serving "really fresh sushi and sashimi". "The decor's basic but that's part of the charm". / SE10 9UW; www.zaibatsufusion.co.uk; @ong_teck; 11 pm; closed Mon.

Zaika, Tamarind Collection W8 £68 4 4 4

1 Kensington High St   020 7795 6533   6–1A

"Stunning Indian food" wins consistent high ratings for this impressive venue, opposite Kensington Gardens. Some feel that "the high ceilings (it was formerly a bank) detract from the ambience", but most reports say it's "all-round great". / W8 5NP; www.zaikaofkensington.com; @ZaikaLondon; 10.45 pm, Sun 9.45 pm; closed Mon L; credit card deposit required to book; set weekday L £38 (FP), set pre-theatre £44 (FP).

Zayane W10 NEW £46 4 4 4

91 Golborne Road   020 8960 1371   7–1A

A modern North African restaurant, in the northerly reaches of Portobello. Heading up the kitchen is Chris Bower (ex-head chef of Tunbridge Wells's lovely Thackeray's) – one or two early reports hail his "terrific European-influenced Moroccan cooking". / W10 5NL; www.zayanerestaurant.com; 10 pm.

Zelman Meats £58 5 4 4

Harvey Nichols, Knightsbridge, SW1   020 7201 8625   6–1D NEW
2 St Anne's Ct, W1   020 7437 0566   5–2A NEW

"Goodman's cool and interesting little sibling...." – this "trendy industrial-style" steakhouse (on the cutely tucked-away site that was briefly Rex & Mariano, RIP) is proving "a brilliant addition to Soho": a "simple, but perfectly executed concept" combining "wonderful, well-cooked meat", plus service that's "knowledgeable, enthusiastic and friendly", all at a price that's "relatively affordable". / see web for detail.

Zest, JW3 NW3 £49 3 3 3

341-351 Finchley Rd   020 7433 8955   1–1B

"Creative Middle Eastern cuisine" and cool contemporary styling win fans for this subterranean modern Israeli in West Hampstead. On Sunday they run a "bottomless brunch": not just the "pomegranate mimosa and fresh carrot juice" but food too! / NW3 6ET; Sat-Thu 9.45 pm; closed Fri & Sat L

Zia Lucia N7 [NEW] £31
157 Holloway Road   020 7700 3708   9–2D
A new spot on Holloway Road, featuring (apparently) a unique-for-London selection of 48-hour, slow-fermented Italian pizza doughs. It opened too late for survey feedback, but the early word-on-the-street says it's cracking. / N7 8LX; www.zialucia.com; @zialuciapizza; closed Mon.

Ziani's SW3 £57 [2][3][2]
45 Radnor Walk   020 7351 5297   6 3C
"Ever-buzzy", "squashed" trattoria just off the King's Road, with a "friendly padrone", and "acceptable food" from "the smallest kitchen ever seen". "Reservations can be unreliable at peak times (which are many), but it's where the locals eat or entertain". / SW3 4BP; www.ziani.co.uk; 11 pm, Sun 10 pm.

Zima W1 [NEW] £29
45 Frith Street   020 7494 9111   5–2A
Next door to Soho's legendary Ronnie Scott's jazz club – a new venture from Russian chef Alexei Zimin that combines Russian street food and drink in a kitsch speakeasy-style atmosphere. / W1D 4SD; www.zima.bar; @ZimaLondon; 1 am; closed Mon & Sun; no bookings.

Zoilo W1 £56 [4][2][3]
9 Duke St   020 7486 9699   3–1A
"Innovative sharing-dishes at affordable prices" win rave write-ups from fans of this "small tapas-style Argentinian restaurant", which is tucked-away near Selfridges. The top perches are in the downstairs bar, with views of the chefs at work. / W1U 3EG; www.zoilo.co.uk; @Zoilo_London; 10.30 pm; closed Sun.

Zuma SW7 £80 [4][3][4]
5 Raphael St   020 7584 1010   6–1C
"The big wristwatch brigade" are out in force, especially at the "very cool bar" of this swish haunt, which is "always buzzing with the Knightsbridge set". Its Japanese-fusion morsels are "truly sensational" too, but service has seemed more "inattentive" of late, and "the bill can leave you feeling flat". / SW7 1DL; www.zumarestaurant.com; 10.45 pm, Sun 10.15 pm; booking max 8 may apply.

INDEXES

BREAKFAST
(with opening times)

Central
Al Duca *(9)*
Asia de Cuba *(7)*
Babaji Pide *(Sat & Sun 11)*
Bageriet *(9, Sat 10)*
Balthazar *(7.30 Mon-Fri, 9 Sat & Sun)*
Bar Italia *(6.30)*
Bar Termini *(Mon-Fri 7.30, Sat 9, Sun 10.30)*
Bbar *(9)*
Bernardi's *(8)*
The Berners Tavern *(7)*
Bonhams Restaurant *(8)*
The Botanist: SW1 *(8, Sat & Sun 9)*
Boulestin *(7 M-F, 10 Sat)*
Brown's Hotel *(7, Sun 7.30)*
Bukowski Grill: W1 *(8, Sat 8.30, Sun 9.30)*
Butler's Restaurant *(7-10 (Mon-Fri) 7:30-11 Sat)*
Café in the Crypt *(Mon-Sat 8)*
Café Monico *(8, Sat & Sun 9)*
Carousel *(9)*
The Cavendish *(Sat & Sun 10)*
Cecconi's *(7, Sat & Sun 8)*
Céleste *(6.30)*
The Chiltern Firehouse *(7)*
Chucs: W1 *(7.30, Sat 9.30, Sun 11)*
The Cinnamon Club *(7.30)*
Clipstone *(Sat 11)*
Clives Midtown Diner *(9, Sat & Sun 10)*
Colbert *(8)*
The Collins Room *(7)*
Cut *(7, Sat & Sun 7.30)*
Dalloway Terrace *(7)*
Daylesford Organic: SW1 *(8, Sun 10); Oxford St W1 (9)*
Dean Street Townhouse *(Mon-Fri 7, Sat & Sun 8)*
The Delaunay *(7, Sat & Sun 11)*
Dickie Fitz *(7, Sat 8.30)*
Dishoom: WC2 *(8, Sat & Sun 10)*
Dorchester Grill *(7, Sat & Sun 8)*
L'Escargot *(9)*
Ethos *(8, Sat 11.30, Sun 10)*
Fernandez & Wells: *Beak St W1 (7.30, sat& sun 9); Lexington St W1 (7); St Anne's Ct W1 (8, sat 10); WC2 (sat-sun 9)*
45 Jermyn St *(7, Sat & Sun 8)*
Franco's *(7, Sat 8)*
La Fromagerie Café *(8, Sat 9, Sun 10)*
Galvin, Athenaeum *(7)*
The Goring Hotel *(7, Sun 7.30)*
The Grazing Goat *(7.30)*
Hardy's Brasserie *(Sat & Sun 9)*
Heddon Street Kitchen *(Mon-Fri 7.30 Sat & Sun 10)*
Holborn Dining Room *(Sun-Fri 7, Sat 8)*
Honey & Co *(Mon-Fri 8, Sat 9.30)*
Hubbard & Bell *(7 Mon-Fri / 8 Sat & Sun)*
Hush: WC1 *(8)*
The Ivy Café: W1 *(Mon-Fri 7.30, Sat 8, Sun 9)*
Jar Kitchen *(Sat 10)*

Joe Allen *(Sat & Sun 11)*
Kaffeine: *Great Titchfield St W1 (7.30, Sat 8.30, Sun 9.30)*
Kaspar's *(7)*
Kazan (Café): *Wilton Rd SW1 (8, Sun 9)*
Koya-Bar *(8.30, Sat & Sun 9:30)*
Palm Court *(6.30, Sat & Sun 7)*
Lantana Café: W1 *(8, Sat & Sun 9)*
M Restaurant: SW1 *(7, Sat & Sun 10)*
Mac & Wild *(11)*
Maison Bertaux *(8.30, Sun 9.15)*
maze Grill *(6.45)*
Mister Lasagna *(7)*
Monmouth Coffee Company: WC2 *(8)*
Nopi *(8, Sat & Sun 10)*
Nordic Bakery: *Dorset St W1 (8, Sat & Sun 9); Golden Sq W1 (Mon-Fri 8, Sat 9, Sun 11)*
The Northall *(Sat & Sun 7)*
100 Wardour Street *(11)*
Opso *(Sat & Sun 10)*
The Orange *(8)*
Ottolenghi: SW1 *(8, Sun 9)*
Percy & Founders *(Sat & Sun 7.30)*
The Portrait *(10)*
Princi *(8, Sun 8.30)*
Promenade *(Sat & Sun 7.30)*
Providores *(8 Sat & Sun 9)*
Quo Vadis *(8)*
Le Restaurant de PAUL: WC2 *(Mon-Fri 7, Sat & Sun 8)*
Rib Room *(7, Sun 8)*
Riding House Café *(7.30, Sat & Sun 9)*
The Ritz Restaurant *(7, Sun 8)*
Roux at the Landau *(7)*
San Carlo Cicchetti: W1 *(8, Sat & Sun 9)*
Savini at Criterion *(8)*
Savoy, Thames Foyer *(8)*
Scandinavian Kitchen *(8, Sat & Sun 10)*
Simpsons-in-the-Strand *(Mon Fri 7.30)*
Sophie's Steakhouse: *all branches (Sat & Sun 11)*
Spring Workshop *(7.30)*
tibits *(9, Sun 11.30)*
Tom's Kitchen: WC2 *(Sat & Sun 10)*
Veneta *(9)*
Villandry: W1 *(Sat 8, Sun 9)*
The Wallace *(10)*
Wolfe's Bar & Grill *(11.30)*
The Wolseley *(7, Sat & Sun 8)*
Yalla Yalla: *Green's Ct W1 (Sat & Sun 10)*

West
Adams Café *(8)*
Angelus *(10)*
Annie's: W4 *(Tue-Thu 10, Fri & Sat 10.30, Sun 10)*
Best Mangal: SW6 *(10)*
La Brasserie *(9)*
Bumpkin: SW7 *(11)*
Charlotte's W5: W5 *(9)*
Cheneston's Restaurant *(7.30)*
Chucs: W11 *(8, Sun 11)*
Clarke's *(8)*
Daylesford Organic: W11 *(8, Sun 11)*

BRUNCH MENUS

BUSINESS

BYO

(Bring your own wine at no or low – less than £3 – corkage. Note for £5-£15 per bottle, you can normally negotiate to take your own wine to many, if not most, places.)

LATE

(open till midnight or later as shown; may be earlier Sunday)

Central

Asia de Cuba *(Fri & Sat midnight)*
Assunta Madre
Atelier de Joel Robuchon
Balthazar
Bar Italia *(open 24 hours, Sun 4 am)*
Bar Termini *(Fri & Sat 1 am)*
Bob Bob Ricard *(Sat only)*
La Bodega Negra *(1 am, not Sun)*
Boisdale
Bone Daddies: *Peter St W1 (Thu-Sat midnight)*
Café Monico *(midnight, Fri & Sat 1 am)*
Cantina Laredo *(Fri & Sat midnight)*
Chotto Matte *(Mon-Sat 1 am)*
Chucs: *W1 (Sat only)*
Colony Grill Room
Dean Street Townhouse *(Fri & Sat midnight)*
The Delaunay
Dishoom: *WC2 (Fri & Sat midnight)*
Ember Yard *(Thu-Sat midnight)*
Five Guys: *all branches (Fri & Sat midnight)*
Flat Iron: *all central branches*
The Four Seasons: *Gerrard St W1 (1 am); Wardour St W1 (1 am, Fri & Sat 3.30 am)*
Gaby's
Gelupo *(Fri & Sat midnight)*
Golden Dragon
Goya
Hakkasan Mayfair: *Bruton St W1 (12.30 am); Hanway Pl W1 (Thu-Sat midnight)*
Hard Rock Café *(12.30 am, Fri & Sat 1 am, not Sun)*
Heliot Steak House *(1 am)*
Hubbard & Bell
The Ivy *(Thu-Sat midnight)*
The Ivy Market Grill
Jinjuu *(Thu-Sat 1 am)*
Joe Allen *(Fri & Sat 12.45 am)*
M Restaurant: *all branches*
Maroush: *W1 (12.30 am)*
MEATLiquor: *W1 (midnight, Fri & Sat 2 am)*
MEATmarket
Mister Lasagna *(Fri & Sat midnight)*
Mr Chow
New Mayflower *(4 am)*
Nobu Berkeley *(Thu-Sat midnight)*
100 Wardour Street *(2 am, Thu-Sat 3 am, Sun 5 pm)*
Peyote *(Mon-Thu 1 am, Fri & Sat 2 am)*
Poppies: *W1*
La Porchetta Pizzeria: *WC1 (Fri & Sat midnight)*
Princi
Rossopomodoro: *WC2*
Saint Luke's Kitchen *(1 am)*
Savini at Criterion
Shoryu Ramen: *Denman St W1*
Sketch *(1 am, Sun Midnight)*
Sophie's Steakhouse: *all branches (12.45 am, not Sun)*
Tabun Kitchen
Veneta
VQ: *WC1 (24 hours)*
The Wolseley
Yumi Izakaya *(12.30 am)*
Zelman Meats: *SW1 (Thu midnight, Fri & Sat 1 am)*
Zima *(1 am)*

West

Albertine *(Thu-Sat midnight)*
Anarkali
Best Mangal: *SW6; North End Rd W14 (midnight, Sat 1 am)*
Buona Sera: *all branches*
Casa Cruz *(12.30 am)*
City Barge *(Fri & Sat midnight)*
The Cross Keys
Electric Diner *(Fri & Sat midnight)*
Gifto's Lahore Karahi *(Sat & Sun midnight)*
Habanera *(Fri & Sat midnight)*
Hanger *(Fri & Sat 12.30 am)*
High Road Brasserie *(Fri & Sat midnight)*
Kojawan *(2 am)*
Maroush: *I) 21 Edgware Rd W2 (1.45 am); VI) 68 Edgware Rd W2 (12.30 am); SW3 (3.30 am)*
No 197 Chiswick Fire Stn *(midnight, Fri & Sat 1 am)*
Peyotito *(midnight, Fri & Sat 1 am)*
Pizza East Portobello: *W10 (Fri & Sat midnight)*
Pizza Metro: *all branches (Fri & Sat midnight)*
Rabbit
Romulo Café
Rossopomodoro: *SW10*
Shilpa *(Thu-Sat midnight)*
Sophie's Steakhouse: *all branches (12.45 am, not Sun)*
VQ: *SW10 (24 hours); W11 (Mon-Wed 1am, Thu-Sat 3 am, Sun midnight)*

North

Ali Baba
Ariana II
Banners *(Sat only)*
Dirty Burger: *NW5 (midnight, Fri & Sat 1 am)*
Five Guys Islington: *all branches (Fri & Sat midnight)*
Gallipoli: *all branches (Fri & Sat midnight)*
Gökyüzü *(midnight, Fri & Sat 1 am)*
Grain Store *(Thu-Sat midnight)*
The Junction Tavern *(Fri & Sat midnight)*
Meat Mission
MEATLiquor: *N1 (midnight, Fri & Sat 2 am)*
Melange *(Sat & Sun midnight)*
Le Mercury
One Sixty Smokehouse: *NW6 (Fri & Sat midnight)*
Pizzeria Pappagone
La Porchetta Pizzeria: *NW1 (Fri & Sat midnight); N1, N4 (Sat & Sun midnight)*
Yum Yum *(Fri & Sat midnight)*

OUTSIDE TABLES
(* particularly recommended)

ROMANTIC

CUISINES

An asterisk (*) after an entry indicates exceptional or very good cooking

AMERICAN
Central
The Avenue *(SW1)*
Big Easy *(WC2)*
Bodean's *(W1,WC2)*
Breakfast Club *(W1)*
The Chiltern Firehouse *(W1)*
Christopher's *(WC2)*
Hard Rock Café *(W1)*
Hubbard & Bell *(WC1)*
Jackson & Rye *(W1)*
Joe Allen *(WC2)*
Rainforest Café *(W1)*
Shake Shack *(WC1,WC2)*
Shotgun *(W1)*
Spuntino *(W1)*
temper *(W1)*
Wolfe's Bar & Grill *(WC2)*

Central
Breakfast Club Angel *(N1)*

West
Big Easy *(SW3)*
Bodean's *(SW6)*
Electric Diner *(W11)*
Jackson & Rye Chiswick *(W4)*

North
Bodean's *(N10)*
One Sixty Smokehouse *(NW6)**

South
Bodean's *(SW17, SW4)*
Counter *(SW8)*
Jackson & Rye Richmond *(TW9)*
The Joint *(SW9)**
MeatUp *(SW18)*

East
Big Easy *(E14)*
Bodean's *(EC1, EC3)*
Boondocks *(EC1)*
Breakfast Club *(E1)*
One Sixty Smokehouse *(E1)**
Pitt Cue Co *(EC2)**
Shake Shack *(E20)*
Smokestak *(E1, EC2)**
Walter & Monty *(EC3)*

AUSTRALIAN
Central
Bronte *(WC2)*
Dickie Fitz *(W1)*
Lantana Café *(W1)*

West
Granger & Co *(W11)*
No 197 Chiswick Fire Stn *(W4)*

North
Granger & Co *(N1)*
Lantana Cafe *(NW1)*

South
Flotsam & Jetsam *(SW17)*

East
Granger & Co *(EC1)*
Lantana Café *(EC1)*

BRITISH, MODERN
Central
Alyn Williams *(W1)**
Andrew Edmunds *(W1)*
Aurora *(W1)*
Balthazar *(WC2)*
Barnyard *(W1)*
Bellamy's *(W1)*
The Berners Tavern *(W1)*
Blacklock *(W1)**
Bob Bob Ricard *(W1)*
Bonhams Restaurant *(W1)**
The Botanist *(SW1)*
Le Caprice *(SW1)*
The Cavendish *(W1)*
Caxton Grill *(SW1)*
Clipstone *(W1)*
The Collins Room *(SW1)*
Coopers *(WC2)*
Daylesford Organic *(SW1,W1)*
Dean Street Townhouse *(W1)*
Dorchester Grill *(W1)*
Ducksoup *(W1)*
Ebury *(SW1)*
Fera at Claridge's *(W1)**
45 Jermyn St *(SW1)*
Galvin, Athenaeum *(W1)*
Gordon's Wine Bar *(WC2)*
The Goring Hotel *(SW1)*
The Grazing Goat *(W1)*
Ham Yard Restaurant *(W1)*
Hardy's Brasserie *(W1)*
Hatchetts *(W1)*
Heddon Street Kitchen *(W1)*
Hix *(W1)*
Hush *(W1,WC1)*
The Ivy *(WC2)*
The Ivy Café *(W1)*
The Ivy Market Grill *(WC2)*
Jar Kitchen *(WC2)*
Kitty Fisher's *(W1)**
Langan's Brasserie *(W1)*
Little Social *(W1)*
Mere *(W1)*
Mews of Mayfair *(W1)*
Native *(WC2)**
The Newman Arms *(W1)**
Noble Rot *(WC1)*
The Norfolk Arms *(WC1)*
The Northall *(WC2)*
The Orange *(SW1)*
Ormer Mayfair *(W1)*
Percy & Founders *(W1)**
Picture Marylebone *(W1)**
Pollen Street Social *(W1)*
Polpo at Ape & Bird *(WC2)*
Portland *(W1)**
The Portrait *(WC2)*
The Punchbowl *(W1)**
Quaglino's *(SW1)*
Quo Vadis *(W1)*
Rail House Café *(SW1)*

Roux Parliament Sq *(SW1)**
Roux at the Landau *(W1)*
Saint Luke's Kitchen *(WC2)*
Seven Park Place *(SW1)**
Seven Stars *(WC2)*
Fortnum & Mason *(W1)*
Shampers *(W1)*
Social Eating House *(W1)**
Spring Restaurant *(WC2)*
Tate Britain *(SW1)*
10 Greek Street *(W1)**
The Thomas Cubitt *(SW1)*
Tom's Kitchen *(WC2)*
Tredwell's *(WC2)*
Villandry *(W1)*
The Vincent Rooms *(SW1)*
Vinoteca Seymour Place *(W1)*
VQ *(WC1)*
Wild Honey *(W1)*
The Wolseley *(W1)*

West
The Abingdon *(W8)*
The Anglesea Arms *(W6)*
Babylon *(W8)*
Belvedere *(W8)*
Bluebird *(SW3)*
The Brackenbury *(W6)*
Brinkley's *(SW10)*
The Builders Arms *(SW3)*
Charlotte's Place *(W5)*
Charlotte's W4 *(W4)*
Charlotte's W5 *(W5)*
City Barge *(W4)*
Clarke's *(W8)**
Claude's Kitchen *(SW6)**
The Dartmouth Castle *(W6)*
Daylesford Organic *(W11)*
The Dock Kitchen *(W10)*
The Dove *(W6)*
Duke of Sussex *(W4)*
Ealing Park Tavern *(W5)*
Elystan Street *(SW3)*
The Enterprise *(SW3)*
The Five Fields *(SW3)**
The Frontline Club *(W2)*
Harwood Arms *(SW6)**
The Havelock Tavern *(W14)*
Hedone *(W4)**
High Road Brasserie *(W4)*
The Hour Glass *(SW3)*
The Ivy Chelsea Garden *(SW3)*
Ivy Kensington Brasserie *(W8)*
Julie's *(W11)*
Kensington Place *(W8)*
Kensington Sq Kitchen *(W8)*
Kitchen W8 *(W8)**
The Ladbroke Arms *(W11)*
Launceston Place *(W8)**
The Ledbury *(W11)**
Magazine *(W2)*
Manuka Kitchen *(SW6)*
Marianne *(W2)**
maze Grill *(SW10)*
Medlar *(SW10)**
Megan's Delicatessen *(SW6)*
Mustard *(W6)*
Parabola *(W8)*

Paradise by Way of KG *(W10)*
The Pear Tree *(W6)*
The Phoenix *(SW3)*
Princess Victoria *(W12)*
Rabbit *(SW3)**
Restaurant Ours *(SW3)*
Salt & Honey *(W2)*
The Sands End *(SW6)*
The Shed *(W8)*
Six Portland Road *(W11)**
Tangerine Dream *(SW3)*
Tom's Kitchen *(SW3)*
The Tommy Tucker *(SW6)*
Vinoteca *(W4)*
VQ *(SW10,W11)*
The Waterway *(W9)*

North
The Albion *(N1)*
The Booking Office *(NW1)*
Bradley's *(NW3)*
The Bull *(N6)*
Caravan King's Cross *(N1)*
Chriskitch *(N1,N10)**
Crocker's Folly *(NW8)*
The Drapers Arms *(N1)*
Fifteen *(N1)*
Frederick's *(N1)*
Grain Store *(N1)**
The Haven *(N20)*
Heirloom *(N8)*
Hill & Szrok *(N1)**
The Horseshoe *(NW3)*
The Ivy Café *(NW8)*
The Junction Tavern *(NW5)*
The Landmark *(NW1)*
The Lighterman *(N1)*
Market *(NW1)*
Odette's *(NW1)**
Oldroyd *(N1)**
Parlour Kensal *(NW10)**
Perilla *(N16)*
Pig & Butcher *(N1)**
Plum + Spilt Milk *(N1)*
Red Lion & Sun *(N6)*
Rotunda *(N1)*
Season Kitchen *(N4)*
Smoke & Salt *(N1)*
The Wells *(NW3)*
The Wet Fish Café *(NW6)*

South
Albion *(SE1)*
Aqua Shard *(SE1)*
The Bingham *(TW10)*
Bistro Union *(SW4)*
Blueprint Café *(SE1)*
The Brown Dog *(SW13)*
Brunswick House Café *(SW8)*
The Camberwell Arms *(SE5)**
Cannizaro House *(SW19)*
Chapters *(SE3)*
Chez Bruce *(SW17)**
Counter Culture *(SW4)**
Craft London *(SE10)**
The Crooked Well *(SE5)*
The Dairy *(SW4)**
The Depot *(SW14)*
The Dysart Petersham *(TW10)**

Earl Spencer *(SW18)*
Edwins *(SE1)*
Elliot's Café *(SE1)*
Emile's *(SW15)*
Fields *(SW4)*
40 Maltby Street *(SE1)**
Franklins *(SE22)**
The Garrison *(SE1)*
The Glasshouse *(TW9)*
The Green Room *(SE1)*
Guildford Arms *(SE10)*
Hood *(SW2)**
House Restaurant *(SE1)*
The Ivy Brasserie *(SE1)*
The Ivy Café *(SW19)*
Lamberts *(SW12)**
The Lido Café *(SE24)*
The Light House *(SW19)*
Magdalen *(SE1)*
The Manor *(SW4)**
May The Fifteenth *(SW4)*
Menier Chocolate Factory *(SE1)*
Oblix *(SE1)*
Olympic *(SW13)*
Oxo Tower *(SE1)*
Oxo Tower *(SE1)*
The Palmerston *(SE22)*
Pear Tree Cafe *(SW11)*
Peckham Ref' Rooms *(SE15)*
The Perry Vale *(SE23)*
Petersham Hotel *(TW10)*
Petersham Nurseries *(TW10)*
Pharmacy 2 *(SE11)*
Le Pont de la Tour *(SE1)*
Rivington Grill *(SE10)*
RSJ *(SE1)*
Salon Brixton *(SW9)**
Sea Containers *(SE1)*
Skylon *(SE1)*
Skylon Grill *(SE1)*
Soif *(SW11)*
Sonny's Kitchen *(SW13)*
Story *(SE1)*
The Swan at the Globe *(SE1)*
The Table *(SE1)*
Tate Modern Restaurant *(SE1)*
Tate Modern *(SE1)*
Tried & True *(SW15)*
Trinity *(SW4)**
Tulse Hill Hotel *(SE24)*
Union Street Café *(SE1)*
Upstairs at John The Un' *(SE15)*
The Victoria *(SW14)*
View 94 *(SW18)*
Waterloo Bar & Kitchen *(SE1)*

East

Anglo *(EC1)**
The Anthologist *(EC2)*
Bird of Smithfield *(EC1)*
Bistrotheque *(E2)*
Bob Bob Exchange *(EC3)*
The Botanist *(EC2)*
The Boundary *(E2)*
Bread Street Kitchen *(EC4)*
Café Below *(EC2)*
Caravan *(EC1)*
The Chancery *(EC4)**

Chiswell St Dining Rms *(EC1)*
City Social *(EC2)*
The Clove Club *(EC1)**
The Culpeper *(E1)*
Darwin Brasserie *(EC3)*
The Don *(EC4)*
Duck & Waffle *(EC2)*
Eat 17 *(E17)**
Ellory *(E8)*
The Empress *(E9)**
Farley Macallan *(E9)*
Fenchurch Restaurant *(EC3)*
The Frog *(E1)*
Galvin HOP *(E1)**
The Gun *(E14)*
High Timber *(EC4)*
Hilliard *(EC4)**
Hoi Polloi *(E1)*
Humble Grape *(EC4)*
Hush *(EC4)*
Jones & Sons *(E8)**
The Jugged Hare *(EC1)*
Legs *(E9)*
Leyton Technical *(E10)*
Lyle's *(E1)**
The Mercer *(EC2)*
Merchants Tavern *(EC2)*
The Morgan Arms *(E3)**
The Narrow *(E14)*
Northbank *(EC4)*
One Canada Square *(E14)*
1 Lombard Street *(EC3)*
P Franco *(E5)*
Paradise Garage *(E2)**
Pidgin *(E8)**
Poco *(E2)*
Princess of Shoreditch *(EC2)*
The Richmond *(E8)*
Rivington Grill *(EC2)*
Rochelle Canteen *(E2)*
Rök *(EC2)**
Sager + Wilde *(E2)*
St John Bread & Wine *(E1)**
Sign of the Don *(EC4)*
Smith's Wapping *(E1)*
Smiths of Smithfield *(EC1)*
Smiths of Smithfield *(EC1)*
3 South Place *(EC2)*
Tom's Kitchen *(E1, E14)*
The Trading House *(EC2)*
Urban Coterie *(EC1)*
Vinoteca *(EC1)*
The White Swan *(EC4)*
The Woodford *(E18)*

BRITISH, TRADITIONAL

Central

Brown's Hotel *(W1)*
Brown's Hotel *(W1)*
Butler's Restaurant *(W1)*
Corrigan's Mayfair *(W1)*
Dinner *(SW1)*
Great Queen Street *(WC2)*
The Guinea Grill *(W1)**
Hardy's Brasserie *(W1)*
Holborn Dining Room *(WC1)*
The Keeper's House *(W1)*
The Lady Ottoline *(WC1)*

Randall & Aubin *(W1)*
Rib Room *(SW1)*
Rules *(WC2)**
Savoy Grill *(WC2)*
Scott's *(W1)**
Shepherd's *(SW1)*
Simpsons-in-the-Strand *(WC2)*
Tate Britain *(SW1)*
Wiltons *(SW1)*
The Windmill *(W1)*

West
Bumpkin *(SW3, SW7)*
Cheneston's Restaurant *(W8)*
Churchill Arms *(W8)*
Ffiona's *(W8)*
The Hampshire Hog *(W6)*
Hereford Road *(W2)**
Maggie Jones's *(W8)*
The Swan *(W4)*

North
The Gilbert Scott *(NW1)*
Piebury Corner *(N7)*
St Johns *(N19)*
York & Albany *(NW1)*

South
The Anchor & Hope *(SE1)**
Butlers Wharf Chop House *(SE1)*
Canton Arms *(SW8)**
Jolly Gardeners *(SW18)*
The Lord Northbrook *(SE12)*
Oxo Tower *(SE1)*
Oxo Tower *(SE1)*
The Plough *(SW14)*
Roast *(SE1)*
The Swan at the Globe *(SE1)*

East
Albion *(E2)*
Albion Clerkenwell *(EC1)*
Bumpkin *(E20)*
Coin Laundry *(EC1)*
The Fox & Anchor *(EC1)*
Hix Oyster & Ch' Hs *(EC1)*
The Marksman *(E2)*
Paternoster Chop House *(EC4)*
E Pellicci *(E2)*
The Quality Chop House *(EC1)*
St John *(EC1)**
St John Bread & Wine *(E1)**
Simpson's Tavern *(EC3)*
Sweetings *(EC4)*

DANISH
Central
Sticks'n'Sushi *(WC2)**

West
Snaps & Rye *(W10)**

South
Sticks'n'Sushi *(SE10, SW19)**

East
Sticks'n'Sushi *(E14)**

EAST & CENT. EUROPEAN
Central
The Delaunay *(WC2)*
Fischer's *(W1)*
Gay Hussar *(W1)*
Sketch *(W1)*
Texture *(W1)**
The Wolseley *(W1)*

North
Bellanger *(N1)*
Black Axe Mangal *(N1)**
German Gymnasium *(N1)*
Kipferl *(N1)*
St Johns *(N19)*

East
The Trading House *(EC2)*

FISH & SEAFOOD
Central
Bellamy's *(W1)*
Bentley's *(W1)*
Bonnie Gull *(W1)**
Burger & Lobster *(SW1,W1)*
Fishworks *(W1)*
Kaspar's *(WC2)*
Olivomare *(SW1)**
One-O-One *(SW1)**
Quaglino's *(SW1)*
Randall & Aubin *(W1)*
Rib Room *(SW1)*
Royal China Club *(W1)**
Salmontini *(SW1)*
Scott's *(W1)**
Sexy Fish *(W1)*
J Sheekey *(WC2)**
J Sheekey Atlantic Bar *(WC2)*
Smith & Wollensky *(WC2)*
Wiltons *(SW1)*
Wright Brothers *(W1)**

West
Bibendum Oyster Bar *(SW3)**
Big Easy *(SW3)*
The Cow *(W2)*
Geales *(W8)*
Kensington Place *(W8)*
Mandarin Kitchen *(W2)**
Outlaw's at The Capital *(SW3)**
The Summerhouse *(W9)*
Wright Brothers *(SW7)**

North
Bradley's *(NW3)*
Carob Tree *(NW5)*
Fish Cafe *(NW3)*
Galley *(N1)**
Lure *(NW5)**
Olympus Fish *(N3)**
Prawn On The Lawn *(N1)**
Toff's *(N10)*

South
Applebee's Café *(SE1)**
Cornish Tiger *(SW11)*
fish! *(SE1)*
Lobster Pot *(SE11)**
Le Querce *(SE23)*

Wright Brothers *(SE1)**

East
Angler *(EC2)*
Burger & Lobster *(EC1, EC4)*
Chamberlain's *(EC3)*
Fish Central *(EC1)*
Fish Market *(EC2)*
Hix Oyster & Ch' Hs *(EC1)*
Royal Exch Grand Café *(EC3)*
Smith's Wapping *(E1)**
Sweetings *(EC4)*
Wright Brothers *(E1)**

FRENCH
Central
Alain Ducasse *(W1)*
Antidote *(W1)*
L'Artiste Musclé *(W1)*
Atelier de Joel Robuchon *(WC2)*
L'Autre Pied *(W1)**
The Balcon *(SW1)*
Bao Fitzrovia *(W1)**
Bar Boulud *(SW1)*
Bellamy's *(W1)*
Blanchette *(W1)**
Boudin Blanc *(W1)*
Boulestin *(SW1)*
Brasserie Zédel *(W1)*
Café Monico *(W1)*
Céleste *(SW1)*
Cigalon *(WC2)*
Clos Maggiore *(WC2)*
Colbert *(SW1)*
Les Deux Salons *(WC2)*
L'Escargot *(W1)*
Frenchie *(WC2)**
Galvin at Windows *(W1)*
Galvin Bistrot de Luxe *(W1)*
Le Garrick *(WC2)*
Gauthier Soho *(W1)**
Le Gavroche *(W1)**
The Greenhouse *(W1)*
Hélène Darroze *(W1)*
Koffmann's *(SW1)**
Marcus *(SW1)*
Margot *(WC2)*
maze *(W1)*
Mon Plaisir *(WC2)*
Les 110 de Taillevent *(W1)*
Orrery *(W1)*
Otto's *(WC1)**
Park Chinois *(W1)*
La Petite Maison *(W1)**
Pétrus *(SW1)*
Pied à Terre *(W1)**
La Poule au Pot *(SW1)*
Prix Fixe *(W1)*
Relais de Venise *(W1)*
Le Restaurant de PAUL *(WC2)*
The Ritz Restaurant *(W1)*
Savoir Faire *(WC1)*
Savoy Grill *(WC2)*
Savoy, Thames Foyer *(WC2)*
Seven Park Place *(SW1)**
Sketch *(W1)*
Sketch *(W1)*
The Square *(W1)*
Terroirs *(WC2)*

28-50 *(W1)*
Villandry *(W1)*
Villandry St James's *(SW1)*
The Wallace *(W1)*

West
Albertine *(W12)*
Angelus *(W2)*
Bandol *(SW10)*
Bel Canto *(W2)*
Belvedere *(W8)*
Bibendum *(SW3)*
La Brasserie *(SW3)*
Brasserie Gustave *(SW3)*
Cheyne Walk Brasserie *(SW3)*
Le Colombier *(SW3)*
L'Etranger *(SW7)*
Gordon Ramsay *(SW3)*
Michael Nadra *(W4)**
Orée *(SW10)**
Quantus *(W4)**
La Trompette *(W4)**
Le Vacherin *(W4)*

North
L'Absinthe *(NW1)*
Almeida *(N1)*
L'Aventure *(NW8)*
Bistro Aix *(N8)**
Bradley's *(NW3)*
La Cage Imaginaire *(NW3)*
Le Mercury *(N1)*
Michael Nadra *(NW1)**
Oslo Court *(NW8)**
Patron *(NW5)*
Petit Pois Bistro *(N1)*
Le Sacré-Coeur *(N1)**
The Wells *(NW3)*

South
Augustine Kitchen *(SW11)*
Boro Bistro *(SE1)*
Brasserie Toulouse-Lautrec *(SE11)*
La Buvette *(TW9)*
Casse-Croute *(SE1)**
Counter *(SW8)*
Gastronhome *(SW11)**
Gazette *(SW11, SW12, SW15)*
Lobster Pot *(SE11)**
Ma Cuisine *(TW9)*
Le Salon Privé *(TW1)**
Soif *(SW11)*
The White Onion *(SW19)*

East
Blanchette East *(E1)**
Bleeding Heart *(EC1)*
Brawn *(E2)**
Café du Marché *(EC1)*
Café Pistou *(EC1)*
Cellar Gascon *(EC1)*
Club Gascon *(EC1)**
Comptoir Gascon *(EC1)*
Coq d'Argent *(EC2)*
The Don *(EC4)*
La Ferme *(EC1)*
Galvin La Chapelle *(E1)*
Lutyens *(EC4)*
Plateau *(E14)*

Provender *(E11)*
Relais de Venise *(E14, EC2)*
Restaurant de Paul *(EC2)*
Royal Exch Grand Café *(EC3)*
Sauterelle *(EC3)*
The Trading House *(EC2)*
28-50 *(EC4)*

FUSION
Central
Asia de Cuba *(WC2)*
Bronte *(WC2)*
Bubbledogs *(W1)**
Carousel *(W1)**
Dabbous *(W1)*
Jikoni *(W1)*
La Porte des Indes *(W1)*
Providores *(W1)*
Twist *(W1)**

West
E&O *(W11)*
Eight Over Eight *(SW3)*
L'Etranger *(SW7)*

North
Caravan King's Cross *(N1)*
The Petite Coree *(NW6)**

South
Caravan Bankside *(SE1)*
Champor-Champor *(SE1)**
Ting *(SE1)*
Tsunami *(SW4)**
Village East *(SE1)*

East
Caravan *(EC1)*
CURIO + TA TA *(E8)*
Jago *(E1)*
The Modern Pantry *(EC1, EC2)*
Typing Room *(E2)**

GAME
Central
Bocca Di Lupo *(W1)**
Boisdale *(SW1)*
Rules *(WC2)**
Wiltons *(SW1)*

West
Harwood Arms *(SW6)**

North
San Daniele del Friuli *(N5)*

South
The Anchor & Hope *(SE1)**

East
Boisdale of Bishopsgate *(EC2)*
Boisdale of Canary Wharf *(E14)*
The Jugged Hare *(EC1)*

GREEK
Central
Estiatorio Milos *(SW1)*
Opso *(W1)*

West
Mazi *(W8)**

North
Carob Tree *(NW5)*
The Greek Larder *(N1)*
Lemonia *(NW1)*
Nissi *(N13)*
Vrisaki *(N22)*

South
Peckham Bazaar *(SE15)**

East
Kolossi Grill *(EC1)*

HUNGARIAN
Central
Gay Hussar *(W1)*

INTERNATIONAL
Central
Café in the Crypt *(WC2)*
Canvas *(SW1)*
Colony Grill Room *(W1)*
Cork & Bottle *(WC2)*
Foley's *(W1)*
Gordon's Wine Bar *(WC2)*
Motcombs *(SW1)*
The 10 Cases *(WC2)*

West
The Admiral Codrington *(SW3)*
The Andover Arms *(W6)*
Annie's *(W4)*
Gallery Mess *(SW3)*
Kensington Wine Rms *(W8)*
Melody at St Paul's *(W14)*
Mona Lisa *(SW10)*
Rivea *(SW7)*

North
Banners *(N8)*
Bull & Last *(NW5)*
8 Hoxton Square *(N1)**
The Haven *(N20)*
Primeur *(N5)**
Salut *(N1)**

South
Annie's *(SW13)*
Joanna's *(SE19)*
London House *(SW11)*
Pedler *(SE15)*
The Plough *(SW14)*
Rabot 1745 *(SE1)*
Tulse Hill Hotel *(SE24)*
Vivat Bacchus *(SE1)*
The Yellow House *(SE16)*

East
Blixen *(E1)*
Eat 17 *(E9)**
Sager + Wilde *(E2)*
Vivat Bacchus *(EC4)*
The Wine Library *(EC3)*

IRISH
West
The Cow *(W2)*

ITALIAN

Central

Al Duca (SW1)
Assunta Madre (W1)
Bar Italia (W1)
Bar Termini (W1)
Il Baretto (W1)
Bernardi's (W1)
Bocca Di Lupo (W1)*
Bocconcino (W1)
Briciole (W1)
C London (W1)
Cacio & Pepe (SW1)*
Café Murano (SW1, WC2)
Caffè Caldesi (W1)
Caraffini (SW1)
Cecconi's (W1)
Chucs (W1)
Ciao Bella (WC1)
Como Lario (SW1)
Il Convivio (SW1)
Da Mario (WC2)
Dehesa (W1)*
Delfino (W1)*
Enoteca Turi (SW1)*
Franco's (SW1)
Fumo (WC2)
Gustoso (SW1)
Latium (W1)*
Locanda Locatelli (W1)*
Luce e Limoni (WC1)
Made in Italy James St (W1)
Mele e Pere (W1)
Mister Lasagna (W1)
Murano (W1)*
Novikov (W1)
Obicà (W1)
Oliveto (SW1)
Olivo (SW1)
Olivocarne (SW1)
Olivomare (SW1)*
Opera Tavern (WC2)*
Orso (WC2)
Ottolenghi (SW1)
Park Chinois (W1)
Polpetto (W1)
Polpo (SW1, W1, WC2)
La Porchetta Pizzeria (WC1)
Princi (W1)
Quattro Passi (W1)
Quirinale (SW1)*
Ristorante Frescobaldi (W1)
Rossopomodoro (W1, WC2)
Sale e Pepe (SW1)
Salt Yard (W1)
San Carlo Cicchetti (W1, WC2)
Santini (SW1)
Sardo (W1)
Sartoria (W1)
Savini at Criterion (W1)
Signor Sassi (SW1)
Theo Randall (W1)
Tozi (SW1)
2 Veneti (W1)
Vapiano (W1)
Vasco & Piero's (W1)
Veneta (SW1)
Vico (WC2)

Il Vicolo (SW1)
Zafferano (SW1)

West

Aglio e Olio (SW10)*
L'Amorosa (W6)*
Assaggi (W2)*
Bird in Hand (W14)
Buona Sera (SW3)
Buoni Amici (W12)
Chucs (W11)
Cibo (W14)*
Clarke's (W8)*
Da Mario (SW7)
Daphne's (SW3)
La Delizia Limbara (SW3)
Edera (W11)
Essenza (W11)
La Famiglia (SW10)
Frantoio (SW10)
Locanda Ottomezzo (W8)
Lucio (SW3)
Made in Italy (SW3)
Manicomio (SW3)
Mediterraneo (W11)
Mona Lisa (SW10)
Nuovi Sapori (SW6)
The Oak W12 (W12, W2)*
Obicà (SW3)
Osteria 60 (SW7)
Osteria Basilico (W11)
Ottolenghi (W11, W8)
Pappa Ciccia (SW6)
Pellicano Restaurant (SW3)
Pentolina (W14)*
Polpo (SW3, W11)
Il Portico (W8)
Portobello Ristorante (W11)
The Red Pepper (W9)
Riccardo's (SW3)
The River Café (W6)
Rossopomodoro (SW10)
Sapori Sardi (SW6)
Scalini (SW3)
Tartufo (SW3)
Theo's Simple Italian (SW5)
Toto's (SW3)
Villa Di Geggiano (W4)
Ziani's (SW3)

North

Anima e Cuore (NW1)*
Artigiano (NW3)
L'Artista (NW11)
La Collina (NW1)
500 (N19)
Giacomo's (NW2)
Melange (N8)
Osteria Tufo (N4)
Ostuni (N6, NW6)
Ottolenghi (N1)
Pizzeria Oregano (N1)
Pizzeria Pappagone (N4)
La Porchetta Pizzeria (N1, N4, NW1)
The Rising Sun (NW7)
Rugoletta (N12, N2)*
San Daniele del Friuli (N5)
Sarracino (NW6)*
Trullo (N1)*

Villa Bianca *(NW3)*

South
A Cena *(TW1)*
Al Forno *(SW15, SW19)*
Antico *(SE1)*
Artusi *(SE15)*
Bacco *(TW9)*
La Barca *(SE1)*
Bibo *(SW15)*
Al Boccon di'vino *(TW9)**
Buona Sera *(SW11)*
Canada Water Cafe *(SE16)*
Donna Margherita *(SW11)*
Figlio Del Vesuvio *(SW17)**
Lorenzo *(SE19)*
Luciano's *(SE12)*
MacellaioRC *(SE1)*
Made in Italy *(SW19)*
Numero Uno *(SW11)*
Osteria Antica Bologna *(SW11)*
Padella *(SE1)**
Pizza Metro *(SW11)*
Pizzeria Rustica *(TW9)*
Pulia *(SE1)*
Le Querce *(SE23)*
Riva *(SW13)**
The Table *(SE1)*
Vapiano *(SE1)*

East
L'Anima *(EC2)*
L'Anima Café *(EC2)*
Apulia *(EC1)*
Bombetta *(E11)*
Il Bordello *(E1)*
Canto Corvino *(E1)**
Caravaggio *(EC3)*
Enoteca Rabezzana *(EC1)*
Gatti's City Point *(EC2)*
Gotto Trattoria *(E20)*
Lardo Bebè *(E8)*
MacellaioRC *(EC1)*
Manicomio *(EC2)*
Obicà *(E14, EC4)*
Osteria *(EC2)*
E Pellicci *(E2)*
Polpo *(EC1)*
La Porchetta Pizzeria *(EC1)*
Rotorino *(E8)*
Rucoletta *(EC2)*
Santore *(EC1)**
Super Tuscan *(E1)**
Taberna Etrusca *(EC4)*
Verdi's *(E1)*

MEDITERRANEAN
Central
Blandford Comptoir *(W1)**
Massimo *(WC2)*
The Ninth *(W1)**
Nopi *(W1)**
The Norfolk Arms *(WC1)*
100 Wardour Street *(W1)*
Riding House Café *(W1)*
Shepherd Mkt Wine Hs *(W1)*

West
Adams Café *(W12)*

The Atlas *(SW6)**
The Cross Keys *(SW3)*
Cumberland Arms *(W14)**
Locanda Ottomezzo *(W8)*
Made in Italy *(SW3)*
Mediterraneo *(W11)*
Raoul's Café *(W9)*
Raoul's Café & Deli *(W11)*
The Swan *(W4)*
Wormwood *(W11)**

North
The Little Bay *(NW6)*
Rubedo *(N16)**
Sardine *(N1)*
Vinoteca *(N1)*

South
The Bobbin *(SW4)*
Fish in a Tie *(SW11)*
The Fox & Hounds *(SW11)**
Gourmet Goat *(SE1)**
Peckham Bazaar *(SE15)**
El Vergel *(SE1)**

East
The Eagle *(EC1)**
Morito *(EC1)*
Rocket Bishopgate *(EC2)*
Rocket Canary Wharf *(E14)*
Vinoteca *(EC1)*

ORGANIC
Central
Daylesford Organic *(SW1,W1)*

West
Daylesford Organic *(W11)*
Squirrel *(SW7)*

East
Smiths of Smithfield *(EC1)*

POLISH
West
Daquise *(SW7)*
Ognisko Restaurant *(SW7)*
Patio *(W12)*

South
Baltic *(SE1)*

PORTUGUESE
West
Lisboa Pâtisserie *(W10)*

East
Eyre Brothers *(EC2)**
The Gun *(E14)*
Taberna do Mercado *(E1)**

RUSSIAN
Central
Bob Bob Ricard *(W1)*
Mari Vanna *(SW1)*
Zima *(W1)*

SCANDINAVIAN
Central
Aquavit *(SW1)*

Bageriet (WC2)
The Harcourt (W1)*
Nordic Bakery (W1)
Scandinavian Kitchen (W1)
Texture (W1)*

West
Flat Three (W11)*

North
Rök (N1)*

SCOTTISH
Central
Boisdale (SW1)
Mac & Wild (W1)*

East
Boisdale of Bishopsgate (FC2)
Boisdale of Canary Wharf (E14)

SPANISH
Central
About Thyme (SW1)
Ametsa (SW1)*
aqua nueva (W1)
Barrafina (W1)*
Barrafina Drury Lane (WC2)*
Barrica (W1)
Cigala (WC1)
Dehesa (W1)*
Donostia (W1)*
Drakes Tabanco (W1)*
Duende (WC2)*
Ember Yard (W1)*
Eneko at One Aldwych (WC2)
Goya (SW1)
Ibérica (SW1,W1)
Lurra (W1)*
Morada Brindisa Asador (W1)
Opera Tavern (WC2)*
El Pirata (W1)
Salt Yard (W1)
Social Wine & Tapas (W1)

West
Cambio de Tercio (SW5)
Capote Y Toros (SW5)
Casa Brindisa (SW7)
Duke of Sussex (W4)
Tamp Coffee (W4)
Tendido Cero (SW5)
Tendido Cuatro (SW6)

North
Bar Esteban (N8)*
Café del Parc (N19)*
Camino King's Cross (N1)
Escocesa (N16)*
El Parador (NW1)*
Trangallan (N16)*

South
Alquimia (SW15)
Boqueria (SW2)
Brindisa Food Rooms (SW9)
Camino Bankside (SE1)
Gremio de Brixton (SW2)
José (SE1)*

Little Taperia (SW17)*
LOBOS Meat & Tapas (SE1)*
Mar I Terra (SE1)
Meson don Felipe (SE1)
Pizarro (SE1)
Tapas Brindisa (SE1)

East
Bravas (E1)
Camino Blackfriars (EC4)
Camino Monument (FC3)
Eyre Brothers (EC2)*
Hispania (EC3)
Ibérica (E14, EC1)
José Pizarro (EC2)*
Morito (E2, EC1)*
Moro (EC1)*
Sagardi (EC2)

STEAKS & GRILLS
Central
Barbecoa (SW1)
Barbecoa Piccadilly (W1)
Beast (W1)
Bentley's (W1)
Bodean's (W1)
Boisdale (SW1)
Bukowski Grill (W1)*
Christopher's (WC2)
Cut (W1)
Flat Iron (W1,WC2)*
Goodman (W1)
The Guinea Grill (W1)*
Hawksmoor (W1,WC2)
Heliot Steak House (WC2)*
M Restaurant (SW1)
MASH Steakhouse (W1)
maze Grill (W1)
Relais de Venise (W1)
Rib Room (SW1)
Rowley's (SW1)
Smith & Wollensky (WC2)
Sophie's Steakhouse (WC2)
34 Mayfair (W1)
Wolfe's Bar & Grill (WC2)
Zelman Meats (SW1,W1)*
Zoilo (W1)*

West
Bodean's (SW6)
Casa Malevo (W2)
Foxlow (W4)
Haché (SW10)
Hanger (SW6)
Hawksmoor (SW3)
MacellaioRC (SW7)
Megan's Delicatessen (SW6)
Popeseye (W14)
Smokehouse Chiswick (W4)
Sophie's Steakhouse (SW10)
West Thirty Six (W10)

North
Foxlow (N16)
Haché (NW1)
Popeseye (N19)
Smokehouse Islington (N1)*
The Wells (NW3)

South
Bodean's *(SW4)*
Bukowski Grill *(SW9)**
Cau *(SE3, SW19)*
Cornish Tiger *(SW11)*
Counter *(SW8)*
Foxlow *(SW12)*
MeatUp *(SW18)*
Naughty Piglets *(SW2)**
Oblix *(SE1)*
Popeseye *(SW15)*
El Vergel *(SE1)**

East
Barbecoa *(EC4)*
Bodean's *(EC1, EC3)*
Boisdale of Bishopsgate *(EC2)*
Boisdale of Canary Wharf *(E14)*
Buen Ayre *(E8)**
Bukowski Grill *(E1)**
Cau *(E1)*
Flat Iron *(EC2)**
Foxlow *(EC1)*
Goodman *(E14)*
Goodman City *(EC2)*
Hawksmoor *(E1, EC2)*
High Timber *(EC4)*
Hill & Szrok *(E8)**
Hix Oyster & Ch' Hs *(EC1)*
Jones & Sons *(E8)**
Jones Family Project *(EC2)*
M Restaurant *(EC2)*
Paternoster Chop House *(EC4)*
Relais de Venise *(E14, EC2)*
Rocket Canary Wharf *(E14)*
Simpson's Tavern *(EC3)*
Smith's Wapping *(E1)**
Smiths of Smithfield *(EC1)*
Smiths of Smithfield *(EC1)*
Smiths of Smithfield *(EC1)*
The Tramshed *(EC2)*

SWISS
Central
St Moritz *(W1)**

VEGETARIAN
Central
Chettinad *(W1)**
Ethos *(W1)*
Malabar Junction *(WC1)*
Mildreds *(W1)*
Ormer Mayfair *(W1)*
Ragam *(W1)**
Rasa *(W1)*
Rasa Maricham *(WC1)*
Sagar *(W1)*
The Square *(W1)*
Texture *(W1)**
tibits *(W1)*

West
Farmacy *(W2)*
The Gate *(W6)**
Sagar *(W6)*

North
Chutneys *(NW1)*
Diwana Bhel-Pouri Hs *(NW1)*

Jashan *(N8)**
Manna *(NW3)*
Rani *(N3)*
Rasa Travancore *(N16)*
Vijay *(NW6)*

South
Ganapati *(SE15)**
Le Pont de la Tour *(SE1)*
Skylon *(SE1)*
Sree Krishna *(SW17)**
Tas Pide *(SE1)*

East
The Gate *(EC1)**
Vanilla Black *(EC4)**

AFTERNOON TEA
Central
Bea's Cake Boutique *(WC1)*
Brown's Hotel *(W1)*
The Collins Room *(SW1)*
Dalloway Terrace *(WC1)*
The Delaunay *(WC2)*
F&M, Diamond Tea Rm *(W1)*
La Fromagerie Café *(W1)*
Galvin, Athenaeum *(W1)*
The Goring Hotel *(SW1)*
Ham Yard Restaurant *(W1)*
Palm Court *(W1)*
Maison Bertaux *(W1)*
Oscar Wilde Bar *(W1)*
Promenade *(W1)*
Le Restaurant de PAUL *(WC2)*
The Ritz *(W1)*
Savoy, Thames Foyer *(WC2)*
Sketch *(W1)*
Villandry *(W1)*
Villandry St James's *(SW1)*
The Wallace *(W1)*
The Wolseley *(W1)*
Yauatcha *(W1)**

West
Cheneston's Restaurant *(W8)*
Magazine *(W2)*

North
Brew House *(NW3)*
The Landmark *(NW1)*

South
The Bingham *(TW10)*
Cannizaro House *(SW19)*
Orange Pekoe *(SW13)*
Oxo Tower *(SE1)*
Petersham Nurseries *(TW10)*
Ting *(SE1)*

East
Restaurant de Paul *(EC2)*

BURGERS, ETC
Central
Bar Boulud *(SW1)*
Bbar *(SW1)*
Bobo Social *(W1)**
Bodean's *(W1)*
Burger & Lobster *(SW1,W1,WC1)*

Clives Midtown Diner (WC1)
Five Guys (WC2)
Goodman (W1)
Hard Rock Café (W1)
Hawksmoor (W1, WC2)
Joe Allen (WC2)
Mac & Wild (W1)*
MEATLiquor (W1)
MEATmarket (WC2)*
Opera Tavern (WC2)*
Patty & Bun (W1)*
Rainforest Café (W1)
Shake Shack (SW1, WC1, WC2)
Tommi's Burger Joint (W1)*
Zoilo (W1)*

West
The Admiral Codrington (SW3)
Big Easy (SW3)
Bodean's (SW6)
Electric Diner (W11)
Haché (SW10)
Tommi's Burger Joint (SW3)*
West Thirty Six (W10)

North
Bill or Beak (NW1)*
Dirty Burger (NW5)
Duke's Brew & Que (N1)*
Five Guys Islington (N1)
Haché (NW1)
Harry Morgan's (NW8)
Meat Mission (N1)
MEATLiquor (N1)
One Sixty Smokehouse (NW6)*

South
Bodean's (SW4)
Dip & Flip (SW11, SW17, SW19, SW9)
Dirty Burger (SW8)
Haché (SW12, SW4)
MEATLiquor (SE22)
Rivington Grill (SE10)
Rox Burger (SE13)*
Sonny's Kitchen (SW13)
Village East (SE1)

East
Bleecker Street Burger (E1)*
Bodean's (EC1, EC3)
Burger & Lobster (EC1, EC4)
Caboose (E1)
Chicken Shop & Dirty
  Burger (E1)
Chuck Burger (E1)
Comptoir Gascon (EC1)
Dirty Burger (E1)
Goodman (E14)
Goodman City (EC2)
Haché (EC2)
Hawksmoor (E1, EC2)
Lucky Chip (E8)
One Sixty Smokehouse (E1)*
Patty & Bun (E2, E8, EC2)*
The Rib Man (E1)*
Rivington Grill (EC2)
Shake Shack (E20)
Smiths of Smithfield (EC1)

CRÊPES
Central
Mamie's (WC2)

FISH & CHIPS
Central
Golden Hind (W1)*
North Sea Fish (WC1)
Poppies (W1)
Seafresh (SW1)

West
The Chipping Forecast (W11)
Geales (W8)
Geales Chelsea Green (SW3)
Kensington Place (W8)
Kerbisher & Malt (W5, W6)

North
Nautilus (NW6)*
Olympus Fish (N3)*
Poppies Camden (NW1)
The Sea Shell (NW1)
Sutton & Sons (N1, N16)*
Toff's (N10)
Two Brothers (N3)
Vintage Salt (N1)

South
Brady's (SW18)
Fish Club (SW11)
fish! (SE1)
Kerbisher & Malt (SW14, SW4)
Masters Super Fish (SE1)

East
Ark Fish (E18)*
Kerbisher & Malt (EC1)
Poppies (E1)
Sutton & Sons (E8)*
Vintage Salt (EC2)

ICE CREAM
Central
Gelupo (W1)*

PIZZA
Central
Il Baretto (W1)
Bocconcino (W1)
Delfino (W1)*
Homeslice (W1, WC2)*
Made in Italy James St (W1)
Mayfair Pizza Company (W1)
Oliveto (SW1)
The Orange (SW1)
Pizza Pilgrims (W1, WC2)*
La Porchetta Pizzeria (WC1)
Princi (W1)
Rossopomodoro (W1, WC2)

West
Bird in Hand (W14)
Buona Sera (SW3)
Da Mario (SW7)
La Delizia Limbara (SW3)
Made in Italy (SW3)
The Oak W12 (W12, W2)*
Osteria Basilico (W11)

Pappa Ciccia (SW6)
Pizza East Portobello (W10)
Pizza Metro (W11)
Pizzicotto (W8)*
Portobello Ristorante (W11)
The Red Pepper (W9)
Rocca Di Papa (SW7)
Rossopomodoro (SW10)
Santa Maria (SW6,W5)*

North
L' Antica Pizzeria (NW3)*
L'Artista (NW11)
Pizza East (NW5)
Pizzeria Oregano (N1)
Pizzeria Pappagone (N4)
La Porchetta Pizzeria (N1, N4, NW1)
Rossopomodoro (N1, NW1)
Sacro Cuore (NW10)*
Sarracino (NW6)*
Sweet Thursday (N1)
Yard Sale Pizza (N4)*
Zia Lucia (N7)

South
Al Forno (SW15, SW19)
Buona Sera (SW11)
Canada Water Cafe (SE16)
Craft London (SE10)*
Donna Margherita (SW11)
Dynamo (SW15)
Eco (SW4)
Figlio Del Vesuvio (SW17)*
The Gowlett Arms (SE15)*
Joe Public (SW4)*
Lorenzo (SE19)
Made in Italy (SW19)
Mamma Dough (SE23, SW9)
Numero Uno (SW11)
Pedler (SE15)
Pizza Metro (SW11)
Pizzeria Pellone (SE24)*
Pizzeria Rustica (TW9)
Rocca Di Papa (SE21)
Rossopomodoro (SW18)
Theo's (SE5)*
The Yellow House (SE16)

East
Il Bordello (E1)
Corner Kitchen (E7)
Crate (E9)
Homeslice (EC1)*
Lardo Bebè (E8)
Pizza East (E1)
Pizza Pilgrims (EC1)*
La Porchetta Pizzeria (EC1)
Rocket Bishopgate (EC2)
Rocket Canary Wharf (E14)
Santore (EC1)*
The Stable (E1)
Yard Sale Pizza (E5)*

SANDWICHES, CAKES, ETC
Central
Bageriet (WC2)
Bea's Cake Boutique (WC1)
Daylesford Organic (W1)
Dominique Ansel (SW1)

Fernandez & Wells (W1,WC2)
La Fromagerie Café (W1)
Kaffeine (W1)
Maison Bertaux (W1)
Maison Eric Kayser (W1)
Monmouth Coffee
  Company (WC2)*
Nordic Bakery (W1)
Scandinavian Kitchen (W1)
Spring Workshop (W1)
Workshop Coffee (W1)

West
Lisboa Pâtisserie (W10)

North
Doppio (NW1)
Ginger & White (NW3)
Greenberry Café (NW1)
Brew House (NW3)
Max's Sandwich Shop (N4)*

South
Ground Coffee Society (SW15)
Kappacasein (SE16)*
Milk (SW12)*
Monmouth Coffee
  Company (SE1)*
Orange Pekoe (SW13)

East
Brick Lane Beigel Bake (E1)*
Dept of Coffee (EC1)
Prufrock Coffee (EC1)
Workshop Coffee (EC1)

SALADS
Central
Kaffeine (W1)

CHICKEN
Central
Bao (W1)*
Billy & The Chicks (W1)
Chicken Shop (WC1)
Clives Midtown Diner (WC1)
On The Bab (WC2)
On The Bab Express (W1)
Randall & Aubin (W1)

West
Cocotte (W2)*

North
Bird Camden (NW1)
Bird Islington (N7)
Chicken Shop (N7, NW5, NW8)
Le Coq (N1)

South
Chicken Shop (SW17)
Chicken Shop & Dirty
  Burger (SW12)
MeatUp (SW18)
Pique Nique (SE1)

East
Bird (E2)
Bird Stratford (E20)
Chick 'n' Sours (E8)

Chicken Shop & Dirty
  Burger *(E1)*
On The Bab *(EC1, EC4)*
Randy's Wing Bar *(F15)*
The Tramshed *(EC2)*

ARGENTINIAN
Central
Zoilo *(W1)**

West
Casa Malevo *(W2)*
Quantus *(W4)**

East
Buen Ayre *(E8)**

BRAZILIAN
East
Sushisamba *(EC2)*

MEXICAN/TEXMEX
Central
La Bodega Negra *(W1)*
Cantina Laredo *(WC2)*
Lupita *(WC?)*
Martha Ortiz *(W1)*
Peyote *(W1)*

West
Habanera *(W12)*
Peyotito *(W11)*
Taqueria *(W11)**

South
El Pastór *(SE1)*

PERUVIAN
Central
Casita Andina *(W1)*
Ceviche Soho *(W1)*
Coya *(W1)*
Lima *(W1)*
Lima Floral *(WC2)*
Pachamama *(W1)*
Señor Ceviche *(W1)*

West
Chicama *(SW10)*

South
MOMMI *(SW4)*

East
Andina *(E2)**
Ceviche Old St *(EC1)*
Sushisamba *(EC2)*

SOUTH AMERICAN
Central
MNKY HSE *(W1)*

West
Casa Cruz *(W11)*
Quantus *(W4)**

South
MOMMI *(SW4)*
El Vergel *(SE1)**

MOROCCAN
West
Adams Café *(W12)*
Zayane *(W10)**

NORTH AFRICAN
Central
The Barbary *(WC2)*
Momo *(W1)*

SOUTH AFRICAN
Central
Bbar *(SW1)*

East
High Timber *(EC4)*

TUNISIAN
West
Adams Café *(W12)*

EGYPTIAN
North
Ali Baba *(NW1)*

ISRAELI
Central
Gaby's *(WC2)*
The Palomar *(W1)**

East
Ottolenghi *(E1)*

KOSHER
Central
Reubens *(W1)*

North
Kaifeng *(NW4)*
Zest *(NW3)*

East
Brick Lane Beigel Bake *(E1)**

LEBANESE
Central
Fairuz *(W1)*
Maroush *(W1)*
Yalla Yalla *(W1)*

West
Chez Abir *(W14)*
Maroush *(SW3)*
Maroush Gardens *(W2)*

South
Arabica Bar & Kitchen *(SE1)*
Meza Trinity Road *(SW17)**
Yalla Yalla *(SE10)*

MIDDLE EASTERN
Central
The Barbary *(WC2)*
Honey & Co *(W1)**
Patogh *(W1)**
Samarkand *(W1)*
Tabun Kitchen *(W1)*

West
Falafel King *(W10)*

East
Berber & Q *(E8)**
Berber & Q Sh' Bar *(EC1)*
Morito *(EC1)**
Pilpel *(E1, EC4)**
Strut & Cluck *(E1)*

PERSIAN
Central
Patogh *(W1)**

West
Alounak *(W14,W2)*
Faanoos *(W4,W5)*
Kateh *(W9)*

South
Faanoos *(SW14)*

SYRIAN
West
Abu Zaad *(W12)*

TURKISH
Central
Le Bab *(W1)**
Babaji Pide *(W1)*
Ishtar *(W1)*
Kazan (Café) *(SW1)*

West
Best Mangal *(SW6,W14)**
Fez Mangal *(W11)**

North
Gallipoli *(N1)*
Gem *(N1)*
Gökyüzü *(N4)**

South
FM Mangal *(SE5)*
Tas Pide *(SE1)*

East
Haz *(E1, EC2, EC3)*
Mangal 1 *(E8)**
Mangal 1.1 *(EC2)*
Oklava *(EC2)**

AFGHANI
North
Afghan Kitchen *(N1)*
Ariana II *(NW6)*

CHINESE
Central
A Wong *(SW1)**
Baozi Inn *(WC2)**
Barshu *(W1)**
The Bright Courtyard *(W1)**
Chilli Cool *(WC1)**
China Tang *(W1)*
The Duck & Rice *(W1)**
Four Seasons *(W1)**
Golden Dragon *(W1)*
The Grand Imperial *(SW1)**
Hakkasan Mayfair *(W1)*
Hunan *(SW1)**
Joy King Lau *(WC2)*
Kai Mayfair *(W1)*

Ken Lo's Memories *(SW1)*
Leong's Legends *(W1)*
Mr Chow *(SW1)*
New Mayflower *(W1)*
New World *(W1)*
Park Chinois *(W1)*
Royal China *(W1)*
Royal China Club *(W1)**
Shuang Shuang *(W1)*
Wong Kei *(W1)*
Yauatcha *(W1)**
Yming *(W1)*

West
Dragon Palace *(SW5)**
The Four Seasons *(W2)**
Gold Mine *(W2)**
Good Earth *(SW3)*
Mandarin Kitchen *(W2)**
Min Jiang *(W8)**
North China *(W3)*
Pearl Liang *(W2)**
Royal China *(SW6,W2)*
Shikumen *(W12)*
Stick & Bowl *(W8)**
Taiwan Village *(SW6)**

North
Good Earth *(NW7)*
Green Cottage *(NW3)*
Kaifeng *(NW4)*
Phoenix Palace *(NW1)*
Singapore Garden *(NW6)*
Xi'an Impression *(N7)**
Yipin China *(N1)*

South
Dragon Castle *(SE17)*
Good Earth *(SW17)*
Hutong *(SE1)*
Silk Road *(SE5)**

East
Chinese Cricket Club *(EC4)*
HKK *(EC2)**
Royal China *(E14)*
The Sichuan *(EC1)**
Sichuan Folk *(E1)**
Yauatcha City *(EC2)**
Yi-Ban *(E16)*

CHINESE, DIM SUM
Central
The Bright Courtyard *(W1)**
Golden Dragon *(W1)*
The Grand Imperial *(SW1)**
Hakkasan Mayfair *(W1)*
Joy King Lau *(WC2)*
New Mayflower *(W1)*
New World *(W1)*
Novikov *(W1)*
Royal China *(W1)*
Royal China Club *(W1)**
Yauatcha *(W1)**

West
Min Jiang *(W8)**
Pearl Liang *(W2)**
Royal China *(SW6,W2)*

Shikumen *(W12)*

North
Jun Ming Xuan *(NW9)*
Phoenix Palace *(NW1)*

South
Dragon Castle *(SE17)*

East
Royal China *(E14)*
Yauatcha City *(EC2)*
Yi-Ban *(E16)*

FILIPINO
West
Romulo Café *(W8)*

GEORGIAN
North
Little Georgia Café *(N1)*

East
Little Georgia Café *(E2)*

HAWAIIAN
Central
Ahi Poké *(W1)*

INDIAN
Central
Amaya *(SW1)*
Benares *(W1)*
Chettinad *(W1)*
Chor Bizarre *(W1)*
Chutney Mary *(SW1)*
The Cinnamon Club *(SW1)*
Cinnamon Soho *(W1)*
Dishoom *(W1,WC2)*
Gaylord *(W1)*
Gymkhana *(W1)*
Imli Street *(W1)*
India Club *(WC2)*
Jamavar *(W1)*
Kricket *(W1)*
Lotus *(WC2)*
Malabar Junction *(WC1)*
Mint Leaf *(SW1)*
Nirvana Kitchen *(W1)*
La Porte des Indes *(W1)*
Punjab *(WC2)*
Ragam *(W1)*
Red Fort *(W1)*
Roti Chai *(W1)*
Sagar *(W1,WC2)*
Salaam Namaste *(WC1)*
Salloos *(SW1)*
Talli Joe *(WC2)*
Tamarind *(W1)*
Trishna *(W1)*
Veeraswamy *(W1)*

West
Anarkali *(W6)*
Bombay Brasserie *(SW7)*
Bombay Palace *(W2)*
Brilliant *(UB2)*
Chakra *(W8)*
Flora Indica *(SW5)*
Gifto's Lahore Karahi *(UB1)*

Indian Zing *(W6)*
Karma *(W14)*
Khan's *(W2)*
Madhu's *(UB1)*
Malabar *(W8)*
Masala Grill *(SW10)*
Noor Jahan *(SW5,W2)*
The Painted Heron *(SW10)*
Potli *(W6)*
Pure Indian Cooking *(SW6)*
Rasoi *(SW3)*
Sagar *(W6)*
Star of India *(SW5)*
Thali *(SW5)*
Zaika *(W8)*

North
Chutneys *(NW1)*
Delhi Grill *(N1)*
Dishoom *(N1)*
Diwana Bhel-Pouri Hs *(NW1)*
Great Nepalese *(NW1)*
Guglee *(NW3, NW6)*
Indian Rasoi *(N2)*
Jashan *(N8)*
Namaaste Kitchen *(NW1)*
Paradise Hampstead *(NW3)*
Rani *(N3)*
Ravi Shankar *(NW1)*
Vijay *(NW6)*
Zaffrani *(N1)*

South
Babur *(SE23)*
Everest Inn *(SE3)*
Ganapati *(SE15)*
Hot Stuff *(SW8)*
Indian Moment *(SW11)*
Indian Ocean *(SW17)*
Indian Zilla *(SW13)*
Kennington Tandoori *(SE11)*
Kricket *(SW9)*
Lahore Karahi *(SW17)*
Lahore Kebab House *(SW16)*
Ma Goa *(SW15)*
Mirch Masala *(SW17)*
Sree Krishna *(SW17)*

East
Café Spice Namaste *(E1)*
Cinnamon Kitchen *(EC2)*
Darbaar *(EC2)*
Dishoom *(E2)*
Gunpowder *(E1)*
Lahore Kebab House *(E1)*
Mint Leaf Lounge *(EC2)*
Needoo *(E1)*
Tayyabs *(E1)*

INDIAN, SOUTHERN
Central
Hoppers *(W1)*
India Club *(WC2)*
Malabar Junction *(WC1)*
Quilon *(SW1)*
Ragam *(W1)*
Rasa *(W1)*
Rasa Maricham *(WC1)*
Sagar *(W1,WC2)*

West
Sagar (W6)
Shilpa (W6)*

North
Chutneys (NW1)
Rani (N3)
Rasa Travancore (N16)
Vijay (NW6)

South
Ganapati (SE15)*
Jaffna House (SW17)*
Sree Krishna (SW17)*

JAPANESE
Central
Anzu (SW1)
The Araki (W1)*
Atari-Ya (W1)*
Bone Daddies (SW1,W1)*
Chisou (W1)*
Chotto Matte (W1)*
Defune (W1)*
Dinings (W1)*
Eat Tokyo (WC1,WC2)*
Engawa (W1)*
Flesh & Buns (WC2)
Ichiryu (WC1)*
Ippudo London (WC2)
Kanada-Ya (SW1,WC2)*
Kiku (W1)
Kikuchi (W1)*
Kintan (WC1)
Koya-Bar (W1)
Kulu Kulu (W1,WC2)
Kurobuta Harvey Nics (SW1)*
Matsuri (SW1)
Murakami (WC2)
Nobu (W1)
Nobu Berkeley (W1)
Oka (W1)*
Oliver Maki (W1)
Roka (W1,WC2)*
Sakagura (W1)
Sake No Hana (SW1)
Salmontini (SW1)
Shoryu Ramen (SW1,W1)
Sticks'n'Sushi (WC2)*
Sumosan (W1)
Sushisamba (WC2)
Taro (W1)
Tokimeite (W1)*
Tokyo Diner (WC2)
Tonkotsu (W1)
Tsunami (W1)*
Umu (W1)
Wazen (WC1)*
Yoshino (W1)*
Yumi Izakaya (W1)

West
Atari-Ya (W3,W5)*
Bone Daddies (W8)*
Chisou (SW3)*
Eat Tokyo (W6,W8)*
Flat Three (W11)*
Inaho (W2)*
Kiraku (W5)*

Kiru (SW3)*
Kojawan (W2)
Kulu Kulu (SW7)
Kurobuta (SW3,W2)*
Maguro (W9)*
Sushi Bar Makoto (W4)
Tokyo Sukiyaki-Tei (SW3)
Tonkotsu (W11)
Tosa (W6)
Yashin (W8)
Yoshi Sushi (W6)
Zuma (SW7)*

North
Asakusa (NW1)*
Atari-Ya (N12, NW4, NW6)*
Dotori (N4)*
Eat Tokyo (NW11)*
Jin Kichi (NW3)*
Oka (NW1)*
Sushi Masa (NW2)

South
Hashi (SW20)*
Matsuba (TW9)
MOMMI (SW4)
Nanban (SW9)*
Sticks'n'Sushi (SE10, SW19)*
Takahashi (SW19)*
Tomoe (SW15)*
Tonkotsu Bankside (SE1)
Tsunami (SW4)*
Yama Momo (SE22)*
Zaibatsu (SE10)*

East
Beer & Buns (EC2)
Bone Daddies (EC1)*
Ippudo London (E14)
K10 (EC2, EC3)*
Pham Sushi (EC1)*
Roka (E14)*
Shoryu Ramen (EC2)
Sosharu (EC1)
Sticks'n'Sushi (E14)*
Sushisamba (EC2)
Sushi Tetsu (EC1)*
Tonkotsu East (E8)
Yum Bun (EC2)*

KOREAN
Central
Bibimbap (W1)
Jinjuu (W1)
Kintan (WC1)
Lime Orange (SW1)
On The Bab (WC2)
On The Bab Express (W1)

West
Kojawan (W2)
Yoshi Sushi (W6)

North
Dotori (N4)*
The Petite Coree (NW6)*

South
Cah-Chi (SW18, SW20)

Matsuba *(TW9)*

East
Bibimbap *(EC3)*
Chick 'n' Sours *(E8)*
On The Bab *(EC1, EC4)*

MALAYSIAN
Central
C&R Café *(W1)*

West
C&R Café *(W2)*
Satay House *(W2)*

North
Roti King *(NW1)*
Singapore Garden *(NW6)*

South
Champor-Champor *(SE1)*

PAKISTANI
Central
Salloos *(SW1)*

South
Lahore Karahi *(SW17)*
Lahore Kebab House *(SW16)*
Mirch Masala *(SW17)*

East
Lahore Kebab House *(E1)*
Needoo *(E1)*
Tayyabs *(E1)*

PAN-ASIAN
Central
Black Roe *(W1)*
Buddha-Bar London *(SW1)*
Hare & Tortoise *(WC1)*
Nopi *(W1)*
Novikov *(W1)*

West
E&O *(W11)*
Eight Over Eight *(SW3)*
Hare & Tortoise *(W14, W4, W5)*
Kojawan *(W2)*
Koji *(SW6)*
Uli *(W11)*

North
Gilgamesh *(NW1)*

South
Hare & Tortoise *(SW15)*

East
Hare & Tortoise *(EC4)*

THAI
Central
Crazy Bear *(W1)*
Kiln *(W1)*
Patara Fitzrovia *(W1)*
Rosa's *(SW1)*
Rosa's Soho *(W1)*
Smoking Goat *(WC2)*

West
Addie's Thai Café *(SW5)*
The Heron *(W2)*
Patara *(SW3)*
Rosa's Fulham *(SW10)*
Sukho Thai Cuisine *(SW6)*
Suksan *(SW10)*

North
Isarn *(N1)*
Yum Yum *(N16)*

South
Awesome Thai *(SW13)*
The Begging Bowl *(SE15)*
Farang *(SE1)*
Kaosarn *(SW11, SW9)*
The Pepper Tree *(SW4)*
Rosa's *(SW9)*

East
Rosa's *(E1)*
Rosa's *(E15)*
Som Saa *(E1)*

VIETNAMESE
Central
Cây Tre *(W1)*
Ho *(W1)*
Viet Food *(W1)*

West
Saigon Saigon *(W6)*

North
CôBa *(N7)*
Salvation In Noodles *(N1, N4)*
Singapore Garden *(NW6)*

South
Bánh Bánh *(SE15)*
Café East *(SE16)*
Mien Tay *(SW11)*

East
Cây Tre *(EC1)*
City Càphê *(EC2)*
Mien Tay *(E2)*
Sông Quê *(E2)*
Viet Grill *(E2)*

TAIWANESE
Central
Bao *(W1)*
Leong's Legends *(W1)*

West
Taiwan Village *(SW6)*

South
Mr Bao *(SE15)*

AREA OVERVIEWS

CENTRAL

Soho, Covent Garden & Bloomsbury
(Parts of W1, all WC2 and WC1)

Price	Name	Cuisine	Rating
£140+	Engawa	Japanese	4 4 4
£110+	Atelier de Joel Robuchon	French	2 2 3
£100+	Smith & Wollensky	Steaks & grills	1 1 2
£90+	Sushisamba	Japanese	3 3 5
£80+	The Northall	British, Modern	3 3 4
	Spring Restaurant	"	3 3 4
	Savoy Grill	British, Traditional	2 3 3
	Kaspar's	Fish & seafood	2 3 3
	Asia de Cuba	Fusion	1 2 2
	MASH Steakhouse	Steaks & grills	2 3 3
	Roka	Japanese	4 3 3
£70+	Christopher's	American	3 2 3
	Social Eating House	British, Modern	4 3 3
	Rules	British, Traditional	4 3 5
	Simpsons-in-the-Strand	"	1 1 1
	J Sheekey	Fish & seafood	4 4 4
	J Sheekey Atlantic Bar	"	3 4 5
	Clos Maggiore	French	3 4 5
	Frenchie	"	4 2 2
	Gauthier Soho	"	5 5 4
	Massimo	Mediterranean	2 2 3
	Nopi	"	4 3 3
	Eneko at One Aldwych	Spanish	– – –
	Hawksmoor	Steaks & grills	3 3 2
	Savoy, Thames Foyer	Afternoon tea	2 3 5
	Yauatcha	Chinese	4 3 3
£60+	Balthazar	British, Modern	1 1 3
	Bob Bob Ricard	"	3 4 5
	Dean Street Townhouse	"	2 3 5
	Ham Yard Restaurant	"	3 4 4
	Hix	"	1 2 2
	Hush	"	2 3 3
	The Ivy	"	3 4 5
	The Portrait	"	2 3 4
	Tom's Kitchen	"	2 2 2
	Tredwell's	"	2 2 2
	Holborn Dining Room	British, Traditional	3 3 4
	Randall & Aubin	Fish & seafood	3 4 4
	Wright Brothers	"	4 3 3

	Antidote	*French*	2	2 2
	Café Monico	"	2	3 4
	Les Deux Salons	"	1	2 1
	L'Escargot	"	3	4 4
	Otto's	"	4	5 3
	Vasco & Piero's	*Italian*	3	4 3
	100 Wardour Street	*Mediterranean*	2	2 3
	aqua nueva	*Spanish*	1	2 2
	Rainforest Café	*Burgers, etc*	2	3 3
	Lima Floral	*Peruvian*	3	2 1
	Red Fort	*Indian*	4	2 2
	Chotto Matte	*Japanese*	4	3 5
	Oliver Maki	"	–	– –
	Patara Soho	*Thai*	3	4 4
£50+	Big Easy	*American*	2	2 3
	Hubbard & Bell	"	3	3 3
	Joe Allen	"	2	2 4
	Shotgun	"	2	2 2
	Andrew Edmunds	*British, Modern*	3	4 5
	Aurora	"	3	4 4
	Ducksoup	"	3	3 4
	The Ivy Market Grill	"	2	2 3
	Noble Rot	"	3	3 3
	Quo Vadis	"	–	– –
	Saint Luke's Kitchen	"	–	– –
	10 Greek Street	"	4	4 3
	Vinoteca	"	2	2 3
	Great Queen Street	*British, Traditional*	3	2 2
	The Lady Ottoline	"	3	2 3
	The Delaunay	*Cent. European*	2	3 4
	Cigalon	*French*	3	4 3
	Le Garrick	"	2	3 4
	Mon Plaisir	"	2	4 4
	Gay Hussar	*Hungarian*	2	3 4
	Cork & Bottle	*International*	2	3 4
	The 10 Cases	"	2	1 3
	Bocca Di Lupo	*Italian*	5	4 4
	Café Murano	"	3	3 3
	Dehesa	"	4	2 3
	Luce e Limoni	"	3	5 3
	Mele e Pere	"	3	3 2
	Obicà	"	3	3 2
	Orso	"	2	3 2
	San Carlo Cicchetti	"	3	3 4
	Vico	"	2	2 1
	Cigala	*Spanish*	2	2 2
	Ember Yard	"	4	4 4
	Opera Tavern	"	4	4 3
	Heliot Steak House	*Steaks & grills*	4	4 4
	Sophie's Steakhouse	"	2	4 3
	Zelman Meats	"	5	4 4
	St Moritz	*Swiss*	4	3 3

261

	Dalloway Terrace	*Afternoon tea*	–	–	–
	Oscar Wilde Bar	"	2	4	4
	La Bodega Negra	*Mexican/TexMex*	3	3	4
	Cantina Laredo	"	3	2	3
	The Palomar	*Israeli*	5	5	4
	Barshu	*Chinese*	4	2	2
	The Duck & Rice	"	4	3	4
	Four Seasons	"	4	1	1
	Lotus	*Indian*	4	4	3
	Flesh & Buns	*Japanese*	3	3	3
	Wazen	"	4	4	2
	Ho	*Vietnamese*	2	2	2
£40+	Bodean's	*American*	2	2	2
	Jackson & Rye	"	1	2	2
	Spuntino	"	3	3	3
	Wolfe's Bar & Grill	"	3	2	2
	Coopers	*British, Modern*	2	3	3
	Jar Kitchen	"	3	3	3
	Native	"	4	4	2
	The Norfolk Arms	"	3	3	3
	Polpo at Ape & Bird	"	2	2	2
	Shampers	"	2	4	5
	VQ	"	2	4	3
	Brasserie Zédel	*French*	1	3	5
	Prix Fixe	"	3	3	2
	Terroirs	"	3	2	4
	Ciao Bella	*Italian*	2	3	5
	Da Mario	"	3	3	3
	Polpetto	"	2	3	3
	Polpo	"	2	2	2
	Barrafina Drury Lane	*Spanish*	5	5	5
	Duende	"	4	2	2
	Morada Brindisa Asador	"	2	2	2
	Mildreds	*Vegetarian*	3	3	3
	Burger & Lobster	*Burgers, etc*	3	3	3
	Rossopomodoro	*Pizza*	3	2	2
	Fernandez & Wells	*Sandwiches, cakes, etc*	3	3	3
	Lupita	*Mexican/TexMex*	3	2	2
	Ceviche Soho	*Peruvian*	3	3	3
	Señor Ceviche	"	3	3	4
	The Barbary	*North African*	–	–	–
	Le Bab	*Turkish*	5	4	3
	New Mayflower	*Chinese*	3	2	2
	Shuang Shuang	"	3	3	3
	Yming	"	3	4	3
	Cinnamon Soho	*Indian*	4	2	2
	Dishoom	"	4	3	4
	Imli Street	"	2	2	2
	Kricket	"	5	4	3
	Malabar Junction	"	3	3	3
	Talli Joe	"	–	–	–

Kintan	Japanese	3	3	3
Murakami	"	3	3	3
Oka	"	4	3	2
Shoryu Ramen	"	3	2	2
Sticks'n'Sushi	"	4	4	4
Yumi Izakaya	"	–	–	–
Jinjuu	Korean	3	3	3
Smoking Goat	Thai	4	3	2

£35+					
Blacklock	British, Modern	5	4	4
Blanchette	French	4	4	5
Le Restaurant de PAUL	"	3	4	4
Savoir Faire	"	3	3	3
Gordon's Wine Bar	International	1	2	5
Bar Termini	Italian	3	4	5
Mister Lasagna	"	–	–	–
Bukowski Grill	Steaks & grills	4	3	2
North Sea Fish	Fish & chips	3	3	2
Bea's Cake Boutique	Sandwiches, cakes, etc	3	2	3
Chicken Shop	Chicken	2	2	3
Yalla Yalla	Lebanese	3	2	3
Tabun Kitchen	Middle Eastern	–	–	–
Joy King Lau	Chinese	3	3	1
New World	"	2	2	2
Sagar	Indian	3	3	2
Salaam Namaste	"	3	4	3
Rasa Maricham	Indian, Southern	3	3	3
Ippudo London	Japanese	3	2	3
Taro	"	3	3	2
On The Bab	Korean	3	3	2
C&R Café	Malaysian	4	2	2
Rosa's Soho	Thai	3	3	2
Cây Tre	Vietnamese	4	3	3
Leong's Legends	Taiwanese	3	2	2

£30+					
Seven Stars	British, Modern	2	3	3
Café in the Crypt	International	2	2	4
Bar Italia	Italian	2	3	5
La Porchetta Pizzeria	"	2	3	3
Princi	"	3	3	4
Pizza Pilgrims	Pizza	4	3	4
Gaby's	Israeli	3	2	2
Chilli Cool	Chinese	4	2	1
Golden Dragon	"	3	2	2
Wong Kei	"	2	2	2
Punjab	Indian	3	2	3
Bone Daddies	Japanese	4	4	4
Ichiryu	"	4	3	2
Koya-Bar	"	3	4	4
Kulu Kulu	"	3	1	1
Tonkotsu	"	2	3	3
Hare & Tortoise	Pan-Asian	3	3	3

	Viet Food	*Vietnamese*	3 3 3
£25+	Breakfast Club	*American*	3 3 2
	Zima	*Russian*	– – –
	MEATmarket	*Burgers, etc*	4 2 2
	Poppies	*Fish & chips*	3 3 3
	Billy & The Chicks	*Chicken*	3 3 2
	India Club	*Indian*	2 2 1
	Hoppers	*Indian, Southern*	4 4 4
	Tokyo Diner	*Japanese*	3 4 3
	Bibimbap	*Korean*	2 2 2
	Bao	*Taiwanese*	4 2 2
£20+	Flat Iron	*Steaks & grills*	4 3 3
	Clives Midtown Diner	*Burgers, etc*	3 4 2
	Patty & Bun	*"*	4 3 2
	Shake Shack	*"*	3 2 2
	Tommi's Burger Joint	*"*	4 4 4
	Homeslice	*Pizza*	4 4 4
	Baozi Inn	*Chinese*	4 2 2
	Eat Tokyo	*Japanese*	4 2 2
£15+	Nordic Bakery	*Scandinavian*	3 4 3
	Maison Bertaux	*Afternoon tea*	3 4 3
	Kanada-Ya	*Japanese*	4 2 2
£10+	Five Guys	*Burgers, etc*	3 2 2
	Bageriet	*Sandwiches, cakes, etc*	3 4 3
£5+	Gelupo	*Ice cream*	5 2 2
	Monmouth Coffee Company	*Sandwiches, cakes, etc*	5 5 4

Mayfair & St James's (Parts of W1 and SW1)

£380+	The Araki	*Japanese*	5 5 4
£130+	Le Gavroche	*French*	5 5 4
	The Greenhouse	*"*	3 4 3
	Hélène Darroze	*"*	3 4 3
	The Ritz Restaurant	*"*	3 4 5
	Sketch	*"*	3 3 5
	The Square	*"*	– – –
£120+	Alain Ducasse	*French*	2 4 3
	Estiatorio Milos	*Greek*	3 3 3
	Promenade	*Afternoon tea*	2 4 4
£110+	Fera at Claridge's	*British, Modern*	4 4 4
	Cut	*Steaks & grills*	1 2 2

	Umu	*Japanese*	3	3	2
£100+	Dorchester Grill	*British, Modern*	3	3	3
	Pollen Street Social		2	2	3
	Galvin at Windows	*French*	2	3	5
	Assunta Madre	*Italian*	2	2	2
	C London	"	1	1	3
	Novikov	"	1	1	2
£90+	Alyn Williams	*British, Modern*	4	5	3
	Corrigan's Mayfair	*British, Traditional*	3	4	4
	Wiltons	"	3	4	4
	Seven Park Place	*French*	4	4	4
	Murano	*Italian*	4	4	3
	Quattro Passi	"	3	3	2
	Theo Randall	"	3	3	1
	Hakkasan Mayfair	*Chinese*	3	2	3
	Kai Mayfair	"	3	2	2
	Park Chinois	"	2	5	4
	Benares	*Indian*	1	1	2
	Nobu	*Japanese*	2	2	2
	Nobu Berkeley	"	3	2	2
	Novikov	*Pan-Asian*	2	1	2
£80+	Butler's Restaurant	*British, Traditional*	3	4	3
	Bentley's	*Fish & seafood*	3	4	4
	Scott's	"	4	5	5
	Sexy Fish	"	2	1	2
	maze	*French*	2	2	2
	La Petite Maison	"	5	4	5
	Sketch	"	2	3	4
	Savini at Criterion	*Italian*	1	1	2
	Goodman	*Steaks & grills*	3	3	3
	Chutney Mary	*Indian*	4	3	4
	Matsuri	*Japanese*	3	3	1
	Roka	"	4	3	3
£70+	The Berners Tavern	*British, Modern*	2	2	4
	Le Caprice	"	3	4	4
	Little Social	"	3	3	4
	Quaglino's	"	1	1	3
	Wild Honey	"	3	3	3
	Brown's Hotel	*British, Traditional*	3	4	4
	Brown's Hotel	"	2	3	3
	Boulestin	*French*	2	2	2
	Cecconi's	*Italian*	2	2	3
	Franco's	"	3	3	3
	Ristorante Frescobaldi	"	3	3	2
	Sartoria	"	2	3	3
	The Guinea Grill	*Steaks & grills*	4	4	4
	Hawksmoor	"	3	3	2
	maze Grill	"	1	2	2

	Rowley's	"	2	2	2
	34 Mayfair	"	2	2	2
	The Ritz	Afternoon tea	2	3	5
	Bocconcino	Pizza	3	3	3
	Peyote	Mexican/TexMex	3	3	2
	Coya	Peruvian	3	2	4
	China Tang	Chinese	3	2	3
	Tamarind	Indian	5	4	2
	Veeraswamy	"	3	3	3
	Sake No Hana	Japanese	3	1	2
	Sumosan	"	–	–	–
	Tokimeite	"	4	4	3
£60+	The Avenue	American	1	2	2
	Hard Rock Café	"	2	2	4
	Bellamy's	British, Modern	3	4	3
	Bonhams Restaurant	"	4	5	3
	Galvin, Athenaeum	"	–	–	–
	Heddon Street Kitchen	"	2	2	2
	Hush	"	2	3	3
	Kitty Fisher's	"	4	4	4
	Langan's Brasserie	"	1	2	4
	Mews of Mayfair	"	3	3	3
	The Wolseley	"	2	3	5
	The Keeper's House	British, Traditional	2	2	2
	Fishworks	Fish & seafood	3	2	2
	The Balcon	French	2	2	2
	Colony Grill Room	International	3	4	4
	Chucs	Italian	3	5	3
	Barbecoa Piccadilly	Steaks & grills	2	2	2
	F&M, Diamond Tea Rm	Afternoon tea	3	3	3
	Momo	North African	3	3	4
	Chor Bizarre	Indian	3	2	4
	Gymkhana	"	5	4	4
	Mint Leaf	"	3	3	4
	Nirvana Kitchen	"	–	–	–
	Black Roe	Pan-Asian	3	3	3
	Patara Mayfair	Thai	3	4	4
£50+	Hatchetts	British, Modern	–	–	–
	Fortnum & Mason	"	2	2	3
	Boudin Blanc	French	2	3	4
	28-50	"	2	3	4
	Villandry St James's	"	1	1	2
	Café Murano	Italian	3	3	3
	Shepherd Mkt Wine Hs	Mediterranean	–	–	–
	Chisou	Japanese	4	4	2
	Kiku	"	3	3	2
£40+	The Punchbowl	British, Modern	4	4	4
	The Windmill	British, Traditional	3	2	3
	L'Artiste Musclé	French	2	2	5

	Al Duca	*Italian*	3 4 3
	Il Vicolo	"	3 3 3
	El Pirata	*Spanish*	3 4 4
	Burger & Lobster	*Burgers, etc*	3 3 3
	Delfino	*Pizza*	4 3 2
	Mayfair Pizza Company	"	3 4 3
	Shoryu Ramen	*Japanese*	3 2 2
	Yoshino	"	4 4 3
£35+	tibits	*Vegetarian*	2 2 3
	Rasa	*Indian, Southern*	3 3 3
£25+	Spring Workshop	*Sandwiches, cakes, etc*	– – –
£15+	Kanada-Ya	*Japanese*	4 2 2

Fitzrovia & Marylebone (Part of W1)

£110+	Pied à Terre	*French*	4 4 3
	Beast	*Steaks & grills*	2 2 2
£100+	Bubbledogs	*Fusion*	5 4 3
	Texture	*Scandinavian*	4 3 3
£90+	Roux at the Landau	*British, Modern*	3 4 4
	Hakkasan	*Chinese*	3 2 3
£80+	The Chiltern Firehouse	*American*	1 2 3
	L'Autre Pied	*French*	4 4 2
	Orrery	"	3 3 3
	Dabbous	*Fusion*	3 3 2
	Locanda Locatelli	*Italian*	4 4 4
	Roka	*Japanese*	4 3 3
£70+	Providores	*Fusion*	3 2 2
	Il Baretto	*Italian*	2 2 2
	Palm Court	*Afternoon tea*	3 3 3
	Royal China Club	*Chinese*	4 3 3
	La Porte des Indes	*Indian*	3 3 5
	Trishna	"	5 3 3
	Defune	*Japanese*	4 3 1
	Kikuchi	"	4 3 2
£60+	Dickie Fitz	*Australian*	2 2 2
	The Cavendish	*British, Modern*	3 3 3
	Portland	"	5 4 3
	Fischer's	*Cent. European*	3 3 4
	Fishworks	*Fish & seafood*	3 2 2
	Galvin Bistrot de Luxe	*French*	3 3 3

Name	Cuisine			
Les 110 de Taillevent	"	3	3	3
Bernardi's	Italian	3	4	3
Caffè Caldesi	"	3	3	3
The Ninth	Mediterranean	4	3	2
The Harcourt	Scandinavian	4	3	4
Lima	Peruvian	3	2	1
Pachamama	"	3	1	2
The Bright Courtyard	Chinese	5	3	2
Gaylord	Indian	3	4	3
Crazy Bear	Thai	2	2	4
Patara Fitzrovia	"	3	4	4

£50+				
Daylesford Organic	British, Modern	2	2	3
The Grazing Goat	"	2	3	3
The Ivy Café	"	2	2	4
Percy & Founders	"	4	3	2
Vinoteca Seymour Place	"	2	2	3
Bonnie Gull	Fish & seafood	4	4	3
28 50	French	2	3	4
Villandry	"	1	1	2
The Wallace	"	2	1	5
Carousel	Fusion	4	5	4
Twist	"	4	4	4
Latium	Italian	4	4	3
Obicà	"	3	3	2
Sardo	"	3	2	2
2 Veneti	"	3	4	3
Blandford Comptoir	Mediterranean	4	4	4
Riding House Café	"	2	2	3
Barrica	Spanish	3	3	3
Lurra	"	4	3	3
Daylesford Organic	Sandwiches, cakes, etc	2	2	3
Zoilo	Argentinian	4	2	3
Reubens	Kosher	2	3	3
Maroush	Lebanese	3	2	2
Dinings	Japanese	4	3	1
House of Ho	Vietnamese	2	2	2

£40+				
Barnyard	British, Modern	2	3	3
Hardy's Brasserie	"	2	3	3
The Newman Arms	"	4	4	4
Picture Marylebone	"	4	4	3
Opso	Greek	3	2	3
Briciole	Italian	3	3	3
Made in Italy James St	"	3	2	3
Rossopomodoro	"	3	2	2
Mac & Wild	Scottish	4	4	3
Donostia	Spanish	5	3	4
Drakes Tabanco	"	4	4	4
Ibérica	"	2	2	3
Salt Yard	"	3	3	3
Social Wine & Tapas	"	3	2	3

	Relais de Venise	*Steaks & grills*	3	2	2
	Bobo Social	*Burgers, etc*	4	4	3
	Burger & Lobster	*"*	3	3	3
	La Fromagerie Café	*Sandwiches, cakes, etc*	3	2	2
	Workshop Coffee	*"*	3	3	4
	Fairuz	*Lebanese*	3	3	3
	Honey & Co	*Middle Eastern*	5	4	2
	Ishtar	*Turkish*	3	3	2
	Royal China	*Chinese*	3	1	2
	Roti Chai	*Indian*	4	3	4
	Tsunami	*Japanese*	5	2	3
£35+	Lantana Café	*Australian*	3	3	3
	Ethos	*Vegetarian*	3	2	3
	MEATLiquor	*Burgers, etc*	3	3	4
	Yalla Yalla	*Lebanese*	3	2	3
	Babaji Pide	*Turkish*	2	2	3
	Chettinad	*Indian*	4	2	3
	Sagar	*"*	3	3	2
	On The Bab Express	*Korean*	3	3	2
£30+	Vapiano	*Italian*	3	2	3
	Atari-Ya	*Japanese*	4	2	2
	Tonkotsu	*"*	2	3	3
£25+	Bao Fitzrovia	*French*	4	2	2
	Golden Hind	*Fish & chips*	4	4	2
	Ragam	*Indian*	4	3	1
	Bibimbap	*Korean*	2	2	2
£20+	Patty & Bun	*Burgers, etc*	4	3	2
	Tommi's Burger Joint	*"*	4	4	4
	Homeslice	*Pizza*	4	4	4
	Patogh	*Middle Eastern*	4	3	3
£15+	Nordic Bakery	*Scandinavian*	3	4	3
£10+	Ahi Poké	*Hawaiian*	–	–	–
	Scandinavian Kitchen	*Scandinavian*	3	3	3
	Kaffeine	*Sandwiches, cakes, etc*	3	5	5

Belgravia, Pimlico, Victoria & Westminster (SW1, except St James's)

£110+	Marcus	*French*	3	2	3
	Pétrus	*"*	3	3	2
£100+	Dinner	*British, Traditional*	3	3	4
	Céleste	*French*	2	3	2

			Rating
	Rib Room	Steaks & grills	2 3 2
£90+	One-O-One	Fish & seafood	4 2 1
	Ametsa	Spanish	4 3 2
£80+	The Collins Room	British, Modern	2 4 5
	The Goring Hotel	"	3 5 4
	Roux Parliament Sq	"	5 5 3
	Koffmann's	French	4 5 3
	Zafferano	Italian	2 2 2
	Hunan	Chinese	5 4 1
	Mr Chow	"	2 2 2
£70+	Caxton Grill	British, Modern	– – –
	Salmontini	Fish & seafood	2 2 3
	Bar Boulud	French	2 3 3
	Canvas	International	2 3 2
	Santini	Italian	2 3 3
	Mari Vanna	Russian	2 2 4
	M Restaurant	Steaks & grills	2 2 2
	Amaya	Indian	5 3 3
	The Cinnamon Club	"	3 3 3
	Quilon	Indian, Southern	4 4 2
	Buddha-Bar London	Pan-Asian	2 2 3
£60+	The Botanist	British, Modern	2 1 2
	45 Jermyn St	"	3 4 4
	The Thomas Cubitt	"	3 4 4
	Olivomare	Fish & seafood	4 3 2
	La Poule au Pot	French	2 2 5
	Il Convivio	Italian	3 3 4
	Enoteca Turi	"	4 5 4
	Olivo	"	3 3 2
	Olivocarne	"	3 3 2
	Quirinale	"	4 4 2
	Sale e Pepe	"	3 4 4
	Signor Sassi	"	3 3 4
	Boisdale	Scottish	2 2 3
	Barbecoa	Steaks & grills	2 2 2
	Oliveto	Pizza	3 2 1
	The Grand Imperial	Chinese	4 3 3
£50+	Daylesford Organic	British, Modern	2 2 3
	Ebury	"	2 2 3
	The Orange	"	3 4 4
	Tate Britain	"	2 3 5
	Shepherd's	British, Traditional	3 3 4
	Colbert	French	1 1 2
	Motcombs	International	2 3 3
	Cacio & Pepe	Italian	4 4 4
	Caraffini	"	3 5 4

	Como Lario	"	2	2	2
	Ottolenghi	"	3	2	2
	About Thyme	Spanish	3	3	3
	Zelman Meats	Steaks & grills	5	4	4
	Bbar	South African	3	4	3
	Ken Lo's Memories	Chinese	3	4	2
	Kurobuta Harvey Nics	Japanese	5	2	2
	Salloos	Pakistani	4	3	2
£40+	Gustoso	Italian	3	5	3
	Polpo	"	2	2	2
	Tozi	"	3	3	3
	Goya	Spanish	3	3	3
	Ibérica	"	2	2	3
	Burger & Lobster	Burgers, etc	3	3	3
	Kazan (Café)	Turkish	3	4	2
£35+	The Vincent Rooms	British, Modern	3	3	3
	Seafresh	Fish & chips	3	4	2
	A Wong	Chinese	5	5	4
	Lime Orange	Korean	3	2	2
	Rosa's	Thai	3	3	2
£30+	Bone Daddies	Japanese	4	4	4
£20+	Shake Shack	Burgers, etc	3	2	2

WEST

Chelsea, South Kensington, Kensington, Earl's Court & Fulham (SW3, SW5, SW6, SW7, SW10 & W8)

£140+	Gordon Ramsay	French	2 4 3
£90+	Vineet Bhatia	Indian	3 2 3
£80+	The Five Fields	British, Modern	5 5 4
	Launceston Place	"	4 5 4
	Cheneston's Restaurant	British, Traditional	2 3 4
	Outlaw's at The Capital	Fish & seafood	4 4 2
	Toto's	Italian	2 3 4
	Zuma	Japanese	4 3 4
£70+	Babylon	British, Modern	2 2 3
	Kitchen W8	"	4 4 2
	maze Grill	"	3 3 3
	Medlar	"	4 4 3
	Bibendum	French	– – –
	L'Etranger	"	3 3 2
	Rivea	International	3 3 2
	Daphne's	Italian	2 2 3
	Lucio	"	3 3 2
	Osteria 60	"	– – –
	Scalini	"	3 2 3
	Cambio de Tercio	Spanish	3 4 3
	Hawksmoor	Steaks & grills	3 3 2
	Min Jiang	Chinese	4 3 5
	Yashin	Japanese	3 2 2
	Koji	Pan-Asian	4 4 3
£60+	The Abingdon	British, Modern	3 3 3
	Bluebird	"	– – –
	Clarke's	"	4 4 4
	Harwood Arms	"	5 3 3
	Ivy Kensington Brasserie	"	2 2 3
	Kensington Place	"	3 3 2
	Restaurant Ours	"	2 4 4
	Tom's Kitchen	"	2 2 2
	Ffiona's	British, Traditional	3 4 4
	Wright Brothers	Fish & seafood	4 3 3
	Bandol	French	3 3 2
	Belvedere	"	2 2 4
	Brasserie Gustave	"	3 4 3
	Cheyne Walk Brasserie	"	3 3 3
	Le Colombier	"	3 4 3
	Mazi	Greek	4 4 4
	Manicomio	Italian	2 2 3

	Theo's Simple Italian	"	– – –
	Locanda Ottomezzo	*Mediterranean*	3 2 3
	Bombay Brasserie	*Indian*	3 3 3
	Zaika	"	4 4 4
	Patara	*Thai*	3 4 4
£50+	Big Easy	*American*	2 2 3
	Brinkley's	*British, Modern*	1 2 3
	Claude's Kitchen	"	4 3 3
	The Enterprise	"	3 3 4
	The Hour Glass	"	3 3 2
	The Ivy Chelsea Garden	"	2 2 5
	The Phoenix	"	2 2 4
	The Sands End	"	2 3 3
	The Tommy Tucker	"	3 3 4
	Bumpkin	*British, Traditional*	2 2 2
	Maggie Jones's	"	2 2 5
	Bibendum Oyster Bar	*Fish & seafood*	4 2 4
	La Brasserie	*French*	2 2 4
	The Admiral Codrington	*International*	1 2 3
	Gallery Mess	"	2 2 3
	Kensington Wine Rms	"	2 3 3
	La Famiglia	*Italian*	2 2 4
	Frantoio	"	2 3 4
	Obicà	"	3 3 2
	Ottolenghi	"	3 2 2
	Pellicano Restaurant	"	3 4 2
	Il Portico	"	3 5 4
	Tartufo	"	3 3 2
	Ziani's	"	2 3 2
	The Cross Keys	*Mediterranean*	3 3 4
	Ognisko Restaurant	*Polish*	3 4 4
	Tendido Cero	*Spanish*	2 3 3
	Tendido Cuatro	"	2 2 2
	MacellaioRC	*Steaks & grills*	3 3 3
	Sophie's Steakhouse	"	2 4 3
	Geales Chelsea Green	*Fish & chips*	1 2 2
	Maroush	*Lebanese*	3 2 2
	Good Earth	*Chinese*	3 2 2
	Romulo Café	*Filipino*	3 3 3
	Chakra	*Indian*	4 2 3
	Masala Grill	"	3 4 4
	The Painted Heron	"	5 4 2
	Star of India	"	4 2 3
	Chisou	*Japanese*	4 4 2
	Kiru	"	4 3 3
	Kurobuta	"	5 2 2
	Tokyo Sukiyaki-Tei	"	– – –
	Eight Over Eight	*Pan-Asian*	3 2 3
	Sukho Thai Cuisine	*Thai*	5 4 3
£40+	Bodean's	*American*	2 2 2

	The Builders Arms	*British, Modern*	2	2	4
	Manuka Kitchen	"	3	2	3
	Megan's Delicatessen	"	2	3	5
	Rabbit	"	4	4	3
	The Shed	"	3	2	4
	VQ	"	2	4	3
	Aglio e Olio	*Italian*	4	3	2
	Buona Sera	"	3	3	3
	Da Mario	"	2	3	4
	Made in Italy	"	3	2	3
	Nuovi Sapori	"	3	4	2
	Polpo	"	2	2	2
	Riccardo's	"	2	3	2
	Sapori Sardi	"	3	2	2
	The Atlas	*Mediterranean*	4	4	4
	Daquise	*Polish*	2	2	2
	Capote Y Toros	*Spanish*	3	4	4
	Casa Brindisa	"	2	2	2
	Hanger	*Steaks & grills*	–	–	–
	La Delizia Limbara	*Pizza*	3	2	2
	Pizzicotto	"	4	4	3
	Rossopomodoro	"	3	2	2
	Royal China	*Chinese*	3	1	2
	Malabar	*Indian*	5	4	3
	Noor Jahan	"	3	3	2
	Pure Indian Cooking	"	–	–	–
	Thali	"	4	3	3
	Suksan	*Thai*	4	3	2
£35+	Churchill Arms	*British, Traditional*	3	3	5
	Haché	*Steaks & grills*	3	4	4
	Rocca Di Papa	*Pizza*	2	2	3
	Best Mangal	*Turkish*	4	3	2
	Rosa's Fulham	*Thai*	3	3	2
	Taiwan Village	*Taiwanese*	4	5	3
£30+	Kensington Sq Kitchen	*British, Modern*	3	4	3
	Tangerine Dream	"	3	2	4
	Mona Lisa	*International*	3	3	2
	Pappa Ciccia	*Italian*	3	4	3
	Santa Maria	*Pizza*	5	4	3
	Dragon Palace	*Chinese*	4	3	2
	Bone Daddies	*Japanese*	4	4	4
	Kulu Kulu	"	3	1	1
	Addie's Thai Café	*Thai*	4	4	3
£20+	Tommi's Burger Joint	*Burgers, etc*	4	4	4
	Stick & Bowl	*Chinese*	4	3	1
	Eat Tokyo	*Japanese*	4	2	2
£10+	Orée	*French*	4	2	3

Notting Hill, Holland Park, Bayswater, North Kensington & Maida Vale (W2, W9, W10, W11)

£130+	The Ledbury	British, Modern	5	5	4
£120+	Marianne	British, Modern	4	3	4
£80+	Flat Three	Japanese	4	4	2
£70+	Assaggi	Italian	4	4	3
£60+	The Dock Kitchen	British, Modern	3	2	3
	Angelus	French	3	4	3
	Chucs	Italian	3	5	3
	Edera	"	3	3	3
	Essenza	"	3	4	3
	Mediterraneo	"	3	2	3
	Wormwood	Mediterranean	4	3	2
	West Thirty Six	Steaks & grills	2	2	3
	Kojawan	Pan-Asian	2	3	4
£50+	Electric Diner	American	2	2	3
	Granger & Co	Australian	3	2	4
	Daylesford Organic	British, Modern	2	2	3
	The Frontline Club	"	–	–	–
	The Ladbroke Arms	"	3	2	4
	Magazine	"	2	3	4
	Paradise by Way of KG	"	3	3	5
	Six Portland Road	"	4	4	3
	The Waterway	"	2	2	4
	The Summerhouse	Fish & seafood	2	3	5
	Bel Canto	French	2	3	4
	The Cow	Irish	3	2	4
	The Oak	Italian	4	3	4
	Osteria Basilico	"	3	2	4
	Ottolenghi	"	3	2	2
	Portobello Ristorante	"	3	4	3
	Farmacy	Vegetarian	–	–	–
	Pizza East Portobello	Pizza	3	3	4
	Casa Malevo	Argentinian	3	4	2
	Peyotito	Mexican/TexMex	–	–	–
	Maroush Gardens	Lebanese	3	2	2
	The Four Seasons	Chinese	4	1	1
	Kurobuta	Japanese	5	2	2
	E&O	Pan-Asian	3	3	3
£40+	Salt & Honey	British, Modern	3	4	2
	VQ	"	2	4	3
	Hereford Road	British, Traditional	4	4	3
	Snaps & Rye	Danish	4	5	3
	Polpo	Italian	2	2	2

			Rating		
	Raoul's Café	Mediterranean	2	2	3
	Pizza Metro	Pizza	3	2	2
	The Red Pepper	"	3	3	2
	Cocotte	Chicken	4	3	3
	Casa Cruz	South American	2	4	4
	Zayane	Moroccan	4	4	4
	Kateh	Persian	3	4	3
	Mandarin Kitchen	Chinese	4	1	1
	Pearl Liang	"	4	4	3
	Royal China	"	3	1	2
	Bombay Palace	Indian	–	–	–
	Noor Jahan	"	3	3	2
	Inaho	Japanese	5	3	1
	Maguro	"	4	4	3
£35+	The Chipping Forecast	Fish & chips	–	–	–
	Taqueria	Mexican/TexMex	4	4	3
	C&R Café	Malaysian	4	2	2
	Satay House	"	3	2	2
£30+	Alounak	Persian	3	2	4
	Gold Mine	Chinese	4	2	2
	Tonkotsu	Japanese	2	3	3
	The Heron	Thai	5	3	1
£25+	Fez Mangal	Turkish	5	4	3
£20+	Khan's	Indian	3	3	3
£10+	Lisboa Pâtisserie	Sandwiches, cakes, etc	3	2	4
£5+	Falafel King	Middle Eastern	3	2	2

Hammersmith, Shepherd's Bush, Olympia, Chiswick, Brentford & Ealing (W4, W5, W6, W12, W13, W14, TW8)

			Rating		
£100+	Hedone	British, Modern	4	3	3
	The River Café	Italian	3	2	4
£70+	La Trompette	French	5	4	3
£60+	Le Vacherin	French	3	2	2
	Villa Di Geggiano	Italian	2	2	2
£50+	No 197 Chiswick Fire Stn	Australian	3	2	4
	The Anglesea Arms	British, Modern	3	4	4
	The Brackenbury	"	3	4	3
	Charlotte's Place	"	3	3	3

	Charlotte's W5	"	3	5	3
	City Barge	"	3	3	4
	Ealing Park Tavern	"	3	3	4
	High Road Brasserie	"	2	2	3
	Vinoteca	"	2	2	3
	The Hampshire Hog	British, Traditional	3	3	4
	Michael Nadra	French	4	4	2
	Melody at St Paul's	International	2	3	3
	Cibo	Italian	4	5	3
	The Oak W12	"	4	3	4
	Foxlow	Steaks & grills	2	2	2
	Smokehouse Chiswick	"	3	3	3
£40+	Jackson & Rye Chiswick	American	1	2	2
	The Dartmouth Castle	British, Modern	3	4	4
	The Dove	"	2	2	4
	Duke of Sussex	"	3	3	4
	The Havelock Tavern	"	3	3	4
	Mustard	"	3	5	4
	The Pear Tree	"	3	3	4
	Princess Victoria	"	3	3	3
	The Andover Arms	International	3	5	5
	Annie's	"	2	3	4
	L'Amorosa	Italian	4	4	3
	Buoni Amici	"	3	3	3
	Pentolina	"	4	5	4
	Cumberland Arms	Mediterranean	4	4	3
	The Swan	"	3	3	5
	Tamp Coffee	Spanish	3	3	3
	Popeseye	Steaks & grills	3	2	2
	The Gate	Vegetarian	4	3	3
	Bird in Hand	Pizza	3	3	4
	Habanera	Mexican/TexMex	3	2	3
	Quantus	South American	4	5	4
	North China	Chinese	3	3	3
	Indian Zing	Indian	4	3	2
	Karma	"	3	3	1
	Potli	"	5	4	3
	Sushi Bar Makoto	Japanese	3	3	4
£35+	Albertine	French	2	4	4
	Patio	Polish	3	5	5
	Chez Abir	Lebanese	3	2	3
	Best Mangal	Turkish	4	3	2
	Shikumen	Chinese	3	3	2
	Anarkali	Indian	3	4	3
	Brilliant	"	3	4	3
	Madhu's	"	5	4	3
	Sagar	"	3	3	2
	Kiraku	Japanese	4	4	2
	Tosa	"	3	3	2
	Yoshi Sushi	"	3	4	2

	Saigon Saigon	*Vietnamese*	3	3	3
£30+	Santa Maria	*Pizza*	5	4	3
	Adams Café	*Moroccan*	3	5	3
	Alounak	*Persian*	3	2	4
	Shilpa	*Indian, Southern*	5	3	2
	Atari-Ya	*Japanese*	4	2	2
	Hare & Tortoise	*Pan-Asian*	3	3	3
£25+	Kerbisher & Malt	*Fish & chips*	3	3	2
	Faanoos	*Persian*	3	3	2
	Gifto's Lahore Karahi	*Indian*	3	2	2
£20+	Abu Zaad	*Syrian*	3	3	2
	Eat Tokyo	*Japanese*	4	2	2

NORTH

Hampstead, West Hampstead, St John's Wood, Regent's Park, Kilburn & Camden Town (NW postcodes)

£70+			
The Landmark	British, Modern	2 4 5
The Gilbert Scott	British, Traditional	2 3 4
Gilgamesh	Pan-Asian	2 2 3

£60+			
The Booking Office	British, Modern	2 2 4
Bradley's	"	3 2 2
Odette's	"	4 4 4
L'Aventure	French	3 3 5
Oslo Court	"	4 5 4
Bull & Last	International	3 2 3
Kaifeng	Chinese	3 3 3

£50+			
One Sixty Smokehouse	American	4 3 4
Crocker's Folly	British, Modern	2 2 3
The Ivy Café	"	2 2 4
Market	"	3 4 2
The Wells	"	2 2 3
The Wet Fish Café	"	3 2 3
York & Albany	British, Traditional	2 2 2
Michael Nadra	French	4 4 2
La Collina	Italian	3 3 3
Villa Bianca	"	2 2 2
Manna	Vegetarian	3 2 2
Pizza East	Pizza	3 3 4
Greenberry Café	Sandwiches, cakes, etc	3 3 3
Good Earth	Chinese	3 2 2
Phoenix Palace	"	3 2 2

£40+			
The Horseshoe	British, Modern	3 3 4
The Junction Tavern	"	3 3 3
Parlour Kensal	"	4 4 4
Lure	Fish & seafood	4 4 3
L'Absinthe	French	2 3 2
La Cage Imaginaire	"	2 2 3
Patron	"	3 4 4
Lemonia	Greek	1 3 4
Anima e Cuore	Italian	4 2 1
Artigiano	"	2 3 3
Ostuni	"	3 3 3
The Rising Sun	"	3 2 3
Sarracino	"	4 2 2
Harry Morgan's	Burgers, etc	2 2 2
Nautilus	Fish & chips	4 3 1
The Sea Shell	"	3 3 2
Rossopomodoro	Pizza	3 2 2
Zest	Kosher	3 3 3

	Jun Ming Xuan	*Chinese, Dim sum*	4	4	2
	Namaaste Kitchen	*Indian*	3	4	2
	Jin Kichi	*Japanese*	5	5	3
	Oka	*"*	4	3	2
	Sushi Masa	*"*	–	–	–
	Singapore Garden	*Malaysian*	3	3	2
£35+	Lantana Cafe	*Australian*	3	3	3
	Fish Cafe	*Fish & seafood*	2	2	3
	Carob Tree	*Greek*	3	5	3
	L'Artista	*Italian*	2	4	4
	Giacomo's	*"*	3	3	2
	El Parador	*Spanish*	4	4	3
	Haché	*Steaks & grills*	3	4	4
	L' Antica Pizzeria	*Pizza*	4	3	3
	Sacro Cuore	*"*	4	3	3
	Bird Camden	*Chicken*	3	2	2
	Chicken Shop	*"*	2	2	3
	Green Cottage	*Chinese*	3	2	2
	Great Nepalese	*Indian*	3	3	2
	Asakusa	*Japanese*	5	3	2
	The Petite Coree	*Korean*	4	5	2
£30+	La Porchetta Pizzeria	*Italian*	2	3	3
	Brew House	*Sandwiches, cakes, etc*	2	2	3
	Ariana II	*Afghani*	3	2	2
	Chutneys	*Indian*	3	2	2
	Guglee	*"*	3	2	2
	Paradise Hampstead	*"*	4	5	4
	Ravi Shankar	*"*	3	2	2
	Vijay	*"*	3	2	1
	Atari-Ya	*Japanese*	4	2	2
£25+	The Little Bay	*Mediterranean*	2	3	4
	Poppies Camden	*Fish & chips*	3	3	3
	Ali Baba	*Egyptian*	3	2	4
	Diwana Bhel-Pouri Hs	*Indian*	3	2	1
£20+	Eat Tokyo	*Japanese*	4	2	2
	Roti King	*Malaysian*	5	2	1
£10+	Bill or Beak	*Burgers, etc*	4	4	–
	Dirty Burger	*"*	3	2	2
	Ginger & White	*Sandwiches, cakes, etc*	2	4	3
£5+	Doppio	*Sandwiches, cakes, etc*	3	3	3

Hoxton, Islington, Highgate, Crouch End, Stoke Newington, Finsbury Park, Muswell Hill & Finchley (N postcodes)

£60+	Fifteen	British, Modern	2 2 3
	Frederick's	"	2 3 4
	Plum + Spilt Milk	"	2 3 4
	German Gymnasium	Cent. European	2 2 3
	Almeida	French	3 2 2
£50+	Granger & Co	Australian	3 2 4
	The Drapers Arms	British, Modern	3 2 2
	Grain Store	"	4 3 3
	The Haven	"	3 4 3
	The Lighterman	"	3 3 4
	Pig & Butcher	"	4 4 4
	Red Lion & Sun	"	3 3 4
	Rotunda	"	3 4 3
	Smoke & Salt	"	– – –
	Bellanger	Cent. European	2 2 3
	Black Axe Mangal	"	5 3 2
	Galley	Fish & seafood	4 3 4
	Bistro Aix	French	4 3 3
	Caravan King's Cross	Fusion	3 2 3
	The Greek Larder	Greek	3 2 2
	8 Hoxton Square	International	4 4 4
	Salut	"	4 4 3
	Melange	Italian	3 3 3
	Ottolenghi	"	3 2 2
	Trullo	"	4 3 3
	Vinoteca	Mediterranean	2 2 3
	Foxlow	Steaks & grills	2 2 2
	Smokehouse Islington	"	4 4 4
	Duke's Brew & Que	Burgers, etc	4 2 3
£40+	Bodean's	American	2 2 2
	The Albion	British, Modern	2 1 3
	The Bull	"	2 3 4
	Heirloom	"	3 3 3
	Hill & Szrok	"	4 4 4
	Oldroyd	"	4 3 2
	Season Kitchen	"	3 3 2
	St Johns	British, Traditional	3 3 5
	Kipferl	Cent. European	3 2 2
	Prawn On The Lawn	Fish & seafood	4 3 3
	Petit Pois Bistro	French	– – –
	Nissi	Greek	3 3 3
	Banners	International	3 4 5
	Primeur	"	4 3 4
	500	Italian	3 4 2
	Osteria Tufo	"	3 4 3
	Ostuni	"	3 3 3

			Rating		
	Pizzeria Oregano	"	3	4	3
	San Daniele del Friuli	"	3	4	3
	Rubedo	Mediterranean	4	4	3
	Rök	Scandinavian	4	2	2
	Café del Parc	Spanish	5	5	4
	Camino King's Cross	"	3	3	3
	Escocesa	"	4	3	2
	Trangallan	"	5	4	4
	Popeseye	Steaks & grills	3	2	2
	Toff's	Fish & chips	3	2	2
	Vintage Salt	"	3	4	3
	Rossopomodoro	Pizza	3	2	2
	Sweet Thursday	"	3	2	3
	Le Coq	Chicken	3	3	3
	Yipin China	Chinese	3	2	1
	Little Georgia Café	Georgian	3	3	3
	Dishoom	Indian	4	3	4
	Zaffrani	"	3	2	2
	Isarn	Thai	4	4	2
	Yum Yum	"	3	2	2
£35+	Le Sacré-Coeur	French	4	4	4
	Vrisaki	Greek	3	3	2
	Pizzeria Pappagone	Italian	3	4	4
	Rugoletta	"	4	3	3
	Bar Esteban	Spanish	4	4	4
	MEATLiquor	Burgers, etc	3	3	4
	Olympus Fish	Fish & chips	4	5	2
	Bird Islington	Chicken	3	2	2
	Chicken Shop	"	2	2	3
	Gallipoli	Turkish	3	4	4
	Delhi Grill	Indian	3	2	2
	Indian Rasoi	"	4	4	3
	Rasa Travancore	Indian, Southern	3	3	3
	CôBa	Vietnamese	4	3	3
£30+	Le Mercury	French	2	2	4
	La Porchetta Pizzeria	Italian	2	3	3
	Meat Mission	Burgers, etc	3	3	4
	Sutton & Sons	Fish & chips	4	3	3
	Two Brothers	"	3	2	2
	Yard Sale Pizza	Pizza	4	3	2
	Zia Lucia	"	–	–	–
	Gem	Turkish	3	4	3
	Gökyüzü	"	4	4	4
	Jashan	Indian	5	4	2
	Rani	"	3	2	2
	Atari-Ya	Japanese	4	2	2
	Salvation In Noodles	Vietnamese	3	2	2
£25+	Breakfast Club Angel	American	3	3	2
	Chriskitch	British, Modern	4	4	3

	Afghan Kitchen	*Afghani*	3 2 2
	Dotori	*Korean*	4 3 2
£20+	Max's Sandwich Shop	*Sandwiches, cakes, etc*	4 3 3
	Xi'an Impression	*Chinese*	4 4 2
£15+	Piebury Corner	*British, Traditional*	3 4 3
£10+	Five Guys Islington	*Burgers, etc*	3 2 2

SOUTH

South Bank (SE1)

£130+	Story	British, Modern	3 3 3
£90+	Aqua Shard	British, Modern	1 1 3
	Ting	Fusion	2 2 3
£80+	Oblix	British, Modern	2 1 5
	Oxo Tower	"	1 1 1
	Hutong	Chinese	3 2 5
£70+	Oxo Tower	British, Modern	1 1 2
	Le Pont de la Tour	"	2 2 4
	Skylon	"	1 1 2
	Skylon Grill	"	2 2 3
	Roast	British, Traditional	2 2 3
	La Barca	Italian	2 2 2
£60+	Sea Containers	British, Modern	2 2 4
	The Swan at the Globe	"	2 2 3
	Butlers Wharf Chop House	British, Traditional	2 2 2
	Wright Brothers	Fish & seafood	4 3 3
	Rabot 1745	International	3 2 2
£50+	Albion	British, Modern	2 2 2
	Blueprint Café	"	2 2 5
	Elliot's Café	"	3 2 3
	40 Maltby Street	"	4 3 3
	The Garrison	"	3 2 4
	House Restaurant	"	2 3 2
	Magdalen	"	3 2 2
	Menier Chocolate Factory	"	2 2 3
	RSJ	"	3 3 2
	Tate Modern	"	2 1 4
	Union Street Café	"	2 3 2
	Waterloo Bar & Kitchen	"	2 1 2
	The Anchor & Hope	British, Traditional	4 3 3
	Applebee's Café	Fish & seafood	4 4 2
	fish!	"	3 2 2
	Caravan Bankside	Fusion	3 2 3
	Champor-Champor	"	4 4 5
	Village East	"	2 2 3
	Vivat Bacchus	International	3 3 3
	MacellaioRC	Italian	3 3 3
	Baltic	Polish	3 4 4
	Pizarro	Spanish	3 3 3
£40+	Edwins	British, Modern	3 4 4

	The Green Room	"		2 2 2
	Boro Bistro	French		3 3 3
	Casse-Croute	"		4 3 4
	Antico	Italian		3 4 3
	Camino Bankside	Spanish		3 3 3
	José	"		5 4 5
	LOBOS Meat & Tapas	"		4 3 2
	Tapas Brindisa	"		2 2 2
	Arabica Bar & Kitchen	Lebanese		3 3 3
	Tas Pide	Turkish		2 3 3
£35+	The Table	British, Modern		3 2 2
	Pulia	Italian		3 4 3
	Meson don Felipe	Spanish		2 3 4
£30+	Vapiano	Italian		3 2 3
	Mar I Terra	Spanish		2 4 2
	El Vergel	South American		4 3 4
	Tonkotsu Bankside	Japanese		2 3 3
£25+	Padella	Italian		4 4 3
	Masters Super Fish	Fish & chips		3 2 2
£10+	Gourmet Goat	Mediterranean		4 4 2
£5+	Monmouth Coffee Company	Sandwiches, cakes, etc		5 5 4

Greenwich, Lewisham, Dulwich & Blackheath (All SE postcodes, except SE1)

£60+	Lobster Pot	Fish & seafood		4 3 4
	Craft London	Pizza		4 3 3
£50+	The Camberwell Arms	British, Modern		4 3 3
	Chapters	"		2 2 2
	Franklins	"		4 3 3
	The Palmerston	"		3 3 3
	Pharmacy 2	"		3 3 3
	Rivington Grill	"		2 2 2
	Babur	Indian		5 5 4
	Yama Momo	Japanese		4 2 3
£40+	The Crooked Well	British, Modern		3 3 4
	Guildford Arms	"		3 3 3
	The Lido Café	"		2 2 4
	Peckham Ref' Rooms	"		3 2 2
	The Perry Vale	"		3 4 3
	The Lord Northbrook	British, Traditional		3 4 4
	Brasserie Toulouse-Lautrec	French		3 3 3

	Peckham Bazaar	Greek	5	3	4
	Joanna's	International	3	4	4
	Tulse Hill Hotel	"	3	2	3
	The Yellow House	"	3	3	2
	Artusi	Italian	3	3	3
	Lorenzo	"	3	3	3
	Luciano's	"	3	3	3
	Cau	Steaks & grills	1	2	2
	Ganapati	Indian	5	4	3
	Kennington Tandoori	"	3	3	3
	Sticks'n'Sushi	Japanese	4	4	4
£35+	Upstairs at John The Un'	British, Modern	–	–	–
	Canada Water Cafe	Italian	3	4	3
	Le Querce	"	3	4	3
	MEATLiquor	Burgers, etc	3	3	4
	Pedler	Pizza	3	4	4
	Rocca Di Papa	"	2	2	3
	Theo's	"	4	3	3
	Yalla Yalla	Lebanese	3	2	3
	Dragon Castle	Chinese	3	3	2
	Everest Inn	Indian	4	3	3
	Zaibatsu	Japanese	4	5	2
	The Begging Bowl	Thai	5	4	3
£30+	The Gowlett Arms	Pizza	4	3	4
	FM Mangal	Turkish	3	3	2
	Bánh Bánh	Vietnamese	4	5	3
	Mr Bao	Taiwanese	3	2	2
£25+	Rox Burger	Burgers, etc	4	3	3
	Mamma Dough	Pizza	3	4	4
£20+	Pizzeria Pellone	Pizza	4	3	2
	Silk Road	Chinese	5	2	2
	Café East	Vietnamese	4	2	2
£5+	Kappacasein	Sandwiches, cakes, etc	5	2	2

Battersea, Brixton, Clapham, Wandsworth Barnes, Putney & Wimbledon
(All SW postcodes south of the river)

£70+	Chez Bruce	British, Modern	5	5	4
	Trinity	"	5	5	4
£60+	Gastronhome	French	5	4	3
	The White Onion	"	3	2	2
	London House	International	3	3	2
	Riva	Italian	4	4	2

FSA Ratings: from **1** (Poor) to **5** (Exceptional)

£50+					
The Brown Dog	*British, Modern*	3	2	3
Cannizaro House	"	2	3	3
The Ivy Café	"	2	2	4
Lamberts	"	5	5	4
The Light House	"	3	3	3
The Manor	"	4	3	3
May The Fifteenth	"	3	3	3
Olympic	"	2	2	4
Sonny's Kitchen	"	2	2	3
The Victoria	"	2	3	4
Soif	*French*	3	3	3
Bibo	*Italian*	3	3	3
Numero Uno	"	3	3	3
The Fox & Hounds	*Mediterranean*	4	4	4
Alquimia	*Spanish*	3	3	2
Cornish Tiger	*Steaks & grills*	3	3	3
Foxlow	"	2	2	2
Naughty Piglets	"	5	5	3
Good Earth	*Chinese*	3	2	2

£40+					
Bodean's	*American*	2	2	2
Counter	"	2	3	3
Bistro Union	*British, Modern*	3	3	3
Brunswick House Café	"	2	3	5
The Dairy	"	5	4	4
The Depot	"	2	2	5
Earl Spencer	"	3	2	4
Emile's	"	3	4	2
Hood	"	4	3	2
Salon Brixton	"	4	3	3
Canton Arms	*British, Traditional*	4	3	4
Jolly Gardeners	"	3	2	3
The Plough	"	3	4	5
Augustine Kitchen	*French*	3	4	2
Annie's	*International*	2	3	4
Buona Sera	*Italian*	3	3	3
Donna Margherita	"	3	3	2
Made in Italy	"	3	2	3
Osteria Antica Bologna	"	3	3	3
Pizza Metro	"	3	2	2
The Bobbin	*Mediterranean*	3	4	4
Brindisa Food Rooms	*Spanish*	2	2	2
Gremio de Brixton	"	3	2	3
Cau	*Steaks & grills*	1	2	2
Popeseye	"	3	2	2
Fish Club	*Fish & chips*	3	2	2
Rossopomodoro	*Pizza*	3	2	2
MOMMI	*Peruvian*	2	3	3
Indian Zilla	*Indian*	4	2	2
Kricket	"	5	4	3
Ma Goa	"	4	4	2
Nanban	*Japanese*	4	3	2

	Sticks'n'Sushi	"	4	4	4
	Takahashi	"	5	3	3
	Tomoe	"	4	3	2
	Tsunami	"	5	2	3
£35+	Gazette	French	2	2	3
	Fish in a Tie	Mediterranean	2	3	2
	Bukowski Grill	Steaks & grills	4	3	2
	Haché	Burgers, etc	3	4	4
	Dynamo	Pizza	3	3	3
	Eco	"	3	3	4
	Chicken Shop & Dirty Burger	Chicken	2	2	3
	Indian Moment	Indian	3	4	3
	Indian Ocean	"	3	3	3
	Hashi	Japanese	4	4	3
	Cah-Chi	Korean	3	4	2
	Rosa's	Thai	3	3	2
£30+	Counter Culture	British, Modern	4	4	4
	Fields	"	3	3	3
	Boqueria	Spanish	3	4	4
	Little Taperia	"	4	4	1
	Brady's	Fish & chips	3	3	3
	Al Forno	Pizza	2	4	4
	Ground Coffee Society	Sandwiches, cakes, etc	3	3	3
	Meza Trinity Road	Lebanese	4	4	3
	Hare & Tortoise	Pan-Asian	3	3	3
	The Pepper Tree	Thai	3	3	3
	Mien Tay	Vietnamese	4	2	2
£25+	The Joint	American	5	3	3
	Figlio Del Vesuvio	Italian	4	4	2
	Dip & Flip	Burgers, etc	3	2	2
	Kerbisher & Malt	Fish & chips	3	3	2
	Mamma Dough	Pizza	3	4	4
	Orange Pekoe	Sandwiches, cakes, etc	3	4	4
	Faanoos	Persian	3	3	2
	Sree Krishna	Indian	4	3	2
	Lahore Karahi	Pakistani	4	2	2
	Mirch Masala	"	5	2	1
	Awesome Thai	Thai	3	4	3
	Kaosarn	"	4	4	3
£20+	Hot Stuff	Indian	3	5	3
	Lahore Kebab House	Pakistani	5	2	2
£15+	Flotsam & Jetsam	Australian	3	4	4
	Tried & True	British, Modern	3	3	3
	Jaffna House	Indian, Southern	5	3	2
£10+	Dirty Burger	Burgers, etc	3	2	2

FSA Ratings: from **1** (Poor) to **5** (Exceptional)

	Joe Public	*Pizza*	4 2 3
	Milk	*Sandwiches, cakes, etc*	4 3 3

Outer western suburbs
Kew, Richmond, Twickenham, Teddington

£70+	The Glasshouse	*British, Modern*	3 4 2
£60+	The Bingham	*British, Modern*	3 4 4
	The Dysart Petersham	*"*	4 4 3
	Petersham Hotel	*"*	3 3 5
	Petersham Nurseries	*"*	2 1 3
	Al Boccon di'vino	*Italian*	4 4 5
£50+	A Cena	*Italian*	3 3 3
£40+	Jackson & Rye Richmond	*American*	1 2 2
	La Buvette	*French*	3 3 3
	Ma Cuisine	*"*	3 2 3
	Le Salon Privé	*"*	4 4 4
	Bacco	*Italian*	3 3 3
	Pizzeria Rustica	*Pizza*	3 3 2
	Matsuba	*Japanese*	3 3 2

EAST

Smithfield & Farringdon (EC1)

Price	Restaurant	Cuisine	Ratings
£90+	The Clove Club	*British, Modern*	5 4 4
£80+	Club Gascon	*French*	4 3 2
£70+	Smiths of Smithfield	*Steaks & grills*	2 2 2
	Sosharu	*Japanese*	2 3 2
£60+	Anglo	*British, Modern*	4 3 2
	Bird of Smithfield	"	2 2 2
	Chiswell St Dining Rms	"	2 2 2
	The Jugged Hare	"	3 2 3
	Urban Coterie	"	– – –
	St John	*British, Traditional*	5 4 3
	Bleeding Heart	*French*	3 3 5
£50+	Granger & Co	*Australian*	3 2 4
	Vinoteca	*British, Modern*	2 2 3
	Albion Clerkenwell	*British, Traditional*	2 2 2
	The Fox & Anchor	"	3 3 4
	Café du Marché	*French*	3 3 4
	Caravan	*Fusion*	3 2 3
	The Modern Pantry	"	2 2 2
	MacellaioRC	*Italian*	3 3 3
	Moro	*Spanish*	5 4 3
	Foxlow	*Steaks & grills*	2 2 2
	Hix Oyster & Ch' Hs	"	2 2 2
	Smiths of Smithfield	"	2 2 1
	Sushi Tetsu	*Japanese*	5 5 4
£40+	Bodean's	*American*	2 2 2
	Coin Laundry	*British, Traditional*	– – –
	The Quality Chop House	"	3 4 3
	Café Pistou	*French*	3 2 2
	Comptoir Gascon	"	3 3 3
	La Ferme	"	3 2 2
	Enoteca Rabezzana	*Italian*	2 2 2
	Polpo	"	2 2 2
	Santore	"	4 3 3
	Ibérica	*Spanish*	2 2 3
	The Gate	*Vegetarian*	4 3 3
	Burger & Lobster	*Burgers, etc*	3 3 3
	Workshop Coffee	*Sandwiches, cakes, etc*	3 3 4
	Ceviche Old St	*Peruvian*	3 3 3
	The Sichuan	*Chinese*	4 2 2
£35+	Lantana Café	*Australian*	3 3 3

	Apulia	*Italian*	3 3 3
	Morito	*Spanish*	4 4 4
	Pham Sushi	*Japanese*	5 3 1
	On The Bab	*Korean*	3 3 2
	Cây Tre	*Vietnamese*	4 3 3
£30+	Smiths of Smithfield	*British, Modern*	2 2 3
	Fish Central	*Fish & seafood*	3 3 2
	Cellar Gascon	*French*	3 3 3
	Kolossi Grill	*Greek*	3 5 2
	La Porchetta Pizzeria	*Italian*	2 3 3
	The Eagle	*Mediterranean*	4 3 5
	Pizza Pilgrims	*Pizza*	4 3 4
	Berber & Q Sh' Bar	*Middle Eastern*	– – –
	Bone Daddies	*Japanese*	4 4 4
£25+	Kerbisher & Malt	*Fish & chips*	3 3 2
£20+	Homeslice	*Pizza*	4 4 4
£15+	Dept of Coffee	*Sandwiches, cakes, etc*	3 5 4
£10+	Prufrock Coffee	*Sandwiches, cakes, etc*	3 2 4

The City (EC2, EC3, EC4)

£90+	Sushisamba	*Japanese*	3 3 5
£80+	City Social	*British, Modern*	3 3 5
	Fenchurch Restaurant	*"*	3 3 3
	Angler	*Fish & seafood*	3 3 3
	Coq d'Argent	*French*	2 2 2
	Goodman City	*Steaks & grills*	3 3 3
£70+	Duck & Waffle	*British, Modern*	2 2 5
	1 Lombard Street	*"*	2 2 2
	Sweetings	*Fish & seafood*	2 2 4
	Lutyens	*French*	2 2 2
	L'Anima	*Italian*	3 3 3
	Hawksmoor	*Steaks & grills*	3 3 2
	M Restaurant	*"*	2 2 2
	HKK	*Chinese*	5 4 2
	Yauatcha City	*"*	4 3 3
£60+	The Botanist	*British, Modern*	2 1 2
	Bread Street Kitchen	*"*	2 2 3
	The Chancery	*"*	4 4 3
	Darwin Brasserie	*"*	2 2 4
	The Don	*"*	3 3 2

High Timber	"	3	4	3
Hush	"	2	3	3
The Mercer	"	2	2	2
Merchants Tavern	"	3	4	4
3 South Place	"	3	3	3
The White Swan	"	3	3	2
Chamberlain's	Fish & seafood	2	3	2
Sauterelle	French	3	3	4
Caravaggio	Italian	2	3	3
Gatti's City Point	"	3	3	3
Manicomio	"	2	2	3
Boisdale of Bishopsgate	Scottish	2	2	2
Eyre Brothers	Spanish	5	3	3
Barbecoa	Steaks & grills	2	2	2
Vanilla Black	Vegetarian	4	2	2
Chinese Cricket Club	Chinese	3	3	1
Darbaar	Indian	4	4	3
Mint Leaf Lounge	"	3	3	4
£50+	Northbank	British, Modern	2	2	3
	Princess of Shoreditch	"	3	3	3
	Rivington Grill	"	2	2	2
	Sign of the Don	"	2	3	4
	Paternoster Chop House	British, Traditional	2	1	1
	Fish Market	Fish & seafood	3	2	2
	Royal Exch Grand Café	French	2	2	4
	28-50	"	2	3	4
	The Modern Pantry	Fusion	2	2	2
	Vivat Bacchus	International	3	3	3
	L'Anima Café	Italian	3	2	3
	Obicà	"	3	3	2
	Osteria	"	2	2	2
	Taberna Etrusca	"	2	3	3
	Hispania	Spanish	3	3	3
	José Pizarro	"	4	3	2
	Jones Family Project	Steaks & grills	3	4	4
	The Tramshed	"	2	3	4
	Oklava	Turkish	4	4	3
	Cinnamon Kitchen	Indian	3	2	3
£40+	Bodean's	American	2	2	2
	Pitt Cue Co	"	5	4	4
	The Anthologist	British, Modern	2	2	3
	Café Below	"	2	2	3
	Humble Grape	"	3	4	4
	Rök	"	4	2	2
	The Trading House	"	3	4	4
	Simpson's Tavern	British, Traditional	2	3	5
	Rucoletta	Italian	2	2	1
	Rocket Bishopgate	Mediterranean	3	3	3
	Camino Blackfriars	Spanish	3	3	3
	Relais de Venise	Steaks & grills	3	2	2

	Burger & Lobster	Burgers, etc	3 3 3
	Vintage Salt	Fish & chips	3 4 3
	Shoryu Ramen	Japanese	3 2 2
£35+	Restaurant de Paul	French	3 4 4
	Haché	Burgers, etc	3 4 4
	Haz	Turkish	2 2 2
	Beer & Buns	Japanese	3 3 4
	K10	"	4 4 3
	On The Bab	Korean	3 3 2
£30+	The Wine Library	International	1 3 5
	Mangal 1.1	Turkish	– – –
	Hare & Tortoise	Pan-Asian	3 3 3
£25+	Walter & Monty	American	– – –
	Hilliard	British, Modern	4 4 3
	Bibimbap	Korean	2 2 2
£20+	Flat Iron	Steaks & grills	4 3 3
	Patty & Bun	Burgers, etc	4 3 2
£15+	City Càphê	Vietnamese	3 2 1
£10+	Smokestak	American	5 3 –
	Pilpel	Middle Eastern	4 4 2
	Yum Bun	Japanese	5 3 –

East End & Docklands (All E postcodes)

£80+	Galvin La Chapelle	French	3 3 4
	Typing Room	Fusion	4 5 3
	Goodman	Steaks & grills	3 3 3
	Roka	Japanese	4 3 3
£70+	The Woodford	British, Modern	3 4 4
	Plateau	French	2 2 3
	Hawksmoor	Steaks & grills	3 3 2
£60+	The Boundary	British, Modern	1 1 3
	The Gun	"	3 2 4
	Lyle's	"	5 4 3
	Pidgin	"	5 5 4
	Tom's Kitchen	"	2 2 2
	Wright Brothers	Fish & seafood	4 3 3
	Canto Corvino	Italian	4 4 4
	Boisdale of Canary Wharf	Scottish	2 2 3

£50+			
Big Easy	American	2 2 3
One Sixty Smokehouse	"	4 3 4
Bistrotheque	British, Modern	3 3 4
Ellory	"	2 4 3
Galvin HOP	"	4 4 3
Hoi Polloi	"	2 1 2
Jones & Sons	"	4 3 4
Legs	"	– – –
The Morgan Arms	"	4 3 3
The Narrow	"	2 2 3
One Canada Square	"	2 3 3
The Richmond	"	3 3 3
Rochelle Canteen	"	3 2 4
Smith's Wapping	"	4 3 4
Albion	British, Traditional	2 2 2
Bumpkin	"	2 2 2
The Marksman	"	3 2 3
St John Bread & Wine	"	5 3 2
Brawn	French	5 4 4
Blixen	International	3 4 4
Sager + Wilde	"	3 3 4
Il Bordello	Italian	3 4 5
Obicà	"	3 3 2
Super Tuscan	"	4 4 3
Pizza East	Pizza	3 3 4
Buen Ayre	Argentinian	4 2 2
Ottolenghi	Israeli	3 2 2
Café Spice Namaste	Indian	5 5 4

£40+			
The Culpeper	British, Modern	2 2 3
The Empress	"	4 4 4
Paradise Garage	"	4 4 3
Poco	"	– – –
Jago	Fusion	3 2 2
Gotto Trattoria	Italian	– – –
Lardo Bebè	"	3 2 2
Rotorino	"	2 3 3
Verdi's	"	3 3 3
Rocket Canary Wharf	Mediterranean	3 3 3
Taberna do Mercado	Portuguese	5 4 3
Bravas	Spanish	3 3 2
Ibérica	"	2 2 3
Cau	Steaks & grills	1 2 2
Hill & Szrok	"	4 4 4
Relais de Venise	"	3 2 2
Lucky Chip	Burgers, etc	3 2 2
Ark Fish	Fish & chips	4 4 2
Corner Kitchen	Pizza	3 2 3
Andina	Peruvian	4 3 4
Berber & Q	Middle Eastern	4 3 5
Strut & Cluck	"	– – –
Royal China	Chinese	3 1 2

	Sichuan Folk	"	4	4	2
	Yi-Ban	"	3	3	3
	Little Georgia Café	Georgian	3	3	3
	Dishoom	Indian	4	3	4
	Gunpowder	"	4	4	4
	Sticks'n'Sushi	Japanese	4	4	4
	Som Saa	Thai	5	2	3
	Viet Grill	Vietnamese	3	2	2
£35+	Eat 17	British, Modern	4	4	3
	Leyton Technical	"	3	2	4
	P Franco	"	–	–	–
	Sager + Wilde	"	2	4	4
	Blanchette East	French	4	4	5
	Provender	"	3	4	3
	Eat 17	International	4	4	3
	Morito	Spanish	4	4	4
	Bukowski Grill	Steaks & grills	4	3	2
	Bird Stratford	Chicken	3	2	2
	Chicken Shop & Dirty Burger	"	2	2	3
	Haz	Turkish	2	2	2
	Ippudo London	Japanese	3	2	3
	Rosa's	Thai	3	3	2
£30+	Farley Macallan	British, Modern	–	–	–
	Caboose	Burgers, etc	2	3	4
	Sutton & Sons	Fish & chips	4	3	3
	The Stable	Pizza	2	2	3
	Yard Sale Pizza	"	4	3	2
	Chick 'n' Sours	Chicken	3	2	3
	Randy's Wing Bar	"	–	–	–
	Tonkotsu East	Japanese	2	3	3
	Tayyabs	Pakistani	4	2	3
	Mien Tay	Vietnamese	4	2	2
	Sông Quê	"	3	2	2
£25+	Breakfast Club	American	3	3	2
	Chuck Burger	Burgers, etc	–	–	–
	Poppies	Fish & chips	3	3	3
	Crate	Pizza	3	2	3
	Mangal 1	Turkish	5	4	3
	Needoo	Pakistani	4	2	2
£20+	Patty & Bun	Burgers, etc	4	3	2
	Shake Shack	"	3	2	2
	Lahore Kebab House	Pakistani	5	2	2
£15+	E Pellicci	Italian	3	4	5
	Bleecker Street Burger	Burgers, etc	5	2	2
£10+	Smokestak	American	5	3	–

	Dirty Burger	*Burgers, etc*	3	2	2
	The Rib Man	"	5	4	–
	Pilpel	*Middle Eastern*	4	4	2
£5+	Brick Lane Beigel Bake	*Sandwiches, cakes, etc*	4	1	1

MAPS

MAP I – LONDON OVERVIEW

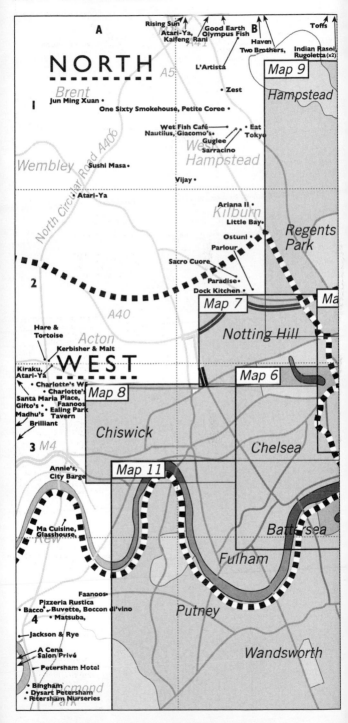

MAP I – LONDON OVERVIEW

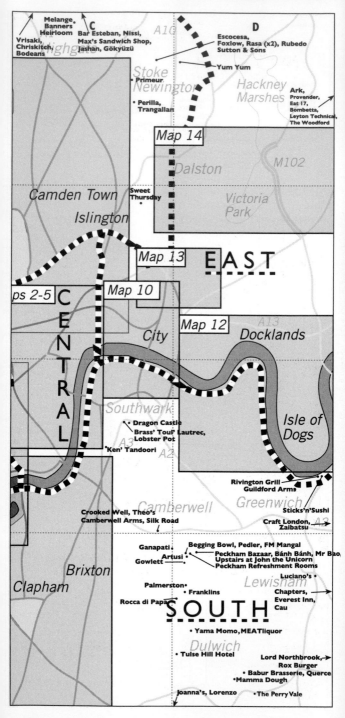

Melange, Banners, Heirloom **C**

Vrisaki, Chriskitch, Bodeans

Bar Esteban, Nissi, Max's Sandwich Shop, Jashan, Gökyüzü

Highgate

A10 **D**

Escocesa, Foxlow, Rasa (x2), Rubedo Sutton & Sons

Yum Yum

Stoke Newington

Primeur

Hackney Marshes

Ark, Provender, Eat 17, Bombetta, Leyton Technical, The Woodford

Perilla, Trangallan

Map 14

Dalston

M102

Camden Town

Sweet Thursday

Islington

Map 13

Victoria Park

E A S T

Map 10

ps 2-5 **C E N T R A L**

City

Map 12

Docklands

A13

Southwark

Dragon Castle

Brass' Tou Lautrec, Lobster Pot

A3

'Ken' Tandoori

A2

Isle of Dogs

Rivington Grill Guildford Arms

Camberwell

Greenwich

Sticks'n'Sushi

Craft London, Zaibatsu

A3

Crooked Well, Theo's, Camberwell Arms, Silk Road

Ganapati

Begging Bowl, Pedler, FM Mangal

Artusi

Peckham Bazaar, Bánh Bánh, Mr Bao, Upstairs at John the Unicorn Peckham Refreshment Rooms

Gowlett

Lewisham

Luciano's

Palmerston

Franklins

Chapters, Everest Inn, Cau

Rocca di Papa

Brixton

S O U T H

Clapham

Yama Momo, MEATliquor

Dulwich

Tulse Hill Hotel

Lord Northbrook, Rox Burger

Babur Brasserie, Querce

Mamma Dough

Joanna's, Lorenzo

The Perry Vale

MAP 2 – WEST END OVERVIEW

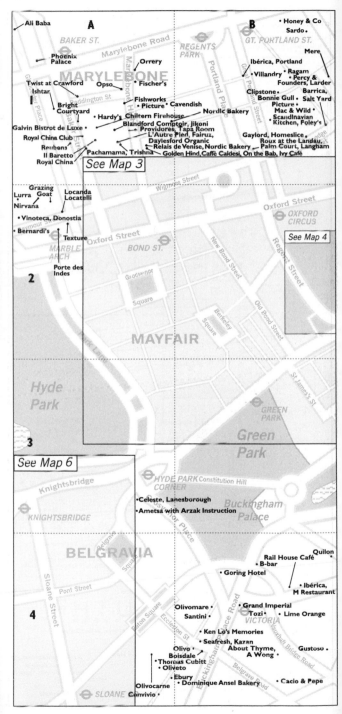

MAP 2 – WEST END OVERVIEW

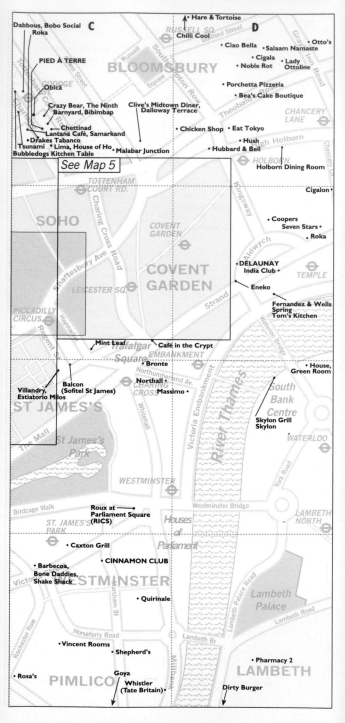

Dabbous, Bobo Social **C**
Roka

Hare & Tortoise
RUSSELL SQ
Chilli Cool

PIED À TERRE

BLOOMSBURY

D

Ciao Bella • Otto's
Salaam Namaste
Cigala Lady
Noble Rot Ottoline

GOODGE
Obica

Porchetta Pizzeria
Bea's Cake Boutique

Crazy Bear, The Ninth
Barnyard, Bibimbap

CHANCERY
LANE

Clive's Midtown Diner,
Dalloway Terrace

Chettinad
Lantana Café, Samarkand
Drakes Tabanco
Tsunami • Lima, House of Ho
Bubbledogs Kitchen Table

Chicken Shop • Eat Tokyo

High Holborn
• Hush

Malabar Junction

Hubbard & Bell

HOLBORN
Holborn Dining Room

See Map 5

TOTTENHAM
COURT RD.

Cigalon •

SOHO

Charing Cross Road

COVENT
GARDEN

Coopers
Seven Stars •
Roka •

COVENT
GARDEN

Shaftesbury Avenue
LEICESTER SQ.

Aldwych
DELAUNAY
India Club •

TEMPLE

PICCADILLY
CIRCUS

Haymarket
Regent St.

Strand
Eneko

Fernandez & Wells
Spring
Tom's Kitchen

Mint Leaf • Café in the Crypt

Trafalgar
Square
EMBANKMENT

Bronte •

House,
Green Room

Villandry,
Estiatorio Milos

Balcon
(Sofitel St James)

Northall •
CHARING
CROSS
Massimo •

South
Bank
Centre

ST JAMES'S

Whitehall

Skylon Grill
Skylon

WATERLOO

The Mall

St James's
Park

Victoria Embankment

River Thames

York Road

WESTMINSTER

Birdcage Walk

Westminster Bridge

LAMBETH
NORTH

ST. JAMES'S
PARK

Roux at
Parliament Square
(RICS)

Houses
of
Parliament

• Caxton Grill

CINNAMON CLUB

• Barbecoa,
Bone Daddies,
Shake Shack

WESTMINSTER

Marsham St

Lambeth Palace Road

Lambeth
Palace

• Quirinale

Lambeth Road

Horseferry Road

Lambeth Br.

Millbank

• Vincent Rooms

• Shepherd's

• Pharmacy 2

• Rosa's

PIMLICO

Rochester Row

Victoria

Goya
Whistler
(Tate Britain) •

LAMBETH

Dirty Burger

MAP 3 – MAYFAIR, ST JAMES'S & WEST SOHO

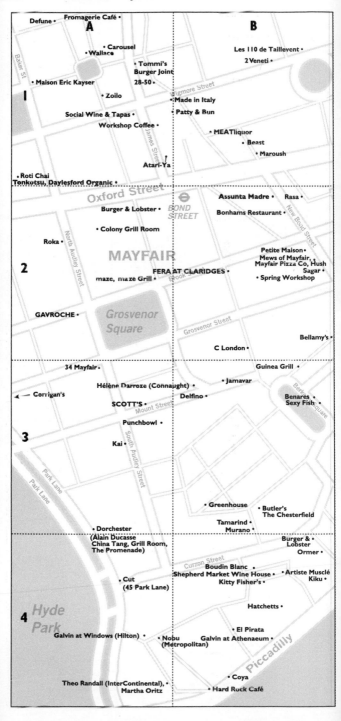

A

Defune •

Fromagerie Café •

• Carousel

• Wallace

• Tommi's Burger Joint

28-50 •

• Maison Eric Kayser

• Zoilo

Social Wine & Tapas •

Workshop Coffee •

Atari-Ya •

• Roti Chai
Tenkotsu, Daylesford Organic •

1

Baker St

Wigmore Street

James Street

Oxford Street

B

Les 110 de Taillevent •

2 Veneti •

• Made in Italy

• Patty & Bun

• MEATliquor

• Beast

• Maroush

2

Burger & Lobster •

• Colony Grill Room

Roka •

MAYFAIR

maze, maze Grill •

FERA AT CLARIDGES •

GAVROCHE •

Grosvenor Square

North Audley Street

James's Street

Brook Street

BOND STREET

Assunta Madre • Rasa •

Bonhams Restaurant •

Petite Maison •
Mews of Mayfair,
Mayfair Pizza Co, Hush
Sagar •
• Spring Workshop

Grosvenor Street

New Bond Street

Bellamy's •

C London •

3

34 Mayfair •

← Corrigan's

Hélène Darroze (Connaught) •

SCOTT'S •

Punchbowl •

Kai •

Mount Street

South Audley Street

• Jamavar

Delfino •

Guinea Grill •

Benares •
Sexy Fish •

Berkeley Square

Greenhouse •

Tamarind •
Murano •

• Butler's
The Chesterfield

4

Hyde Park

Park Lane

• Dorchester

(Alain Ducasse
China Tang, Grill Room,
The Promenade)

• Cut
(45 Park Lane)

Galvin at Windows (Hilton) •

• Nobu
(Metropolitan)

Theo Randall (InterContinental),
Martha Oritz

Curzon Street

Boudin Blanc •
Shepherd Market Wine House •
Kitty Fisher's •

Hatchetts •

• El Pirata

Galvin at Athenaeum •

• Coya

• Hard Rock Café

Burger &
Lobster •

Ormer •

• Artiste Musclé
Kiku •

Piccadilly

MAP 3 – MAYFAIAR, ST JAMES'S & WEST SOHO

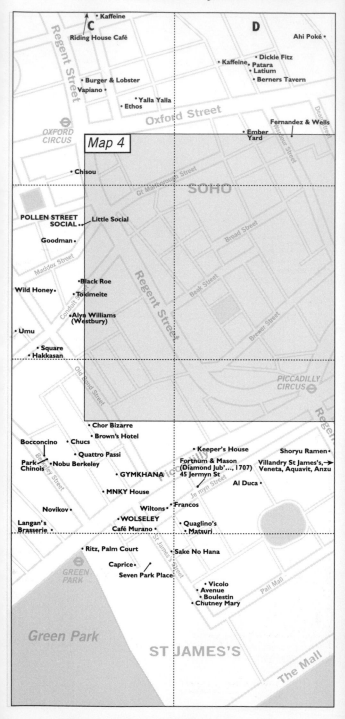

C

D

• Kaffeine

Riding House Café

• Ahi Poké •

• Dickie Fitz
• Kaffeine, Patara
• Latium
• Berners Tavern

• Burger & Lobster
Vapiano •

• Yalla Yalla
• Ethos

OXFORD STREET

Fernandez & Wells

OXFORD CIRCUS

• Ember Yard

Map 4

• Chisou

SOHO

Gt Marlborough Street

POLLEN STREET SOCIAL •• Little Social

Broad Street

Goodman •

Maddox Street

• Black Roe

Beak Street

Wild Honey •

• Tokimeite

Conduit Street

• Alyn Williams (Westbury)

Brewer Street

• Umu

• Square
• Hakkasan

Old Bond Street

PICCADILLY CIRCUS

• Chor Bizarre
• Brown's Hotel

Bocconcino • • Chucs
Park • Quattro Passi
Chinois •Nobu Berkeley

• Keeper's House

Shoryu Ramen •

Fortnum & Mason
(Diamond Jub'..., 1707)
45 Jermyn St

Villandry St James's,→
Veneta, Aquavit, Anzu

• GYMKHANA

Al Duca •

Je myn Street

• MNKY House

Novikov •

• Wiltons •Francos

Langan's
Brasserie •

• WOLSELEY
Café Murano •

• Quaglio's
• Matsuri

• Ritz, Palm Court

Caprice •

Seven Park Place

GREEN PARK

• Sake No Hana

• Vicolo
• Avenue
• Boulestin
• Chutney Mary

Pall Mall

Green Park

ST JAMES'S

The Mall

MAP 4 – WEST SOHO

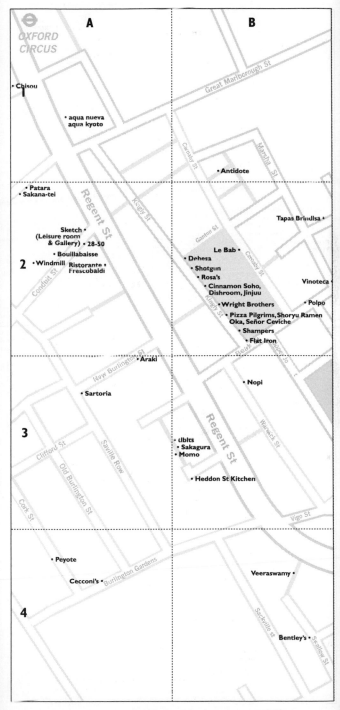

OXFORD CIRCUS

A
B

• Chisou

• aqua nueva
aqua kyoto

• Antidote

• Patara
• Sakana-tei

Tapas Brindisa •

Sketch •
(Leisure room
& Gallery) • 28-50
• Bouillabaisse
• Windmill   Ristorante •
Frescobaldi

Le Bab •
• Dehesa
• Shotgun
• Rosa's
• Cinnamon Soho,
Dishroom, Jinjuu
• Wright Brothers
• Pizza Pilgrims, Shoryu Ramen
Oka, Señor Ceviche
• Shampers
• Flat Iron

Vinoteca •

• Polpo

• Araki

• Nopi

• Sartoria

• tibits
• Sakagura
• Momo

• Heddon St Kitchen

• Peyote

Veeraswamy •

Cecconi's •

Bentley's •

MAP 4 – WEST SOHO

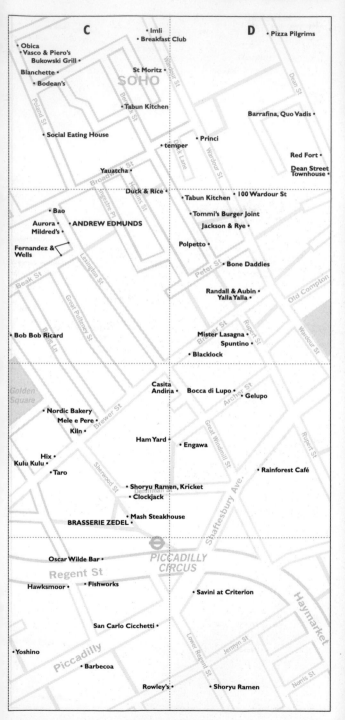

C

D

• Imli
• Breakfast Club

• Pizza Pilgrims

• Obica
• Vasco & Piero's
   Bukowski Grill •
Blanchette •
   • Bodean's

• St Moritz

SOHO

Wardour St

Barrafina, Quo Vadis •

Poland St

• Tabun Kitchen

• Social Eating House

• Princi
• temper

Dean St

Red Fort •

Broadwick St

Dean St

Wardour St

Dean Street
Townhouse •

Duck Lane

Yauatcha •

Berwick St

Duck & Rice •

• Tabun Kitchen   • 100 Wardour St

Theatre Pl

• Bao

• Tommi's Burger Joint

Aurora •
Mildred's •

• ANDREW EDMUNDS

Jackson & Rye •

Polpetto •

Fernandez &
Wells

Lexington St

Peter St

• Bone Daddies

Old Compton

Beak St

Randall & Aubin •
Yalla Yalla •

Wardour St

Great Pulteney St

Lower Marsh Ln

• Bob Bob Ricard

Brewer St

Mister Lasagna •
Spuntino •
• Blacklock

Rupert St

Golden
Square

Casita
Andina •

Bocca di Lupo •

Archer St

• Gelupo

• Nordic Bakery
   Mele e Pere •
      Kiln •

Brewer St

Ham Yard •   • Engawa

Great Windmill St

Rupert St

Hix •
Kulu Kulu •
   • Taro

Sherwood St

• Rainforest Café

• Shoryu Ramen, Kricket
   • Clockjack

Denman St

Shaftesbury Ave.

• Mash Steakhouse

BRASSERIE ZEDEL •

Oscar Wilde Bar •

**PICCADILLY
CIRCUS**

Regent St

Haymarket

Hawksmoor •   • Fishworks

• Savini at Criterion

San Carlo Cicchetti •

Jermyn St

• Yoshino

Piccadilly

Lower Regent St

Norris St

• Barbecoa

Rowley's •   • Shoryu Ramen

MAP 5 – EAST SOHO, CHINATOWN & COVENT GARDEN

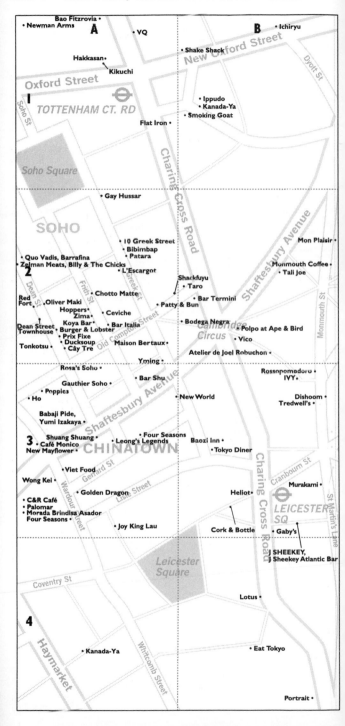

MAP 5 – EAST SOHO, CHINATOWN & COVENT GARDEN

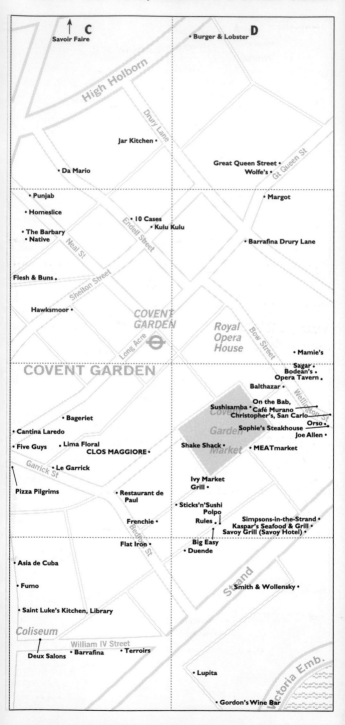

C

D

Savoir Faire

• Burger & Lobster

High Holborn

Drury Lane

Jar Kitchen •

Great Queen Street •
Wolfe's •

Gt Queen St

• Da Mario

• Punjab
• Homeslice

• Margot

Endell Street

• 10 Cases
• Kulu Kulu

• The Barbary
• Native

• Barrafina Drury Lane

Neal St

Flesh & Buns •

Shelton Street

Hawksmoor •

COVENT
GARDEN

Long Acre

Royal
Opera
House

Bow Street

COVENT GARDEN

• Mamie's

Sagar •
Bodean's •
Opera Tavern •

Wellington St

Balthazar •

• Bageriet

On the Bab •
Sushisamba • Café Murano
Christopher's, San Carlo
Sophie's Steakhouse

Orso •

• Cantina Laredo

Covent
Garden
Market

Joe Allen •

• Five Guys
• Lima Floral
CLOS MAGGIORE •

Shake Shack •

• MEATmarket

Garrick St

• Le Garrick

Pizza Pilgrims

Ivy Market
Grill •

• Restaurant de
Paul

• Sticks'n'Sushi
Polpo
Rules •

Bedford St

Frenchie •

Simpsons-in-the-Strand •
Kaspar's Seafood & Grill •
Savoy Grill (Savoy Hotel) •

Flat Iron •

Big Easy •
• Duende

• Asia de Cuba

Strand

• Fumo

Smith & Wollensky •

• Saint Luke's Kitchen, Library

Coliseum

William IV Street

Deux Salons • Barrafina • Terroirs

• Lupita

Victoria Emb.

• Gordon's Wine Bar

MAP 6 – KNIGHTSBRIDGE, CHELSEA & SOUTH KENSINGTON

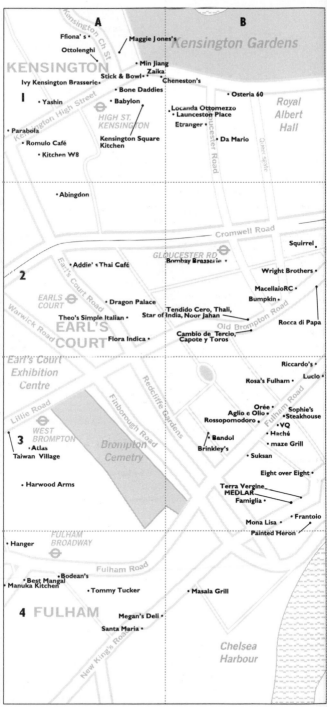

A

B

Kensington Gardens

Ffiona's

Maggie Jones's

Ottolenghi

Min Jiang

KENSINGTON

Stick & Bowl

Zaika

Cheneston's

Ivy Kensington Brasserie

Osteria 60

Royal Albert Hall

Bone Daddies

1

Yashin

Babylon

Locanda Ottomezzo

Parabola

Launceston Place

Romulo Café

HIGH ST. KENSINGTON

Etranger

Kitchen W8

Kensington Square Kitchen

Da Mario

Abingdon

Cromwell Road

Squirrel

GLOUCESTER RD

2

Addie's Thai Café

Bombay Brasserie

Wright Brothers

EARLS COURT

Dragon Palace

MacellaioRC

Bumpkin

Theo's Simple Italian

Tendido Cero, Thali, Star of India, Noor Jahan

Rocca di Papa

EARL'S COURT

Flora Indica

Cambio de Tercio, Capote y Toros

Old Brompton Road

Earl's Court Exhibition Centre

Riccardo's

Luclo

Rosa's Fulham

Orée

Sophie's Steakhouse

WEST BROMPTON

Aglio e Olio

Rossopomodoro

VQ

3

Atlas

Haché

Taiwan Village

Brompton Cemetery

Bandol

maze grill

Brinkley's

Suksan

Harwood Arms

Eight over Eight

Terra Vergine

MEDLAR

Famiglia

Mona Lisa

Frantoio

Painted Heron

FULHAM BROADWAY

Hanger

Fulham Road

Bodean's

Best Mangal

Manuka Kitchen

Tommy Tucker

Masala Grill

4 FULHAM

Megan's Deli

Santa Maria

Chelsea Harbour

MAP 6 – KNIGHTSBRDIGE, CHELSEA & SOUTH KENSINGTON

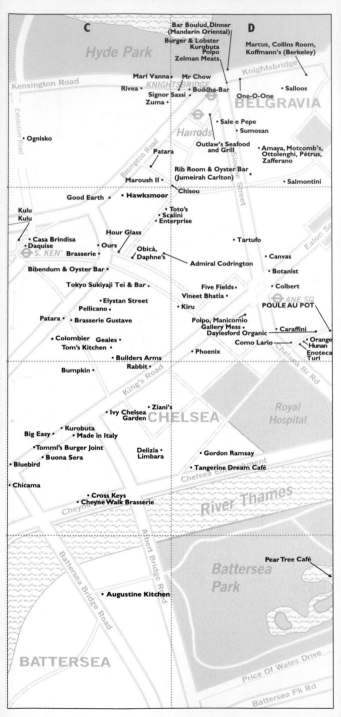

C

D

Hyde Park

Kensington Road

Exhibition Road

Bar Boulud, Dinner
(Mandarin Oriental)
Burger & Lobster
Kurobuta
Polpo
Zelman Meats

Marcus, Collins Room,
Koffmann's (Berkeley)

Knightsbridge

Mari Vanna   Mr Chow
Rivea   KNIGHTSBRIDGE
Signor Sassi   • Buddha-Bar
Zuma

One-O-One   • Salloos

BELGRAVIA

• Sale e Pepe

Harrods   • Sumosan

• Ognisko

Patara

Outlaw's Seafood
and Grill

• Amaya, Motcomb's,
Ottolenghi, Pétrus,
Zafferano

Brompton Road

Maroush II •

Rib Room & Oyster Bar
(Jumeirah Carlton)

Sloane Street

• Salmontini

Chisou

Good Earth   • Hawksmoor

Kulu
Kulu

• Toto's
• Scalini
• Enterprise

• Casa Brindisa
• Daquise
S. KEN'   Brasserie

Hour Glass
• Ours

Obicà,
Daphne's

• Tartufo

Eaton Sq

Bibendum & Oyster Bar •

Admiral Codrington

• Canvas

• Botanist

Tokyo Sukijaji Tei & Bar •

Five Fields •

• Colbert

• Elystan Street
Pellicano •

Vineet Bhatia •

SLOANE SQ

Patara •
• Brasserie Gustave

• Kiru

POULE AU POT

• Colombier
Tom's Kitchen

Geales •

Polpo, Manicomio
Gallery Mess •
Daylesford Organic
Como Lario

• Caraffini

• Orange
Hunan
Enoteca
Turi

Chelsea Br Rd

• Builders Arms
Rabbit •

• Phoenix

Bumpkin •

King's Road

• Ziani's

• Ivy Chelsea   CHELSEA
Garden

Royal
Hospital

Big Easy •   • Kurobuta
• Made in Italy

• Tommi's Burger Joint
• Buona Sera

Delizia
Limbara

• Bluebird

• Gordon Ramsay

Chelsea Embankment

• Tangerine Dream Café

• Chicama

• Cross Keys
• Cheyne Walk Brasserie

Cheyne Walk

River Thames

Battersea
Bridge Rd

Albert Bridge Rd

• Augustine Kitchen

Battersea
Park

Pear Tree Café

BATTERSEA

Price Of Wales Drive

Battersea Pk Rd

MAP 7 – NOTTING HILL & BAYSWATER

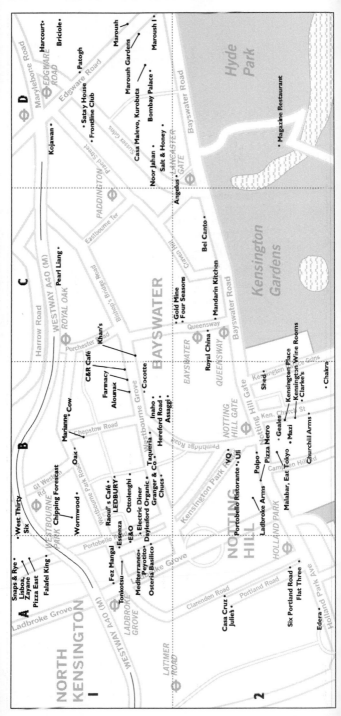

MAP 8 – HAMMERSMITH & CHISWICK

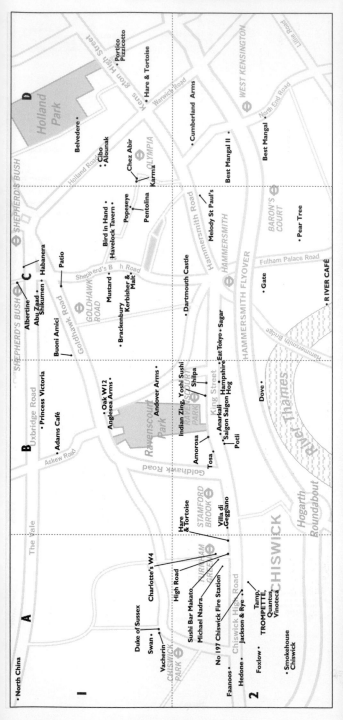

MAP 9 – HAMPSTEAD, CAMDEN TOWN & ISLINGTON

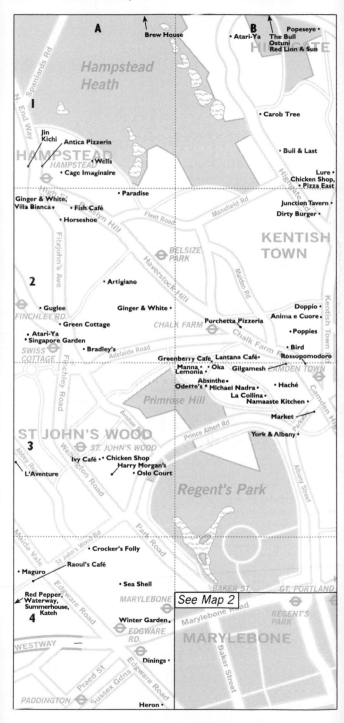

A

Brew House

B

• Atari-Ya
Popeseye •
The Bull
Ostuni
Red Lion & Sun

HIGHGATE

Hampstead Heath

1

• Carob Tree

Jin Kichi
Antica Pizzeria
• Wells
• Cage Imaginalre

HAMPSTEAD
HAMPSTEAD

N. End Way

Spaniards Rd

• Bull & Last

Lure •
Chicken Shop, •
• Pizza East

High St

• Paradise

Ginger & White, •
Villa Bianca •
• Fish Café
• Horseshoe

Fleet Road

Mansfield Rd

Junction Tavern •
Dirty Burger •

Rosslyn Hill

BELSIZE PARK

KENTISH TOWN

2

Fitzjohn's Ave

• Artigiano

Haverstock Hill

• Guglee
FINCHLEY RD.

Ginger & White •

Maiden Rd

Kentish Town Rd

Doppio •
Anima e Cuore •

• Green Cottage
CHALK FARM

Porchetta Pizzeria •

• Poppies

• Atari-Ya
• Singapore Garden

Chalk Farm Rd

• Bird
Rossopomodoro •

SWISS COTTAGE

• Bradley's

Adelaide Road

Greenberry Café •
Manna •
Lemonia •
Odette's •

Lantana Café •

Absinthe •
• Michael Nadra
La Collina •
Namaaste Kitchen •

• Oka   Gilgamesh •

CAMDEN TOWN

• Haché

Finchley Road

Market •

Camden High St

Prince Albert Rd

Primrose Hill

York & Albany •

ST JOHN'S WOOD
ST. JOHN'S WOOD

Wellington Road

3

L'Aventure

Abbey Road

Ivy Café •
• Chicken Shop
Harry Morgan's
• Oslo Court

Regent's Park

Albany Street

4

Maida Vale

Crocker's Folly •

Raoul's Café

• Maguro

St John's Wood Rd

Park Road

• Sea Shell

BAKER ST.   GT. PORTLAND

MARYLEBONE

See Map 2

REGENT'S PARK

Red Pepper,
Waterway,
Summerhouse,
Kateh

Edgware Road

Winter Garden •
EDGWARE RD.

Marylebone Road

MARYLEBONE

WESTWAY

• Dinings

Baker Street

Praed St

Sussex Gdns

Edgware Road

PADDINGTON

Heron •

MAP 9 – HAMPSTEAD, CAMDEN TOWN & ISLINGTON

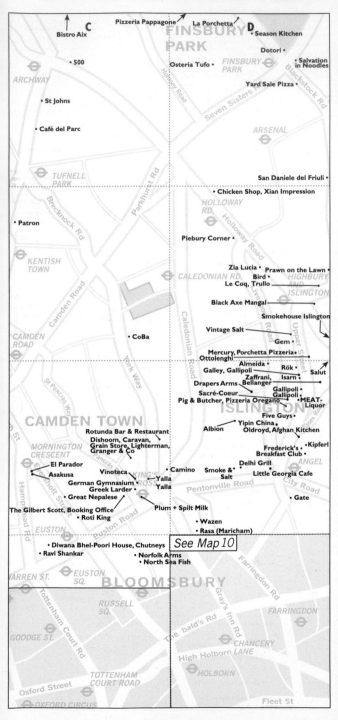

Bistro Aix

C

Pizzeria Pappagone

La Porchetta

D

Season Kitchen

FINSBURY
PARK

Dotori

• 500

Osteria Tufo

FINSBURY
PARK

Salvation
in Noodles

ARCHWAY

Yard Sale Pizza

• St Johns

Seven Sisters

ARSENAL

• Café del Parc

Holloway Road

TUFNELL
PARK

San Daniele del Friuli

Parkhurst Rd

HOLLOWAY
RD.

Chicken Shop, Xian Impression

Brecknock Rd

Holloway Road

• Patron

KENTISH
TOWN

Piebury Corner

Zia Lucia • Prawn on the Lawn
Bird •
Le Coq, Trullo

Camden Road

CALEDONIAN RD.

HIGHBURY
AND
ISLINGTON

Black Axe Mangal

Smokehouse Islington

CAMDEN
ROAD

York Way

• CoBa

Vintage Salt

Upper St

Gem

Caledonian Road

Mercury, Porchetta Pizzeria •
Ottolenghi

Almeida •   Rök •
Galley, Gallipoli   Isarn   Salut
Zaffrani,
Drapers Arms, Bellanger
Gallipoli
Sacré-Coeur   Gallipoli
Pig & Butcher, Pizzeria Oregano • MEAT-
Liquor

St Pancras Way

ISLINGTON

Five Guys •

CAMDEN TOWN

Yipin China •
Oldroyd, Afghan Kitchen

Albion

Frederick's • Kipferl
Breakfast Club •

MORNINGTON
CRESCENT

Rotunda Bar & Restaurant
Dishoom, Caravan,
Grain Store, Lighterman,
Granger & Co

Camden Road

• El Parador
Asakusa

Vinoteca

German Gymnasium •
Greek Larder •
• Great Nepalese

• Camino

Delhi Grill

ANGEL

Yalla
Yalla

Smoke &
Salt

Little Georgia Cafe

Hampstead Rd

Eversholt St

The Gilbert Scott, Booking Office
• Roti King

Pancras Rd

Euston Road

Plum + Spilt Milk

Pentonville Road

• Gate

City Road

EUSTON

• Wazen
• Rasa (Maricham)

See Map 10

WARREN ST.

EUSTON
SQ.

• Diwana Bhel-Poori House, Chutneys
• Ravi Shankar

• Norfolk Arms
• North Sea Fish

Farringdon Rd

BLOOMSBURY

Tottenham Court Rd

RUSSELL
SQ.

Gray's Inn Rd

FARRINGDON

GOODGE ST.

The bald's Rd

CHANCERY
LANE

High Holborn

HOLBORN

TOTTENHAM
COURT ROAD

Oxford Street

OXFORD CIRCUS

Fleet St

MAP 10 - THE CITY

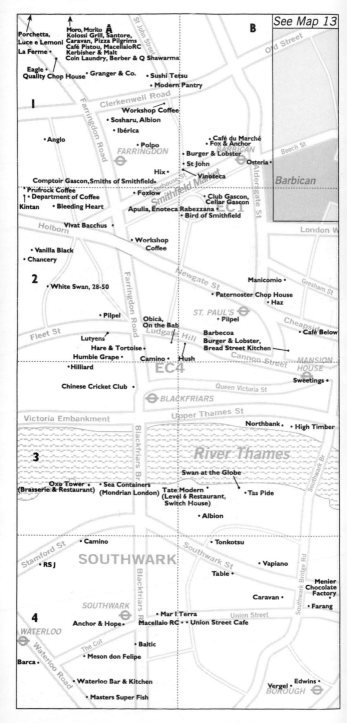

A

B

See Map 13

Porchetta,
Luce e Lemoni
La Ferme

Moro, Morito
Kolossi Grill, Santore,
Caravan, Pizza Pilgrims
Café Pistou, MacellaioRC
Kerbisher & Malt
Coin Laundry, Berber & Q Shawarma

Old Street

Eagle
Quality Chop House
• Granger & Co.

• Sushi Tetsu

• Modern Pantry

1

Clerkenwell Road

Beech St

• Workshop Coffee

• So.sharu, Albion

• Ibérica

• Anglo

FARRINGDON

• Polpo

• Café du Marché
• Fox & Anchor
• Burger & Lobster
• St John   Osteria •
Hix •   • Vinoteca

Barbican

Comptoir Gascon, Smiths of Smithfield
• Prufrock Coffee
• Department of Coffee
Kintan   • Bleeding Heart

• Foxlow
Smithfield Market
• Club Gascon,
Cellar Gascon
Apulia, Enoteca Rabezzana •
• Bird of Smithfield

Aldersgate St

EC1

London W

Vivat Bacchus •

Holborn

• Workshop
Coffee

Newgate St

Gresham St

• Vanilla Black
• Chancery

2

• White Swan, 28-50

Manicomio •

• Paternoster Chop House
• Haz

Cheapside

Farringdon Road

ST. PAUL'S ⊖

• Pilpel

Obicà,
On the Bab

Ludgate Hill

• Pilpel

Barbecoa
Burger & Lobster,
Bread Street Kitchen

• Café Below

Fleet St

Lutyens •
Hare & Tortoise •
Humble Grape •

• Camino • Hush

Cannon Street

MANSION
HOUSE

• Hilliard

EC4

Queen Victoria St

Sweetings •

Chinese Cricket Club •

⊖ BLACKFRIARS

Victoria Embankment

Upper Thames St

Northbank •   • High Timber

3

River Thames

Blackfriars Br

Southwark Br

Oxo Tower •
(Brasserie & Restaurant)

• Sea Containers
(Mondrian London)

Swan at the Globe •

Tate Modern
(Level 6 Restaurant,
Switch House)

• Tas Pide

• Albion

• Camino

Stamford St

• Tonkotsu

Southwark St

• RSJ

SOUTHWARK

• Vapiano

Table •

Menier
Chocolate
Factory

Southwark Bridge Rd

SOUTHWARK

Caravan •

• Farang

Blackfriars Road

• Mar I Terra

Union Street

Anchor & Hope • Macellaio RC • • Union Street Cafe

4

WATERLOO ⊖

The Cut

• Baltic

Waterloo Road

Barca •

• Meson don Felipe

• Waterloo Bar & Kitchen

Vergel •   Edwins •

BOROUGH

• Masters Super Fish

MAP 10 – THE CITY

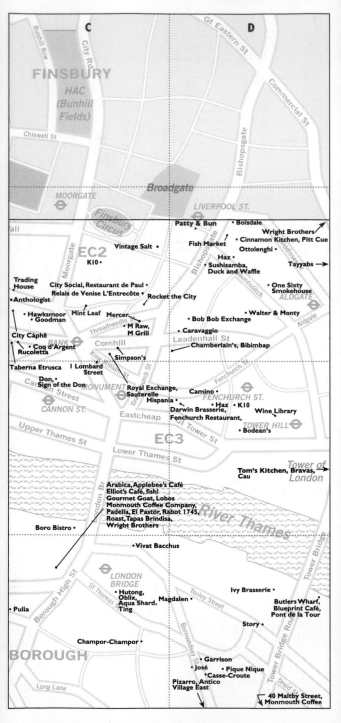

C

D

Gt Eastern St

Bunhill Row

City Road

FINSBURY

HAC
(Bunhill
Fields)

Commercial St

Bishopsgate

Chiswell St

Broadgate

MOORGATE

LIVERPOOL ST.

Finsbury
Circus

Patty & Bun • Boisdale

EC2

Moorgate

Vintage Salt •

K10 •

Wright Brothers →

Fish Market • Cinnamon Kitchen, Pitt Cue

Ottolenghi •

Houndsditch

Haz •
Sushisamba, Tayyabs →
Duck and Waffle

Trading
House •

City Social, Restaurant de Paul •
Relais de Venise L'Entrecôte •

• One Sixty
  Smokehouse

• Anthologist

• Rocket the City

ALDGATE

• Hawksmoor
  • Goodman

Mint Leaf •

Mercer •

• Walter & Monty

Threadneedle St

City Càphê •

M Raw,
M Grill •

• Bob Bob Exchange

Aldgate

• Coq d'Argent
Rucoletta

Cornhill

• Caravaggio

Leadenhall St

BANK

King William St

• Chamberlain's, Bibimbap

Taberna Etrusca •

I Lombard
Street

Simpson's •

Gracechurch St

Fenchurch St

Carey St

Don,
Sign of the Don •

MONUMENT

Royal Exchange,
Sauterelle

Camino •

FENCHURCH ST.

CANNON ST.

Cannon Street

Hispania •

Eastcheap

• Haz • K10

Darwin Brasserie,
Fenchurch Restaurant,

Wine Library •

Upper Thames St

Gt Tower St

TOWER HILL

EC3

• Bodean's

Lower Thames St

River Thames

Tom's Kitchen, Bravas, →
Cau

Tower of
London

London Br

Arabica, Applebee's Café
Elliot's Café, fish!
Gourmet Goat, Lobos
Monmouth Coffee Company,
Padella, El Pastór, Rabot 1745,
Roast, Tapas Brindisa,
Wright Brothers

Tower Bridge

Boro Bistro •

River Thames

• Vivat Bacchus

London Br

LONDON
BRIDGE

Ivy Brasserie •

Borough High St

St Thomas St

• Hutong,
  Oblix,
  Aqua Shard,
  Ting

Tooley Street

Magdalen •

Butlers Wharf, •
Blueprint Café,
Pont de la Tour

• Pulia

Story •

Bermondsey St

Tower Bridge Road

Champor-Champor •

• Garrison

BOROUGH

José • • Pique Nique

• Casse-Croûte

Long Lane

Pizarro, Antico
Village East

← 40 Maltby Street,
   Monmouth Coffee

Druid St

MAP 11 – SOUTH LONDON (& FULHAM)

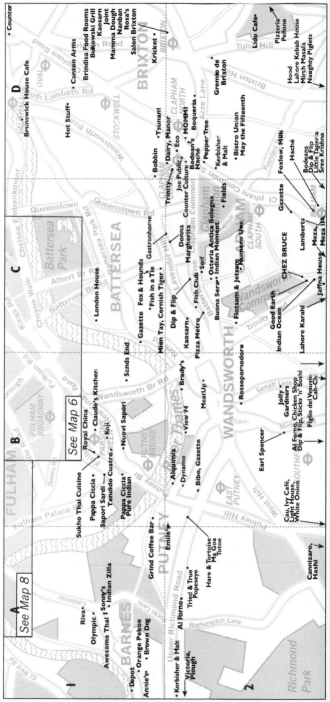

MAP 12 – DOCKLANDS

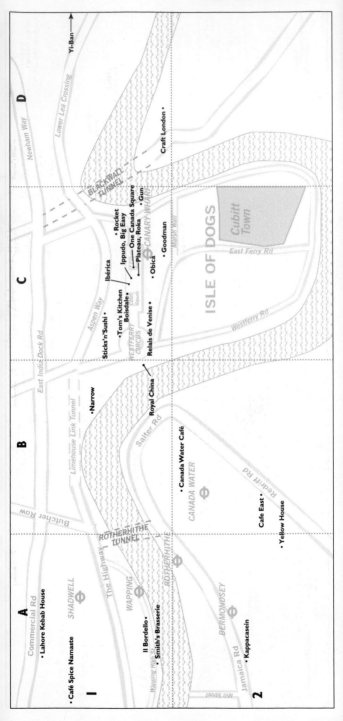

MAP 13 – SHOREDITCH & HOXTON

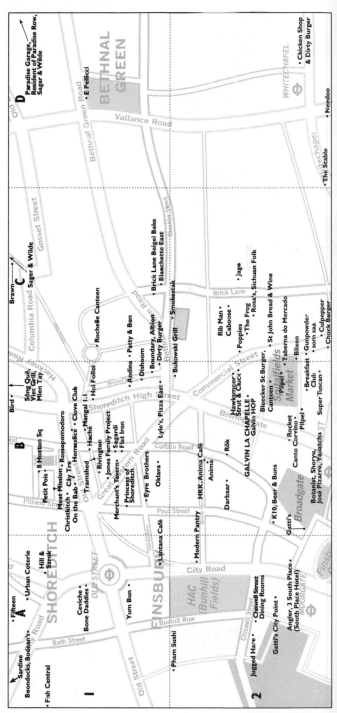

Paradise Garage, Resident of Paradise Row, Sagar & Wilde

E Pellicci

BETHNAL GREEN

Old

Bethnal Green Road

Vallance Road

WHITECHAPEL

Chicken Shop & Dirty Burger

Needoo

The Stable

WHITECHAPEL

Gosset Street

Brick Lane Beigel Bake

Blanchette East

Glenister Street

Jage

Brawn

Columbia Road

Sager & Wilde

C

Rochelle Canteen

Brick Lane

Rib Man
Caboose

The Frog
Rosa's, Sichuan Folk

St John Bread & Wine

Taberna do Mercado

Poppies

Culpepper
Chuck Burger

Andina · Patty & Bun

Dishoom

Boundary, Albion
Dirty Burger

Bukowski Grill

Smokestak

D

Hackney Road

Bird

Hoxton Road

Song Quê,
Viet Grill,
Miên Tay

Hoi Polloi

Shoreditch High Street

Commercial Street

Spitalfields Market

Bilxen
Breakfast · Gunpowder
Club · som saa

8 Hoxton Sq

Meat Mission · Rossopomodoro

Christditch · Cây Tre
On the Bab · Homeslice · Clove Club

Tramshed · Mangal I

Hâché

Bishopsgate

Bleecker St Burger,
Canteen ·
Rocket ·
Canto Corvino ·
Pilpel

Hawksmoor,
Strut & Cluck
Galvin HOP

Super Tuscan

B

Petit Pois

Rivington
Jones Family Project

Princess of
Shoreditch

Sagardi
Flat Iron

Lyle's, Pizza East

Great Eastern Street

Eyre Brothers

Oklava ·

Curtain Road

HKK, Anima Café

Anima ·

Rök ·

GALVIN LA CHAPELLE

Rocket ·
Canto Corvino ·
Pilpel

Botanist, Shoryu,
José Pizarro, Yauatcha ST

Broadgate

SHOREDITCH

Merchant's Tavern

Pitfield Street

Lantana Café

Modern Pantry

Darbaar ·

K10, Beer & Buns

Paul Street

Gatti's

Fifteen

Urban Coterie

Hill & Szrok

Ceviche ·
Bone Daddies ·

OLD STREET

City Road

FINSBURY

HAC (Bunhill Fields)

Broadgate

Finsbury

MOORGATE

A

Sardine

Beondocks, Bodean's

Kingsland Road

Fish Central

Yum Bun ·

Bunhill Row

Bath Street

Angler, 3 South Place,
(South Place Hotel)

Chiswell Street
Dining Rooms

Gatti's City Point ·

Pham Sushi ·

Jugged Hare ·

Chiswell Street

Old Street

1

2